COMPUTERS AND MAN

Third Edition

RICHARD C. DORF
University of California, Davis

BOYD & FRASER PUBLISHING COMPANY
San Francisco, California

Richard C. Dorf
COMPUTERS AND MAN
Third Edition

Library of Congress Catalog Card Number: 82-70804

ISBN: 0-87835-121-3

1 2 3 4 • 5 4 3 2

CONTENTS

PREFACE TO THE THIRD EDITION

Computers and information-processing systems influence our lives in many ways. They have become part of the foundation supporting our technological industry and our society. There are approximately one-half million computers in operation in the US, while there were just 10,000 a decade ago. Students of the Seventies could neglect the study of computers and information systems, but it will be increasingly difficult to qualify as a broadly educated person in this decade or the future without experiencing at least an introduction to computers, their application, and their impact on society. The purpose of this book is to provide just such an introduction.

This book is meant to serve as a textbook in a first course on the introduction to computing. It is structured to meet the needs of a student who does not possess any background in computing or advanced mathematics. It is assumed that the textbook and the coordinate course would be open to all students in colleges and universities whatever their major or year of advancement. Increasingly, such a course will be offered during the first or second year of college, but at present it is offered to students at any level depending on their curriculum. The book is written to follow the course description developed by the Association for Computing Machinery (ACM), published in the March, 1979 issue of the *Communications of ACM*. The suggested catalog description provided by ACM is given below.*

Communications of the ACM, March, 1979, Vol. 22, Number 3, page 162.

There is a great need and demand for computer science material by students who do not intend to major in computer science. Faculty of computer science departments must be willing to offer different courses for those students than for majors when that is appropriate. Service courses should be offered by computer science faculty rather than by faculty in other departments. This, of course, implies that the courses must be made appealing by providing appropriate computer science content in a manner that is attuned to the needs, levels, and backgrounds of the students taking such courses.

CSS 1. Computer Applications and Impact (3-0-3)

A survey of computer applications in areas such as file management, gaming, CAI, process control, simulation, and modeling. Impact of computers on individuals and society. Problem solving using computers with emphasis on analysis, formulation of algorithms, and programming. Projects chosen from various application areas of student interest.

The primary purpose of this book is to introduce the use of algorithms and computers to solve important problems. In addition, a large number of applications of computers are examined. Finally, the social impact of computers as tools in our society is discussed.

Several contemporary topics have been added to the Third Edition. The minicomputer and the microcomputer are discussed. Also, several new applications of computers are presented, including the new approach to distributed processing. The Third Edition thus makes an attempt to keep up with the very rapid developments in the applications of computers as well as those of modern computer equipment.

Science should be taught not to spectators but to participants; therefore, we should teach computer science rather than teach *about* computer science. Thus, when one learns computer science, he is learning to deal with the kinds of problems which computers are used to solve. Therefore, good challenging problems are the best vehicle for learning computing and computer science. This is the basic aim of this book.

The problems in this text have a classroom aspect and a laboratory dimension. That is, we shall want to think about any given problem first, and then proceed to the laboratory or computer center and act upon our thoughts and tentative solution proposal. The best course to introduce the computer consists of thought and action; most problem solutions will result from an iterative process of thought and action. The problems in this book are an aid toward this process.

We are often asked if this subject is socially relevant—that is, does it have some bearing on the grievous problems facing the world? Also, is the subject self-rewarding, real, or meaningful and thus personally relevant? It is the belief of the author that the study of computers and information processing can be both socially and personally relevant. Here is an opportunity for the student to bring knowledge and concern together in solving some of the problems of industry, education, and society. When we are able to concentrate on the unknown while resting on a base of knowledge, we shall be able to sense where we are going and then make progress toward our goal.

In conclusion, I would like to express my sincere appreciation to my wife and daughters, who love a book as much as I do. Therefore, I wish to dedicate this book to Joy, Christine and Renée as a partial response to their love.

RICHARD C. DORF

Davis, California, March, 1982

1

INTRODUCTION

1.1 COMPUTERS AND COMPUTER SCIENCE

The computer exercises such an important and widespread influence on our society today that every educated person should study the basic disciplines underlying its operation and application. Just as a student will study the basis of economics or psychology, for example, so also he will study the fundamentals of computer science. As a scholarly discipline, computer science is no more than 25 years old; yet one may not find a discipline more important as a preparation for life and work in the last three decades of the twentieth century.

Wherever there are phenomena, and these phenomena are of interest to man, there can be a science to describe and explain those phenomena. There are computers and applications of computers, and the phenomena resulting from these applications. Computer science, therefore, is the study of computers and the phenomena resulting from their use.[1] We can give a more specific definition of computer science after we first describe a computer.

A computer is a device capable of accepting information or data, processing the information, and providing the results as an output. More specifically, a computer can be described as follows:

COMPUTER (1) A data processor that can perform substantial computation, including numerous arithmetic or logic operations, without intervention by a human operator during the process. (2) A device capable of solving problems by accepting data, performing described operations on the data, and supplying the results of these operations. Various types of computers are calculators, digital computers, and analog computers.

A visual representation, or schematic diagram, shows how the computer processes information.

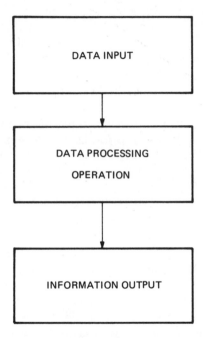

FIGURE 1–1   Information processing system.

Now, with a definition of a computer in mind, let us return to the discussion of the discipline of interest in this book, that of computer science. In one sense, computer science is what computer scientists do, just as mathematics is what mathematicians do. What do computer scientists do? They (1) develop and design computers; (2) work on ways to improve the operation of computers; (3) study the use of computers to solve problems of society and industry, and (4) study the choice of practical ways to utilize computers.[2] As Professor Richard Hamming indicates, "computer engineering" might be a more suitable name for the discipline, except for confusion from the term "engineering." In any case, the computer is the information processing device which is the foundation for the discipline of computer science. A useful definition of computer science is:

COMPUTER SCIENCE (1) The study of computers and the phenomena resulting from their use. (2) The art and science of representing, storing, processing, and presenting information.

The study of the discipline of computer science is appropriate for any college student. It may lead to an understanding of an introductory nature as partially provided by this textbook, or to study of a major nature and perhaps a bachelor's or graduate degree in computer science. The Association for Computing Machinery has developed syllabi for thirty courses which provide a foundation for the study of the discipline, if one chooses to major in the field; these courses also provide non-majors with a clear comprehension of the subject.[3] This approach is similar to the study of economics, which a student may adopt as a major, or study in a first course on the basic tenets of the discipline.

There has been much discussion in the past decade of the information explosion—that is, the exponential growth of knowledge at a rate which is forcing us to specialize ever more narrowly. However, there is hope that computer science, which is intimately concerned with information processing, will provide a new framework for information, and will aid our ability to synthesize and integrate information. This means that the reader will often find other terms, such as "computer and information sciences" or the "science of information processing" used interchangeably with "computer science." See Figure 1-2.

The knowledge industries, which produce and distribute ideas and information rather than goods and services, are analyzed in an important book by Peter Drucker.[4] Drucker reports that these information processing industries account for one-third of the US Gross National Product and they are expected to account for one-half of the GNP during the 1980s. As Drucker points out, the demand for professional workers in the knowledge industry appears insatiable. He states, "In addition to a million computer programmers, the information industry in the US will need in the next fifteen years another half-million systems engineers, system designers, and information specialists."

The application of computers to society and industry is resulting in an information processing revolution. As Marshall McLuhan states, "The computer is by all odds the most extraordinary of all the technological clothing ever devised by man, since it is the extension of our central nervous system. Beside it, the wheel is a mere hula-hoop, though that is not to be dismissed entirely."*

The student of computer science should learn not only the operation and application of computing devices, but also the consequences of their introduction into our society. Just as the release and control of atomic energy has resulted in what has been called the atomic age since 1944, so the release and control of information may result in the period after 1980 being labeled the computer age. It has been proposed that a National Computer Year be proclaimed on the model of

*From WAR AND PEACE IN THE GLOBAL VILLAGE by Marshall McLuhan and Quentin Fiore. Copyright © 1968 by Marshall McLuhan, Quentin Fiore and Jerome Agel. By permission of Bantam Books, Inc.

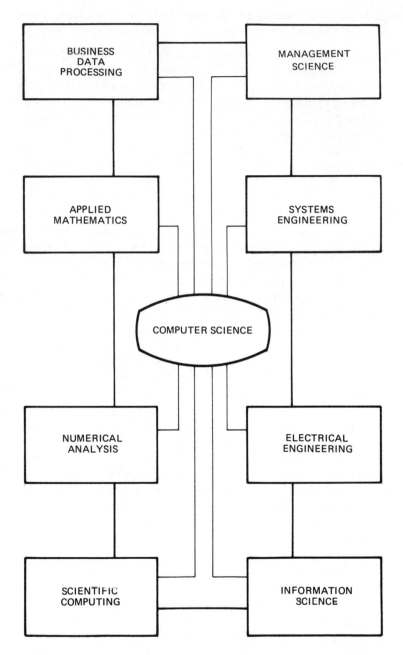

FIGURE 1–2   The relationship of computer science to other sciences.

the successful International Geophysical Year of the past. The aim of the year, proposed by the Association for Computing Machinery, is that specialists from computer science, law, education, industry, and many others should join to explore the various roles the computer could play over the next decade. A presidential proclamation for a National Computer Year would challenge the entire nation to examine the impact of the computer on our society and its potential for enabling progress in the decade of the 80s. Eventually, computer systems will be developed for use in libraries, hospitals, schools, production lines, the legislatures, and so on. Computers can assist in overcoming the stock market paperwork crisis and soaring medical costs; easing overburdened court calendars; and making out-of-date transportation systems efficient, for example. A National Computer Year would be further indicative of the information processing revolution and the pervasiveness of the computer age.[6]

1.2   THE GROWTH OF THE NUMBER OF COMPUTERS AND THEIR APPLICATIONS

Computer products and services make up the fastest-growing major industry in the world. Computer market sales grew from an estimated $339 million in 1955 to over $50 billion in 1980. They are expected to exceed $100 billion in 1985. [7] Computer systems increase the efficiency of government and industry and assist in the solution of complex problems. Without the use of computers, some tasks, such as landing a man on the moon and returning him safely to earth, would be impossible. The computer has become an indispensable part of our economy, and the growth of the computer industry is reasonably assured. The estimated value of computer equipment shipped by American manufacturers is shown in Table 1–1.[7]

TABLE 1–1

Estimated Value of Computer Equipment Shipped by American Manufacturers (Values in $ Millions)

Year	Computers	Peripheral Equipment	Computer Services	Supplies	Total
1955	155	14	15	155	339
1960	1,620	105	125	370	2,220
1965	3,650	175	450	660	4,935
1968	9,050	300	970	960	11,300
1971	13,300	700	1,800	1,200	17,000
1973	18,500	1,000	2,500	1,400	23,400
1975	22,000	1,500	4,000	1,500	29,000
1980	34,000	2,000	16,000	2,000	54,000

It has been estimated that the cumulative value of digital computers in use by business and government in 1980 in the world equaled $100 billion.

The top ten industrial firms in the computer industry are listed in Table 1-2, which shows the market held by each firm in 1979. By far the largest and most influential firm is International Business Machines Corporation, which held 66% of the market. This share declined to 51% by 1980.[8]

Table 1-2
Computer Sales in the U.S. by Computer Firm

Company	1974 (Millions of dollars)	1979 (Millions of dollars)	Compound Growth (Percent)
1. IBM	10,510	18,338	11.8%
2. NCR	1,122	2,634	18.3%
3. Burroughs	1,293	2,376	13.1%
4. Sperry Univac	1,294	2,360	12.8%
5. Control Data	1,101	2,273	15.6%
6. Digital Equipment	422	1,804	33.7%
7. Honeywell	856	1,453	11.2%
8. Hewlett-Packard	390	1,092	22.9%

IBM had a total 1979 revenue of $18 billion, which accounted for one half of the total revenue of the United States computer industry. IBM holds about 68% of the world computer market. Honeywell and Sperry Univac hold respectively about 10% and 8% of the world market.

In 1970 Honeywell purchased the computer division of General Electric Company. In 1971 Sperry Univac purchased the computer division of RCA. Thus, both Honeywell and Sperry Univac grew through merger in order to increase their competitiveness with IBM, the leader of the industry.

IBM is clearly the computer industry leader, holding about 68% of the world market. The question is raised: Is this concentration in one firm excessive, or can only a giant company carry out the necessary research and development necessary in the computer field? IBM is growing at 12% per year, and it may achieve revenues of $40 billion by the mid-1980s. The United States Department of Justice is suing under antitrust laws to break IBM into several competing companies. The Justice Department's aim is to make IBM price its products and services separately through many separate companies. These questions will not be answered for several years: Is IBM a monopoly? And, if it is, what action is required?

Total data processing and computer-associated expenditures grew to $82 billion by 1980. Table 1-3 illustrates that the percent of the Gross National Product expended for data processing has continually increased.

The total of computers in the world is estimated to be about 600,000. Of this number, it is estimated that 500,000 are in use in the United States.

Table 1-3
U.S. Data Processing Expenditures

Year	Expenditure ($ Billion)	Percent of Gross National Product*
1970	21	2.1
1975	41	3.2
1980	82	5.2
1985 (estimate)	164	8.3

*Expressed in constant 1970 dollars.

During the growth of the number of computers during the past decade, the number of applications of computers to the needs of our society has also grown. The computer or information processing system has served such uses and applications as these:

- Control of new management and labor relationships
- Development of speedups that make planning mandatory
- Weapon against crime
- Means of dealing with many problems simultaneously
- Medical diagnostician, doctor, and druggist
- Cupid for ideal matches
- Marriage monitor and arbiter
- Substitute for salesman
- Immigration counselor
- Promoter of executive drop-outs
- Misunderstood teen-ager
- Encyclopedic legal counsel
- Nemesis of the bookie
- Ad man
- Author of Haiku
- Highway designer
- Management consultant
- Bank teller and credit rater
- Librarian
- Internal Revenue Service accountant
- Registrar for college students

Certainly it is clear that the computer has become the information machine of our age which itself is characterized by knowledge industries. As McLuhan suggests, the computer has become, to a great extent, the central nervous system of our society. It assists man in calculating, storing information, and making decisions. As the wheel introduced great changes in our world culture, so will the information machine. This book will show how computers are used and what their impact on society has been—and will be.

"I'M FIRMLY CONVINCED THAT BEHIND EVERY GREAT MAN IS A GREAT COMPUTER."

FIGURE 1–3 © Sidney Harris. Used with permission.

CHAPTER 1 PROBLEMS

P1–1. Give a definition of a computer in your own words.

P1–2. Give a definition of computer science.

P1–3. Name several knowledge industries.

P1–4. In what way or ways do you agree with McLuhan's statement that the computer is an extension of man's central nervous system?

P1–5. Name several uses for computers in industry and society that do not appear in the partial list in section 1-2.

P1–6. Based on the estimated number of computers in use in the United States, how many people does each computer serve on the average? How many people does the computer at your college serve?

CHAPTER 1 REFERENCES

1. A. Newell, A. J. Perlis, and H. Simon, "Computer Science," *Science*, Sept. 22, 1967, pp. 1373–1374.
2. R. W. Hamming, "One Man's View of Computer Science," *Journal of the Association for Computing Machinery*, Vol. 16, No. 1, Jan. 1969, pp. 3–12.
3. Report of the Curriculum Committee on Computer Science, *Communications of the Association for Computing Machinery*, Vol. II, No. 3, March, 1968, pp. 152–172.
4. P. F. Drucker, *The Age of Discontinuity*, Harper & Row, New York, 1968.
5. M. McLuhan and Q. Fiore, "War and Peace in the Global Village," Bantam Books, New York, 1968.
6. M. L. Dertouzas and J. Moses, *The Computer Age*, The MIT Press, Cambridge, Mass., 1980.
7. M. Blumenthal, "DP Outlays to Exceed $50 Billion," *Computerworld*, February 25, 1980, p. 1.
8. H. Seneker, "IBM: The Empire Strikes Back," *Forbes*, June 23, 1980, pp. 40–44.
9. J. Nussbaum, "Computers and Cyclicality," *Datamation*, April 1980, pp. 160–162.
10. "The Datamation 100—The Top 100 U.S. Companies in the DP Industry," *Datamation*, July 1980, pp. 87–182.
11. G. W. Brock, *The U.S. Computer Industry*, Ballinger Publishing Co., Cambridge, Massachusetts, 1975.
12. J. T. Soma, *Computer Industry: An Economic-Legal Analysis of Its Technology and Growth*, Lexington Books, Lexington, Massachusetts, 1976.
13. E. J. Laurie, *Computers, Automation and Society*, Irwin, Inc., Homewood, Illinois, 1979.
14. "The Age of Miracle Chips," *Time*, February 20, 1978, pp. 44–59.

2

A HISTORY OF COMPUTERS

2.1 PREHISTORIC AND EARLY CALCULATING DEVICES

Although the computer age may be said to have existed only since 1945, when the first electronic computer was introduced, man has apparently always had a need to process data and to calculate. The known history of computers and calculating machines in western civilization reaches back a thousand years before the birth of Christ, at which time the abacus was in use.

As you read the accounts of the development of computers, keep in mind the different ways of dealing with problems used by the various inventors; that is, think of how they conceived of the operations of mathematics and computation. Also, remember the effects the computing systems had on those who used them—for, as it has been pointed out many times, machines shape their users as much as the men who make them shape the machines.*

For centuries, man has tried to use power from other sources to do his work. One of the oldest forms of engineering is found in long-established efforts to make machines that will carry and change the nature of power and speed. Wind-

*Some of this chapter is based on material from *Technology in Western Civilization, Volume II: Technology in the Twentieth Century*, edited by Melvin Kranzberg and Carroll W. Pursell, Jr. Copyright © 1967 by The Regents of the University of Wisconsin. Used by permission of Oxford University Press, Inc.

mills, gear wheels, belts and pulleys, and block and tackle are devices which alter, transmit, and reduce or increase the magnitude of power or speed or both.

Gear wheels, however, have another function which early inventors were quick to notice. They can be adapted to count rotations. Clockworks depend on this principle. So does the odometer in your car, which measures the miles the car has traveled. It has evolved from a counting device described in an account dating back possibly two thousand years. This device, called Hero's odometer, is also found on one form or another in modern instruments for metering gas and electricity. It depends on the action of the pegged counting wheel. A schematic drawing of this device is shown below.

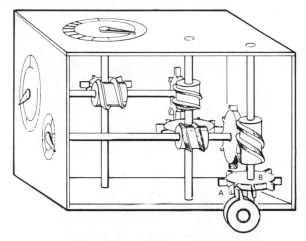

FIGURE 2–1   Hero's odometer.

In Figure 2–1, the pegged counting wheel A turns with the axle of the vehicle upon which the odometer is mounted (or it turns with a rotor shaft if the device is metering flow). Each time A revolves it moves B, the first wheel in the gear train, one peg. This motion is carried forward by other gears. Pointers attached to their shafts show how many revolutions each gear makes. These can be arranged to give direct readings in whatever quantities are being measured.

Equipment for counting or calculating has existed far longer than the odometer described above. The best example for our purposes is the abacus. It employs two principles which have probably been part of human experience from its earliest emergence. The first is the use of things to act as counters: stones, chips of wood, or fingers, for instance. These counters represent the abstract idea of quantity. A primitive shepherd could place a pebble in his pouch for each sheep when he let the flock out every morning. When the sheep returned at night, he could then remove a pebble for each sheep that crowded into the sheepfold. If there were pebbles left over, the shepherd knew there were sheep unaccounted for.

The second principle is the use of position to show different kinds of quantities. As the flock grew larger, the pebble system could become unwieldy. The shepherd (or his overseer, since Parkinson's Law has been in effect from earliest times) would place a pebble in a different counting place for each group of six sheep or ten, or twenty. This procedure was adopted in early counting boards, and finally on counting frames on which small beads were strung. The pebbles of the counting boards were called *calculi*, from which our modern term *calculate* and related words are derived. The modern abacus finds extensive use in oriental countries. There is an annual competition for schoolchildren in Japan to find the most accurate and dextrous student of this art; complicated arithmetic and mathematical computations can be done with surprising speed on this counting frame.

FIGURE 2-2   An abacus. *Courtesy of The Smithsonian Institution.*

Calculating machines have also existed in forms from prehistoric times. One of the most fascinating calculating devices was built by stone age men. It is an attraction for tourists today. The ancient British stone monument, on the Salisbury Plain in southern England, is called Stonehenge. An astronomer and a team of computer scientists have analyzed the probable origins and use of Stonehenge; they have also published a theory of explanation.[2, 3] According to Hawkins, Stonehenge was built between 1900 and 1600 B. C. It required 1,497,680 mandays to construct.

Why was Stonehenge built? With the aid of a computer, Hawkins examined the possible correlations of the alignments of the stones and the rise and set points of any heavenly bodies during the period 2000—1500 B. C. This avenue for examination was supported by the fact that if you stand in the center of Stonehenge

FIGURE 2–3 Stonehenge. *Courtesy of Varian Data Machines.*

on a clear midsummer morning (around June 22) you will see the sun rise almost exactly over the stone called "The heelstone." With the aid of the electronic computer, Hawkins was able to draw some startling conclusions about this ancient stone calculating device.

Apparently, Stonehenge may have been built as an excellent astronomical observatory, possibly used to predict the changes of the seasons. Prehistoric people were deeply concerned by eclipses of the sun and moon, and Stonehenge could have provided means for predicting them, too. The scientists who have studied this remarkable monument are astonished at the skill and precision with which the huge structure was assembled by primitive men who had no engineering devices to help them, but who were moved by a need for a device to aid their calculations.

More recent evidence of man's need for computing equipment was discovered in a society scarcely more modern technologically than the neolithic one in which Stonehenge was built.* In the Peruvian Andes, about 500 years ago, the ruling Incas had established a "perfect" society—one for which all needs were supplied according to an elaborate system of information. This information was the basis for the Inca's decisions. The entire region over which the Incas ruled was divided and redivided, and all important facts were recorded from the level of individual families on up, through an elaborate system of counting and reporting on knotted cords called *quipus*. (The word *quipu* means "to knot"; the basic record was a knot in a cord.) These cords were assembled by the regional and district officers of a vast bureaucracy and carried by runners over a fully developed highway system to the capital at Cuzco. From there, requests for more information, and orders to be carried out, were sent back and forth.

This system was perfected through four centuries and 13 successive reigns of Incas, until the Inca society was destroyed by the Spaniard Francisco Pizarro.

*Adapted with permission from "The Almost-Perfect Decision Device," from *Input for Modern Management*, Volume IV, Number 2, 1968. Published by Sperry Rand Univac.

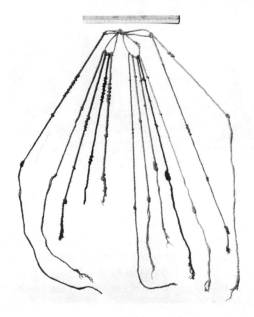

FIGURE 2–4   A *quipu. Courtesy The American Museum of Natural History.*

The computing system they had devised never failed the Incas. In fact, the last orders to go from an Inca ruler to his subjects by *quipu* were those that brought back enough gold to fill the prison cell of the Inca named Atahuallpa. The gold was ordered to pay the ransom for the release of the Inca. The world knows of the Spanish treachery. Even after the invaders had killed Atahuallpa and placed a puppet ruler on his throne, the system of computing and accounting based on the *quipu* continued to function—perhaps too well. In the greedy hands of the Spanish conquerors, the *quipu* system became a tool of easy enslavement and exploitation.

2.2   FROM MECHANICAL DEVICES TO MODERN COMPUTERS

The practical applications of counting devices seemed to justify their invention and existence from prehistoric times. Nevertheless, there have always been persons who were interested in the abstract ideas behind the practical considerations; from such theoreticians have come many contributions with great practical potential. One person who enjoyed working with numbers, and who put this enjoyment to use in a manner which produced practical benefits, was John Napier (1550–1617). This Scottish scholar observed that he could make tables of the results of multiplications. He also observed the relationship between arithmetic series and geometric series which can be seen in the table below.

TABLE 2-1
Two Kinds of Series

Arithmetic series:	1	2	3	4	5	6	7
Geometric series based on 2:	2	4	8	16	32	64	128

Napier invented and named the *logarithm*, which allows us to represent any member of the second series by a member of the first series. You can see that 2 multiplied by itself 5 times ("raised to the fifth power") is 32. We can express this fact by saying that the logarithm to the base 2 of 32 is 5. This expression is written $\log_2 32 = 5$. Similarly, $\log_2 8 = 3$.

We can *add* the logarithms of any two numbers to get the logarithm of their product. For instance, $\log_2 4 = 2$, and $\log_2 32 = 5$. Adding these logarithms, we get $2 + 5 = 7$; 7 is the logarithm of the product of 4×32, or 128. Had we multiplied 4×32, we would have obtained the same answer. In simple problems of this nature, the advantage of logarithms is not easily seen. However, for very large numbers and complicated calculations, a system in which multiplication is replaced by simple addition, for which the answers can be read easily from tables, has obvious advantages.

Napier put these advantages to use in a simple invention which had come to be called "Napier's bones" (from the ivory from which it was constructed) or "Napier's rods." He transcribed the results of multiplications from tables onto a series of rods. By arranging the rods side by side and matching up the numbers he wanted to multiply, Napier could read off the answer very quickly without having to do any calculations at all. In setting up this device, Napier combined the ideas of representing abstract quantities by numerical symbols and of showing their values by relative position on a measuring device—the system used by anyone who makes a yardstick.

The system of representing distance and motion by a point moving along a line, which came to us through Greek geometry, was next employed by Edmond Gunter, who marked off Napier's logarithms on a line and then added the logarithms by using a pair of dividers. By 1654 (Napier having published information about his rods in 1617), Robert Bissaker placed the Gunter-Napier lines on sliding wooden strips, or rules, thus inventing the first form of the modern slide rule. Within two hundred years the slide rule was perfected, providing an extremely versatile hand calculating device still very much in evidence today.

By 1700, then, the numerical, or *digital* calculator, represented by the abacus, and the *analog* calculator, represented by the slide rule, were in common use.*

Digital refers to digits, which are the counting numbers (in informal usage; technically, "numbers" are abstractions and integers are the symbols for them). The digital computer works with numbers, while the *analog* computer works with quantities, such as lengths on rulers, that stand for numbers. You can measure two feet digitally by marking off 24 inches on a yardstick; analogically, by putting

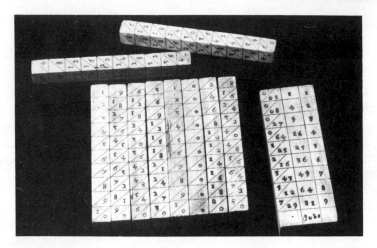

FIGURE 2–5   Napier's bones. *Courtesy of The Smithsonian Institution.*

To these useful machines, Blaise Pascal (1623–1662) added a third which combined characteristics of both: the numerical adding machine. Pascal was working as a tax clerk. He found it wearying to add the three kinds of coins with which he had to deal, so he invented a counting machine which was similar in some ways to Hero's odometer.

In Pascal's machine, which showed numbers printed on the rotating gears, the adjacent wheels had pins like the one in Hero's machine. When the first wheel was rotated one time, a pin on its edge advanced the wheel in the next place to the left, just as the modern odometer changes its indication from, say, 09 (miles) to 10 (miles). Both addition and subtraction could be performed on Pascal's instrument. Although it was not carefully made and therefore was occasionally inaccurate, it became the prototype for counting devices which can be found everywhere today. An especially handy mechanical adder is often used by modern shoppers to calculate their expected bills; another is used to count crowds passing through a gate; others calculate the numbers of copies turned out by duplicating machines. Of his invention, Pascal himself wrote in 1649:

> Dear reader, this notice will serve to inform you that I submit to
> the public a small machine of my invention, by means of which
> you alone may, without any effort, perform all the operations of
> arithmetic, and may be relieved of the work which has often

two one-foot rulers end-to-end. You can measure the passage of a minute digitally by counting 60 seconds, one at a time; analogically, by observing the circular displacement of the minute hand around one-sixtieth of the clock face. Napier's bones worked with digits, so his was a digital computing system. Gunter's measurements were analogous to numbers; the larger distances stood for larger numbers. His was an analog computing system.

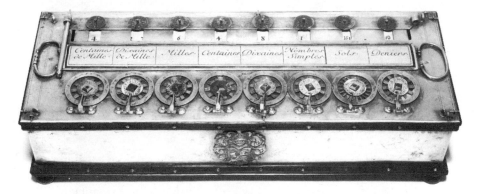

FIGURE 2–6 Pascal's adder. *Courtesy of IBM Corporation.*

times fatigued your spirit, when you have worked with the counters or with the pen. As for simplicity of movement of the operations, I have so devised it that, although the operations of arithmetic are in a way opposed the one to the other—as addition to subtraction, and multiplication to division—nevertheless they are all performed on this machine by a single unique movement. The facility of this movement of operation is very evident since it is just as easy to move one thousand or ten thousand dials, all at one time; if one desires to make a single dial move, although all accomplish the movement perfectly. The most ignorant find as many advantages as the most experienced. The instrument makes up for ignorance and for lack of practice, and even without any effort of the operator, it makes possible shortcuts by itself, whenever the numbers are set down.

Gottfried Wilhelm von Leibniz (1646–1716) was next to advance the design of mechanical calculating devices. His machine, built in 1694, was based on the principle of repeated addition. Instead of multiplying 25 by 7, Leibniz added 25 to 25 seven times. His machine was not constructed well, and therefore was not entirely reliable, but it was a refinement of ideas of earlier centuries. There are many adaptations of Leibniz's machine in modern office calculating equipment.

Note that none of the machines described so far could do anything other than compute or store information put into them by their human operators (or by outside agents, as in the case of the rotating wheel in Hero's odometer). In this sense, we may say that all of these devices were *passive*.

Neither Leibniz nor Pascal was an engineer. It took many years before engineers turned their talents to making equipment that was precise enough to ensure accuracy in computing machinery. However, improvements were soon to come from the clock making industry, which was refining its machine parts steadily from crude wooden works to dependable and rugged metal ones. In the eighteenth and nineteenth centuries, major advances were made in metalworking and in shaping tools and gears to fine tolerances, so that eventually precision clockwork machinery could be built. The same skills could also be applied to machinery necessary for calculators and eventually for computers.

It can be seen that by the eighteenth century two influences combined to provide the force from which the modern computer has evolved. The first was that of the counting system, whether by markers, counters, or rotating gears. The second was that of the mechanical precision which came with the manufacture of refined instruments.[22]

By the early twentieth century, mechanical calculators had become very important as tools of science and commerce. Probably the most significant inventor and contributor to this development was a gifted English mathematician, Charles Babbage (1792–1871). In many ways Babbage may be considered the grandfather of the computer—yet his work was to lead only to failure. Babbage was a theoretician. By 1823, he had evolved several basic concepts for what he called a "Difference Engine." Babbage had intended this machine, in the spirit of his age, to relieve man of constant drudgery. The Difference Engine was designed to calculate with numbers, to store information, to select different ways of solving problems according to the most efficient approaches,* and to deliver printed solutions to problems both during the solutions and at their conclusions. Unlike the abacus, Pascal's adder, and Leibniz's multiplier, Babbage's machine would not need constant attention and information from its human operator. It would·

FIGURE 2–7   Charles Babbage. *Photo Courtesy of Science Museum, London.*

*It is not uncommon for modern computers to provide solutions to problems—solutions which the programmers did not have in mind. Choosing the most effective of alternate routes to a solution is called *branching*.

be entirely automatic. Furthermore, Babbage saw his engine as one composed of several smaller engines, each working together with the others, each performing its own separate chore: the "mill," which did the arithmetic; the receiver, to take in information; the printer, to put out information; a device to transfer information from one component to another; and a "store" of information. One can grasp the magnitude of the problems Babbage faced, and perhaps a little of the overreaching ambition that brought him to grief, by reading his own description, written in *The Life of a Philosopher* in 1864:

> Every formula which the Analytical Engine can be required to compute consists of certain algebraical operations to be performed upon given letters, and of certain other modifications depending on the numerical value assigned to those letters. There are therefore two sets of cards, the first to direct the nature of the operations to be performed—these are called operation cards: the other to direct the particular variables on which those cards are required to operate—these latter are called variable cards. Now the symbol of each variable or constant is placed at the top of a column capable of containing any required number of digits. Under this arrangement, when any formula is required to be computed, a set of operation cards must be strung together, which contain the series of operations in the order in which they occur. Another set of cards must then be strung together, to call in the variables into the mill, in the order in which they are required to be acted upon. Each operation card will require three other cards, two to represent the variables and constants and their numerical values upon which the previous operation card is to act, and one to indicate the variable on which the arithmetical result of this operation is to be placed. But each variable has below it, on the same axis, a certain number of figure-wheels marked on their edges with the ten digits: upon these any number the machine is capable of holding can be placed. Whenever the variables are ordered into the mill, these figures will be brought in, and the operation indicated by the preceding card will then be performed upon them. The result of this operation will then be replaced in the store.

Although Babbage's machine, which called for the elements found in modern computers, resembled a human intelligence in some of its characteristics, it would have depended entirely on the instructions fed into it by the operator. Nevertheless, it represented a significant advance over earlier machines. The astonishing fact about its development, however, is that it was never built! Babbage spent his life dealing unsuccessfully with the engineering difficulties atten-

210. Métier Jacquard.

FIGURE 2–8   Jacquard's loom. Program cards, attached to each other in belt fashion, fed from the floor into the loom. *Courtesy of IBM Corporation.*

dant upon making such a complicated machine. His plans were too ambitious. Modern computer experts have concluded from his papers that the machine would have worked if it had been built, but fate did not allow Babbage that successful culmination to his career.

In the eighteenth century, French artisans had become highly skilled in manufacturing intricately-designed fabrics on looms. The machinery for weaving the designs was directed by a method perfected by Joseph Jacquard (1752–1834) early in the nineteenth century. Jacquard used cards punched with holes to position threads for the weaving process. A hole allowed a hooked wire, containing a thread, to be inserted into the pattern. If no hole was present, no wire emerged and no colored thread was allowed into the pattern during that operation of the loom. For each operation, a card was provided; the whole collection of cards made up a program which directed the weaving.

The punched card appealed to manufacturers of calculating equipment. In 1890, The United States Census was compiled with the aid of Hollerith computing machines, named for Herman Hollerith, an inventor who had adapted the punched card system to the special needs of census-taking. Hollerith had added electrical sensing equipment to take advantage of the information holes in the punched cards.*

By 1937, the punched card operation, combined with electrical drive mechanisms (also added by Hollerith), had become so efficient that they suggested timely application to the newest form of computing machine, then taking

---

*Hollerith's company was to become the International Business Machines Corporation.

FIGURE 2–9 Hollerith equipment. *Courtesy of IBM Corporation.*

shape in the imagination of Howard Aiken, an instructor in applied mathematics who also held a doctorate in physics. (Aiken repeated much of what Babbage had accomplished nearly 100 years before. However, he learned of Babbage's work three years after beginning his own—thus needlessly duplicating the efforts of his predecessor!) [9]

Aiken worked out a plan to set mechanical calculators to working on mathematical problems in controlled sequences. He set up a project to develop the necessary equipment, and with the support of International Business Machines Corporation and Harvard University, and assistance from four co-workers from IBM, he built the first computer. This machine, called International Business Machines Automatic Sequence Controlled Calculator, and also known as the Harvard Mark I computer, was presented to Harvard in August, 1944. It was the first information-processing machine.

The Mark I was electrically-powered. Instructions and data were fed into it by punched paper tape. The components worked on electrical, electronic and mechanical principles. Although the machine was very large, and limited in speed and applications by comparison with modern machines, it was the first to possess all the characteristics of a true computer.

The first electronic computer was built in 1946 by J. P. Eckert and J. W. Mauchly at the University of Pennsylvania. The nearly instantaneous working of electronic components made it possible for this machine, called ENIAC,* to multiply two ten—digit numerals in three thousandths of a second, compared to

*Electronic Numerical Integrator and Computer. The use of acronyms like ENIAC increased rapidly from this point, with engineers vying with each other to find names that would yield interesting or catchy acronyms. It was not long before a MANIAC appeared, for instance.

FIGURE 2–10   Mark I. *Courtesy of IBM Corporation.*

roughly three seconds for Mark I. ENIAC contained 18,000 vacuum tubes; it was huge, taking up the walls of a room 20 by 40 feet in size. Its use was limited to the special problems of ballistics. The designers avoided the mistakes that had caused Babbage to fail, among them those which come from trying to accomplish too much at one time. [19, 20, 21, 23, 24]

A machine constructed at the University of Iowa by John Atanasoff between 1939 and 1942 also contends for honor as the first electronic computer. [20]

Mark I and ENIAC were digital computers. Analog computers also became available at about the same time, in part through the need for machinery to control guns and radars in World War II. Among such devices were the servomechanisms which translated motion into signals to which either machines or men could respond. Automatic-cannon gunsights, for instance, were built so that, as the gunner tracked his target, a computing device would cause the sight image to change, forcing the gunner to "lead" his target sufficiently to hit it in motion.

It may be said that the modern electronic computer is not so much directly related to the earlier forms of calculating machines as it is a result of their evolution under the influence of new technology in radio, radar, and telephone transmissions. Eventually, computer designers refined the various components of the computer system (described by Babbage a century before) by introducing

FIGURE 2–11   ENIAC. *Courtesy of UNIVAC Division of Sperry-Rand Corporation.*

transistors and printed circuits. This made possible smaller and still more efficient machinery.

Calculation in modern machines is usually carried out in the binary system, which can be adapted to carry both instructions and data to the machine. This possibility arises from the latter-day application of a system of logic invented by the English mathematician, George Boole (1815–1864). The Boolean system shows how statements can be related to each other logically. It provides a way of working through difficult problems, and its fundamental simplicity suits it well to applications involving switches and electrical circuits—as in telephone switching and digital computers.

In the mid-40s, John Von Neumann, a brilliant mathematician at Princeton University, demonstrated how binary logic and arithmetic could be made to work together in calculating and in forming stored programs. Von Neumann demonstrated that one could encode instructions to the machine in the same language used for the data it processed. This especially important demonstration made it possible to mix instructions and data in the program; both could also be stored in the computer.

These arrangements make possible the design, construction, and operation of units which can be employed separately or added to each other in many combinations. They also make it possible to store programs and data in memory com-

FIGURE 2–12   John Von Neumann with the IAS computer, completed in 1952 under his direction. *Courtesy of The Smithsonian Institution.*

ponents which are compact, accurate, and easily accessible. Finally, Von Neumann's legacy of proof also makes it possible for computers to transmit information to, and to receive it from, other computer installations. A company can purchase a large central computer and can program all of its different operations—from manufacturing through sales and inventory control, for instance—through the application of the computer language in the binary means of expression.

SUMMARY

Each man stands upon the shoulders of the man who preceded him. While Eckert and Mauchly developed the first electronic computer, they had the developments of their predecessors to build upon. Those previous developments are numerous; some of them are listed in chronological order in Table 2-2. From the time of the first calculator and decision device to the most recent electronic computer, man has done "the impossible." In Chapter 15, we examine what may develop in the future. However, we are certainly impressed by the developments of the past. In the next chapter, we examine the nature of computers and how they work.

TABLE 2-2

Historical Development of Calculating Machines
(Dates are approximate.)

1600 B. C.	Stonehenge
1000 B. C.	Abacus
1400 A. D.	Quipu
1617	Napier's "bones"
1642	Pascal's calculator
1673	Liebniz's calculator
1801	Jacquard's punched-card looms
1822	Babbage's difference engine
1890	Hollerith's punched-card tabulators
1911	Monroe Calculator, first mass-produced desk calculator
1930	Electric desk calculators
1937	Aiken's Mark I
1942	Atanasoff's electronic machine
1945	Von Neumann's proposal for a stored-program computer
1946	ENIAC computer
1950	MIT WHIRLWIND computer
1954	Univac I computer commercially available
1955	IBM 650 computer commercially available

CHAPTER 2 PROBLEMS

P2-1. Calculating machines have helped man through the ages. What two ideas were used to develop an abacus?

P2-2. What calculation was possible using Napier's bones? On what principle was it based?

P2-3. What limited the practical success of Liebniz's multiplier and Pascal's mechanical adder?

P2-4. What was the prime contribution of Jacquard toward the development of a modern computer? Can you name a musical instrument which uses the same device Jacquard introduced?

P2-5. What was the prime contribution of Hollerith and of Von Neumann?

P2-6. Mechanical desk calculators are used extensively today. When was the first commercially mass-produced calculator available? On what mechanical principle does the mechanical calculator work?

P2-7. The *quipu* was an information device used by the Incas. How was information stored and transmitted?

P2-8. If those who constructed Stonehenge had 1,000 men working six days per week, how many years would it have taken to construct Stonehenge, according to Hawkins' estimate?

CHAPTER 2 REFERENCES

1. T. M. Smith, "Origins of the Computer" in *Technology in Western Civilization*, Volume II, edited by M. Kranzberg and C. W. Pursell, Jr., Oxford University Press, New York, 1967.
2. G. S. Hawkins, "The Secret of Stonehenge," *Harper's Magazine*, June 1964, pp. 96–99.
3. G. S. Hawkins, *Stonehenge Decoded*, Doubleday Publishing Co., Garden City, New York, 1965.
4. "The Almost-Perfect Decision Device," from *Input for Modern Management*, Sperry Rand Univac, New York, Volume IV, Number 2, 1968, pp. 3–7.
5. E. K. Yasake, "Fragments of Computer History," *Datamation*, Sept., 1976, pp. 131–135.
6. P. Morrison and E. Morrison, *Charles Babbage and his Calculating Engines*, Dover Publications, Inc., New York, 1961.
7. J. Bernstein, *The Analytical Engine*, Alfred Knopf, Inc., New York, 1963.
8. D. W. Kean, *The Author of the Analytic Engine*, Thompson Book Co., Washington, D. C., 1966.
9. H. Aiken, "Proposed Calculating Machine," reprinted in *IEEE Spectrum*, Vol. 1, No. 8, 1964.
10. A. H. Taub, ed., *John Von Neumann: Collected Works*, Macmillan Co., New York, 1963.
11. B. Randall, *The Origins of Digital Computers*, Springer-Verlag, New York, 1974.
12. M. V. Wilkes, "How Babbage's Dream Came True," *Nature*, Vol. 257, Oct. 16, 1975, pp. 541–544.
13. H. H. Goldstine, *The Computer from Pascal to Von Neumann*, Princeton University Press, Princeton, New Jersey, 1974.
14. H. Tropp, "The Effervescent Years: A Retrospective," *IEEE Spectrum*, February, 1974, pp. 70–81.
15. H. D. Huskey and V. R. Huskey, "Chronology of Computing Devices," *IEEE Transactions on Computers*, Dec. 1976, pp. 1210–1222.
16. M. Harmon, *Stretching Man's Mind: A History of Data Processing*, Mason/Charter, New York, 1975.
17. C. Eames and R. Eames, *A Computer Perspective*, Harvard University Press, Cambridge, Massachusetts, 1974.
18. T. M. Smith, "Project Whirlwind," *Technology and Culture*, July, 1976, pp. 447–464.
19. "Computers and Space—A History," *Electronics*, April 17, 1980, pp. 323–414.
20. W. D. Gardner, "Will the Inventor of the First Digital Computer Please Stand Up?" *Datamation*, February 1974, pp. 88–90.

21. A. Dahl, "The Last of the First," *Datamation*, June 1978, pp. 145–149.
22. M. Gleiser, "Men and Machines Before Babbage," *Datamation,* October 1978, pp. 125–130.
23. K. C. Redmond and T. M. Smith, *"Lessons from Project Whirlwind,"* October 1977, pp. 50–59.
24. N. Metropolis, *A History of Computing in the 20th Century*, Academic Press, New York, 1980.

3

THE NATURE OF COMPUTERS AND COMPUTING

3.1 INFORMATION PROCESSING AND THE ELECTRONIC DIGITAL COMPUTER

The electronic computer allows man to increase his productivity and permits him to do tasks he would be unable to complete without the computer. As we found in Chapter 1, the computer is a machine capable of (1) accepting data; (2) performing described operations on the data, and (3) providing the results of these operations. Thus the computer also permits man to improve his output per unit of time, or productivity. We can say that the computer's two most important contributions as a tool are to increase (1) the speed of operation, and (2) accuracy and quality of operation in terms of productivity.

Of course, when we consider these two factors, we realize that the computer enables us to accomplish tasks that we would probably never even attempt manually. For example, if the number of input data is greater than several million and the time necessary to accomplish a task is greater than fifty years, we would probably never attempt it. Yet it is just such tasks that we can ask the computer to accomplish.

Symbols are the basis of any language. The computer accepts and processes symbols in order to provide information. The symbols that today's computers process are the letters of the alphabet and numbers, as well as several useful algebraic and business symbols.

In this text, we consider the uses and applications of the electronic digital computer. The term *computer* has already been discussed in Chapter 1 and reviewed above. The term *electronic* implies that the computer is powered by electrical and electronic devices rather than by mechanical ones or those affected by heat or air pressure. Here *digital* refers to discrete, noncontinuous quantities, as contrasted with continuous quantities. For example, the computer accepts individual numbers, or signs, or other symbols. This set of statements leads to the definition:

ELECTRONIC DIGITAL COMPUTER An information-processing device that accepts and processes data represented by discrete symbols. It is constructed primarily of electric or electronic devices.

A typical electronic digital computer, the IBM 3033 Data Processing System, is shown in Figure 3–1. The electronic devices which constitute the computer are identified by function in Figure 3–1. We can use the computer to process the input data by sorting them, or by completing a calculation, for example. Of course, there are many ways to accomplish a given task; the two advantages we seek are increased *speed* and increased *quality* of processing. The process of ac

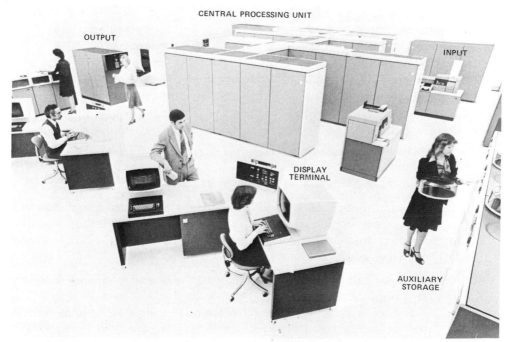

FIGURE 3–1 The IBM 3033, first delivered in 1979. *Courtesy IMB Corporation.*

counting, for instance, is a good example of a task most readily accomplished by a digital computer system. Over the years accounting has shifted in great part from ledgers to punched cards, and then to computer processes.

Information processing is a series of planned actions and operations upon input data, taken to achieve a desired result. The actions taken may be illustrated by a common data processing operation which a person usually accomplishes manually but which is increasingly accomplished automtically by data processing service companies: completing a Federal Income Tax Form.

Recall Figure 1–1, which shows the data input, the data processing action, and finally the information output. In the case of the IRS form, the output information required is the amount of tax owed. The data input is the person's salary or wages and income; deductions; and other information, such as the number of dependents. This is the series of planned actions taken upon the input data to calculate the tax due:

(1) Provide the necessary input data.
(2) Record the input data on the Tax Form 1040 worksheet.
(3) Examine the Tax Instruction Booklet for the necessary instructions.
(4) Carry out the necessary arithmetic calculations.
(5) Record the tax due on the correct line on the Form 1040.

As is often the case, the tax calculation will require carrying out steps 3 and 4 several times* prior to recording the tax due in step 5, since we must consult the instructions at different stages. This example of information processing is illustrated graphically in Figure 3–2.

In the preceding example, information-processing required:

(1) Data input
(2) Storage and retrieval of data, and instructions for data-processing actions
(3) Arithmetic steps
(4) Output of result
(5) Control of all steps above by the individual taxpayer

Now, if we want to construct an automatic information-processor, we shall find it necessary to carry out the same steps to complete the processing. A computer follows a similar process. It is composed of five basic units, as shown in Figure 3–3. The five basic units or functions are:

(1) An *input* unit or function which accepts the necessary input data and instructions
(2) A *storage* or *memory* unit in which computer instructions and the data as well as intermediate results are stored

*Each time a task is carried out, the carrying-out is called an *iteration*.

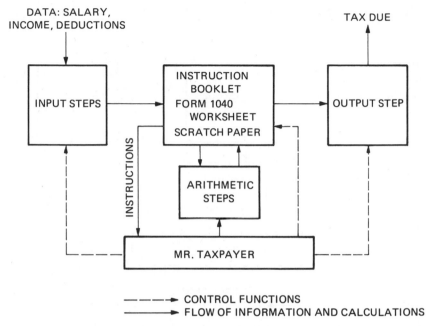

FIGURE 3–2   The information processing operation for calculating income tax.

(3) An *arithmetic* unit in which numbers can be added, subtracted, compared in size to other numbers, etc.

(4) An *output* unit which provides the desired result in a suitable form, such as a printed number

(5) A *control* unit which controls the other four units, directs their order of operation and supervises the overall operation of the computer

The several devices which may accomplish the function of input, output, and storage for the IBM 3033 are shown with labels in Figure 3–1. The arithmetic and control functions are accomplished by the central processing unit, located in the module on which the console is mounted.

The basic unit of the electronic digital computer is the arithmetic unit. It performs the arithmetic operations accurately, reliably, and at high speed. However, the high-speed ability of the arithmetic unit would be wasted if for each operation it had to go back to the input unit for the same information at every step. The storage unit holds the data, the instructions and the intermediate results of the calculations. (The incorporation of instructions in the storage unit for ready and high-speed accessibility is the stored-program concept introduced by John Von Neumann.) Since the instructions are in the memory, just as the intermediate calculation results are, it is possible for the computer to modify the instructions themselves as the calculation progresses.

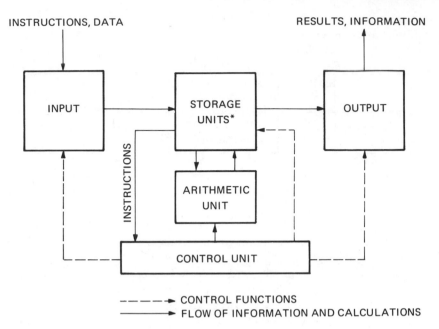

FIGURE 3–3   The five basic units of an electronic digital computer.

*Instructions may be stored in the storage units (see text). This feature makes it possible to build programs within programs, which in turn enables the computer to work very rapidly without requiring many repeated references to input.

The control unit supervises the flow of information and calculations and requests from memory the instructions and data necessary at each stage in the calculation sequence. The control functions are shown as dotted lines in Figure 3–3.

The input and output units serve as connections between the user and the machine. The input device may also serve as the output device, as in the case of the typewriter shown in Figure 3–1. We may also enter data on a magnetic tape, punched cards, or other media. Note the output line printer shown in Figure 3–1. We consider some specific input and output devices in Chapter 10.

3.2   THE NATURE OF COMPUTERS

An electronic digital computer possesses three advantages which make it extremely useful. They are:

(1) High speed of operation
(2) Precision and accuracy
(3) Reliability

Modern digital computers are constructed of electronic devices which enable the computer to complete an arithmetic calculation in approximately one-millionth of a second—or less! The increase in the speed of computers is shown in Figure 3—4a, which gives the number of additions per second. Figure 3—4b shows the speed of storage in the central processing unit, in thousands of additions per second.

Computer size decreased by a factor of 10,000 from 1955 to 1980; see Figure 3—4c. An integrated electronic central storage unit is as small as one-tenth of one cu. ft. (173 cu. in. or 2,830 cu. cm.). This is the size of a small box approximately five inches on a side. For example, one such small integrated circuit device, which cost $3,400 in 1980, provides computer power equivalent to that of the IBM 701, which cost $1 million in 1952. As an indication of the size of a modern computer, a typical small computer is shown in Figure 3—5. These small computers are commonly called minicomputers. They provide the power and speed of many large computers of only five years ago. A complete small computer system is shown in Figure 3—6; it uses small punched cards. The system, called the IBM System/3, is designed especially for small business use. Through the utilization of high-speed electronic devices, notably transistors and solid-state devices, the speed and size of electronic digital computers has improved dramatically during the past decade. If the trends continue, we shall have a computer the size of a shoe box capable of a billion additions per second—by the end of this decade. [4]

In 1979, IBM announced a new 4300 series which increased the internal speed five times over that of the System/370, which IBM had announced in 1970. As an article in the *Wall Street Journal* indicates, there are many more announcements of faster and smaller computers to be expected in the next several years. For example, see Figure 3—9.

The second advantage of an electronic digital computer is the great precision available in the calculation process. The *precision* of a computer may be defined in this way:

PRECISION The degree of exactness or discrimination with which a quantity is stated. The amount of detail used in representing the data.

Precision is to be compared with *accuracy*. For example, four-place numerals are less precise than six-place numerals; nevertheless, a properly computed four-place numeral might be more accurate than an improperly computed six-place numeral. The *accuracy* of a computer is defined as follows:

ACCURACY The degree of freedom from error; that is, the degree of conformity to truth or to a rule.

As an exercise, consider two computers which are to add the number exactly one (1) to the number exactly zero (0). We expect a result exactly equal to one. The output we receive from computer A is 1.00 and from computer B is 1.0000. Which is more precise?

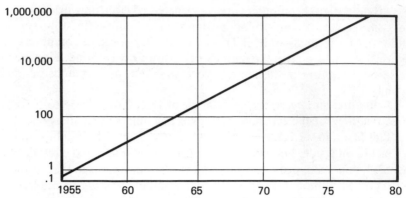

FIGURE 3–4a   Computing power in the United States.

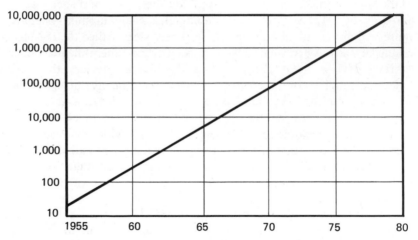

FIGURE 3–4b   CPU/Storage speed in thousands of additions per second.

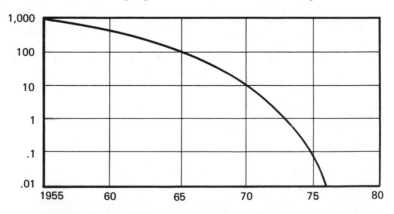

FIGURE 3–4c   CPU/Storage size in cubic feet.

FIGURE 3–5   The TRS-80 Model III personal business computer utilizes BASIC
language and two floppy disks, which are placed in the machine through
doors above and below the name plate. This computer sells for about
$3000. *Courtesy of Tandy Corporation.*

Now consider computers C and D and give them the same calculation to perform. The result from computer C is 1.000 and from computer D is 1.0100.
Which computer is more precise and which is more accurate? Consider your
answer before reading the following explanation.

Computer B is more *precise* than computer A, since it provides an answer
with great detail, with four decimal places for B as contrasted with two decimal
places in the case in A. Computer D is more precise than computer C since it provides four decimal places while C provides only three decimal places. However,
computer C is more accurate, since we know that the exact or truthful answer is
1.0000, and the answer from computer D is in error in the second decimal place.

We strive to obtain and utilize computers which are both precise and accurate. Computers with both characteristics can be bought, but the limitation on extreme accuracy and precision is the excessive cost for computers which give both.
Typically, a computer is able to perform calculations with numbers to a precision
and accuracy of ten decimal places.

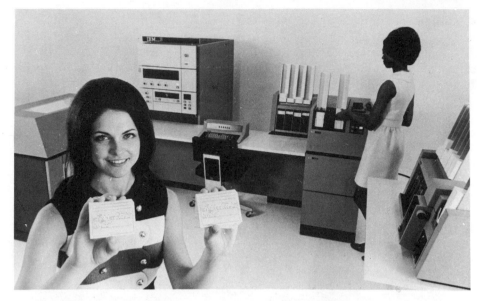

FIGURE 3-6   The IBM System/3, which utilizes a small punched card and is designed for small-business use. The card is one-third the size of the familiar punched card, but it holds 20 percent more information. *Courtesy IBM Corporation.*

The third advantage of the electronic digital computer is *reliability*, which is defined:

RELIABILITY The quality of freedom from failure, usually expressed as the probability that a failure will not occur in a given amount of use.

The reliability of a typical computer might be expressed as a 95 percent probability that it will *not* miscalculate one error in one week, and that it will *not* cease functioning within a month. (A computer is not affected by fatigue, boredom, or numbers with many decimal places as a man carrying out similar calculations would be. Thus, a computer is immensely more reliable than a man in completing long, difficult calculations.) [9]

Now let us consider some of the disadvantageous characteristics of electronic digital computers. Three of these characteristics are:

(1) Limited inherent intelligence
(2) Limited language-handling capacity
(3) High cost

We say that the computer has limited inherent intelligence because it must be told what to do. (As we shall find in Chapter 14, man is developing an artificial intelligence capability for special-purpose computers. Nevertheless, in general, the digital computer can do only what man has instructed it to do.)

Also, the computer possesses a very limited language-handling capacity at present. Typically, its vocabulary is limited to a hundred words or so, and its grammar is primitive, However, computers are being developed which will have expanded language capabilities. At present, only a very small subset of the English language can be addressed to a computer—perhaps that possessed by a student in first grade.

The cost of computing power is illustrated in Figure 3–7, which shows the central storage coast in dollars per million additions. Notice how the cost of storage has decreased by a factor of five hundred over the past decade. Generally, new and faster models of computers, in a given series, have appeared every four years on the average. Computer purchasers have almost always found it economically advantageous to change to the newer models. For example, a model may cost twice as much, but its speed will be four times as great, justifying the added cost.

A relationship between the computing power (essentially speed) and the cost of the computer has been deduced by Grosch: [3]

$$\text{Cost of computer} = \text{constant} \times \sqrt{\text{computing power}}$$

This relationship, often called Grosch's Law, has been faithfully followed during the years 1944 to 1980. Computing power increases as the cost squared.

$$\text{Computing power} = \text{constant} \times (\text{cost})^2$$

For example, if we double the cost, we can obtain four times the computing power. Of course, larger computers do demand larger operating staffs, which increase operating costs somewhat.

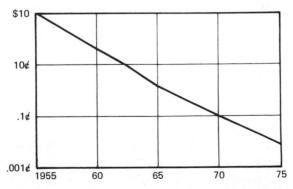

FIGURE 3–7   CPU/Storage cost per million additions.

FIGURE 3–8   The Amdahl 470 V/6 has a memory cycle speed of 32.5 nanoseconds. The
computer uses a video display operator's console. The memory consists of
semi-conductor integrated circuits. *Courtesy Amdahl Corporation.*

In summary, we find there are basically three advantages and three disadvantages in electronic computers. They are as follows:

Advantages	*Disadvantages*
High Speed	Limited Intelligence
High Precision and Accuracy	Limited Language Capability
Reliability	Cost

A large computer system is shown in Figure 3–8. This machine, the Amdahl 470 V/6, has a memory speed of 32.5 nanoseconds. It can add more than a million numbers each second. It sells for $4 million and leases for $100,000 per month. These speeds and costs are illustrative of the large general-purpose computers of the early 1980s.

As we shall find in the following chapters, the advantages far outweigh the disadvantages in a great number of needs and applications in industry, government, education, and business. There are many activities that we could not accomplish without the computer; like all helpful friends, however, it possesses mixed characteristics. Nevertheless, the nature and structure of the electronic digital computer is such that it is helpful and beneficial to man, as we shall continually discover in the ensuing chapters.

FIGURE 3–9   The IBM System/370 Model 148 was first made available in 1977. The Model 148 provides a main memory of two million characters. It uses a visual display console to provide information on the status of the central processor. *Courtesy IBM Corporation.*

CHAPTER 3 PROBLEMS

P3–1.   What are the primary contributions of the digital computer?

P3–2.   Consider one of the following applications of computers to a process familiar to you and substantiate the two primary contributions of the computer in this application.

  (a) registering for college courses
  (b) checking, recording, and balancing checking accounts
  (c) billing credit card accounts

P3–3.   Complete the definitions:

  (a) An electronic digital computer is a device that accepts and processes data that is represented by:
  (b) The accuracy of a computer is defined as the degree of freedom from:
  (c) The reliability of a computer is defined as the quality of:

P3–4.   What is the function of the memory unit of a computer?

P3–5.   According to Grosch's Law, what would be the cost of a future computer which would operate at one hundred million additions per second if the present computer in a specific line operates at four million additions per second and costs two million dollars?

P3–6.   The computer has permitted man to increase his output per hour and the quality of his output. The increase in productivity in the United States for the years 1947 to 1966 is shown in Figure P3–6. Estimate the percentage growth of productivity for the decade 1955 to 1965 and compare it with the percentage growth in computing power in the United States.

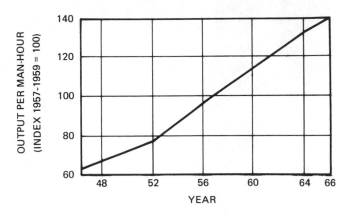

FIGURE P3–6   Productivity, 1947 to 1966. Source: *Automation*, June, 1970, p. 53.

CHAPTER 3 REFERENCES

1. M. Sheils, "And Man Created the Chip," *Newsweek*, June 30, 1980, pp. 50–60.
2. D. L. Stein, "Price/Performance, Semiconductors, and the Future," *Datamation*, November 1979, pp. 14–20.
3. N. Graham, *The Mind Tool*, West Publishing Co., St. Paul, Minnesota, 1976.
4. C. Evans, *The Micro Millennium*, The Viking Press, New York, 1980.
5. M. L. Dertouzos and J. Moses, *The Computer Age*, The MIT Press, Cambridge, Massachusetts, 1980.
6. G. B. Shelly and T. J. Cashman, *Introduction to Computers and Data Processing*, Anaheim Publishing Co., Fullerton, California, 1980.
7. D. L. Slotnik and J. K. Slotnik, *Computers: Their Structure, Use and Influence*, Prentice-Hall, Inc., Englewood Cliffs, New Jersey, 1979.
8. C. W. Gear, *Computer Organization and Progamming*, 3rd Edition, McGraw-Hill Book Co., New York, 1980.
9. R. Longbottom, *Computer System Reliability*, Wiley and Sons, Inc., New York, 1980.

4

PROBLEM SOLVING AND ALGORITHMS

4.1 PROBLEM SOLVING

The computer is capable of solving problems by accepting data, performing prescribed operations on the data, and supplying the results of these operations. In this chapter we consider the process of problem solving. In ensuing chapters, we may then discuss the specific application of the computer to solving problems.

The solution of mathematical problems proceeds through these four basic stages:

1. Precise formulation
2. Development of a mathematical model
3. Mathematical analysis
4. Computation of a solution

The first step is the precise formulation of the problem to be solved. This step requires an explicit statement of the problem so we can proceed to the second step, which is the development of a mathematical model. To get a model, we must identify the relationships among the variables under consideration. The third step is to apply the methods and procedures of mathematical analysis. The final step is to carry out the necessary computation to obtain the desired result. Note that it is not beneficial to expend time and energy calculating a result to a precision beyond the inherent accuracy of the model.

Let us consider the solution of a specific problem.

EXERCISE 4–1

You wish to travel from Davis, California to San Francisco in your automobile on the freeway in the shortest possible time. Find the shortest possible time for the trip, assuming you will not exceed the speed limit and the freeway is unobstructed.

Stage 1. The problem is to calculate the shortest time for the trip. Assume travel at the maximum lawful speed over the entire distance, with neither delay nor obstruction.

Stage 2. A model of an automobile traveling on a freeway must be developed in terms of the speed and distance traveled. We recall the physical relationship

$$d = s \times t \qquad\qquad (4-1)$$

$$\text{where } d = \text{distance traveled}$$
$$s = \text{average speed of travel}$$
$$t = \text{time spent in traveling}$$

Stage 3. We want to know the shortest time necessary to travel the distance, so we solve equation 4–1 for time (t), obtaining

$$t = \frac{d}{s} \qquad\qquad (4-2)$$

Stage 4. Now we complete the calculation process by substituting the proper distance and speed. The distance from Davis to San Francisco is 75 miles, and the speed limit on the freeway is 55. We find that

$$t = \frac{75 \text{ miles}}{55 \text{ miles/hour}} = 1.36 \text{ hours}$$

Therefore, 1.36 hours is the shortest possible time to travel the distance.

Now that we have completed the exercise, we find that we accomplished several steps in the problem process under the first and second stages. Let us restate the four stages of problem solving with the subsidiary steps noted:

1. Precise formulation
   a. Recognize the problem.
   b. Identify the important variables.
   c. Formulate a precise problem statement.
2. Development of a mathematical model
   a. Make idealizations and assumptions about the variables and their relationships.
   b. Formulate a mathematical model.
3. Mathematical analysis
4. Computation of a solution
   a. Compute some specific results.
   b. Check these results for accuracy by comparing them with some known measured results.

c. Check the precision of the results and compare the precision and accuracy with appropriate standards.

One is often required to solve problems which are not entirely mathematical but which can be formulated precisely. An example of this type of problem occurs in the game of checkers. A mathematical model which represents the process of playing the game can be set up so that one can analyze the various possible moves in the game mathematically. Such a model has been used to obtain computer solutions to the game. In effect, the computer uses the mathematical models to "play" checkers. This type of problem solving will be treated more thoroughly in Chapters 9 and 14.

The computer, therefore, may be used to solve problems other than those mathematical in nature if a mathematical model of the problem can be developed. For instance, the solution to the problem of pollution in rivers, or the arrangement of the trial docket of a courtroom can be obtained.

Stage Four of the solution is typically accomplished by a computer. In the next section we examine how we can develop precise computer approaches to the solution of problems.

4.2 ALGORITHMS

In order for a computer to provide a solution to a problem, we must have a precise, unambiguous procedure for the solution of the problem. An algorithm is such a procedure, defined as:

ALGORITHM A complete, unambiguous procedure for solving a specified problem in a finite number of steps.

The word *algorithm* is derived from the name of a ninth-century Arab mathematician, al-Khowarizmi. He developed methods for solving problems which used specific, step-by-step instructions.[1] al-Khowarizmi wrote the celebrated book *Kitab al jabr w al-mugabala (Rules for Restoration and Reduction)*; the word *algebra* stems from the title of his book. An algorithm is like a recipe used in the kitchen or a set of specific procedures for completing an income tax form.

An algorithm must have all the following characteristics to be useful. It should be:

1. Unambiguous
2. Precisely defined
3. Finite
4. Effective

As an example, consider an algorithm for boiling an egg. A *poor* algorithm for this process is:

Put the egg in a pan of water and boil; then remove it and serve.

This is an ambiguous, poorly-defined procedure. A better, more effective algorithm is:

1. Place three inches of water in a pan.
2. Place the egg in the pan.
3. Place the pan on the stove and turn on the heat.
4. Bring the water to a boil.
5. Boil the water for three minutes.
6. Remove the egg.
7. Turn off the heat under the pan.
8. Serve the egg.

This procedure is finite; each step is clearly defined and limited. The whole procedure is also finite in length. It may be improved in effectiveness, perhaps, by adding "Add salt to the water" between steps 3 and 4. If we add that step, it must be precise, however, giving the quantity of salt to be added.

Governments publish thousands of instruction booklets to help people understand certain regulations or requirements, such as the completion of income tax forms. Upon reading the tax instruction booklet, you may wonder if good algorithmic procedure was followed in developing the directions. Strings of qualifiers such as *unless*, *providing*, and *except* are extremely troublesome to the person who must follow through all the complicated paths to a final solution. In the next section, we demonstrate how we can follow a path to a solution of a complicated income tax problem.

AN ALGORITHM FOR COMPUTING PRODUCTS

First, consider the elementary problem of computing a product of two numbers, for example 33 and 15. In school, we all learned an algorithm for this calculation which utilizes the memorized multiplication tables. The elementary school algorithm for calculating the product is:

1. Write the two numbers, one immediately below the other.
2. Draw a line beneath the two numbers.
3. Using the multiplication table, multiply the first numeral (on the right) of the bottom number by the top number, making sure to carry the proper digits, and enter the answer below the line.
4. Repeat step 3 for the second numeral of the bottom number and enter the answer below that of step 3, shifted one place to the left.
5. Draw a line below the two products and add them.

We could write this algorithm with even more precision and detail if we wished. Now let us carry out the calculation.

$$
\begin{array}{r}
33 \\
\times\ 15 \\
\hline
165 \\
33 \\
\hline
495
\end{array}
$$

We would probably find it easier to carry out the calculation than it is to write down all the steps in such an algorithm. (For example, write down all the steps in the process for dividing 234 by 13.)

We often have more than one algorithm available for solving a problem. Naturally, we wish to utilize the most effective algorithm. By "effective" we mean the algorithm which requires the smallest computer (in terms of memory and arithmetic unit size) and utilizes the shortest time on the computer. Effectiveness, then, is basically the cost of the solution, since we can state:

cost of solution = size of the computer × time for calculation

THE RUSSIAN PEASANT ALGORITHM

Consider again obtaining the product of 33 × 15 by different algorithms. A method of obtaining the product which requires only the use of the "times two" multiplication table is called the Russian peasant algorithm. This method involves continually doubling one factor while halving the other, noting where the halving leaves a remainder. The algorithm is:

1. Write the two numbers on a horizontal line, leaving room for a column between them.
2. Double the smaller number; write the result below the smaller number.
3. Halve the larger number and write down the resulting whole number below the larger number while indicating if there was a non-zero remainder beside the larger number.
4. Repeat steps 2 and 3 until the result of halving will not yield a whole number.
5. Add the multiples of the smaller number on lines where remainders do occur. This is the result.

The calculation for 33 × 15 by the Russian peasant algorithm follows:

$$
\begin{array}{rl}
33\ R & 15 \rightarrow\ \ 15 \\
16 & 30 \\
8 & 60 \\
4 & 120 \\
2 & 240 \\
1\ R & 480 \rightarrow\ \underline{480} \\
& 495
\end{array}
$$

R (indicating a non-zero remainder) occurs on line 1, since we divide 33 by two, obtaining 16 plus a remainder. One cannot be divided by 2 to give a whole number, so we stop at this line, with the 1 counted as having a remainder. In using this algorithm it may be simpler to write the results of doubling one factor below the original number only when there occurs a remainder with the number being halved. For example, the product 45 × 17 might be written as shown.

$$45 \; R \quad 17$$
$$22$$
$$11 \; R \quad 68$$
$$5 \; R \; 136$$
$$2$$
$$1 \; R \; \underline{544}$$
$$765$$

AN AGE-DIVINING ALGORITHM

Let us consider algorithm for finding a volunteer's age. Using a paper and pencil or a calculator, the volunteer completes these steps:

1. Write his or her age.
2. Subtract any one-digit number.
3. Multiply the result of step 2 by 9.
4. Add the age to the product obtained in step 3.
5. Hand the result of step 4 to you.

You will be able to tell the person's age by adding the last two digits in the result of step 4 to get the ones place. Use the next digit in the tens place.

SALARY AGORITHM

We wish to calculate the weekly salary paycheck for a single individual who works at an hourly rate of pay and who receives overtime pay after 40 hours. Let us assume that the overtime pay is one and a half times normal for all overtime hours. The algorithm is:

1. Write the worker's identification number (or name), the hours worked, and the rate of pay.
2. If hours exceed 40, proceed to step 4; otherwise, proceed to step 3.
3. Salary = hours worked times rate of pay. Proceed to step 5.
4. Salary = 40 times rate of pay plus (hours worked minus 40) times rate of pay times 1.5.
5. Write the identification number and salary.

This algorithm can be more readily discerned if we use arithmetic equations. We will use *ID* for identification number, *H* for hours, *R* for rate of pay and *S* for salary. Then the algorithm is:

1. Write *ID, H, R*
2. *If (H − 40) > 0*   proceed to step **4**, otherwise continue to step **3**
3. *S = H × R*   proceed to step **5**
4. *S = 40 × R + (H − 40) × R × 1.5*
5. Write *ID, S*

THE EUCLIDEAN ALGORITHM

Consider the following problem:

Given two positive integers, *A* and *B*, find their greatest common divisor. (The greatest common divisor of two positive integers is the largest integer that divides both the positive integers without yielding a non-zero remainder.)

One way of computing the greatest common divisor of *A* and *B* consists of listing all divisors of *A* and *B* and picking out the largest divisor that appears in both of the lists. Using this brute-force algorithm, find the greatest common divisor of 72 and 20.

Divisors of 72: 1, 2, 3, 4, 6, 8, 9, 12, 24, 36

Divisors of 20: 1, 2, 4, 5, 10

This process yields a greatest common divisor of 4. If you worked it out, it took you 46 calculation steps.

The Euclidean algorithm finds the greatest common divisor of two numbers. It appears in the Fifth Book of Euclid, dating back to 300 B. C. [2] One form of the steps in this algorithm is:

1. Write down the numbers, say *A* and *B*, in that order on a line.
2. Compare the two numbers and determine whether the first equals, is less than, or is greater than the second.
3. If the numbers are equal, then each of them is the required result. If not, proceed to the next step.
4. If the first number is smaller than the second, exchange them; proceed.
5. Subtract the second number from the first and replace the two numbers under consideration by the subtrahend (the former second number) and the remainder respectively. Proceed to instruction 2.

Note that the process terminates at step **3** when the two numbers are equal.

The process for 72 and 20 is as follows:

Calculation	*Comments*
72, 20	
72 − 20 = 52 = remainder	Subtraction

$$20, 52$$
$$52, 20 \qquad \text{Interchange}$$
$$52 - 20 = 32 \qquad \text{Subtraction}$$
$$20, 32$$
$$32, 20 \qquad \text{Interchange}$$
$$32 - 20 = 12$$
$$20, 12$$
$$20 - 12 = 8$$
$$12, 8$$
$$12 - 8 = 4$$
$$8, 4$$
$$8 - 4 = 4$$
$$4, 4 \qquad \text{Stop}$$

Thus, 4 is the greatest common divisor. This process consumed 15 steps. It is shorter than the algorithm which enumerated all divisors of each number.

Since the division process can be reduced to repeated subtractions, the Euclidean algorithm was given in the foregoing as a subtraction process. It can also be written as a division process which requires even fewer calculation steps. The Euclidean algorithm in this form involves repeated dividing and finding remainders until we reach the remainder 0. Each step produces a remainder smaller than the remainder from the previous step. Eventually we must obtain the remainder 0. The remainder *before* 0 is the greatest common divisor.

1. Write down A and B in that order on a line, with A the larger of the two.
2. Divide A by B yielding a first remainder $R1$.
3. Write down B and $R1$.
4. Divide B by $R1$ yielding a second remainder $R2$.
5. Write down $R1$ and $R2$.
6. Continue until the remainder equals zero. Then the remainder of the preceding division step is equal to the greatest common divisor.

Taking the numbers 72 and 20 again, the procedure is:

Calculation	*Comments*
72, 20	
$72 = 3 \cdot 20 + 12$	Dividing by 20, remainder = 12
20, 12	
$20 = 1 \cdot 12 + 8$	Remainder = 8
12, 8	
$12 = 1 \cdot 8 + 4$	Remainder = 4
8, 4	
$8 = 1 \cdot 4 + 4$	Remainder = 4
4, 4	
$4 = 1 \cdot 4 + 0$	Remainder = 0

In 10 steps this time, we again found that the greatest common divisor is 4. Clearly, of the three algorithms we have considered, this is the most efficient algorithm for finding the greatest common divisor.

Let us restate Euclid's algorithm in a more mathematical fashion, using an equation. The algorithm may be written as:

1. Write down A and B in that order with the larger number first.
2. Calculate $A = Q \cdot B + R$, where $Q =$ an integer and $R =$ remainder.
3. If $R = 0$, then the greatest common divisor is equal to B. If R is not equal to zero, then proceed to the next step.
4. Replace A with B and B with R.
5. Return to step 1 and continue.

As a final example, let us find the largest common divisor of 162 and 126.

A	B	*Calculation*
162	126	$162 = 1 \cdot 126 + 36$
126	36	$126 = 3 \cdot 36 + 18$
36	18	$36 = 2 \cdot 18 + 0$

The largest common divisor is 18. We use this form of the Euclidean algorithm in succeeding chapters.

4.3   FLOW CHARTS

Following the well worn dictum that a picture is worth a thousand words, we can develop a method of representing an algorithm graphically by means of a flow chart. The definition of a flow chart is:

> FLOW CHART A graphic representation of the definition, analysis, or solution of a problem, in which symbols are used to represent operations, data, flow, equipment, and so on.

A flow chart consists of a diagram containing selected symbols such as lines connecting boxes that contain statements of operation or decision. The boxes represent the steps in the algorithm, and the connecting lines represent the flow through the steps. The diagrams are usually drawn so that one starts on the top and moves toward the bottom. Arrows on connecting lines show the direction of flow on the chart. An algorithm may have several possible flow charts.

A flow chart is a blueprint of the logic of the solutions to any problem. A set of the symbols used in this text is shown in Figure 4–1. A rectangle indicates the action of processing. A diamond indicates a decision or logical choice; it may have two or more branches exiting from it. The other symbols are explained in Figure 4–1.

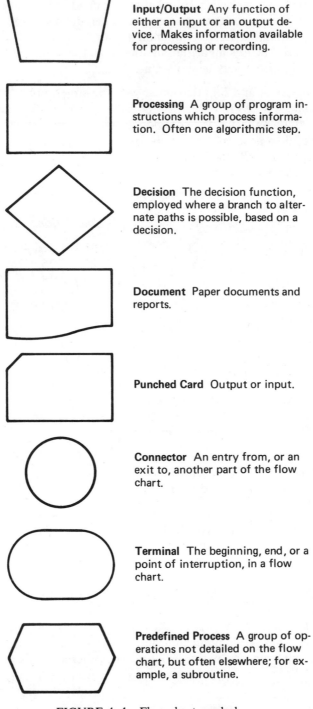

Input/Output Any function of either an input or an output device. Makes information available for processing or recording.

Processing A group of program instructions which process information. Often one algorithmic step.

Decision The decision function, employed where a branch to alternate paths is possible, based on a decision.

Document Paper documents and reports.

Punched Card Output or input.

Connector An entry from, or an exit to, another part of the flow chart.

Terminal The beginning, end, or a point of interruption, in a flow chart.

Predefined Process A group of operations not detailed on the flow chart, but often elsewhere; for example, a subroutine.

FIGURE 4–1   Flow chart symbols.

Four reasons for using flow charts are:

1. The flow chart shows the logic of a problem displayed in pictorial fashion, by which means the algorithm may be checked for correctness.
2. The flow chart is a means of communication to other students, teachers, and to later users. A flow chart is a compact means of recording an algorithmic solution to a problem.
3. The flow chart allows the problem-solver to break his problem into parts and to chart the solution to each part for analysis and study. The parts can be connected to make a master chart.
4. The flow chart records the solution to a problem. It is a permanent record of the solution which can be consulted at a later time.

Flow charts can represent the algorithmic solution to problems of all types. A detailed flow chart for placing a telephone call is shown in Figure 4–2. This flow chart contains enough detail so a person could, with the aid of the chart, place a phone call without any prior knowledge of the process.

The general form a flow chart will take in the solution of problems is shown in Figure 4–3. We usually have input data, which is then used in a calculation process. As a result of the calculation, we substitute some information into prearranged variables. These variables are then tested against some criterion. If the test is satisfied, an output is provided. If the test is not met, the process returns to the calculation phase and continues.

Consider the problem of finding the largest of three numbers: A, B, and C. Think how you would do it by comparing one number with another. Now, examine a flow chart which represents the problem solution (Figure 4–4). Note how the flow chart may represent pictorially what you would have been required to express in several hundred words. Also, you can check each path by using test data. Try the flow chart for the sets of A, B, C as follows: [3, 8, 4]; [7, 3, 4]; [2, 1, 5].

Let us consider the salary algorithm again and obtain the flow chart. A calculation is required to determine if the number of hours worked exceeds 40; and, considering this calculation, we decide whether overtime pay is required. The flow chart is shown in Figure 4–5. A decision symbol is used to determine whether to branch to the overtime pay calculation. After the appropriate salary calculation is obtained, an output is recorded for the identification number and the salary to be paid.

In the previous section we studied Euclid's algorithm for obtaining the greatest common devisor of two numbers, A and B. The flow chart representing Euclid's algorithm appears in Figure 4–6. Review the algorithm, stated in the last section, if you need to. The first step in the algorithm is to write down A and B, assuming A is larger than B. The second step is to calculate $A = Q \cdot B + R$ when Q is an integer and R is the remainder. Then, R is tested to find if $R = 0$. If so, we output B as the greatest common divisor. If not, we replace A with B and B with R. On the flow chart, we have used a common notation for replacement: an ar-

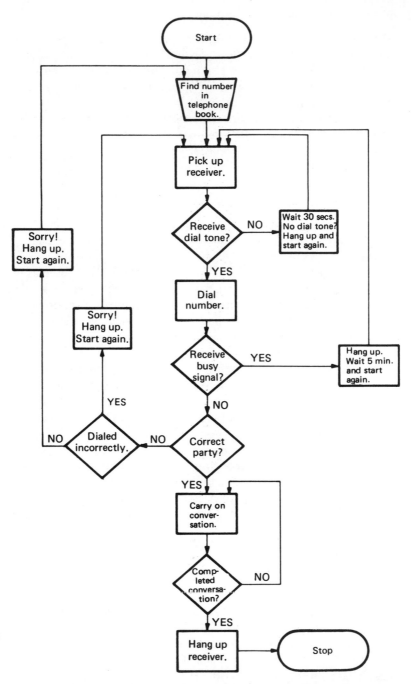

FIGURE 4–2   Flow chart for placing a telephone call.

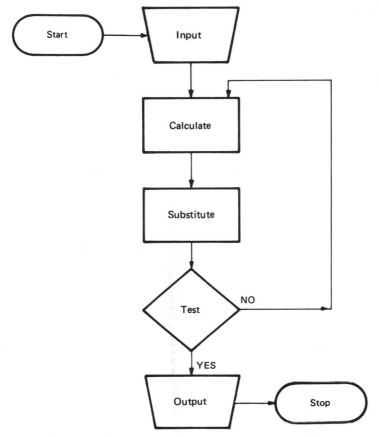

FIGURE 4–3 The general form of a flow chart for the solution of a problem.

row. Thus, $A \leftarrow B$ implies that A is replaced with B. Then after replacement we return to the calculation step and continue.

Note in the flow chart that we assumed A is always greater than B when it is received as input. If we do not want to bother to require the user to make sure every time that A is greater than B, then we can add two flow chart symbols between the input symbol and the calculation symbol. What would those two symbols be? The revised flow chart with this increased detail for Euclid's algorithm is shown in Figure 4–7. If we do not insure against these small errors in lack of detail, a new user would find the flow chart useless. What if a new person tried Figure 4–6 with the pair [18, 72]? Clearly, we need to provide for all contingencies on a flow chart.

Algorithms and flow charts are not restricted to mathematical problems. The flow chart form of an algorithm is extremely helpful in assisting a person through a labyrinth of instructions. For example, the instructions for special cases in the

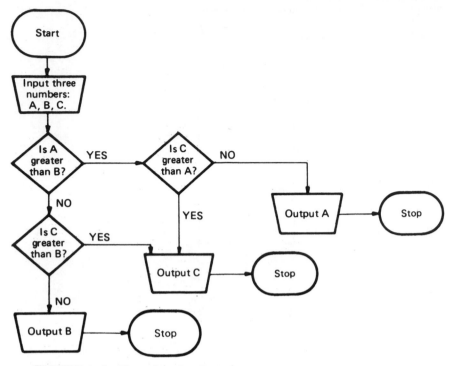

FIGURE 4–4   Flow chart for finding the largest of three numbers.

income tax booklet often confuse the reader.[4] For instance, the instructions stating who must file an estimated tax are provided. Then the problem statement is provided in two different cases. The flow chart representing the instructions is provided in Figure 4–9. Compare the effort and confusion in solving this problem with and without the flow chart. Determine your answer to both problems before proceeding to the next paragraph.

EXERCISE 4–2

Here is an extract from the 1970 U.S. Internal Revenue Service instructions for who must make a declaration of estimated income tax.[4]

(In reading this extract, it should be remembered that this is not taken from the tax law itself—it was specifically produced to help people decide whether they must make an estimated tax declaration.)

Declaration of Estimated Tax for Individuals

1. Purpose of declaration-vouchers—The declaration-vouchers are provided for paying currently any income tax (including self-employment tax) due in excess of the tax withheld. Therefore, declarations are required only from individuals

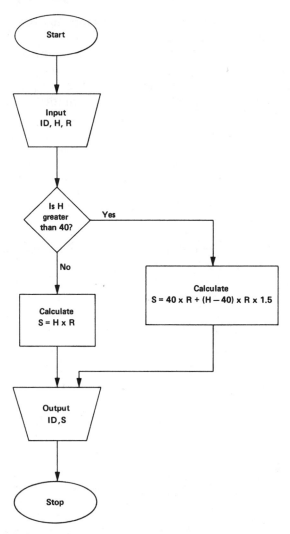

FIGURE 4–5   Flow chart for the salary algorithm for an employee with an hour rate of pay R.

whose wages or other income exceed the amounts specified in instruction 2. In general, the definitions of income, deductions, exemptions, etc., are the same as those on Form 1040.

2. Who must make a declaration—Under the law every citizen of the United States or resident of the United States, Puerto Rico, Virgin Islands, Guam, and American Samoa shall make a declaration of his estimated tax. If his total

estimated tax (line 14 of worksheet) is $40 or more and he:

    (a) can reasonably expect gross income to exceed—

        (1) $10,000 for a head of household or a widow or widower entitled to the special tax rates;

        (2) $5,000 for other individuals;

        (3) $5,000 for a married individual not entitled to file a joint declaration;

        (4) $5,000 for a married individual entitled to file a joint declaration, and the combined income of both husband and wife can reasonably be expected to exceed $10,000; or

    (b) can reasonably expect to receive more than $200 from sources other than wages subject to witholding.

. . .

7. Changes in income, exemptions, etc.—Even though your situation on April 15 is such that you are not required to file, your circumstances may change so that you will be required to file a declaration later. In such case the time for filing is as follows: June 15, if the change occurs after April 1 and before June 2; September 15, if the change occurs after June 1 and before September 2; January 15, 1971, if the change occurs after September 1. The estimated tax may be paid in equal installments of the remaining payment dates.

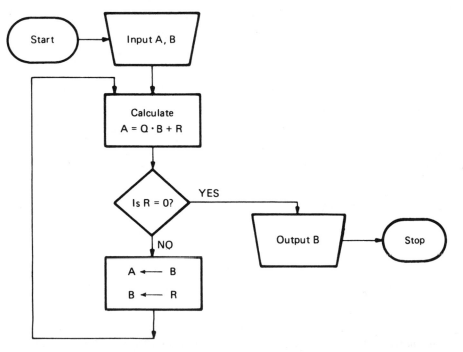

FIGURE 4–6   Flow chart for Euclid's algorithm for obtaining the greatest common divisor of two numbers.

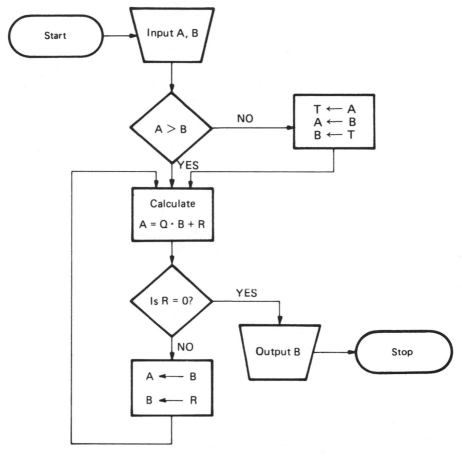

FIGURE 4–7   A more detailed flow chart for Euclid's algorithm.

The Problem

Mary Black won a $200 prize in a television quiz program. She has no other income and files a joint return with her husband, who earns $11,000 a year in wages. They calculate that the tax on her winnings will be about $50. Does she have to file an estimated tax declaration?

Another Try

Now try the problem again with one change—suppose Mary Black earned $5,000 a year in wages and her husband $6,000. Except for that, the situation is the same. Does she have to file an estimated tax declaration now?

If you followed the flow chart in Figure 4–8 carefully, you found that in the first problem Mrs. Black does not file an estimated tax declaration. However, in the second problem, Mrs. Black's total personal income is $5,200 and she does have to file an estimated tax declaration.

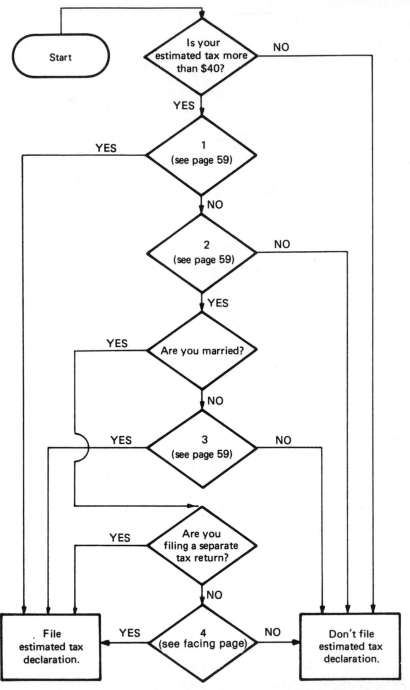

FIGURE 4–8   Flow chart for estimated tax. Reprinted from *Psychology Today*, April, 1970. Copyright © Communications/Research/Machines/Inc.

1. Will you receive
   more than $200
   from sources other
   than wages subject
   to withholding?

2. Is your personal
   income (regardless
   of whether you are
   single or married)
   more than $5000?

3. Are you the head
   of a household or
   a widow or widower
   with a total income
   of $10,000 or more
   and entitled to special
   taxes?

4. Are you filing a joint
   tax return, and is your
   combined income more
   than $10,000?

FIGURE 4–8   (Continued)

The advantages of the flow chart algorithm are evident to anyone who would have to decipher the instructions without the aid of a flow chart. The flow chart has three main advantages over the continuous prose form. First, the reader is called upon to make a sequence of simple decisions, often of a yes-no nature. Second, each decision is about a specific issue; the problem of deciding what is relevant is greatly simplified. Finally, in working through the flow chart one does not have to remember his previous decisions. The use of algorithms in flow chart form for instructions for various tasks allows workers and others to shorten the time to complete a task and to reduce the number of errors in the problem solving process.

Algorithms and their pictorial representation as flow charts are a necessary part of the problem solving process using computers. The solution of problems requires a well defined process. The problems to be solved by computer using algorithmic methods are not limited to numerical problems, as we found in the problem of Mrs. Black and the tax declaration. Lady Lovelace, a friend of Charles Babbage, had a comment on the use of computers and algorithms in 1844:

> Many persons who are not conversant with mathematical studies imagine that because the business of (Babbage's Analytical Engine) is to give its results in numerical notation, the nature of its processes must consequently be arithmetical and numerical, rather than algebraical and analytical. This is an error. The engine can arrange and combine its numerical quantities exactly as if they were letters or any other general symbols; and in fact it might bring out its results in algebraical notation, were provisions made accordingly.

In this chapter we have found that in order to solve a problem we must develop a precise formulation of the problem, a mathematical model and an algorithm for the solution of the problem. The analytical engine which is the object of study in this book, the electronic digital computer, is a powerful engine indeed. In the next chapter, we consider how we can communicate with the computer through an algorithmic process. The computer is able to accomplish the steps in our algorithms and flow chart representations. It remains only to learn how to arrange for the computer to accomplish the algorithmic process; this is the essence of the ensuing three chapters. As Bertalanffy states:*

> In somewhat different terms, the algorithmic system becomes a calculating machine, as conversely every calculating machine is materialization of an algorithm. Suitable data being fed in, the machine runs according to pre-established rules and eventually a result drops out which was unforeseeable to the individual mind with its limited capacities.

CHAPTER 4 PROBLEMS

P4–1. You are a police detective called to the scene of a crime. One clue you discover is a bullet lodged in a wooden wall stud. The bullet has penetrated three inches into the wood and the wood is pine. Formulate and solve the problem of determining the type and size of weapon from which the bullet was fired.

P4–2. You and a friend attend an auction in which you write down your bids and compare them. High bidder gets $20 and pays the other the amount of the higher bid. Tie bidders split $20. How much do you bid in order to maximize the amount you get? Formulate the problem and a model. Then analyze and calculate your bid.

P4–3. You and two friends have $32 to spend on a weekend in the city. Your friend John has $4 more than your friend Bill. Furthermore, your friend Bill has $2 more than you do. How much does each of you have to spend?

P4–4. Using the problem method, analyze whether you should live in the residence hall at your college, in a local rooming house or in a shared apartment with two students. Make a choice based on the ratio of dollar cost to the square feet of space allocated to you. For example, if you paid $300 for a room of 10 square feet, the ratio would be $\frac{300}{10} = 30$.

P4–5. It is said that Immanuel Kant was a bachelor of such regular habits that the good people of Königsberg would adjust their clocks when they saw him stroll past certain landmarks.

One evening Kant was dismayed to discover that his clock had run down. Evidently his manservant, who had taken the day off, had forgotten to wind it. The great philosopher did not reset the hands because his watch was being repaired and he had no way of knowing the correct time. He walked to the home of his friend Schmidt, a merchant who lived a mile or so away, glancing at the clock in Schmidt's hallway as he entered the house.

After visiting Schmidt for several hours Kant left and walked home with a slow, steady gait that had not varied in twenty years. He had no notion of how long this return trip took. (Schmidt had recently moved into the area and Kant had not yet timed himself on this walk.) Nevertheless, when Kant entered his house, he immediately set his clock correctly.

How did Kant know the correct time?*

*Reprinted from *New Mathematical Diversions from Scientific American*, by Martin Gardner. By permission of the publisher, Simon and Schuster, Inc.

P4–6. In about 250 B. C. Eratosthenes constructed an algorithm for finding all the prime numbers between 1 and some specified integer N. A prime number is a positive integer, other than 1, that is exactly divisible only by itself and 1. For example, the prime numbers less than 10 are 2, 3, 5, and 7. Thus, the problem is to find all the prime numbers up to N. The algorithm developed by Erathosthenes, called the *Sieve of Eratosthenes*, proceeds as follows[6]:

1. Write down all the integers in numerical order from 2 through N. Call this the *basic* list. For example, assuming $N = 10$, the basic list is

   2, 3, 4, 5, 6, 7, 8, 9, 10

2. Record, in what we shall call the *prime list* (to distinguish it from the basic list), the first uncrossed number in the basic list. (There will be no number crossed out in the basic until we decide the first M in the prime list.) Call it M, then cross it and every *Mth* number thereafter off the basic list. Continuing the example, we have $M = 2$; we then cross off every second number in the list:

   2, 3, 4, 5, 6, 7, 8, 9, 10

3. If M is less than $\sqrt{N}$, return to *step 2*; if M is $\geqslant \sqrt{N}$, then add all the remaining uncrossed-out numbers to your prime list and stop. In the example, $M = 2$, which is less than $\sqrt{10}$, so we return to step 2 and repeat it. The first uncrossed number is 3. The prime list is now 2, 3. Repeating step 2:

   2, 3, 4, 5, 6, 7, 8, 9, 10

   Now $M = 3$, which is still less than $\sqrt{10}$, so we return again to step 2 and repeat it. The first uncrossed number is 5. The prime list is now 2, 3, 5. M is 5, which is greater than $\sqrt{10}$. We add all the remaining uncrossed-out numbers (there is only one, 7) to our prime list, and we are through; our list is 2, 3, 5, 7.

The prime list we have prepared is, in fact, the desired list of primes less than N.

For another example, what are all the primes between 2 and 8? We write the basic list:

2 3 4 5 6 7 8

We record 2 as a prime number and cross off every even number, obtaining

2 3 4 5 6 7 8

Since 3 is not less than $\sqrt{8}$, we add 3, 5 and 7 to the list of prime numbers, obtaining 2, 3, 5 and 7 as the prime numbers between 2 and 8.

1. Determine all the prime numbers between 2 and 18.
2. Draw a flow chart of the algorithm.

P 4 −7. Often we wish to find the sum of *N* numbers where *N* is specified. The sum is the output, and the numbers are available one at a time from *N* punched cards. The number read from each card is called *X* and the card is the *I*th card. The sum is called *S*. In the algorithm, we need a counter to indicate what card we are counting, so we know when we come to *N*. Also, we need to set *S* equal to zero initially. A flow chart for this algorithm is shown in Figure P4−7. Complete the algorithmic steps in the flow chart by entering the missing items in each block.

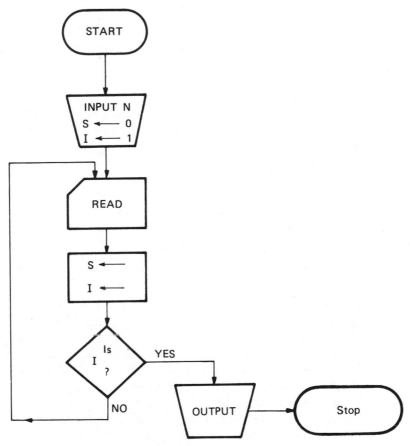

FIGURE P4−7   Flow chart for finding the sum of N numbers.

P4−8. Even the simplest of household tasks can present complicated problems in operational research. Consider the preparation of toast in a form of electric toaster often found in diners. This toaster is an older type, with hinged doors on its two sides. It holds two pieces of bread at once but toast each of them on one side only. To toast both sides it is necessary to open the doors and reverse the slices.

It takes three seconds to put a slice of bread into the toaster, three seconds to take it out and three seconds to reverse a slice without removing it. Both hands are required for each of these operations, which means that it is not possible to put in, take out, or turn two slices simultaneously. Nor is it possible to butter a slice while another slice is being put into the toaster, turned, or taken out. The toasting time for one side of a piece of bread is thirty seconds. It takes twelve seconds to butter a slice.

Each slice is buttered on one side only. No side may be buttered until it has been toasted. A slice toasted and buttered on one side may be returned to the toaster for toasting on its other side. The toaster is warmed up at the start. In how short a time can three slices of bread be toasted on both sides and buttered?*

Draw a flow chart to assist in determining the length of time in which the three slices of bread can be toasted on both sides and buttered.

P4-9. The following problem statement concerns the application of a grant upon the death of the insured under British Ministry of Pensions. Complete the flow chart and determine if the late contributions count for either Mr. Doe or Mrs. Doe.[4] See figure P4-9.

Mr. and Mrs. John Doe, a young couple, were involved in a car crash. Mrs. Doe was killed outright. Mr. Doe, who was self-employed, died in a hospital a month later. Mr. Doe's accountant paid a backlog of late contributions for both Mr. and Mrs. Doe to the national insurance plan a few days before Mr. Doe's death.

A British Ministry of Pensions and National Insurance leaflet set out the qualifications for a small grant payable on death in this way:

"Contributions paid late cannot normally count for death grant (other than towards yearly average) unless they were paid before the death on which the grant is claimed and before the death of the insured person if that was earlier. But if the insured person died before the person on whose death the grant is claimed, contributions, which although paid late, have already been taken into account for the purpose of a claim for a widow's benefit or retired pension, will count towards death grant." (Leaflet N1 48, *Late Paid or Unpaid Contribution*, MPN1 1963.)

---

*Reprinted from *New Mathematical Diversions from Scientific American*, by Martin Gardner. By permission of the publisher, Simon and Schuster, Inc.

Will the late contributions count toward a death grant for Mr. Doe? for Mrs. Doe?**

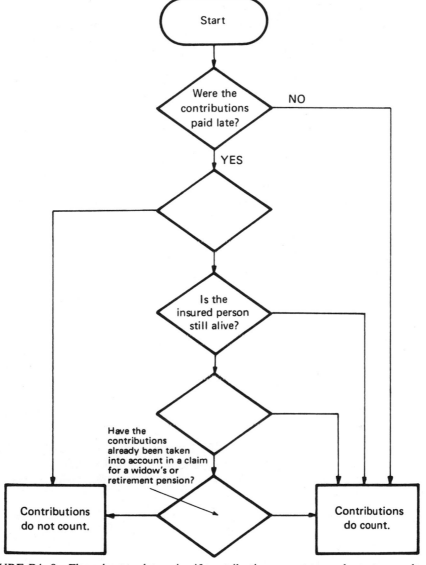

FIGURE P4–9   Flow chart to determine if contributions count toward grant upon death of insured. Reprinted from *Psychology Today*, April, 1970. Copyright © Communications/Research/Machines/Inc.

**From I. K. Davies, "Algorithms." Reprinted from PSYCHOLOGY TODAY Magazine, April, 1970. Copyright © Communications/Research/Machines/Inc.

P4–10.   An algorithm is used to generate a sequence. Determine the algorithm and generate the next two entries in the sequence.

0.5   2   4.5   8   ?   ?

P4–11.   An algorithm is shown in Figure P4–11 for finding and providing as output all the factors of a number N. In this algorithm, we use a predefined process which yields the integer part of any number and is labeled as INT (b). Thus, if b = 3.47, INT (b) = 3. Follow through the algorithm in order to find all the factors for $N = 6$.

P4–12.   You must arrive at a decision concerning your activities this evening. Assuming you like to swim, play tennis and go to the movies, draw a flow chart to enable you to make a decision based on the following criteria:

1. You will go swimming if the temperature is greater than 80°.
2. You will go to the movies if the temperature is greater than 90° and you like the movie.
3. You will play tennis if the temperature is greater than 60° and less than 85° and there is a court available.
4. If all else fails, you will stay home and complete the problems in Chapter 4.

P4–13.   It is interesting to deduce the algorithm being used to generate a sequence. Consider the sequence below. Determine the algorithm and generate the next two entries in the sequence.

77   49   36   ?   ?

P4–14.   Determine the basis for the operation of the age-divining algorithm given in the text.

P4–15.   An algorithm for calculating the square root of a number N follows:

1. Start with a guess equal to $N/5$.
2. Calculate the next estimate of the root by the formula

$$R_{I+1} = \frac{(N/R_I) + R_I}{2}$$

where I starts at zero and progresses in integer values until the difference between R_{I+1} and R_I is smaller than some preset amount. First, try the algorithm for $N = 100$. Then draw a flow chart of the algorithm.

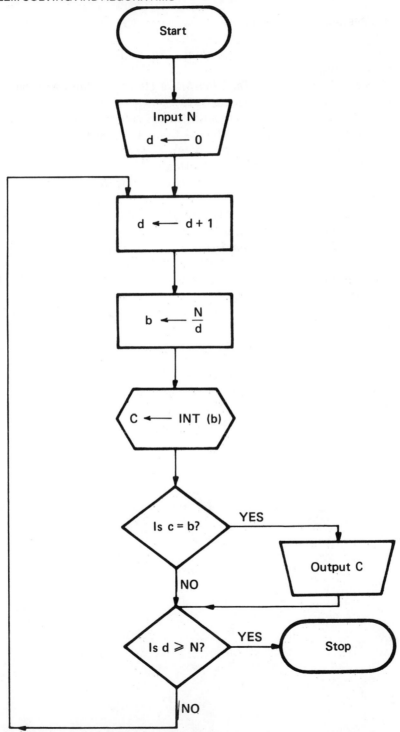

FIGURE P4–11   Flow chart for finding all the factors of a number N.

CHAPTER 4 REFERENCES

1. D. Knuth, *Fundamental Algorithms*, Addison-Wesley Publishing Co., Reading, Mass., 1968.
2. S. K. Stein, *Mathematics: The Man-Made Universe*, Third Edition, W. H. Freeman and Co., San Francisco, 1975.
3. A. Forsythe, T. Keenan, E. Organick, W. Stenberg, *Computer Science: A First Course*, Second Edition, Wiley & Sons, Inc., New York, 1975.
4. I. K. Davies, "Algorithms," *Psychology Today*, April, 1970, p. 53.
5. L. von Bertalanffy, *Robots, Men and Minds*, Braziller Inc., New York, 1967.
6. H. Maisel, *Introduction to Electronic Computers*, McGraw-Hill Book Co., New York, 1969.
7. G. B. Kolata, "Analysis of Algorithms: Coping with Hard Problems," *Science*, November 8, 1974, pp. 520–521.
8. N. Wirth, *Algorithms & Data Structures = Programs*, Prentice-Hall Inc., Englewood Cliffs, New Jersey, 1976.
9. N. Stern, *Flowcharting: A Tool for Understanding Computer Logic*, Wiley and Sons, Inc., New York, 1975.
10. L. I. Kronsjo, *Algorithms: Their Complexity and Efficiency*, Wiley and Sons, Inc., New York, 1979.
11. G. Sting and J. Gips, *Algorithmic Aesthetics*, University of California Press, Berkeley, 1979.
12. S. Baase, *Computer Algorithms: Introduction to Design and Analysis*, Addison-Wesley Publishing Co., Reading, Massachusetts, 1978.
13. H. R. Lewis and C. H. Papadimitriou, "The Efficiency of Algorithms," *Scientific American*, January 1978, pp. 50–62.

5

PROGRAMMABLE CALCULATORS, MINICOMPUTERS, AND MICROCOMPUTERS

5.1 PROGRAMMABLE CALCULATORS

In the preceding chapter we learned that following the development of an algorithmic approach to a problem, often using a flow chart, it becomes necessary to write a detailed set of instructions for the computer. This set of instructions, called a *program*, must include instructions for transcription of the data, coding for the computer and output of the results. In this section of Chapter 6, we consider the programming of electronic calculators.

Many computing problems require complex calculations, but involve only a moderate amount of input data and output results. The programmable electronic calculator is often used to solve such problems. It costs less than a computer, but it has a much greater capacity than a mechanical desk calculator. The programmable calculator is like a small personal electronic computer; it is easy to program and to operate. Also, the calculator can provide results for complicated calculations within seconds.

Electronic digital calculators are constructed like electronic digital computers. We have defined a computer as a data processor that can perform substantial computation, including numerous arithmetic or logic operations, without intervention by a human operator during the run. Although the programmable electronic calculator fits within this definition, and can therefore be considered a small computer, we observe current convention and call it an electronic calculator from this point on.

The electronic calculator is the result of historical development of calculators during the last several hundred years, culminating in operable machines in this century.[1] Babbage (see above) came close to providing a working mechanical calculator, but his project was abandoned in 1842. Thomas Hill built an "Arithmometer" in 1857; his machine lacked precision. Other inventors made calculators that worked, but they were slower than clerks adding in their heads, unfortunately for the inventors. In 1872, however, a former bank clerk named William S. Burroughs made the first practical calculator. In 1879 D. E. Felt marketed his "Comptometer." The Marchant calculator shown in Figure 5–1 was patented in 1911. This instrument, called the Marchant Pony, required

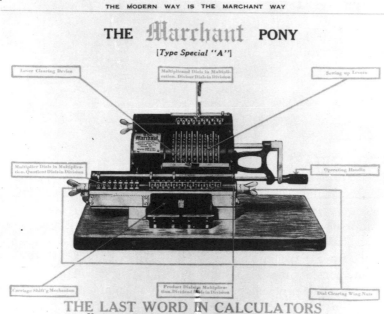

FIGURE 5–1 The Marchant Pony Calculator and operating instructions. *Courtesy of Hewlett-Packard Corporation.*

FIGURE 5–2 The manually-operated CURTA calculator. *Courtesy of the Curta Company, Van Nuys, California.*

human intervention during the calculation run; thus it does not meet our definition of a computer. An interesting example of a small contemporary hand-held calculator is shown in Figure 5–2. This device, the CURTA calculator, also requires human intervention in the calculation run. It adds, subtracts, multiplies, divides, squares, cubes, and extracts square roots. It uses eight-digit precision for multiplication. Babbage would be proud of such a calculator!

By the 1920s, automatic motor-driven calculators made by Burroughs, Monroe, Marchant, and Friden were in use in this country. Electronic calculators began to appear in the 1960s.

5.2 PROGRAMMABLE DESKTOP CALCULATORS

The distinction we can make for contemporary electronic calculators, bringing them closer to computers, is that they are programmable; that is, the instructions and data may be entered and stored within the calculator and then the run may be ordered to proceed without intervention. The stored-program concept, you will recall, was one of the primary developments of the late 1940s which made possible our present-day computers.

Many manufacturers produce programmable calculators; some have distinct advantages. Some characteristics of desktop electronic calculators are given in Table 5–1.

TABLE 5-1

Typical Characteristics of Desktop Electronic Calculators

1. *Size:*   desktop calculator size, typically 15 in. x 20 in. x 10 in. high
2. *Price:*   less than $8,000
3. *Speed:*   addition -.001 seconds; multiplication -.01 seconds
4. *Attachments:*   capable of accommodating an output printer
5. *Electronic:*   transistor or integrated circuit electronic construction
6. *Storage:*   196 to 960 instruction steps
7. *Accuracy:*   ± 1 part in the tenth digit of a number
8. *Number of digits of input data and output results:*   12
9. *Program Recording:*   tape cassette, magnetic card or punched cards

Programmable desktop electronic calculators, you can see, have small size, low price, reasonable calculation speed and high accuracy within the limits of the instruction steps allowed. One disadvantage is that the operator must enter all the data into the calculator. This means that each data item is equivalent to an instruction step. Thus, the electronic calculators are restricted to problems with relatively few input data items. Since every program contains many steps, there is a physical limitation to the amount of information we can feed in and utilize.

Programming an electronic calculator is an excellent introduction to programming computers. We can readily learn the language used for a particular calculator and step the calculator through all of the calculation processes. For instance, the Hewlett-Packard 85 personal computer, shown in Figure 5−3, is constructed of integrated circuits. This device is called a personal computer. It is suited for use by scientists and engineers. This computer uses the BASIC language and includes a central processor, keyboard, cathode-ray tube display, printer, and tape cartridge. [10]

Another useful desktop programmable calculator is the IBM 5120, shown in Figure 5−4. The 5120 may actually be classified as a small computer. It uses the BASIC or APL language and it displays the program and results on a visual display screen. This portable computer weighs less than 50 pounds. It uses a tape cartridge for storing data or programs.

The desktop computer or programmable calculator can be a very useful tool for the business person, scientist, or professional. A less costly but similar device is the handheld programmable calculator.

The small personal computer sells for several thousand dollars. It is available in computer stores such as Radio Shack.[9] These small computers are used by small businesses as well as in the home.

5.3   THE POCKET PROGRAMMABLE CALCULATOR

A pocket-size programmable calculator is available from several manufacturers. These small devices, which fit into one's pocket or hand, are useful to the

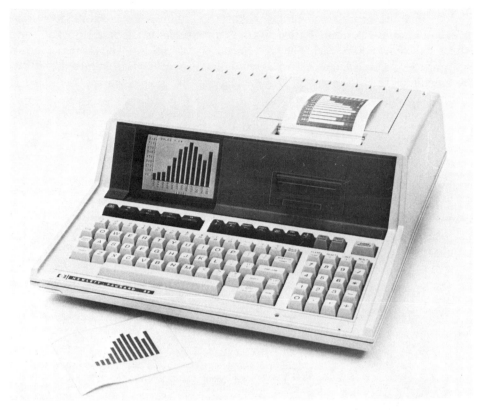

FIGURE 5-3   The Hewlett-Packard 85. This personal computer is designed for the engineer, scientist, accountant and analyst. The system includes a cartridge tape drive and a printer. Using the BASIC language, it sells for about $3200.

TABLE 5-2

The ENIAC and Pocket Calculators Compared

	ENIAC	*HP 67*	*TI 59*
Word Size	10 decimal digits	10 decimal digits	10 decimal digits
Data Memory Size	20 registers	26 registers	150 registers
Program Memory Capacity	750 instructions	224 instructions	300 instructions
Multiplications per Second	360	15	250
Cost	$480,000	$750	$300
Power Required	50,000 watts	$1/2$ watt	1 watt
Size	4,000 cu. ft.	25 cu. in.	29 cu. in.

student and the professional alike. Like large computers, these devices store information and operating instructions in their memories. Small pocket computers sell for less than $800. They have a variety of options. The HP-67 is shown in Figure 5–5. This calculator uses a small magnetic card inserted into the side of the calculator to read-in the program. The data is entered via the keyboard at appropriate points in the program.

The sale of programmable calculators amounted to about $300 million in

FIGURE 5–4   The IBM 5120 is a small portable computer that uses either the BASIC or the APL language. A visual display screen is provided as well as an optional printer for output. The floppy disk can store programs and data for later use. It is inserted in the slot above the operator's right hand. *Courtesy IBM Corporation.*

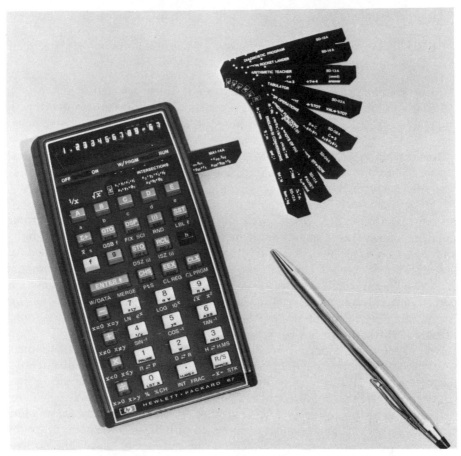

FIGURE 5-5   The Hewlett-Packard Model 67 programmable calculator uses a magnetic card to input the program. The HP 67 can accommodate up to 224 program steps. It has 26 data-storage registers. The display shows 10 digits plus a two-digit exponent in scientific notation. *Courtesy Hewlett-Packard Corporation.*

1980. Texas Instruments manufactures a model 59 which competes with the HP-67 we show here. Several programmable pocket-size calculators sell for less than $200. The Hewlett-Packard Model 65 or 67 or the Texas Instruments Model 59 have about the same power as the original ENIAC computer, as shown in Table 5-2. [2]

5.4   CHARACTERISTICS OF ELECTRONIC CALCULATORS

The ideal pocket or desktop electronic calculator should be easy to learn to operate. One should be able to program it for complex calculations without extensive training or special computer languages.

All programmable calculators are based on the use of a *register*.

REGISTER   A device capable of storing a specified amount of data, such as a ten-digit number.

Most programmable calculators have about ten to thirty registers.

The trigonometric, logarithmic and exponential functions are produced with a single keystroke each, since they are stored internally in a read-only-memory:

READ-ONLY-MEMORY (ROM)   A storage unit into which the information is placed at the time of manufacture. Such information is available at any time. It can be modified only with difficulty.

Read-only-memories are often used in small computers and electronic calculators, since they are small, rapid, and relatively inexpensive. The read-only-memory also stores the algorithms necessary to accomplish instructions called for by a simple keystroke. For example, the algorithm for accomplishing the square root of a number is stored in the read-only-memory. Also, the useful constant π is stored in the read-only-memory. It is clear that a read-only-memory is one cornerstone of an electronic programmable calculator or small computer. A small electronic ROM is shown in Figure 5–6.

One of the most important features of electronic calculators is the tremendous range of numbers that they can accommodate without special attention from the operator. It is not necessary to worry about where to place the decimal point to obtain the maximum accuracy. The numbers in an electronic calculator are stored, and all operations are accomplished, in what is called *floating point arithmetic*. A floating point number is expressed with the decimal point following the first digit and an exponent representing the number of places the decimal point should be moved—to the right if the exponent is positive, or to the left if the exponent is negative. Sometimes floating point arithmetic is called *scientific notation*.

FLOATING POINT NOTATION   A writing system in which numbers are expressed as significant digits, together with an exponent of the base 10 which indicates the location of the decimal point.

Thus, a floating point number shown on this 10-digit machine would appear as:

$$\pm \text{ F.FFFFFFFFF} \times 10^{XX}$$

The number consists of a plus or minus sign, a 10-digit number (all F's here), the decimal point following the first digit and the exponent (XX) of the base 10. Not all numbers require ten digits, of course. Table 5–3 illustrates the conversion of numbers to floating point form.

TABLE 5-3

Floating Point Coding of Numbers

Item	Number	Floating Point Form
a	123.4567	$+ 1.234567 \times 10^2$
b	0.0012345	$+ 1.2345 \times 10^{-3}$
c	−1,230,000	$- 1.23 \times 10^6$
d	4,000,000,000,000	$+ 4. \times 10^{12}$
e	−0.000000000050	$- 5. \times 10^{-11}$
f	123,456,789.423	$+ 1.234567894 \times 10^8$
g	−0.0000521	
h	98765.4321987	

Examining Table 5–3, we can gain some insight into the usefulness of floating point notation. All electonic calculators and digital computers have a limited number of digits that can be accommodated. Item *a* shows that the floating point notation simply accommodates just the digits and indicates the place of the decimal point by means of the exponent 10^2. Since 10^2 equals 100, we should move the decimal point two places to the right. Similarly, in Item *b*, 10^{-3} equals .001; for it, we should move the decimal point three places to the left.

Item *d* illustrates the usefulness of floating point, since the number of digits in 4,000,000,000,000 is 13 and this number could not be accommodated in this form in a 10-digit machine. In Items *d* and *e*, we omit the zeros following the digits 4 and 5 respectively; they are assumed to be zero if omitted. Item *f* is a 12-digit number. The actual number accommodated in the 10-digit calculator is shown with the last two digits, 32, omitted. These additional two digits cannot be accommodated. They are also omitted in calculation. It is clear that the precision of calculations by a computer or electronic calculator is limited by the number of digits that can be accommodated. Complete Items *g* and *h* before proceeding to the next paragraph. You may check your answers with the footnote on the following page.

The limitation of the number of digits accommodated by a specific machine is important. The number of characters a computer will accommodate is called a *word*:

WORD　　A sequence of characters considered as an entity.

Since any sequence of characters accommodated by the HP9100 are the plus or minus sign, the decimal point, up to ten digits and the exponent with its sign, a word in this calculator appears as:

$$\pm \text{ F.FFFFFFFFF} \pm XX$$

Since the word has a certain specified fixed length in any given machine, we call it the *word length*. The word length of the HP9100 is 14. This word length of 14 characters assumes the decimal point. In other machines it is assumed that the

FIGURE 5–6   Several Read Only Memory integrated circuits are shown with sugar crystals in a teaspoon. These ROMs are used in the IBM 5100 computer. They employ a Metal Oxide Semiconductor Field Effect Transistor (MOSFET). Each chip is 0.23 inches across. *Courtesy IBM Corporation.*

decimal point always follows the $\mp$ sign. In that case the word length required is again 14 characters, and any number is written $\mp$ .FFFFFFFFFF $\mp$ XX.

What are the largest and smallest numbers that can be stored in a computer with a 14-character word? Since the exponent can accommodate two digits we can have

$$\pm \text{F.FFFFFFFFF} \pm \text{XX}$$

Where XX = 99, the largest positive number would be

$$+ 9.999999999 \times 10^{+99}$$

and the smallest

$$+ 1. \times 10^{-99}$$

Clearly, almost all the numbers we would want to use can be accommodated within the exponents +99 to −99.

Item g -5.21×10^{-5}
Item h $+9.876543219 \times 10^{4}$

Electronic calculators and digital computers also accommodate numbers in *fixed point notation*:

FIXED POINT NOTATION   A system of writing numbers in which the position of the decimal point is fixed with respect to one end of the numerals according to some convention.

The convention for calculators is to display the decimal point in its proper position within the 10-digit number, assuming, of course, that the number in question can be accommodated within ten digits. The number 5.3361×10^3 is displayed in fixed point notation as

5336.1

Fixed point notation is a commonly used and understood notation, but its disadvantage is the limited size of the numbers that can be used. The difference in the range of numbers available with 10 digits for fixed and floating point is given in Table 5–4, which shows why floating point notation is preferable.

TABLE 5-4
The Range of Numbers for 10-Digit Fixed and Floating Point Notation

	RANGE
Fixed Point	$10^{10}-1 \geqslant$ number $\geqslant 1 \times 10^{-10}$
Floating Point	$10^{100}-1 \geqslant$ number $\geqslant 1 \times 10^{-99}$

The concepts of floating and fixed point numbers, registers and words are used with digital computers of all sizes.

Electronic calculators employ a code to translate instructions into logic that can be interpreted by the machine. Most codes or sets of instructions use one instruction for each line of code. An abbreviation or symbol is frequently used for an instruction. The code uses *mnemonic symbols*:

MNEMONIC SYMBOL   A sign chosen to assist the human memory. For example, an abbreviation such as MPY for "Multiply."

5.5 MINICOMPUTERS

Small computers called *minicomputers* have grown increasingly common in industry, education, and commerce. Minicomputers are characterized by their relatively smaller size and lower cost compared to general purpose computers. A minicomputer is developed primarily for data processing for a single application. The cost of minicomputer systems is shown in Table 5–5, where such cost is compared with the cost of larger systems. The IBM 5100 shown in Figure 5–4 may be classified as a minicomputer because it is small and relatively inexpensive.

Minicomputers have become attractive because they offer a low-cost system that can be dedicated to an independent application. By 1980, minicomputers accounted for about one-half of all computer systems in use in the United States. Approximately 100,000 minicomputer systems were sold in 1980 in this country. The market for minicomputer sales is growing about 20% per year, and it is estimated that 80% of the computers in use in 1985 will be minicomputers.

TABLE 5-5
Cost of Computer Systems

	1976	*1980*
General Purpose Computer	$50,000–$2 million	$40,000–$1 million
Minicomputer	$5,000–50,000	$2,000–$40,000
Microcomputer	$500–$5,000	$100–$2,000

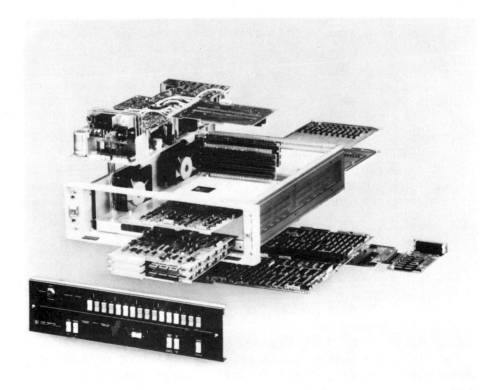

FIGURE 5-7 The Hewlett-Packard 21MX computer uses a modular design, illustrated here by the two separated sections. This minicomputer uses a sixteen-bit word; it costs about $9,000. It has 8,000 words of main memory. *Courtesy Hewlett-Packard Corporation.*

TABLE 5-6

Minicomputer Characteristics

Size: 6 inches × 20 inches × 30 inches (suitcase size)
Word length: 16 binary digits
Addition time for two numbers: 2 microseconds
Cost: $15,000
Size of Main Memory: 8,000 words

A typical minicomputer has the characteristics given in Table 5–6. The cost of expanding the central storage (main memory) will expand the cost of the system. In addition, appropriate input-output devices will be required for most systems. The modular design of a minicomputer is illustrated in Figure 5–7.

A complete minicomputer system includes input and output devices and expanded storage devices. A minicomputer system with several devices is shown in Figure 5–8.

For some problems it is useful to interconnect several minicomputers to achieve inexpensive and reliable systems. [4] Each computer carries out a separate task, and the set of minicomputers substitutes for one larger computer.

The availability of small low-cost minicomputers has led to the use of computers by hobbyists. Several stores in the United States now sell minicomputers and their components to hobbyists. One small computer, the Altair 8800, sells for less than $400 in kit form. The Altair 8800 has an eight-bit word, and it adds two numbers in two microseconds. A system with 4,000 words of memory and a keyboard input device costs less than $2,000.

5.6 MICROCOMPUTERS

Since 1975 small, inexpensive computer systems have been available. They provide significant computing power at relatively slower speeds compared to minicomputers. These small computers are called *microcomputers*; they are results of the effort to develop hand-held calculators.

The microcomputer is based upon a *microprocessor*, which can be constructed from integrated circuit devices (chips). They provide the functions characteristic of the central processing unit of a computer.[5] The microprocessor consists of the arithmetic unit and the control unit of a computer. (See Figure 3–3.) When the main memory and input-output functions are added to the microprocessor, the system is called a microcomputer.[6] When all the functions of a microcomputer are available, the small computer can compete with a minicomputer for some applications. The input-output and main memory functions are typically provided by one or more integrated circuits.

The characteristic microcomputer is typically a device containing a small

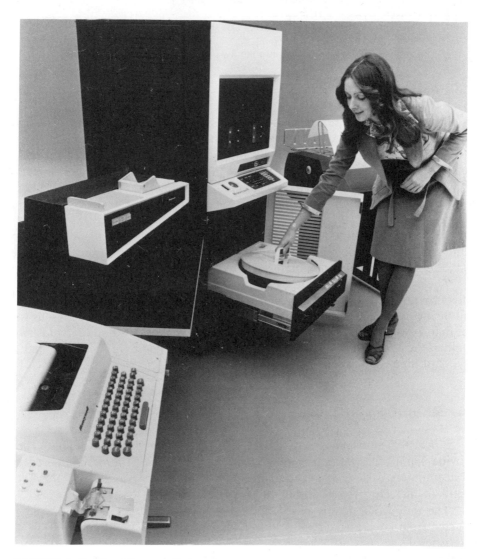

FIGURE 5–8   The Honeywell Level 6 minicomputer system includes (from left): teleprinter, tabletop card reader, magnetic cartridge disk unit, magnetic tape cassettes, and printer. The operator is loading the magnetic cartridge disk unit. *Courtesy Honeywell Inc.*

FIGURE 5-9 The Zilog Z80 central processing unit or microprocessor appeared in 1980. The microprocessor appears as one integrated circuit. *Courtesy of Zilog Corporation.*

main memory. It can add two eight-bit numbers in five microseconds. It costs about $300. The microcomputer is slower than a minicomputer, and often it has an eight-bit word length. Several microprocessor kits are available. They enable a hobbyist to build a microcomputer. The organization of a minicomputer or a microcomputer is shown in Figure 5-11. Any hardware device other than the central processing device and main memory is called a *peripheral*. The peripherals include input and output devices as well as auxiliary memory devices. The data and control bus is a set of lines (wires) used for communication between the devices. [20] A microcomputer incorporating a microprocessor is shown in Figure 5-10.

The microcomputer was first available commercially in 1971, and the number of microcomputers exceeded the number of large computers and minicomputers by 1975. It is estimated that over one million microcomputers are in use today. [8] A typical microcomputer weighs one pound, consumes two watts of power, and costs less than $100. Microcomputers, in contrast to minicomputers, trade computing power for economic and size advantages. The evolution of minicomputers and microcomputers is shown in Figure 5–12. The comparison of a minicomputer and a typical microcomputer is illustrated in Table 5–7.

TABLE 5-7
Features of Minicomputers and Microcomputers

Feature	Minicomputer	Microcomputer
Word Size (bits)	32	8
Speed of Execution	Medium (1 μs)	Slow (10 μs)
Random access memory (bits)	64 K	16 K
Programming	Efficient	Slow

FIGURE 5–10 The HP Series 9000 System 45 features a powerful central processor and a built-in mass memory. It incorporates a 12-inch CRT display, BASIC language programming and hard-copy printing. *Courtesy of Hewlett-Packard Journal.*

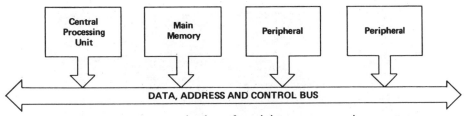

FIGURE 5–11 The organization of a minicomputer or microcomputer.

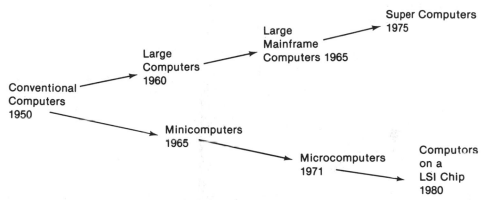

FIGURE 5–12 The evolution of computers has followed two diverging paths. Large, general-purpose computers have grown in power while decreasing in cost for a fixed number of operations. Smaller minicomputers have declined in price and size, permitting their use in dedicated, special-purpose applications.

Microprocessors are used in control units for microwave ovens, television sets, and videogames. They are also used with instruments in data acquisition and display. [5] With the price of microprocessors constantly falling, they will cause the use of microcomputers to increase in heretofore unimagined ways. [8]

SUMMARY

In this chapter we have reviewed the characteristics and advantages of electronic programmable calculators. While discussing programmable calculators, we have considered floating point and fixed point numbers and the concept of registers. We have found that electronic calculators are powerful calculating machines; they rival digital computers for solving mathematical problems with small amounts of input data. While programmable calculators are not general purpose computers, they can assist in the solution of problems. They have many

FIGURE 5–13 The first scientific calculator into which alphanumeric formulas can be entered as written, the Sharp EL-5100 displays numbers, letters, and symbols on the screen. This calculator sells for approximately $80.

features, such as program storage, claimed by the larger, more expensive digital computers.

We have also examined the characteristics of minicomputers, which now account for one half of the computers in use in the United States. We have reviewed the new microcomputer, which promises to revolutionize technology and to introduce the computer to many uses.

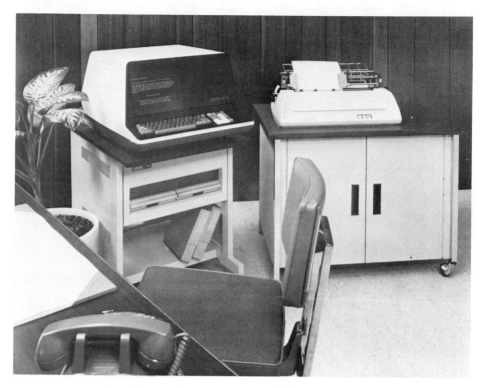

FIGURE 5–14 The DEC WD 78 is a minicomputer useful for business and industry. This personal business computer is sold through computer stores. *Courtesy of Digital Equipment Corporation.*

CHAPTER 5 PROBLEMS

P5–1. List some of the advantages and disadvantages of the programmable electronic calculator. A calculator is shown in **Figure P5–1.**

P5–2. What is the typical accuracy of an electronic calculator? Compare the accuracy of a programmable electronic calculator with the accuracy of a mechanical desk calculator available at your school.

P5–3. Define *register*, *read-only-memory*, and *word*.

P5–4. A specific machine can accommodate five numerical digits in fixed point notation, and five numerical digits, a decimal point, and a two-digit

FIGURE P5-1. A powerful personal calculator, the HP 34-C.[11, 12] Note the key labelled SOLVE, which solves for the roots of an equation. Also note the key used for evaluating an integral.

exponent in floating point form. Thus, for this machine we have

Input Number	Floating Point	Fixed Point
432.56	4.3256×10^2	432.56
5,637.822	5.6378×10^3	5,637.8
−0.01459		
+8384,446		
Maximum allowable		
Minimum allowable		
+939423.1		

Complete the table of entries for the fixed point and floating point representation of the input numbers.

P5-5. List some mnemonic symbols used by the telephone company, your bank, and other organizations. Examine your utility bills and salary stubs for mnemonic symbols.

P5–6. For the latest electronic programmable calculator, determine the price-to-performance ratio where the performance is measured by the number of additions performed per second.

P5–7. Language translators are available in the form of hand-held calculators. Examine the operation of such a device.

P5–8. An algorithm for calculating the factorial of a number *n* is called Stirling's approximation. This approximation is quite suitable for a calculator or desk-top computer. First divide n by e (the Naperian number) and raise this result to the power n. Then multiply by the square root of the product of twice the number and π. Find 9! by this method and compare with the correct result, which is 362.880.

CHAPTER 5 REFERENCES

1. L. D. Shergalis, "Calculators," *Hewlett-Packard Journal*, Sept. 1968, Palo Alto, California, p. 2.

2. G. Otto and George A. Miller, "A Pocket ENIAC," *Datamation*, June, 1974, p. 26.

3. E. W. McWhorter, "The Small Electronic Calculator," *Scientific American*, March, 1976, pp. 88–96.

4. A. L. Robinson, "Multiple Minicomputers: Inexpensive and Reliable Computing," *Science*, January 31, 1975, pp. 337–338.

5. J. G. Posa, "Microcomputer Does It All," *Electronics*, October 1979, p. 82.

6. S. Crespi–Reghizzi, "A Survey of Microprocessor Languages," *Computer*, January 1980, pp. 48–66.

7. S. L. Snorer and M. A. Spikell, *How To Program Your Programmable Calculator*, Prentice-Hall Inc., Englewood Cliffs, New Jersey, 1979.

8. A. Allison, "Follow Three Simple Rules to Improve Software Productivity," *Electronic Design News*, March 20, 1980, pp. 167–171.

9. G. Bylinsky, "The Computer Stores Have Arrived," *Fortune*, April 24, 1978, pp. 151–155.

10. T. R. Lynch, "A New World of Personal/Professional Computation," *Hewlett-Packard Journal*, July 1980, pp. 3–6.

11. W. M. Kahan, "Handheld Calculator Evaluates Integrals," *Hewlett-Packard Journal*, August 1980, pp. 23–32.

12. W. M. Kahan, "Personal Calculator Has Key to Solve Any Equation f(x) = 0.," *Hewlett-Packard Journal*, December 1979, pp. 20–26.

13. K. D. Wise, K. Chen, and R. E. Yokely, *Microcomputers: A Technology Assessment to the Year 2000*, Wiley and Sons, New York, 1980.

14. W. S. Benett and C. F. Evert, Jr., *Microcomputers: Hardware/Software Design*, Dekker, Inc., New York, 1980.
15. M. E. Sloan, *Introduction to Minicomputers and Microcomputers*, Addison-Wesley Publishing Co., Reading, Massachusetts, 1980.
16. C. A. Ogden, *Microcomputer Management and Programming*, Prentice-Hall, Inc., Englewood Cliffs, New Jersey, 1980.
17. G. A. Gibson and Y. Liu, *Microcomputers for Engineers and Scientists*, Prentice-Hall, Inc., Englewood Cliffs, New Jersey, 1980.
18. J. Doerr, "Microcomputers," *Proceedings of the IEEE*, February 1978, pp. 117–130.
19. R. N. Noyce and M. E. Hoff, "A History of Microprocessors," *IEEE Micro*, February 1981, pp. 1–10.
20. N. Graham, *Introduction to Computer Science: A Structured Approach*, West Publishing Co., St. Paul, Minnesota, 1980.

6

COMPUTER COMPONENTS

6.1 INTRODUCTION

In the preceding chapter, we considered the binary number system used in digital computers, computer arithmetic and the algebra of binary variables. The internal operation of a computer, based on binary arithmetic and algebra, is realized physically by means of computer components. It is the purpose of this chapter to describe the components used within computers and some of the trends in their evolution.

Basically, a computer consists of input and output units, storage units and a central processing unit as shown in Figure 6-1. The central processing unit includes the control function and the arithmetic function. The input and output devices transmit information between the computer and the user. The storage unit retains the instructions, data and intermediate results within its memory. We devote the next section of this chapter to the electronic components used to build the computer units, and the trends in their evolution. Section 6.3 deals with the input and output units available for use with digital computers. Section 6.4 discusses the developments and trends in the construction of storage units and memories.

A computer is a system of interconnected components, combined into what is called a *hardware system*; this is a collection of physical parts such as

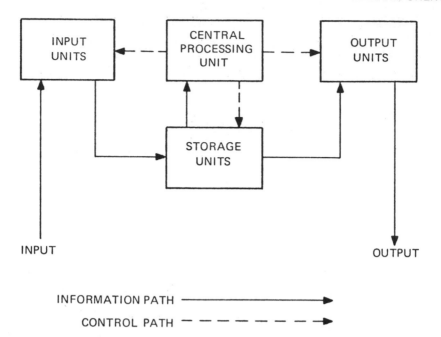

FIGURE 6-1   The four major units of a computer hardware system, with their information and control paths.

mechanical, electrical and electronic devices. The hardware system consists of input and output devices, the main storage units, together known as the memory,
and the central processing unit.

Computer components have been improved rapidly during the past decade,
leading to a markedly improved digital computer. In many ways, the development of reliable, fast, and small components has brought us to a plateau of quality computers. What new trends in computer developments will occur we can only
attempt to predict.

6.2 ELECTRONIC COMPONENTS FOR COMPUTERS

The electronic digital computer is built primarily of electronic components,
which, as we have explained above, are those devices whose operation is based on
the phenomena of electronic and atomic action and the physical laws of electron
movement. An *electronic circuit* is an interconnection of electronic components
arranged to achieve a desired purpose or function.

During the past two decades, the computer has grown from a fledgling
curiosity to an important tool in our society. At the same time, electronic circuit
developments have advanced rapidly; they have had a profound effect on the

computer. The computer has been significantly increased in reliability and speed of operation, and also reduced in size and cost. These four profound changes have been primarily the result of vastly improved electronic circuit technology. As Maurice V. Wilkes said in his 1967 Association for Computing Machinery Turing Lecture:

> An event of first importance in my life occurred in 1946, when I received a telegram inviting me to attend in the late summer of that year a course on computers at the Moore School of Electrical Engineering in Philadelphia. I was able to attend the latter part of the course, and a wonderful experience it was. No such course had ever been held before, and the achievements of the Moore School, and other computer pioneers, were known to few. There were 28 students from 20 organizations. The principal instructors were John Mauchly and Presper Eckert. They were fresh from their triumph as designers of the ENIAC, which was the first electronic digital computer, although it did not work on the stored program principle. The scale of this machine would be impressive even today—it ran to over 18,000 vacuum tubes. Although the ENIAC was very successful—and very fast, it had severe limitations which greatly restricted its application as a general purpose computing device. In the first place, the program was set up by means of plugs and sockets and switches, and it took a long time to change from one problem to another. In the second place, it had internal storage capacity for 20 numbers only. Eckert and Mauchly appreciated that the main problem was one of storage, and they proposed for future machines the use of ultrasonic delay lines. Instructions and numbers would be mixed in the same memory in the way to which we are now accustomed. Once the new principles were enunciated, it was seen that computers of greater power than the ENIAC could be built with one tenth the amount of equipment.

Electronic vacuum tubes were used in the earliest computers. They were replaced by solid-state electronic devices toward the end of the 1950's. A *solid-state component* is a physical device whose operation depends on the control of electric or magnetic phenomena in solids; for example, a transistor, crystal diode, or ferrite core. Solid-state circuits brought about the reliability and flexibility required by the more demanding applications of computers in industry. Probably the most important solid-state device used in computers is the semi-conductor, which is a solid-state element which contains properties between those of metal or good conductor, and those of a poor conductor, such as an insulator. Perhaps the best-known semi-conductor is the transistor. (See below.)

The advances in electronic circuit technologies have resulted in changes of "orders of magnitude" where an order of magnitude is equal to a factor of ten.

The number of installed computers grew from 5000 in 1960 to approximately 500,000 in 1980. Also, the number of circuits employed per computer installation has significantly increased, as is illustrated by Figure 6–2. The first computers

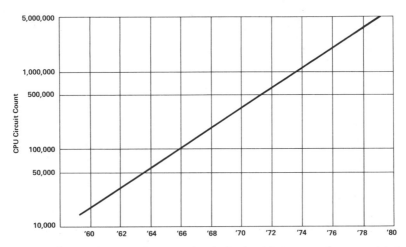

FIGURE 6–2   The number of solid-state circuits in the CPU versus the year of delivery.

using solid-state devices employed 20,000 circuits. Today computers using transistors may have more than one million circuits.[1] The trend is likely to continue; it has been made possible by the continued decrease in size, power dissipation, cost, and improved reliability of solid-state circuits. The increase in the speed of operation of logic circuits is shown in Figure 6–3. Note that what was used in a "high performance" computer in 1975 became commonly used in 1980. The speed of the logic circuits is given in nanoseconds, 10^{-9} seconds. Table 6–1 lists the common names for the measures of time.

TABLE 6-1

Time Interval Measurements and their Commonly-Used Name and Symbol

ms = Milliseconds = 10^{-3} seconds = .001 seconds
μs = Microseconds = 10^{-6} seconds = .000001 seconds
ns = Nanoseconds = 10^{-9} seconds
ps = Picoseconds = 10^{-12} seconds

Figure 6–4 shows the marked improvement of the time for an addition in a computer. Along with the increase in speed has been the increase in the performance of a computer in terms of its speed and cost. A plot of a performance

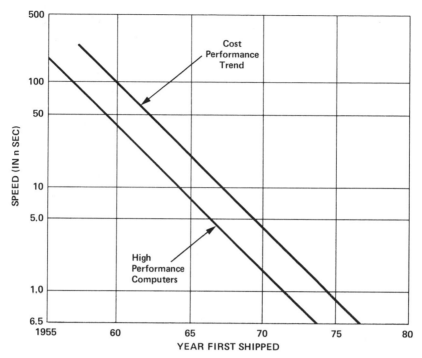

FIGURE 6-3   The speed of operation of a computer logic circuit in nanoseconds versus the year shipped.

measure P is shown in Figure 6–5, where

$$P = 1/(\text{Add time} \times \text{average computer rental cost})$$

Figure 6–6 is a photo of a circuit board for computer memory. This circuit is used for random access memory. When assembled, hundreds of these boards are used in the central processing unit of a computer.

The reliability of an electronic circuit is essential to the overall reliable operation of a computer, which contains thousands of such circuits. The improvement in the reliability of electronic components for a fifteen-year period is shown in Figure 6–7. The improvement in reliability is shown as a function of the system failure rate per logic gate; there has been an improvement of almost four orders of magnitude during the fifteen-year period.

Several trends are evident today in system design. Probably the most important requirements in future systems will be for data integrity and high reliability. With the increasing use of computers in all aspects of economic life, there must be absolute guarantees that records cannot be destroyed, and, furthermore, that the system cannot fail in such a manner that its services become unavailable. Attempts will be made to design computer systems that "fail softly," much in the manner of a telephone switching network, which has a high probability of being able to process calls even with faulty components in the system.[1]

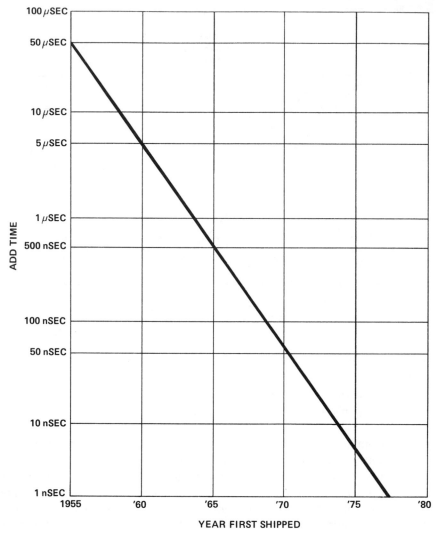

FIGURE 6–4   The add time of a computer.

The size of computers has dramatically decreased during the past twenty years because the size of electronic components has decreased and packaging techniques have improved. The density of circuits per square inch is shown in Figure 6–8 for the period 1960–1980.[1] There was a change of four orders of magnitude during the period 1960 to 1975. *Packing density* is the number of components per cubic measure of volume. A chart of the packing density of electronic components is shown in Figure 6–9.[3] The standard of packing of logical components is the neuron density in a human brain. Circuit fabrication using electron

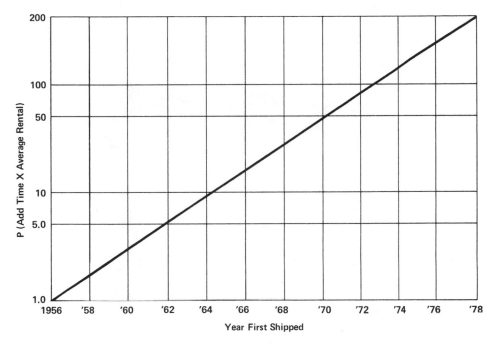

FIGURE 6–5   The performance measure of a computer.

beam methods may in the future enable us to improve the packing density of circuits significantly within a computer.

In 1980, expenditures for electronic components and computer hardware
were approximately $16 billion. Of this amount, the expenditure for solid-state
components is estimated as $5.0 billion, with the remaining expenditure for in-
put/output equipment and storage units. Expenditures for semiconductors have
grown from $1 billion in 1964 and may reach $8 billion in 1984.[2]

While the electronic circuits have been continually improved with respect to
size, speed, cost and reliability, one must ask if there is any ultimate limit of performance. The answer in part depends upon the transistor. The modern high-
performance computer was made possible by the utilization of the transistor as a
computer component beginning in 1957. The transistor is a solid-state semiconducting device, using germanium or silicon, that performs dynamic functions
such as amplification or switching. The transistor is much faster than the vacuum
tube, and it also uses less power (and energy). The lower power consumed by the
transistor is at least as important as its greater speed. It permits many more
elements to be packed into a given space, and thus makes more powerful computers possible within a given physical space for a computer.

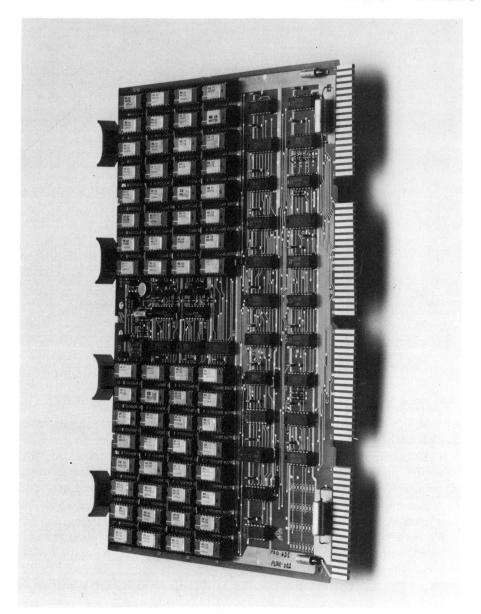

FIGURE 6–6   The National NS-11 memory storage circuit board provides 16,000 words
of storage with each word equal to 16 bits. The access time is 800 nanoseconds and the board measures 8.9 × 10.4 inches. *Courtesy National
Semiconductor Corporation.*

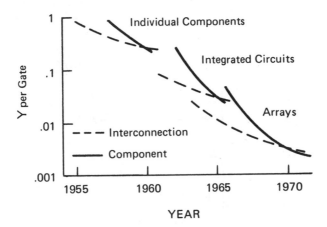

FIGURE 6-7   The improvement of the reliability of circuits during a fifteen-year period. The abcissa is a logscale showing a measure of reliability where Y is a function of system failure rate.

One limit that appears to be formidable is the wavelength of light. It is assumed that we cannot fabricate any component smaller than one wavelength. Also, the propagation of computer information is limited to the speed of light and the delay introduced by sending information along lengths of wires in computer circuits. A delay of two nanoseconds is contributed by each foot of interconnecting wire. The introduction of electron-beam technologies may reduce this problem.

The unforeseen has always led us to underestimate the limits of the existing technology, not realizing that new technologies may develop which will lead to new performance. As J. P. Eckert, the developer of ENIAC, points out[5]:

> In the early days of computers, I had many examples of people who told me why computers wouldn't work. I think the first expert that came around was from the Ordnance Department, and he asked, "How much power does the machine take?" And we replied, "Over 100 kw." He then asked how big the room was, and we told him "thirty by fifty feet." He thought about it for a while and said, "It's impossible to get that much power out of a room that size."

> Dr. Pender, the Dean of Electrical Engineering School at the University of Pennsylvania, used to come down to the laboratory regularly and say, "Nobody around here ever gets twenty tubes to work at one time. How do you guys propose to get all these thousands of tubes to work at once?"

Although the early critics were proved wrong, Keyes points out that thermal limitations place the upper limit of computer speeds at only one order of

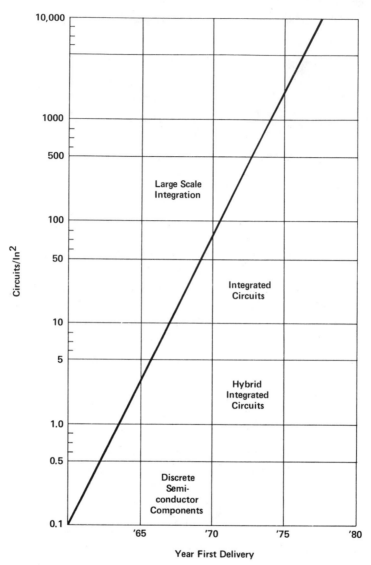

FIGURE 6–8   The density of computer circuits versus year delivered. Several microcomputers achieved 100,000 circuits/in² in 1980.

magnitude above the fastest speeds allowed by today's circuits.[5] Although
power levels have remained essentially the same since early application of the
transistor, faster logic circuitry has demanded such higher power densities (closer
component packaging leads to higher power densities) that the problem of power
dissipation appears to present an almost insurmountable barrier to higher speeds.
The only solution appears to be lowering the computer operating temperatures.

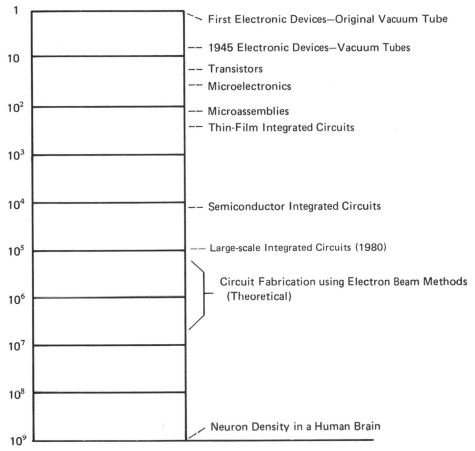

FIGURE 6–9   A chart of packing density of electronic components. The human brain is
the most-packed computer so far known.

The computer's speed is limited by the physical operation of its components, such as the element known as the binary flip-flop device. If solid-state phenomena are used, involving electronic motion, speed is determined by the inertia of electrons. Electrons have a natural response time no faster than 10^{-15} second. Perhaps some other phenomena (such as optical phenomena) will be utilized in the future for logic circuits.

Also, there will be some limit to the packing density that can be achieved with existing technology. In nature we find that the bacterial DNA molecule can store 3000 bits with a density of 3×10^{19} bit/cm³. Nature stores genetic information in DNA molecules made up of long sequences of nucleotides of four different species. The information is, in fact, stored redundantly since the nucleotides occur in correlated pairs. This redundancy provides a means of replication as well as a means for preserving the integrity of the stored information so that repairing mechanisms within the cell can restore damaged sections of the molecule. The packing density of information within the human brain is also impressive. The brain can store 10^{13} bits at a density of 10^{10} bit/cm³.

The miniaturization of electronic computer components has been made possible by the availability of solid state components, which made possible revolutionary improvements in the reliability, size, and power consumption. A further dramatic change has been a reduction in cost well below what would have been possible with vacuum-tube technology. These changes have had a major impact on the computer industry, which has in turn stimulated the semi-conductor industry. A new generation, or standard, of computer equipment appeared approximately every five years during the period 1954 to 1964. With each succeeding generation there has been a reduction by a factor of 10 in the cost per arithmetic operation, and a reduction by a factor of about 10 in the rate of failure of components. The reduction in the cost per operation has increased the range of problems that can be handled economically by electronic computers and hence has rapidly widened the market, while the increase in reliability has made it possible to build larger systems without the problem of constant component failure. The extremely rapid buildup of demand for computational power and the fact that computers can be built from relatively few and conceptually simple digital logic circuits used in enormous repetition has made the technological development rapid as well.

The first-generation computers appeared commercially in 1954. They used vacuum tubes as electronic components. A typical system had 2000 logic circuits in its central processing unit, with a mean time to failure, per circuit, of 1 percent per 1000 hours. The equipment was fairly large in size and consumed quite a large amount of electric power.

The second-generation computers appeared in 1959; they used transistors as the electronic component. The transistors and other components were connected in a manner similar to that of the first-generation machines. However, the reliability was increased by a factor of 10 and the power consumption was reduced.

The third-generation computers appeared in 1964 using *integrated circuits*, which are combinations of interconnected circuit elements inseparably associated on or within a continuous layer of material, which is called a *substrate*. An integrated circuit is shown in Figure 6–10. The photograph is magnified about 80 times. The actual chip is 1/10 the size of a small fingernail.

The current evolutionary step in electronics is the emerging development of *large-scale integration* (LSI), which is a term used to describe the technology consisting of arrays of logic cells, formed in a batch process, to realize a complete function. The concept of LSI emerged from the rapid evolution of the batch fabrication technology of silicon transistors. When scientists learned to fabricate hundreds and thousands of transistors next to each other on a one-inch slice of silicon, the idea presented itself of adding cross-connections and separating them into blocks containing all the interacting parts of a large gate or flip-flop. As this became a reality, engineers found they could place hundreds of such blocks of functions on one slice of silicon. Again, the thought was obvious—how many of

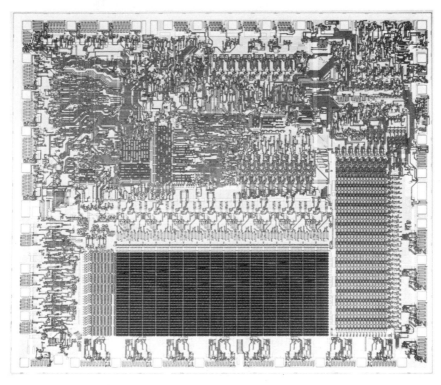

FIGURE 6-10   The Intel 8748 single-chip eight-bit microcomputer contains 20,000 transistors. The microphotograph shows a chip that measures 0.221 × 0.261
inches. The microcomputer contains a central processing unit, programmable read-only memory, random-access memory, and an input/output
interface. © Intel Corporation.

these might one be able to interconnect and leave together on one chip?[4]

The number of circuits involved in an array may be 100 to 2000. A photo of
an integrated circuit which provides two complete serial registers is shown in
Figure 6-11. The circuit is less than 0.1 inch on a side. The cost of such devices,
when employed in large systems, is as low as $.05 per bit. The cost of developing
and producing an LSI circuit decreases as the amount of integration is increased.
Figure 6-12 shows the level of integration for the period 1960-1980. The flat
portion of the curve represents the time when single discrete components were
used. Higher performance circuits are fabricated to closer tolerances so that the
number of circuits that can be integrated at the chip level with reasonable yield
will be lower than those designed for more modest performance. The complexity

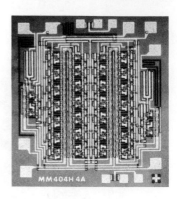

FIGURE 6–11   A photomicrograph of a
               Dual 100 Bit Bynamic Se-
               rial Register, which uses
               metal oxide semiconduc-
               tor (MOS) construction.
               The device shown is actu-
               ally .076″ by .091″ in
               size. *Courtesy of National
               Semiconductor Corp.*

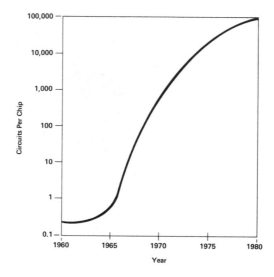

FIGURE 6–12   The level of circuit integration during the period 1960–1980. The num-
               ber of circuits per chip of material is shown.

of integrated circuits is also illustrated by Figure 6–13, which shows the number
of active elements (transistors) per chip during a twenty-year period.[4]

One of the expected advantages of LSI is a reduced cost for a given function.
The reduction in the estimated average price per logic function of an integrated
circuit is shown for the sixteen-year period 1964–1980 in Figure 6–14. [4]
Another illustration of the expected performance per dollar is shown in Figure
6–15. In this figure the performance ratio is shown as the switching rate of a
logic circuit in bits per second for a given dollar cost.

The reliability of a computer function can be increased by utilizing LSI,

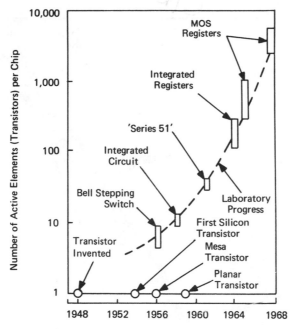

FIGURE 6–13   The number of active elements (transistors) per chip versus year of laboratory accomplishment.

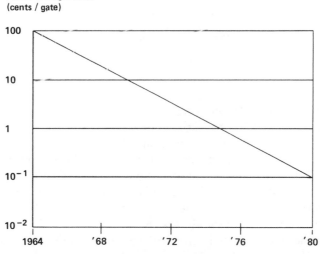

FIGURE 6–14   The reduction of the estimated average price per logic function of an integrated circuit in cents for a 16-year period. The cost was reduced by a factor of 1000 during this time.

CIRCULAR

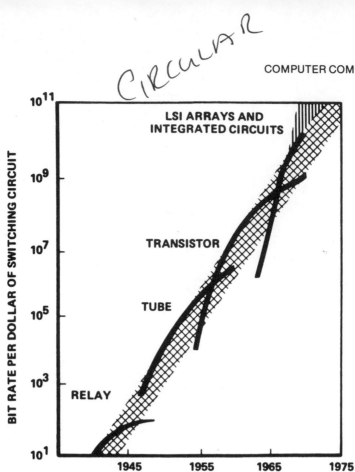

FIGURE 6–15   The switching rate of a logic function per dollar cost for a thirty-year period. The switching rate is given in bits/second. From *Proceedings of the Fall Joint Conference, 1969. Courtesy of American Federation of Information Processing Societies.*

since, as the circuit density increases, the number of interconnections at all levels of packaging decreases. Since every mechanical connection is a potential failure, it is important to minimize the number of interconnections necessary. For example, for a computer system requiring 10,000 gates, the reduction of mechanical connections is from 150,000 for discrete devices to 20 for LSI.

The definite advantages and gains from LSI are (1) reduction of the cost per bit; (2) tolerance of large parameter variations; (3) reduced power consumption per logic gate; (4) increased speed of operation, and (5) increased reliability due to its reduced number of mechanical interconnections. Whether all these advantages come to fruition is a matter for the future to judge. As LSI arrives, then the fourth generation of computers will arrive with it.

Whether the next electronic circuit development and application for computers is LSI, electron beam electronics or some other electronic or optical technique, the future will undoubtedly lead to smaller, faster, and more reliable computers. The electronic components are the bricks in the foundation of the computer. The history of the development of the computer has paralleled the development of new electronic devices, and we can expect this relationship to continue for the decade of the 80s.

6.3 INPUT/OUTPUT SYSTEMS AND PERIPHERAL EQUIPMENT

The four main units of a digital computer, shown in Figure 6–1, are the central processing unit, the input units, the storage units and the output units. The process of transferring information into the main storage unit is known as an *input* operation, and the process of transferring the results from the main storage unit to the user is known as an *output* operation.

INPUT/OUTPUT SYSTEM   A general term for the equipment for transferring the information into the main storage of the computer and out of storage to the user.

The input/output system (commonly called the I/O system) enables the computer to communicate with the computer operators, the programmers and the user. I/O operations are important to the overall efficient operation of the computer. In addition, I/O devices proved auxiliary storage media to handle input information which is too large to be contained in main storage at one time.

The input/output system essentially consists of:

(1) I/O hardware devices for sensing input information and recording the output information
(2) communication devices for transmitting the information between the I/O devices and the main storage
(3) control mechanism for initiating, supervising, and terminating the I/O process.

The input/output equipment is a major portion of the equipment other than the CPU and main storage units. The computer equipment other than the CPU and main storage units is called the *peripheral equipment*: it consists of any units of equipment, distinct from the central processing unit and the main storage unit, which may provide the system with outside communication. The primary portion of the peripheral equipment is the I/O system. Auxiliary storage units make up the remaining major peripheral equipment. Often, if is difficult to determine when an auxiliary storage unit is serving as input/output intermediate storage and when it is serving as an auxiliary storage unit to the CPU. In this section we consider the role and operation of input/output systems and most perpheral equipment.

Input/output systems are often quite complex. They include some logic circuits within the equipment because there are problems inherent in transferring information between relatively low-speed I/O devices and a high-speed storage unit and CPU. I/O devices are in part mechanical and therefore inherently slower than the electronic CPU and storage units. The I/O devices typically transfer information within intervals of milliseconds, while the CPU and main storage operate within intervals of microseconds. Information may be defined in terms of binary digits (bits); thus, an information transfer rate would be defined as bits per second. Many I/O devices operate in the range of 10–1000 bits/second, while a CPU and main storage unit operate within the range 10^5–10^8 bits per second. Thus, there is an inherent problem in the difference of speeds of a factor of 10^4 or more. Synchronizing the operation of I/O devices with the operation of transferring information to and from main storage is a very important design consideration. In some cases, the slow operating speeds of the I/O devices relative to the fast internal speeds of the CPU have caused applications to be called *input/output bound* or *limited*.

With the growth of time-sharing computing and networks of computers which require many peripherals per CPU, it is predicted that 76 percent of the expenditures for computers will be for peripheral equipment by 1982. The expenditures for peripherals amounted to $4.3 billion in 1968 out of a total expenditure for computers of $7 billion. Sales of peripheral equipment reached an expenditure of $16 billion in 1980.

Input/output systems are built with one common objective: to move information between peripheral devices and main storage. The digital computer can handle, arrange, extract, correlate, and otherwise manipulate information at an all-but-incomprehensible rate. It can also perform arithmetic calculations so rapidly that it can provide answers to questions that would necessarily remain unanswered without it. But the information must be given to the computer before it can manipulate, and it must be told what manipulations to perform. A question must first be posed to the computer, and the programmer must describe to it the arithmetic steps required for calculating the answer. Finally, when the computer has performed the operation, the results must be returned to the user in an intelligible way if they are to be useful. This is the input/output problem: how to get information of all sorts from the form in which we understand it into the computer in a form which it requires and then to do the same thing in reverse.

Information is provided as input or output through I/O media. Input media range from punched cards to voice input. Output media range from a printed page to microfilm and visual displays. Some I/O media in common use are the following:

- switches
- punched cards
- punched paper tapes
- magnetic tapes
- optically-readable printed characters

- magnetic ink characters
- cathode ray tubes (CRT)
- microfilms
- printed pages

Each medium requires a code or specific arrangement of symbols to represent information. The relationship of each input or output medium to its translation device and the main storage unit and the CPU is shown in Figure 6−16. This list, while not all-inclusive, is illustrative of the range of I/O peripherals available.

The most common input medium has been the punched card. A mechanical keypunch has been used since its development in 1880 by Hollerith. An example of an early keypunch is shown in Figure 6−17. A keypunch for preparing punched cards is still a dominant input preparation device. Of course, punched cards have been in use for well over 100 years; a photo of Jacquard's original card is shown in Figure 6−18.

A modern keypunch machine is shown in Figure 6−19. The 80-column punched card with its code for the numbers and the alphabet is shown in Figure 6−20. Information is represented in a punched card by a code of holes in a given column, which represents a character. That can be seen by examining the figure. The speed of preparation of punched cards is limited to the speed of typing, which is commonly one to five characters per second. However, the punched cards are prepared off-line; that is, without any connection to the computer.[10] Prepared and checked, the cards are read into the computer by a punched-card reader. The card reader reads one card at a time, and can process hundreds of cards per minute. A punched card reader and punch are shown in Figure 6−21. This device can read cards as input and, at another time, it can punch cards as output.

The primary medium for output useful to humans is a printed document. A printed page of output can be produced by a line printer as shown in Figure 6−22. A line printer, such as that shown in the figure, operates by impact printing and prints one line at a time at the rate of several hundred to a thousand lines per minute.[11] An example of a printout from a line printer is shown in Figure 6−23.

Punched paper tape serves much the same purpose as punched cards. Data are recorded as arrangements of punched holes, precisely arranged along the length of a paper tape. Paper tape is a continuous recording medium, as compared to cards, which are fixed in length. Thus, paper tape can be used to record data in records of any length, limited only by the capacity of the storage medium into which the data is to be placed or from which the data is received. Data punched in paper tape are read by a paper-tape reader and recorded by a paper-tape punch. A high-speed paper-tape reader is shown in Figure 6−24.

Magnetic tape is a primary I/O medium used as an intermediary for input to main storage and output from main storage. Typically, many programs are

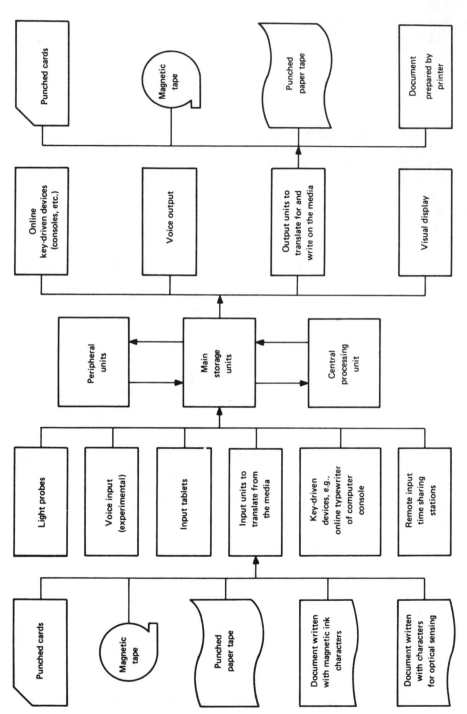

FIGURE 6–16   Input/output media and hardware.

FIGURE 6–17 Mechanical keypunch, circa 1901. *Courtesy of IBM Corporation.*

FIGURE 6–18 Jacquard's original card. *Courtesy of IBM Corporation.*

FIGURE 6–19 An IBM Model 29 Keypunch. *Courtesy of IBM Corporation.*

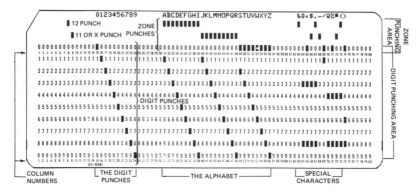

FIGURE 6–20   A punched card with the code displayed for the numbers, alphabet and special characters.

FIGURE 6–21   A punched-card reader and punch. *Courtesy of IBM Corporation.*

entered onto magnetic tape off-line from the computer. Then magnetic tape is entered into the computer. This makes it possible to enter many programs at one time at a high rate of transfer. This process is also followed for the output step. Thus magnetic tape units offer high-speed entry of data into the computer system, as well as efficient, extremely fast recording of processed data from the system. Highly reliable input/output data rates of up to 680,000 numeric characters per second are possible.

Information is recorded on magnetic tape as magnetized spots called *bits*.

FIGURE 6–22   An IBM Model 1403 Printer. *Courtesy of IBM Corporation.*

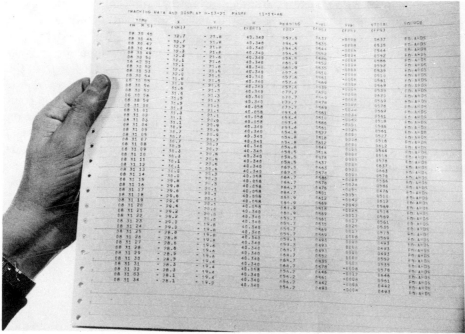

FIGURE 6–23   A portion of a computer printout detailing second-by-second progress
of the first successful rocket-powered flight of the HL-10 "wingless lift-
ing body" aircraft November 13, 1968 at NASA's Edwards, California
Flight Research Center. Radar readings communicated to a GE-225 information system were processed instantaneously, and results were
transmitted to the computer center. Numerical data simultaneously
recorded on magnetic tape were transferred to this printout later.
Courtesy of General Electric Co.

FIGURE 6–24   The NCR Model
472 Paper Tape
Reader. *Courtesy
of the National
Cash Register
Corp.*

The recording can be retained indefinitely, or the recorded information can be erased automatically and the tape reused many times with continued high reliability. So that tape can be easily handled and processed, it is wound on individual reels. Tape is usually 1/2 inch wide; it is supplied in lengths up to 2400 feet per reel. Data is recorded in parallel channels or tracks along the length of the tape. There are seven or nine tracks on the 1/2 inch tape. The tracks across the width of the tape provide one row of data. The spacing between the vertical rows is automatically generated during the writing operation and varies depending on the character density used for recording. Character densities up to 1600 characters per inch are commonly achieved. An example of a magnetic tape system is shown in Figure 6–25.

Another method of representing data on paper media for machine processing is with magnetic ink characters—a language readable by both man and machine, as shown in Figure 6–26 for a paycheck. The numbers printed along the bottom edge of the paycheck are magnetically readable. The shape of the characters permits easy visual interpretation; the special magnetic ink allows reading or interpretation by machine. The printing, or inscribing, of the magnetic ink characters is accomplished by a machine. An example of a machine for reading magnetic ink characters is shown in Figure 6–27, which shows a Honeywell document reader-sorter. Magnetic ink character readers are used extensively in the banking industry.

The punched card used with the Hollerith code offers a maximum of 80 characters and has minimal error detection capability. It is also limited in man-readable printout without secondary operations; the utility bill you receive must be both printed and punched under current conditions.

An equivalent card magnetically imprinted can give up to 700 characters with 10 lines of data at 70 characters per line. This is an improvement of about 9 to 1 over mechanically-punched cards, along with the advantage of full interpretation

FIGURE 6–25   The IBM 2415 Magnetic Tape System (rear), shown with the IBM disc
storage device (front). *Courtesy of IBM Corporation.*

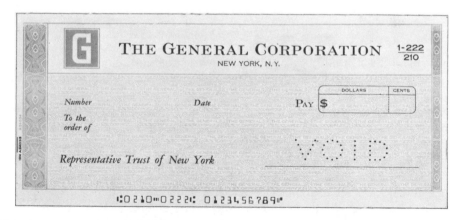

FIGURE 6–26   A paycheck with magnetic ink characters imprinted on the bottom edge
of the check.

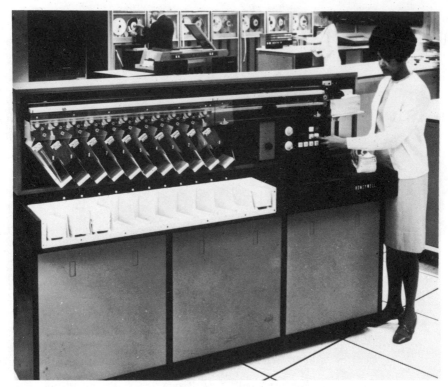

FIGURE 6–27   The Honeywell Type 232 MICR Reader-Sorter, which can be operated as a free-standing unit or on-line to any Series 200 computer. This unit reads magnetic ink-encoded documents at speeds up to 600 documents per minute and sorts them into 11 different pockets (10 accept and one reject). *Courtesy of Honeywell Corp.*

in one operation. In addition to this, the hardware requirements for printing a card are much simpler, less expensive and faster than the techniques available for punching cards.[12]

A recently developed method of representing data on paper for input to a computer uses optically-readable characters. In industry and business, a large amount of data must be entered into the computer. One option is to use cards marked by hand and read by a mark-sensing device such as shown in Figure 6–28, with an example of a mark-sense card in Figure 6–29.

Optical character reading (OCR) machines that can read almost any type of printed material at a rate of up to 14,000 characters per second have been developed. OCR equipment is expensive for high-speed reading machines; more modest reading rates are obtained with cheaper devices. OCR machines can read

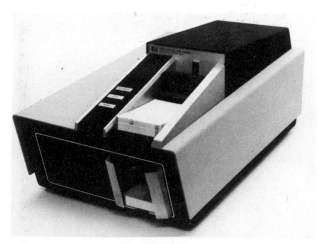

FIGURE 6−28 The Hewlett-Packard Optical Mark Reader Model 2761A, which is capable of reading 250 cards per minute, or 455 characters per second.

FIGURE 6−29 A mark-sense card for examinations.

typed and printed material, and script-reading devices are being developed. An example of an OCR machine is shown in Figure 6−30. The paper form is shown passing the reading wheel in Figure 6−31.

An output device of growing usefulness and availability is the visual display. Visual display units in several sizes, capacities, speeds, and capabilities to handle complexities of information permit the user of a computing system to see graphic reports on a cathode ray tube that would take many times longer to produce by normal printing methods. The use of a visual display unit at a system-operator console is a typical application. Another is the retrieval and presentation of a record as a result of an inquiry. An example of a visual display unit is shown in

FIGURE 6–30   The OPSCAN 100 optical reader, which automatically reads marked
sheets at a rate of 2,400 per minute and transfers the information to
magnetic tape or storage. *Courtesy of Optical Scanning Corp.*

FIGURE 6–31 The
paper form passing
through the optical
scanning wheel of the
OPSCAN 100.
*Courtesy of Optical
Scanning Corp.*

Figure 6–32. A data communication system incorporating several input and output devices is shown in Figure 6–33. This modular system, shown with some of
its component options, can handle punched cards, paper tape, manual keyboard
input, magnetic tape cartridges, a magnetic character reader, a visual display and
a medium-speed printer. The system shown in Figure 6–33 has card reader (upper right), display station (center) and printer (foreground).

FIGURE 6–32 The
IBM Model 3277 display
station. This visual dis-
play device can be used
by business, industry,
and government. The ter-
minal is capable of dis-
playing 24 lines with 80
characters per line, for a
total of 1,920 characters.
Courtesy IBM Corp.

FIGURE 6–33 The Tektronix 4025 computer display terminal. Up to 1,024 (horizontal)
by 780 (vertical) points may be displayed on the eleven-inch screen.
Charts, graphs, diagrams, and lines of words may be displayed. A unit
that produces a copy of the display is shown at right. *Courtesy
Tektronix, Inc.*

The off-line process of transferring data into machine readable from and recording it on some form of intermediate memory, such as tape, has grown in use during the past decade. During the period 1965–1975, two forms of keyboard-to-magnetic tape devices were developed for data input. The first device is primarily a direct unit-for-unit replacement for keypunch equipment employing a keyboard entry of data, bypassing the mechanical punching of cards, and recording the keyed-in data electronically on magnetic tape. The second device employs a typewriter keyboard for the recording of data (usually textual data) on magnetic tape in cartridges or cassettes.[12] It is claimed that a 1/3 to 1/2 improvement in operator efficiency is achieved due to simpler set up and operation. The acceptance of such keyboard-to-tape devices is impressive; over 300,000 units were in operation by 1980. One such keyboard-to-tape device is shown in Figure 6–34. These units can be used for data entry on the floor of a factory, for example. A device which enters the data on a tape cassette or a flexible disk is shown in Figure 6–35.

In recent years numerous developments have been pursued that will enable human beings and computer systems to communicate with each other. For example, time-sharing computer systems enable individual computer users to utilize a computer simultaneously. Time-sharing systems and other remote access-immediate response computer systems provide the power of the computer to users located remotely from the computer. One of the basic components of such a system is a *terminal* for input and output use. A terminal serves to provide the operator with a connection to the computer, and to control the format and transmission of information. One such terminal is the common Teletype Model 33ASR, shown in Figure 6–36. The Teletype Model 40, shown in Figure 6–37,

FIGURE 6–34   The KB-800 Datascribe, a data recorder which enables an operator to enter data directly onto computer-compatible magnetic tape. *Courtesy of Vanguard Data Systems.*

FIGURE 6–35 The Sycor Model 340 terminal, equipped with a microprocessor, cathode ray tube (CRT), and typewriter-like keyboard. The 340 includes two cassette tape recorders, shown to the right of the CRT, as well as a flexible disk recorder to the right of the keyboard. The flexible disk has an access time of 93 milliseconds. It is capable of storing up to 486,000 characters. One tape cassette is capable of storing 250,000 characters of data. *Courtesy Sycor, Inc.*

FIGURE 6–36   The Teletype Model 33 ASR. A paper punch input device is shown on the left of the device. *Courtesy of Teletype Corp.*

is a recent solid-state model, with an impact printer operating at 314 lines per minute. Small terminals hand-carried in an attaché case can be connected to a computer through a telephone headset acoustically coupled to the terminal. One such portable terminal is shown in Figure 6–38. These terminals allow the user

FIGURE 6–37 The Tele-
type Model 40 Terminal includes a line printer operating
at up to 400 characters per
second. The terminal is used
for message preparation, editing, and on-line transmission
and reception. The display
screen has a 24 line capacity
with up to 80 characters per
line. The Model 40 can store
up to 5,760 characters. *Cour-*
tesy Teletype Corporation.

FIGURE 6–38 A person can "talk" with the company computer from the convenience
of his office by using a Honeywell COM-PACT computer terminal, a
device that is acoustically coupled through any standard telephone. The
computer, through its audio response unit, provides answers that the
user hears through the terminal's speaker. The portable unit can be
operated by its own batteries or plugged in to any 110-volt electric
outlet. *Courtesy of Honeywell Electronic Data Processing Division.*

to dial the computer he wishes to use by telephone and to communicate with it, whatever his location. The terminals typically communicate at 10 characters a second or less. Portable hand-held terminals are now available, and it is expected that their use will grow rapidly in the 1980s. One terminal is shown in Figure P6–21.

The number of all kinds of terminals in use in 1980 was estimated to be 2,000,000, and it is predicted that there will be three million terminals in use in 1988 for on-line input, conversational time-sharing and remote batch computing.[13] The trend in terminals, as well as with most peripheral equipment, is to include more digital circuitry built into the terminal. This trend may be accelerated by the availability of LSI in the next few years.

The output of a computer must necessarily be readable by humans. The medium selected should be in keeping with the way the data will be utilized. Thus, archival files—where minimum physical size and high information density are important—might require microfilm output. On the other hand, a readout of the status of a process that has only temporary significance could best be obtained from a line or strip printer, or perhaps a CRT terminal. Output printers offer insufficient speed of reproduction and they use massive amounts of paper. For these reasons, the use of microfilm offers many advantages. A computer output microfilm device (COM) is any unit of hardware which produces a microfilm record from information provided by a computer. (Microfilm is any film up to 105 mm—commonly 16mm film—with images that must be enlarged 8 to 40 times to be equivalent to normal paper documents. Microfilm can be in rolls or chips, or can be mounted in other carriers.)

Alphanumeric COM devices are primarily used as substitutes for impact printers. Whereas an impact printer can produce 2400 characters per second, COM devices can write characters at rates up to 500,000 characters per second. Since a large percentage of the information generated is for reference only, there are extensive savings in the cost of film compared to paper. Binding expenses, as well as storage and shipping costs, are also minimized by the reduction in the bulk and weight of the recording medium.

Graphic COM devices are used to make bar charts, graphs, and drawings. Typesetting characters, company logos, and half-tone pictures are further examples of graphic output. The programming capability of COM devices also makes them well adapted for producing animated movies, an application that is becoming increasingly popular.[14]

The distinct advantages of COM relative to impact printers are shown in Figures 6–39 and 6–40.[15] COM gives hard copy output after the film has been exposed and processed. A computer output microfilmer is shown in Figure 6–41. The model shown is a relatively lower-priced unit which films alphanumerics at a rate of 13,000 lines per minute. It is estimated that expenditures for COM were $100 million in 1970 and increased to one and one-half billion dollars by 1980. It is estimated that 5,000 COM units were in use in 1980.

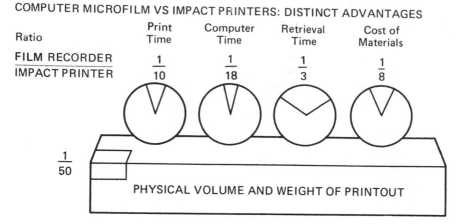

Ratio	Print Time	Computer Time	Retrieval Time	Cost of Materials
FILM RECORDER / IMPACT PRINTER	$\frac{1}{10}$	$\frac{1}{18}$	$\frac{1}{3}$	$\frac{1}{8}$

COMPUTER MICROFILM VS IMPACT PRINTERS: DISTINCT ADVANTAGES

$\frac{1}{50}$

PHYSICAL VOLUME AND WEIGHT OF PRINTOUT

FIGURE 6–39   The distinct advantages of computer output microfilm relative to an output printer. From *Proceedings of the Fall Joint Computer Conference, 1969. Courtesy of American Federation of Information Processing Societies.*

The primary application of COM devices is information storage for random, infrequent retrieval. COM is used at Houston's Manned Spacecraft Center for many applications as shown in Figure 6–42, for storing massive amounts of data and documents.[16] A comparison of the costs of computer microfilm and continuous paper output is given in Table 6–2.[15] Furthermore, a COM information retrieval system compares very favorably with a time-sharing computer system, as shown in Figure 6–43. The comparison depends upon the numbers of pages that must be stored, the number that must be brought up to date each month and the number of users of the system. The active use of microfilm for the storage and retrieval of information in daily use has been practiced by some users and companies for years. For the most part, these have been extremely large users (*e.g.*, Social Security Administration). In the future we can expect a growing use of computer output microfilm systems.

It would be helpful if we could talk directly with computers. Recently, there has been some development of devices that can lead ultimately to computer input units capable of recognizing human speech, and to computer output units capable of generating "voices." A computer system that can identify words in continuous speech of an unknown speaker is beyond the current state of the art in speech recognition. However, limited speech-recognition systems have been developed capable of responding to a vocabulary of 20 to 40 words.[6, 7, 8] The user must train the system to recognize his or her enunciation of the words. The problems involved in the design of voice response systems are less formidable than those en-

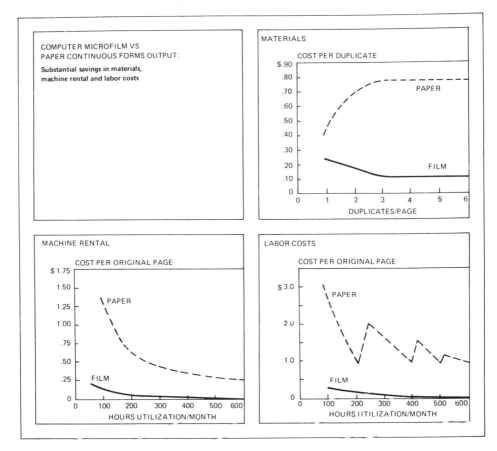

FIGURE 6-40 The substantial savings in materials, machine rental and labor costs for computer microfilm versus continuous paper output. From *Proceedings of the Fall Joint Computer Conference, 1969. Courtesy of American Federation of Information Processing Societies.*

countered in the development of voice recognition systems. Voice-recognition systems are difficult to design since they must account for each person's variation in speech patterns, pitch and intensity.

Voice-response systems are based on analog recording of a few selected phrases and words or on digitally-controlled synthesis of speech. One commercially available system, the IBM 7772, consists of 15 digitally-controlled frequencies, or voice pitches, covering the telephone voice band. The audio signals are combined and applied to the listener's telephone set. Voice-response systems are often used with remote-access computer systems.

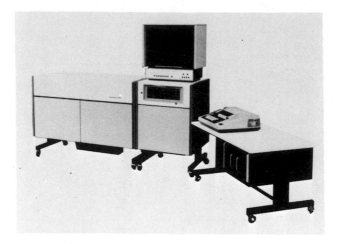

FIGURE 6–41   The Model 4560 Computer Microfilmer can record up to 20,000 lines per
minute on 16 mm. film. The information is provided as tape input on
the tape transport unit shown above the center cabinet. COM can store
500 times the capacity of paper printouts in a given storage volume.
Courtesy Stromberg Datagraphix, Inc.

Voice-recognition systems will probably be developed first for specialized
applications such as manned space flight.[16] The human voice is a desirable
means of communication with a computer since it uses a human's natural
language, leaves his limbs free for other purposes, and is more rapid than typing
at a terminal.

Currently, voice-response systems are being used as a voice answering service
for banks, insurance companies and other businesses. The use of an audio
response unit is more suitable than the use of a CRT display, a Teletype or some
other type of printer in areas where short and simple replies to remote inquiries
are required and where no need exists for computer interaction or hard-copy output as in a telephone booth, in a patrol car, or on board a plane. The selection of
a particular type of audio device must be based on the area of application and
whether it fits the requirement of a limited vocabulary and relatively simple
responses. Perhaps voice I/O systems for computers will be common within this
decade.

A useful and common output device is the computer graphic plotter. This
device provides the user with visual plots, graphs and drawings on paper. One example of a graphic plotter is shown in Figure 6–44. A pen is driven by electronic
circuitry controlled by the computer. It writes directly on paper. Plotter accuracy
is about ± .01 inch and plotters operate at speeds from 20 inches/minute to 1500
inches/minute. Two drawings obtained from computer plotter output are shown

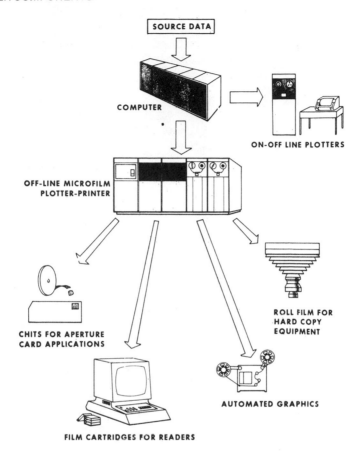

SOURCE DATA

COMPUTER

ON-OFF LINE PLOTTERS

OFF-LINE MICROFILM
PLOTTER-PRINTER

CHITS FOR APERTURE
CARD APPLICATIONS

ROLL FILM FOR
HARD COPY
EQUIPMENT

AUTOMATED GRAPHICS

FILM CARTRIDGES FOR READERS

FIGURE 6–42 The Manned Spacecraft Center's Computer Output Microfilm Unit, which is used to store the massive records of space flight.

in Figures 6–45a and 6–45b. The plotter is a very useful tool for permanently recording graphic relationships.

Remote-access computer systems, such as time-sharing computers, require a communication facility to connect the remote terminal to the CPU and main storage. This peripheral device, while not an I/O device, is a fundamental portion of the I/O system in a remote-access system. As Mr. Sam Wyly recently stated:

> In the immediate future, knowledge, rather than capital, labor or raw materials, will become the major source of economic growth. Knowledge, not things, will become the new basis of productivity. It will become the force which drives our economy. And the computer, as the central organizer and repository of in-

TABLE 6-2
Comparison of Costs of Computer Microfilm and
Continuous Paper Output

5,000 PAGES	VOLUME	APPROXIMATE ANNUAL STORAGE COST
MICROFILM	0.10 Ft^3	$0.05
PAPER	4.50 Ft^3	$4.15

5,000 PAGES	WEIGHT	APPROXIMATE FIRST CLASS MAIL COST
MICROFILM	3.0 Lbs.	0.03¢ / mile
PAPER	150.0 Lbs.	4.05¢ / mile

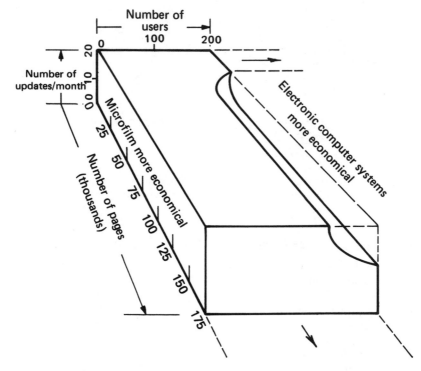

FIGURE 6-43   Computer-generated microfilm versus time-sharing computer systems as a storage and retrieval system. From *Proceedings of the Fall Joint Computer Conference, 1969. Courtesy of American Federation of Information Processing Societies.*

FIGURE 6–44 The CAL-COMP 565 Plotter drawing a learning curve. *Courtesy of California Computer Products, Inc.*

FIGURE 6–45a Copy of a Model 100 plot. *Courtesy of Strobe Inc.*

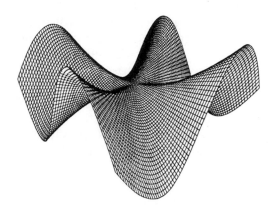

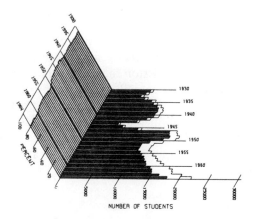

FIGURE 6–45b Three-axis graph showing relationship between two sets of data—University of Washington. *Courtesy of California Computer Products, Inc.*

formation, will play a massive role in this new society. But it is an exercise in futility to have massive data banks if we don't have the data transmission capacity to make their information immediate, accessible, and universal. Unless we find a fast, efficient, reliable means of transporting digital data (*i.e.*, knowledge) between computers, data banks, and terminals, we will severely limit our opportunities to make the computer a major intrument in human service... .

Several alternate approaches to communication between remote access I/O devices and the CPU I/O system are shown in Figure 6–46. Common carrier telephone channels are used for data transmission, and it has been estimated that in the near future half of the information transmitted over telephone lines will be digital computer data, as contrasted with human voice transmission. One device often used with telephone connections is called a *modem*, which is a contraction of "modulator-demodulator," and is one name ("data set" is the other) for the units which modulate the series of data from a computer or terminal for transmission through the common carrier network. If a computer has only one port, or connection, to the network, a modem at the computer site and one modem at each remote site are the only required communications peripherals. In Table 6–3, we have a comparison of the communication speeds of a human, a communication transmission system and a computer. Notice that a telephone is limited to transmitting at rates of 120 to 400 characters/second, while a human is limited to typing at one to five characters per second. Clearly, the computer which accepts data at speeds up to 10^6 characters/second has a sufficient amount of time to accommodate many input channels from numerous simultaneous users.

The computer operator uses many of the input/output devices and peripherals. A recent study of the operator's activities shows that he spends about half of his time with activities related to the I/O units and peripherals. In this study, the operators stated their preferences for equipment location in the computer room.

In Table 6–4, a summary of the approximate cost and range of speed of various input/output devices is given. During the next five years, it is expected that the number of remote terminals and data transmission facilities will increase markedly. Also, it is expected that microfilm equipment will replace many of the slower impact line printers. Furthermore, the number of Optical Character Readers and keyboard-to-tape recorders in use will increase significantly.[4] Input/output systems are an important portion of a computer system. While they may be peripheral in location, they are central in importance to the proper and efficient functioning of a computer system.

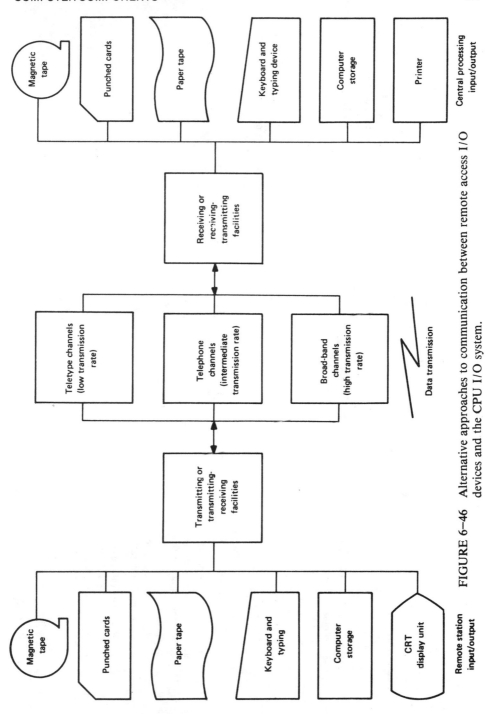

FIGURE 6-46 Alternative approaches to communication between remote access I/O devices and the CPU I/O system.

TABLE 6-3

A Comparison of the Communication Speeds of a Human, a Communication Transmission System and a Computer

Man	*Transmission System*	*Machine* (Third Generation Digital Computer)
A. His Communication Capabilities 　1. Sensing Senses 　　a. Speech: 5–20 char/sec 　　b. Handwriting: 3–10 char/sec 　　c. Typing: 1–5 char/sec 　2. Receiving Senses 　　a. Sight 　　　–Pictorial: Very fast 　　　–Reading: 10–15 char/sec 　　b. Hearing: Fast B. His Memory Capabilities 　a. Total Storage: Up to $(10)^{15}$ char 　b. Prompt Recall: 1–10% of total 　c. Speed of Recall: 　　–Up to 10% fast; remainder slow (and inaccurate) C. His Psychological Reactions 　a. Rational – Likely predictable 　b. Emotional – Unlikely predictable	A. Terminal I/O Equipment 　1. Telecom Typewriter 　　Printing Speed: 10–15 char/sec 　　Char/line: 72–156 　2. Cathode Ray Tube (CRT) 　　Display Speeds: 240–100,000 char/sec 　　Total no. of char: 1,000–4,000 　3. Remote Batch Printers 　　Printing Speed: 600–660 char/sec B. Telephone Network 　1. Voice Grade – Single Channel 　　Speed: 120–400 char/sec 　2. Broad Bank – Multi-Channel 　　Speed: Up to 23,000 char/sec	A. Central Processing Unit 　1. Execution rate 10^6–10^8 　2. Memory cycle time: Microsec to nanosec 　3. Core memory capacity: 10^5–10^7 B. Peripheral Storage 　1. Access Speed: Up to $300(10)^3$ char/sec 　2. Capacity: Up to $1.60(10)^9$ char

TABLE 6-4

Input/Output Devices

Name	Approximate Cost 1	Speed Range 2
Teletypewriter	Low	10 characters/second
Punched Paper Tape Reader	Low	100–1000 characters/second
Punched Paper Tape Punch	Low	100–300 characters/second
Punched Card Readers	Medium	100–1600 cards/minute
Punched Card Punches	Medium	60–500 cards/minute
Line Printers	Medium	200–1200 lines/minute
Mark Sensing	Low-Medium	100–1000 cards/minute
Magnetic Character Reader	Medium	300 mag. cards/minute = 2700 punch cards/minute
Optical Character Reader	High	2400 sheets/hour
Graphical Plotters	Low-Medium	20–1500 inches/minute
Visual Displays	Medium-High	60 frames/second
Computer Output Microfilmer	High	10–30,000 lines/minute

[1]Low cost = $1,000 – $5,000
Medium cost = $5,000 – $25,000
High cost = greater than $25,000

[2]Speed: 5,000 electric typewriters = 30 Impact Line Printers = 1 COM

6.4 STORAGE DEVICES

A major unit of a digital computer is the main storage unit, which is shown in Figure 6–1. A computer also often utilizes auxiliary storage units for aiding the input/output process. This section describes storage devices, some of the components of storage devices, and some of the trends in the development of storage units. The definition of storage is:

STORAGE (1) Holding of information; synonymous with *memory*. (2) Pertaining to a device into which information can be entered, in which it can be held, and from which it can be retrieved.

In this section we consider only storage devices that can be used in conjunction with a computer. Also, we use the term "memory" interchangeably with "storage." Information entered into storage can be either data or instructions.

The ability of computers to process information and to solve problems is often limited by the need for access to data used in the solution of the problem. A single unit of information is the binary digit (bit), which is the measure of information stored in a given memory. The availability of storage has always set a limit on a computer's ability to communicate and to solve problems. Twenty-five years after the first generation of digital computers, the performance of computers is often limited by the size and speed of the memory. In the beginning, a few hundred bits of data-storage seemed like a large memory. Now, our information processing and problem-solving ambitions have grown, and we can use the far larger memories—up to a trillion bits—that are now available.

The main storage unit accepts data from an input unit, exchanges data with and supplies instructions to the central processing unit, and can furnish data to an output unit. All information to be processed by any system must pass through main storage. This unit must therefore have capacity to retain a usable amount of data and the necessary instructions for processing.

Applications may require additional storage. If so, the capacity of main storage is augmented by auxiliary storage units. All information to and from auxiliary storage must be routed through main storage. Storage is arranged somewhat like a group of numbered mail boxes in a post office. Each box is identified and located by its number. Similarly, storage is divided into locations, each with an identifying number and a specified location. A given storage location will hold a specified number of bits. When information is entered into a storage location, it replaces the previous contents of that location. When information is read from a location, the contents remain unaltered. The process of taking or reading information from a storage location is often called *reading out* stored data.

The computer requires some time to locate and transfer information to or from storage. This interval of time required to read data is called access time; it is defined as follows:

ACCESS TIME   (1) The time interval between the instant at which data are called for from a storage device and the instant delivery is completed; that is, the *read time*. (2) The time interval between the instant at which data are requested to be stored and the instant at which storage is completed, which is often called the *write time*.

The access time of a storage unit has a direct bearing on the efficiency of the computer system. The faster the arithmetic speed of a computer, the larger and faster must be the main storage unit.

Thus, these are two primary characteristics of computer main storage units: (1) the capacity of a storage unit, measured in bits, and (2) the access time of a storage unit, measured in seconds. The growth in capacity of storage for different media during the period 1940–1975 is shown in Figure 6–47. The media used for storage have progressed from the vacuum tube and the magnetic drum to advanced thin films and experimental holographic storage. The increase in the capacity has been a factor of approximately 10^8. Optical storage devices are capable of storing 10^8 bits per square inch. In Figure 6–49, we have the relationship between the capacity of various storage media and the related access time.[9]

The main storage unit uses only storage devices that provide an access time of less than 10^{-6} seconds, since the CPU operates at that speed or faster.

A good measure of performance of a storage device is the density-speed factor, where the density of storage is given in bits per cubic volume and the speed is

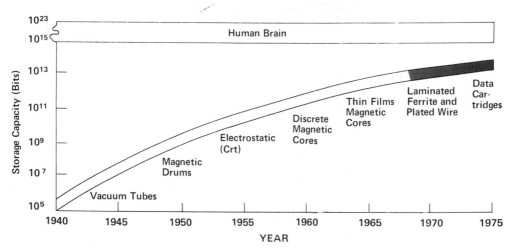

FIGURE 6–47   The capacity of storage media available during the period 1940–1975.

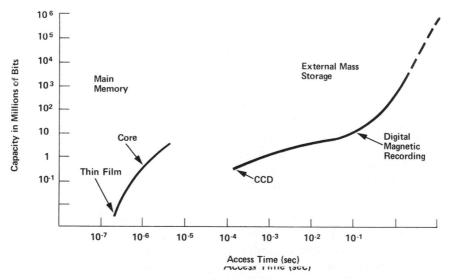

FIGURE 6–48   Capacity of storage media versus access time associated with the media.

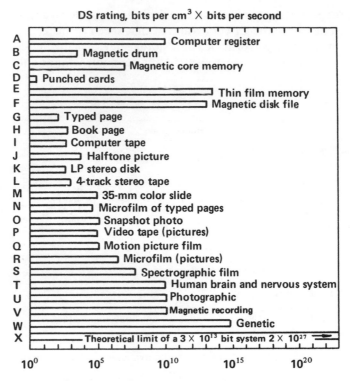

FIGURE 6–49 Density-speed ratings for different information storage methods. Density is given in bits/cm³ and speed in bits/second.

given in the rate of transfer of bits per second. Figure 6–49 illustrates the density-speed ratings for numerous storage devices.[9] The genetic storage of nature is the present standard—but notice that a magnetic disk file and a thin film memory approach it in performance.

Of course, one always pays a price for rapid access to data. The relationship between cost per bit of storage and the access time required is shown in Figure 6–50. [12] Notice that if we wish to decrease the access time from 10^{-3} to 10^{-7} (by a factor of 10^4) then the cost increases, relatively, by a factor of almost 10^3.

Each bit of information is stored in a physical device capable of being in one of two stable states. The binary media can store their binary information in a physical device, a circuit or a region of a physical material. Most main storage units consist of *magnetic core* storage units. A magnetic core is defined as follows:

MAGNETIC CORE   A configuration of magnetic material that is placed in a spatial relationship to current-carrying conductors and whose magnetic properties are to be used for storage purposes.

An example of a magnetic core is shown in Figure 6–51a, where the direction of magnetization is indicated by the arrow. The magnetization is reversed by reversing the current direction, as shown in Figure 6–51b. Thus the magnetic core is capable of two directions of magnetization; it is a binary device. The direction of magnetization is retained when the current is removed; therefore the storage is of

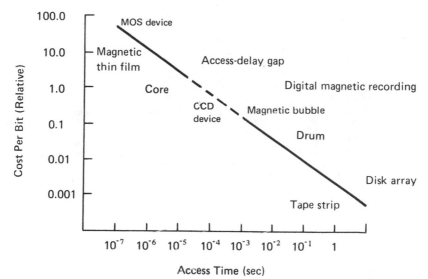

FIGURE 6–50   The cost per bit of access time in a storage unit.

FIGURE 6–51   Magnetic core storage. (a) Core magnetized in one direction. (b) Magnetization of the core reversed by the current, which itself has been reversed.

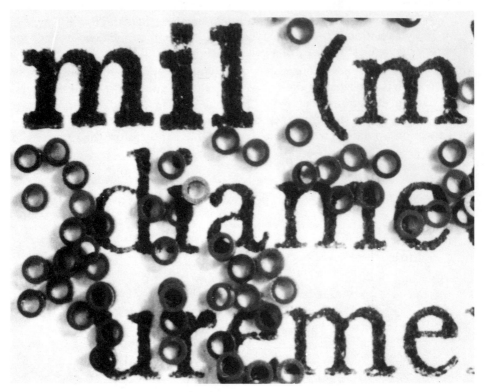

FIGURE 6–52   Magnetic cores of 18 mil diameter. *Courtesy of Ampex Corp.*

a permanent nature. Core storage is the most expensive storage device in terms of cost per storage location. However, core storage also provides the fastest access time; thus, it may be the most economical in terms of cost per machine calculation.

A magnetic core is a tiny ring of ferromagnetic material, a few hundredths of an inch in diameter. Cores are placed like beads on sets of wires. Because any specified location of storage must be instantly accessible, the cores are arranged so that any combination of ones (1's) and zeros (0's) representing a character can be "written" magnetically or read back when needed. A collection of magnetic cores is shown in Figure 6–52. The cores are only 18 thousandths of an inch in diameter.

To magnetize a specific core, two wires run through each core at right angles to each other as shown in Figure 6–53. When half the current needed to magnetize a core is sent through each wire, only the core at the intersection of the wires is magnetized. No other core in the string is affected. Using this principle, a

SENSE WIRE

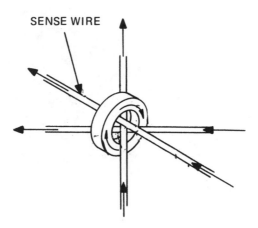

FIGURE 6–53   A magnetic core, with the two magnetizing wires at right angles, and the sense wire.

large number of cores can be strung on a screen of wires, yet any single core in the screen can be selected for storage or reading without affecting any other. In the computer, the cores are magnetized by a pulse of electrical current sent through the two wires, which is said to "flip" the binary element. A sense wire, shown in Figure 6–53, is added to the arrangement for detecting whether a core contains a 1 or a 0. This wire is strung through all the wires in a given plane of cores. A group of cores mounted on sense and write wires is shown in Figure 6–54.

A portion of a complete core memory plane is shown in Figure 6–55. In this figure, each plane carries 4000 cores. Other units use 16,384 cores in each plane, and 70 planes. Such a seventy-core plane would hold approximately one million bits.

By far the majority of main storage units utilize magnetic cores as the storage device. The decrease in the memory access time for magnetic core storage for the period 1953–1973 is shown in Figure 6–56. Also, the cost of a constant size (10^6 bit) core memory has decreased from 20¢ per bit in 1957 to approximately 1¢ per bit in 1980.

The prime requirements for main storage units are rapid access time and reasonably large memory capacity. Magnetic thin-film devices are used for main storage units, since they meet these requirements. A thin film of magnetic material is deposited on a surface and a physical location serves as a memory location. One commercially available thin-film memory uses a thin magnetic film on a beryllium copper wire six thousandths of an inch in diameter. These wires, or metal whiskers, are shown in Figure 6–57. Each wire, .110 inch in length, is used for a single bit in a memory plane. The memory built from the thin-film whiskers operates with an access time of 800 nanoseconds. Thin-film plated wire cost is approximately $.06 per bit, which is greater than the cost of magnetic

FIGURE 6–54   Magnetic cores mounted on the sense and write wires. *Courtesy of Ampex Corp.*

cores. Plated-film wire memories currently possess an access time of 200 to 800 nanoseconds.

Another potential device for use as a main storage unit is a semiconductor memory, particularly a unit fabricated from integrated circuits. As we learned in section 6.2, semiconductor devices are fast and small. The price per bit of semiconductor memories has decreased rapidly over the last decade. The cost of semiconductor memories has declined to approximately one-half cent per bit in 1980. It is therefore competitive with core memories. Semiconductor memory prices have been reduced by large-volume production and the use of large-scale integration (LSI).

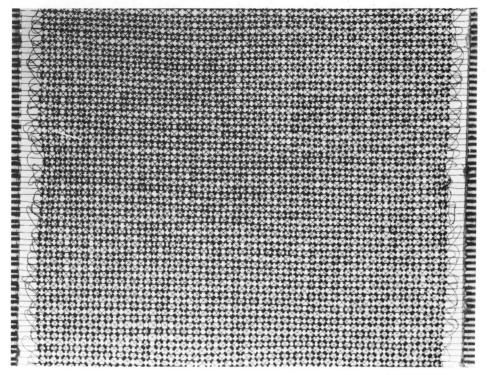

FIGURE 6–55   A portion of a magnetic core memory plane (approximately 1/3 size)
used in an electronic computer. One such plane has more than 4,000
cores, each threaded by four enamel-coated wires. Vertical and horizontal wires carry electrical charges which magnetize or demagnetize
selected cores under control of the computer. Diagonal wires "sense"
which cores are magnetized, thereby enabling the computer to "read"
the contents of its memory while processing data at electronic speeds.
Courtesy of General Electric Co.

The sales of semiconductor memories accounted for approximately $700
million in 1976. This total was estimated to be $2.2 billion in 1980.[3] Further-
more, while the cost of semiconductor memory (per bit) is about the same as for
core memory, the access time for semiconductor memory is about one-tenth that
of core memory. Therefore it is expected that semiconductor memory will account for 80% of the memory market in 1982.[2] An example of an integrated
circuit memory device is shown in Figure 6–58. These integrated circuit devices
are assembled in memory modules as shown in Figure 6–59. This memory unit
has a capacity of approximately 250,000 bits and possesses an access time of 40
nanoseconds. The IBM System 370 Model 145, announced in June, 1970 incorporates a main memory of integrated circuits. The access time of this main
storage is 540 nanoseconds.

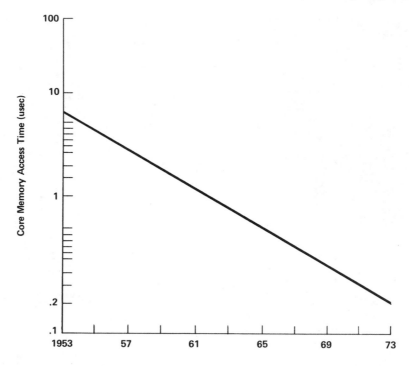

FIGURE 6–56   The memory access time for magnetic core storage for the period 1953–1973.

The question of reliability of semiconductor memories remains to be answered by experience. However, it is expected that semiconductor memories will grown in importance during the 1970s.

Within the next few years, new semiconductor devices, charge-coupled devices (CCDs), may become important components in memory units. CCD units can offer lower cost per bit than semiconductor MOS devices, with somewhat longer access times. (See Figure 6–50.) The CCD units fit between the core and the semiconductor unit and the disk storage unit.

The performance of magnetic cores, magnetic thin-films and integrated circuit memories for 1980 is shown in Figure 6–60.[12] The usefulness of core memories for large, moderate speed main storage memories is clear. The thin-film memories and lower-capacity semiconductor memories will together help to meet the needs for rapid-access memory components.

The main storage unit stores data which is accessible at any time and for which access is independent of the location of the data. A storage device for which access time is independent of the storage location of the data is a *random access* storage device. Random access is defined as follows:

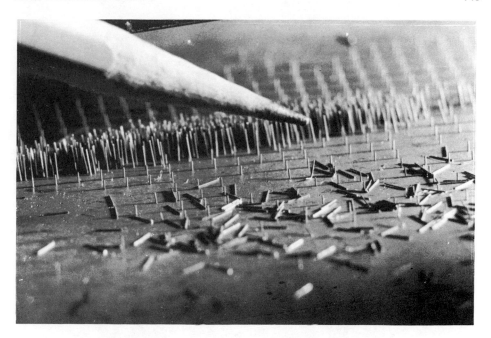

FIGURE 6-57 Thousands of metal "whiskers," the heart of a computer memory developed by NCR, are automatically put in place by a simple, ingenious method. More than 4,600 tiny magnetic coated rods have to be put into solenoid openings in the memory plane. A matrix with corresponding holes is placed over the solenoids. Rods are poured onto the matrix plate and the unit is drawn through a pulsating magnetic field. The rods stand on end and quickly "dance" into the openings. Excess rods are swept off. *Courtesy of National Cash Register Corp.*

RANDOM ACCESS   Obtaining data from, or placing data into, storage when the time required for such access is independent of the location of the data most recently obtained or placed into storage. Synonymous with *direct access*.

Main storage units require that random access is part of the operation of the storage system. This requirement is necessary because of the high speed of the CPU and the necessity of keeping the memory operating at the same rate as the CPU.

There are quite a few applications where the storage of information does not necessitate immediate and random access. Storage units that do not possess the quality of random access may often be used as auxiliary storage. Storage devices not providing random access to a storage location usually store information in a specified sequence and require that the computer proceed sequentially through all the storage locations between the present location of the reading device and the location desired. Storage devices operating in this manner are magnetic tape drives and magnetic data-cell drives.

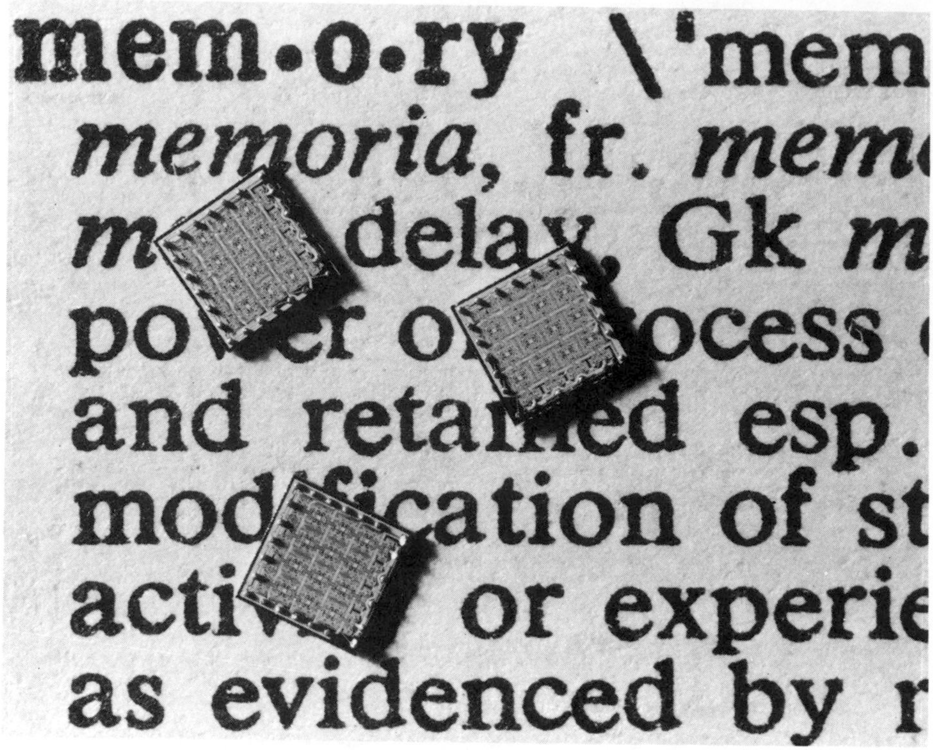

FIGURE 6–58   Memory storage circuits are diffused into the surface of a single silicon chip measuring less than an eighth of an inch square (shown above on a dictionary page*). Each chip—containing 664 individual components such as transistors, diodes, and resistors—provides 64 memory storage cells. These circuits are so minute that 53,000 components can fit into one square inch.

*By permission. From *Webster's Seventh New Collegiate Dictionary* © 1969 by G. & C. Merriam Co., Publishers of the Merriam-Webster Dictionaries.) *Courtesy of IBM Corp.*

Magnetic disk storage units provide computer systems with the ability to record and retrieve stored data sequentially *or* directly with random access. Disk units permit immediate access to specific locations of storage without the need to examine sequentially all recorded data. The magnetic disk is a thin metal disk coated on both sides with magnetic recording material. The disks are mounted on a vertical shaft separated from one another to provide the space necessary for the movement of the read/write arms. The shaft revolves at a high speed, spinning the disks. Information is stored as magnetized spots in concentric tracks on the surface of each disk. Some units have 500 tracks on each surface. The information is accessible for reading or writing by positioning the read/write head on the

FIGURE 6–59 Seventy-two monolithic memory modules, together with drive and sense modules, are packaged on a 7″ × 9″ multilayered pluggable card (left) with a 512-word × 18-bit capacity. Sixteen storage cards and four logic and terminating cards make up the basic storage unit (background) of 2,048 words × 72 bits. Two units form the complete one-quarter million bit memory. Access time for this memory is 40 nanoseconds. *Courtesy of IBM Corp.*

access arm between the spinning disks. Each time new information is stored, the old information is erased. The IBM 2311 disk drive shown in Figure 6–61 uses an interchangeable disk pack which can be seen through the plastic cover. Six disks are mounted as a disk pack which can be readily removed from the 2311 Disk Drive and stored in a library of disk packs in much the same manner as reels of magnetic tape may be stored. The packs are 14 inches in diameter and weigh less than ten pounds. Each of the ten recording surfaces contains 200 data recording tracks. The disks turn at 2,400 revolutions per minute. Up to 7.25 million characters of information can be stored in each disk pack.

The access time of disk storage units ranges from 10 to 100 milliseconds. The capacity of disk units ranges from 10^7 to 5×10^9 bits. The approximate storage cost is $.0005 per bit. Thus, disk storage units provide bulk storage at a low cost per bit and possess a relatively slow access time.

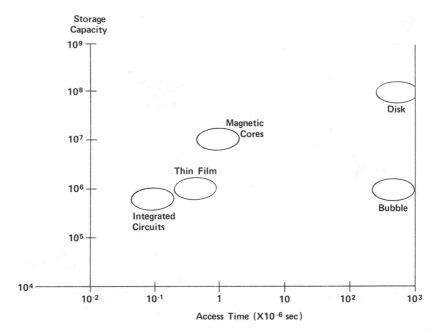

FIGURE 6–60 The memory storage capacity versus access time for several technologies.

For massive amounts of storage a number of disk units are combined, as in Figure 6–62. This unit consists of six drives and a control unit. Any of the drives can be on line at a time. The device uses disk packs that are built into the unit. All components, including reading heads, arms and disks are fixed in the unit, so they cannot be removed. Each disk unit provides up to 317 million bytes of storage.

Within the past few years, a new form of disk storage has been introduced using a *flexible*, or *floppy*, *disk*. Floppy disks, about the size of 45-rpm records, are made of flexible plastic. Floppy disk systems can store two million bits, with access times of about one-half second.[13] The IBM 374 data entry terminal is shown in Figure 6–63 with a floppy disk.

For bulk storage, data cartridges are often used. The IBM 3850 mass storage system combines the random-access characteristics of disk devices with the economy of tape drives. Housed in honeycomb storage compartments, these hand-size cartridges hold up to 770 inches of three-inch-wide magnetic tape in cylinder form. The IBM 3850 is shown in Figure 6–64.

Magnetic tape is a very commonly used auxiliary storage medium. In addition, magnetic tape units are often used as input/output devices in order to avoid

FIGURE 6–61   The IBM 2311 disk storage drive, showing the disk pack and the access arms. *Courtesy of IBM Corp.*

FIGURE 6–62   The IBM 3350 multiple disk storage system. Instead of using the familiar removable disk (see Figure 6–25), all components, including heads, arms and disks are built into the 3350. Through this approach the 3350 achieves enhanced data density and greater capacity. The 3350 provides up to 317 million bytes of storage per drive. Six drive units are shown in the illustration; they provide up to 1.8 billion bytes. The average access time is 25 milliseconds. *Courtesy IBM Corporation.*

coupling slower I/O units to the central processor and main storage. The input is placed on the tape in an offline operation and all the input is then read into the main storage from the tape. Similarly, the output results will often be stored on tape until a later time when the results are printed out from the stored tape. A library of magnetic tapes is shown in Figure 6–65.

FIGURE 6–63   The IBM
3741 data entry terminal,
with floppy disk storage.
The disk is enclosed in a
semi-stiff plastic jacket, but
it is free to rotate within the
jacket for reading and recording by a head. The disk
is a round piece of oxide-
coated Mylar. The disk ro-
tates at 360 revolutions per
minute; it is capable of storing several million bits. The
access time is about one second. The data content of
nearly 1,900 punched cards
can be recorded on a single
disk. *Courtesy IBM Corporation.*

FIGURE 6–64   The IBM 3850 mass storage system uses data cartridges in honeycomb
compartments. An access device moves the cartridges to a recording
mechanism. The capacity of this device is about 10^{13} bits; it has an access
time of 15 seconds. *Courtesy IBM Corporation.*

Magnetic tape is much faster than punched tape or cards, with read speeds
from five to 100 times greater than cards. Along with its high speed—often in the
order of 10,000 characters per second—magnetic tape has a much greater capacity than the other high-speed I/O devices. This can be a significant edge when
large quantities of data require reloading the I/O device during a run. For example, a 2,400-foot reel of tape having a low packing density of 200 bits per inch will
hold about as much data as 20,000 cards. The operator of a 1,000-card-capacity
card hopper would have to load the cards 20 times to equal the capacity of one
such roll of magnetic tape. The difference would also be reflected in computer
productivity. At higher densities, magnetic-tape capacity grows to that of 400,000
cards.

FIGURE 6–65   Data recorded on magnetic tape may be stored in a tape library. *Courtesy of National Cash Register Co.*

In tape recording, the magnetic material usually consists of tiny needle-like particles of gamma ferric oxide with an average length of about 24 microinches and diameter of 4 microinches. These are mixed with a plastic binder and coated onto a thin strip of "base" material which is usually polyethylene terephthalate, more commonly known as "polyester" or "Mylar." The base material for computer applications is 1 milliinch thick and 1/2 inch wide. Most tape coatings are 0.5 to 0.6 milliinches thick with oxide density of about 1/3 of the total. This material is magnetized by a recording head as the tape passes by the head. Recovering the information from a tape is essentially the reverse of the recording process; the recorded magnetization produces a current in the head winding. Magnetic tape on reels has practically unlimited capacity, but access time is slow because it may be necessary to move much tape or even to change reels to find desired information. Therefore, it is difficult to give an average access time for a tape. We can estimate the average access time by letting the access time equal the ratio of one-half the length of the tape to the tape speed. This estimate assumes that on the average one would have to search through half the length of the tape to locate a specific stored item. On this basis, for a 2400 foot tape operating at 112.5 inches/second, the average access time is approximately 120 seconds. Obviously one does not wish to use tape storage for direct or random access because of this long access time. Magnetic tape is used primarily for storing sequential data—that is, information in a pre-arranged series of stored items. As a sequential input device, a tape drive provides an input speed in the range of 30,000 to

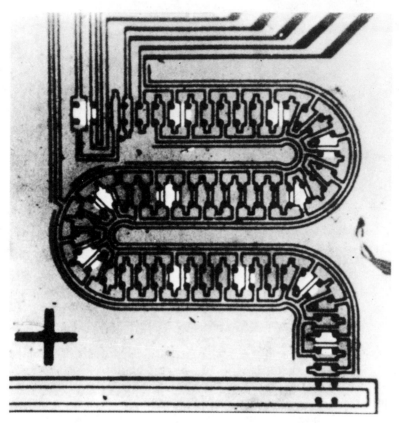

FIGURE 6–66   Tiny computers of the future may accomplish counting, switching, memory and logic functions all within one solid magnetic material, employing new technology now in exploratory development. This actual circuit, on the surface of a sheet of thulium orthoferrite, can move magnetic bubbles, four thousandths of an inch in diameter, through a shift register. *Courtesy of Bell Telephone Laboratories.*

300,000 characters/second. A magnetic tape unit is shown above in Figure 6–25. This unit records 1600 characters/inch of tape.

Recently, tape recorders which use cassettes rather than reels have been developed. Digital cassette tape recorders store the data on a magnetic tape held within an interchangeable cassette. Because they are smaller and more limited in capacity than reel-to-reel tapes, cartridges and cassettes are especially useful where small capacity is sufficient and computer time is not a factor, as is the case with small computers. As I/O devices, they are ideal for low-speed data collection and auxiliary storage. Most cartridges and cassettes are narrower than standard computer tapes and therefore have fewer tracks. Digital cassette recorders are

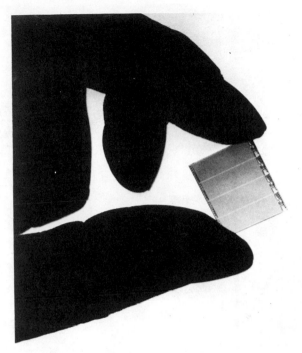

FIGURE 6–67   The INTEL 7110 magnetic bubble memory has a storage capacity of one
                million bits, with an average access time of 41 milliseconds. *Courtesy of
                Intel Corporation.*

potential replacements for punched paper tape since the cost is about the same
and the cassette tape is three to five times as fast. Typical digital cassette
recorders operate at a tape speed of 20 inches/second, record 800 bits/inch, and
have an access time of 20 seconds.

There is a continuing need for improved and less expensive memories. Experimental storage devices are being developed. One such storage device, shown
in Figure 6–66, utilizes magnetic "bubbles" that move. The bubbles are locally-
magnetized areas that can move about in thin plates of orthoferrite, a magnetic
material. In present computer and communication technology, connections between electronic components are a major factor in costs. In the new technology,
the bubbles can be created, erased, and moved anywhere in thin sheets without interconnection. They may interact with one another in a controlled fashion, and
their presence or absence can be detected. Therefore, devices employing the new
technology could be made to perform a variety of functions, such as logic,
memory, switching or counting, all within one solid magnetic material.[10, 13]

The energy needed to manipulate the bubbles either can be applied by
current-carrying conductors or it can be picked up from a surrounding magnetic

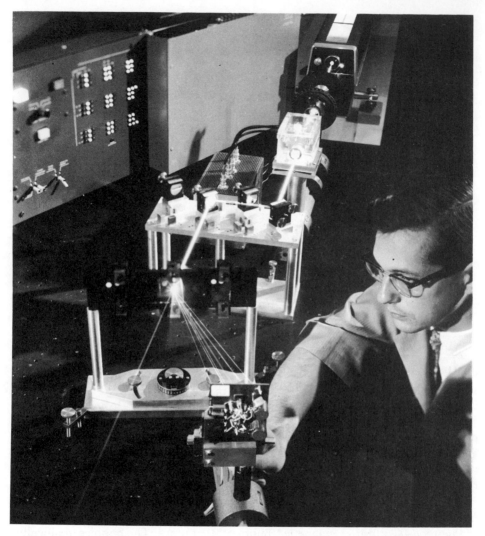

FIGURE 6–68   The feasibility model of an experimental optical memory system, which
transmits blocks of computer-interpretable information in ten-
millionths of a second, is inspected by an engineer. In the experimental
system, information recorded on a holographic plate is produced one
thousand times faster than it is by conventional auxiliary storage
devices. The intensive light of the laser is controlled and directed to a
holographic plate where the beam is split. Informational light beams
emerging from the hologram are directed to a light-sensitive detector array. The optical information is converted to electronic signals and used
by the computer's central processor. More than 100 million bits of information could be placed on a nine square inch holographic plate.
Courtesy of IBM Corp.

field by microscopic "ferromagnetic antennae" in printed patterns distributed over the surface of the material. As the bubbles are moved into precisely defined positions, their presence or absence at different positions can represent binary numbers.

Bubbles of a size corresponding to only a few wavelengths of light can be manipulated. These lead to memory densities of about 1 million bits per square inch. The energy required to move, or switch, such a bubble is minute—a fraction of that needed to switch a transistor. Data rates of 3,000,000 bits per second have been demonstrated with this technology. A commercially available bubble memory device is shown in Figure 6–67.

As digital computers continue to grow in complexity and size, memory storage will have to be increased significantly at no sacrifice in speed. This means the information will have to be packed much more densely. With a laser beam and the new science of holography, an optical memory is being explored whose ultimate storage capacity is predicted to be in excess of 10 billion bits of data, and whose random access time may ultimately be as short as 1 microsecond. Holograms make use of a high-energy laser beam to store or display three-dimensional images. Holograms overcome the shortcomings of optical techniques that employ conventional photography. With the latter, lenses must be used, and microphotographs are vulnerable to dust and scratches, which can cause loss of data. Holograms do not require lenses; they are self-focusing. The image can be easily read by a photodetector, and information is stored redundantly. Even if part of a hologram is destroyed or obscured, the remainder can still contain a complete record of the data stored in it.[15]

The holographic storage array is made on a special recording medium somewhat similar to conventional photographic film. This process starts with the construction of a data mask that represents the contents of a page. Each mask is basically an array of pinholes, blocked where we want zeros and transparent where ones are needed. Each data mask is recorded holographically, one at a time, on the recording medium. Information is retrieved from the memory by projecting the data recorded on the hologram onto a light-sensitive detector. The detector converts the optical information into electronic signals that the computer can process. An experimental laser-holographic memory system is shown in Figure 6–68.

The characteristics of storage units are shown in Table 6–5.[33] The primary characteristic of the main storage devices is the access time of a microsecond or less. The auxiliary storage units possess access times of one-tenth of a second or greater, but provide low-cost bulk storage. The ability of the computer to process information is closely related to the ability to access masses of stored information. The main storage devices provide the computer with a memory which is rapidly accessible and the auxiliary storage devices provide a memory for the masses of data that can be used less often and for which more time can be allowed for obtaining any data item.

TABLE 6-5
Comparison of Storage Unit Characteristics

	Average Capacity (Bits)	Average Access Time (seconds)	Average Cost (cents/bit)
A. Main Storage Units			
1. Magnetic Cores	10^7	1.0×10^{-6}	0.5
2. Thin Magnetic Films	10^6	$.8 \times 10^{-6}$	2
3. Semiconductor Integrated Circuits	10^5	$.1 \times 10^{-6}$	0.5
B. Auxiliary Storage Units			
1. Magnetic Disk Units	10^9	.10	.05
2. Magnetic Data Cartridges	10^{13}	10	10^{-4}
3. Magnetic Tape Drives	10^{10}	100	.01
4. Floppy Disk Units	2×10^6	.50	.01
C. Advanced Storage Devices			
1. Magnetic Bubbles	10^7	1×10^{-3}	.01
2. Holographic Storage (Laser)	10^{10}	1×10^{-6}	10^{-4}

The memory capacities of computer storage devices continue to increase. The capacities of several devices are compared in Table 6-6. These devices still have a long way to go before they approach the human brain in memory capacity.

TABLE 6-6
Memory Capacities

Memory device	Storage capacity (millions of characters)
Human brain	125,000,000
National Archives	12,500,000
IBM 3850 magnetic cartridge	250,000
Encyclopaedia Britannica	12,500
Optical disc memory	12,500
Magnetic (hard) disc	313
Floppy disc	2.5
Book	1.3

Data: RCA Corp. Advanced Technology Laboratories

6.5   MULTIPROGRAMMING AND MULTIPROCESSING

The computer's central processing unit (CPU) can operate many times faster than the input-output devices. Advanced computer systems are arranged so that the CPU can switch from a program which is receiving input or yielding output to performing calculations for another program until it too requires an input or output operation. The sharing of the CPU by several programs is called *multiprogramming*.

> MULTIPROGRAMMING: Procedures for handling several programs by overlapping or interleaving their execution by the central processing unit.

Multiprogramming permits more than one program to be stored in main memory; these programs can be executed as the CPU becomes available. While one program is in the input-output mode, another program can use the CPU. The advantage of this approach is the increase of overall system efficiency, since the system will execute a larger number of programs in a given period when multiprogramming is used.

In some advanced systems a greatly increased number of programs can share main memory through *virtual memory*. Parts of a program in main memory that are not in use and kept in auxiliary storage can be recalled when they are needed. The program is divided into sections called *pages*. Unneeded pages are held in readily-accessible auxiliary storage. Because the pages are so readily available, we think of them as being virtually part of the program. This process by which the pages are held at the ready is called *virtual storage*.

The interconnection of two or more central processing units is called *multiprocessing*.

> MULTIPROCESSING: An arrangement whereby several central processing units share one memory.

Multiprocessing is a powerful tool. Through it the several central processing units that share a single memory can communicate with each other without the need for manual input. This means that the sharing CPUs can provide backup capability for each other. Multiprocessing systems are useful for executing programs that require extensive calculations, because they have great computing power.[14]

CHAPTER 6 PROBLEMS

P6-1.   Define the following items:
(1) hardware system
(2) solid-state component
(3) transistor
(4) microsecond
(5) Input/Output System

P6—2.   Sketch the interconnection of the four major units of a computer system and the information and control paths.

P6—3.   If a computer was the size of a room, 15 feet by 20 feet, in 1955, what size would you expect for an equivalent computer in 1985?

P6—4.   If a given computer worked an average of 10 hours without failure in 1955, what would you expect for an average time to failure for an equivalent computer in 1985?

P6—5.   Using Figure 6—20, determine the difference in the punched card code for the number 3, the letter C, and the special character — the period.

P6—6.   What is the ratio of speed of printing magnetic characters to the rate of punching punched cards in characters per second?

P6—7.   What are the uses of graphic plotters and visual displays? When would you use a graphic plotter and when a visual display if both devices were available in the computer center?

P6—8.   When would you use a computer output microfilmer in preference to line printer, if both were available in the computer center?

P6—9.   List several media that can be used with an input and output unit of a computer.

P6—10.   Define the following items:
          (1) storage location
          (2) access time
          (3) random access

P6—11.   What characterizes the difference between a main storage unit and an auxiliary storage unit?

P6—12.   What is the ratio of the capacity, in bits, of the human brain to the capacity of bulk storage devices such as the disk file or strip file?

P6—13.   What is the ratio of the density-speed rating of the human brain to the density-speed rating of (1) the magnetic disk file (2) the magnetic core memory?

P6—14.   What are the two primary characteristics of a main storage unit?

P6—15.   How many bits can one magnetic core store?

P6—16.   List one advantage and one disadvantage of a semiconductor main storage unit.

P6—17.   What is the speed ratio of a magnetic tape input unit to a punched card input unit for a tape unit which provides 100,000 characters/second?

P6—18.   Determine the ratio of the cost/bit of storage for a magnetic core memory to a magnetic tape drive. Why not replace a computer core storage unit with a tape drive?

P6—19.   Interactive display terminals are widely used. One versatile terminal is shown in Figure P6—19. Visit a local airlines office or computer center and observe the use of such terminals. You can also find such terminals in local computer hobby stores.

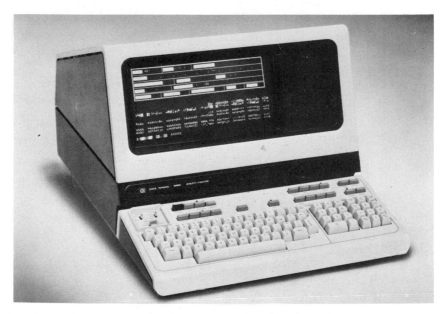

FIGURE P6–19   The HP 2640B interactive display terminal. This input/output device
uses a cathode ray tube to display the characters as shown. The terminal is equipped with 1,024 characters of display memory. It can
store from eight to fifty lines of information, depending on line length.
Courtesy Hewlett-Packard Corporation.

FIGURE P6–21   The MSI/88e
portable terminal, with program
loadable memory, is useful for
ordering, calculation and reporting
of sales, accounting and other kinds
of remote entry data. A program
can be stored in a module which
can be plugged into the terminal.
The device can store up to 48,000
characters of program and data.
Courtesy of MSI Corporation.

P6–20. Voice recognition systems are available for use with computers. Contact either Threshold Technology, Inc. of Delran, New Jersey, or Heuristics, Inc. of Sunnyvale, California for information and cost of a voice recognition system.

P6–21. Portable terminals are used in warehouses and by professionals traveling frequently such as salespeople. A portable terminal is shown in Figure P6–21. Contact a local warehouse or sales firm that uses portable terminals and visit to see such equipment in use.

CHAPTER 6 REFERENCES

1. N. Mokhoff, "Four Targets of VLSI," *IEEE Spectrum*, June 1980, pp. 34–36.
2. "INTEL: The Microprocessor Champ Gambles On Another Leap Forward," *Business Week*, April 14, 1980, pp. 82–93.
3. E. R. Hnatek, "Semiconductor Memory Update," *Computer Design*, February 1980, pp. 147–159.
4. W. D. Frazer, "Potential Technology Implications for Computers and Telecommunications in the 1980s," *IBM System Journal*, Vol. 18, No. 2, 1979, pp. 333–347.
5. F. G. Withington, "Trends in MIS Technology," *Datamation*, Feb. 1970, pp. 108–119.
6. B. LeBoss, "Speech I/O Is Making Itself Heard," *Electronics*, May 22, 1980, pp. 95–105.
7. J. R. Welch, "Automatic Speech Recognition," *Computer*, May 1980, pp. 65–73.
8. G. Kaplan, "Words Into Action," *IEEE Spectrum*, June 1980, pp. 22–26.
9. R. M. White, "Disk-Storage Technology," *Scientific American*, August 1980, pp. 138–148.
10. A. H. Eschenfelder, *Magnetic Bubble Technology*, Springer-Verlag Publishing Company, New York, 1979.
11. H. Shershow, "The Flexible Future of Rigid Disk Drives," *Digital Design*, May 1980, pp. 52–68.
12. E. R. Hnatek, "Semiconductor Update," *Computer Design*, December 1979, pp. 67–77.
13. G. Sollman, "The Coexistence of Floppies and Bubbles," *Mini-Micro Systems*, November 1979, pp. 109–114.
14. M. Satyanarayanan, "Commercial Multiprocessing Systems," *IEEE Computer*, May 1980, pp. 75–95.
15. G. C. Kenney, "An Optical Disk Replaces 25 Mag Tapes," *IEEE Spectrum, February 1979, pp. 33–38.*
16. A. L. Robinson, "Communicating with Computers by Voice," *Science*, February 23, 1979, pp. 734–736.

17. E. K. Yasake, "Voice Recognition Comes of Age," *Datamation*, August, 1976, pp. 65–68.
18. J. H. Gilder, "Novel Ways of Entering Data," *Electronic Design*, May 10, 1975, pp. 46–52.
19. D. W. Cardwell, "Interactive Telecommunications Access by Computer," *Proceedings of the Fall Joint Computer Conference, 1968*, Thompson Book Co., Washington, D.C., 1968, pp. 243–253.
20. J. R. Brown, "Magnetic Core Memories," *Modern Data*, August, 1975, pp. 51–54.
21. "CCD Memory," *Datamation*, February, 1975, pp. 85–88.
22. P. Franson, "Floppy Disks Spin Into Systems," *Electronics*, January 23, 1975, pp. 59–60.
23. J. H. Gilder, "Mass Memories Raising Speed, Dropping Cost and Storing Billions of Bytes," *Electronic Design*, October 25, 1975, pp. 46–50.
24. A. H. Bobeck and H. E. D. Scovil, "Magnetic Bubbles," *Scientific American*, Vol. 224, No. 6, June, 1971, pp. 78–90.
25. "Samples of 92-K Bubble Memories Coming from TI," *Electronics*, September 30, 1976, pp. 29–30.
26. J. E. Juliessen, "Magnetic Bubble Systems Approach Practical Use," *Computer Design*, October, 1976, pp. 81–91.
27. R. S. Eward, "Optical Memories," *Optical Spectra*, August, 1975, pp. 25–28.
28. J. E. Geusic, "Magnetic Bubble Devices: Moving from Lab to Factory," *Bell Laboratories Record*, November, 1976, pp. 263–267.
29. H. S. Stone, Editor, *Introduction to Computer Architecture*, Science Research Associates, Chicago, 1975.
30. M. Well, *Computer Systems Hardware*, Cambridge University Press, New York, 1976.
31. A. M. Ard-Ella and A. C. Meltzer, *Principles of Digital Computer Design*, Prentice-Hall, Inc., Englewood Cliffs, New Jersey, 1976.
32. M. E. Sloan, Computer Hardware and Organization, *Science Research Associates*, Chicago, Illinois, 1976.
33. L. Altman, Memories, *Electronics*, January 20, 1977, pp. 81–96.

7

BUSINESS DATA PROCESSING AND MANAGEMENT INFORMATION SYSTEMS

7.1 BUSINESS DATA PROCESSING

The storage, processing, and reporting of data for business purposes, such as the routine financial transactions of a business, is called *business data processing*. As business operations become more complex, businessmen have found it advantageous to utilize the computer to process much of the data generated in the course of business operations. Business data processing is focused on the processing of *business* data, as they can be distinguished from other forms of data. Thus, business data processing is distinguished from data manipulation for purposes of government, education, or industrial process control. Of course, the line of demarcation is often a hazy one. However, we shall focus on the use of computers in business data processing for financial, accounting, banking and management purposes and thus restrictively define business data processing within these limits.

Business data are processed for output information. The manager or owner of a business operation needs information in order to (1) establish, evaluate and adjust business goals; (2) develop plans and standards and intitiate action, and (3) measure actual performance and take appropriate action when required.[1] These three steps are part of the management process of any business enterprise.

The factors in business management which can be assisted by the utilization of a computer are fourfold.[2] First, there is the physical factor of large masses of data. A business generates data on raw material purchases, assets, accounts payable, inventories, shipping, billings, receipts and taxes, to name a few generators of masses of data.

Second, there is the element of time in the successful operation of a business. Many firms do not practice price competition as often as cost competition. It is extremely important to reduce cost by decreasing time required to produce an item and process the associated records. Business data processing can significantly affect the cost structure of a company where volume production is the rule by reducing the time taken for necessary records and reports.

Third, there is the use of computers to reduce the clerical work force. Clerical workers have increased in number during the past forty years in order to process and analyze data generated in business operations. The introduction of computers enables a business to maintain the cost of clerical operations within tolerable limits.

Finally, the error factor is of great importance. Many clerical recording processes are tedious, and people performing them are prone to errors. Thus, the automation of such processes should lead to reduced errors in the operation of business.

The importance of rapid, low-cost business data processing with a low incidence of error is clear. Management of a business requires reliable and accurate information presented in an understandable form at the time it is needed. This is the natural objective of computer data processing in business.

The processing of business data may include several of the following nine steps:[1]

1. Originating and recording of data in form for computer processing
2. Placing data into appropriate classifications, such as sales data or tax data
3. Rearranging the data after it is classified into a predetermined sequence for processing; often called *sorting*
4. Arithmetic manipulation of the data, called *calculating*
5. Summarizing the data so that resulting reports will be concise and effective
6. Storing of data into appropriate storage locations for future reference
7. Retrieving the data from storage
8. Reproducing or duplicating the data in a report or document
9. Communicating data to a user or to another location in the form of a report or other form

As an example, let us consider the steps required to process sales data from a large department store. The data originates at the point of sale in the form of a sales ticket, which is then coded for machine input. Then the sales ticket, along with other sales tickets, is classified by product sold, location of sale, customer credit or cash payment as well as other data. The data may then be sorted by invoice number or by customer credit card number, for example. The calculation operation then calculates the charge to the customers' credit accounts as well as the total sale of the department store for that day. In this case, the summary step might include the summarizing of all the purchases of the customer. Then the information might be stored to be retrieved later, say at the end of the month, to produce a bill for each customer with a credit account. The process is illustrated graphically in Figure 7–1.

A computer may be used effectively with a business of any moderate size or larger. A computer is most efficiently used in business data processing operations with one or more of the following characteristics:

1. A large volume of input data is generated by business transactions on a regular basis.
2. The data processing operation is repeated many times, making it worthwhile to invest in developing and debugging the computer program.
3. The need for timely information provides the requirement of rapid processing needs.
4. There is a need for reliable and accurate output reports.

Perhaps the characteristic that most distinguishes the processing of scientific data is that business processing operations more normally involve large masses of input data and large amounts of output information. Business data processing is most efficient when a computer is used to perform repetitious tasks with large masses of data at rapid speeds.

The Wall Street Journal recently undertook a research survey project among its subscribers in order to provide information on the present availability and use of computers for business data processing. Two-thirds of the respondents to the survey indicated that their companies now have one or more computers. Over 90% of the large companies possessed a computer while the proportion declined 27% for those companies employing fewer than 100 persons. The leading applications for the computer in the firms responding were accounting (76%); sales analysis (45%); and inventory control (43%). The growth in demand for mid-sized business computers is given in Table 7–1.

Business and industry in the U.S. tripled expenditure for computers and associated operations during the period 1965–1970. Business in the U.S. spent approximately 25.5 billion dollars in 1970 to utilize computers for all purposes.[4] This figure increased to 53 billion dollars in 1980. Of $53 billion expended in 1980, $31 billion was for operating costs, $16 billion for equipment, and $5 billion for services from outside the firms.

The use of computers by business firms is often necessary simply to keep even with the growing masses of data processed by the company. It has been estimated that the absolute number of business transactions and recordings is increasing at a rate between 8% to 15% per year.[5] The mass of data transmitted

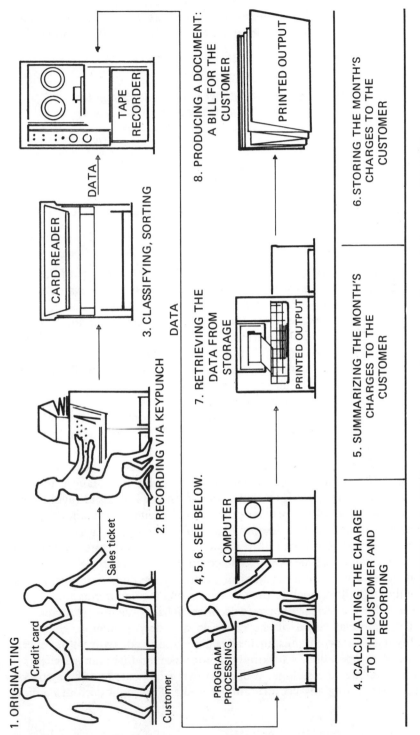

FIGURE 7–1 The business data processing sequence for producing a month's bill for a credit account customer of a department store.

over communications lines has been growing at a rate of 25% a year or more. The problems of the volumes of business data are only partially overcome by large computer systems.

TABLE 7-1
Projected Sales of Mid-Sized Business Computers in the United States Commencing in 1975.

Year	1975	1977	1980	1983
Cumulative Shipments (1000s of units)	1	3	20	50

NOTE: This table applies to general purpose computers that sell in the range of $100,000 to $1 million. The year 1975 serves as the first year in this projection.

Computers are often required not only to handle the masses of data without error, but also to increase the productivity of a business. As an example, consider the airlines which have turned in the best productivity performance during the past 20 years—a classic case of economies of scale. With larger and faster planes, such carriers have been able to book a five-fold gain in operating revenues, to nearly $20 billion, while holding their labor force to less than double its 1960 size. Relatively little of that manpower boost represents additional flight crews. The real managerial problems, such as filling the seats in huge jets, have been on the ground. The only way airlines can approach full capacity is to perform prodigies of scheduling, which requires multimillion–dollar computer installations. With the aid of computers, airlines were able to increase their annual productivity at an average annual rate of 9.5% during the period 1960–1975.

The basic organization of a business is often altered by the introduction of a computer. The changes take time to occur, as did the changes in industrial technology. But the inventions that brought on the industrial revolution about 200 years ago generally improved power or efficiency levels about 10 times in their initial applications. For example, an early steam pump was worth about 10 oxen; an automobile is about 10 times as fast as a horse; and an airplane is 10 times faster than an express train. The computer is a bigger step; it is nearly one million times faster than a mechanical calculator or the human brain. It costs a bank only 1/300th as much to post a check using a computer as to have a ledger clerk do it. Such efficiency comes at a price. Part of the cost is social: It comes from the industrialization of the office in a pattern similar to that found on assembly lines. In large banks, insurance companies and credit billing operations, the paperwork operation is strikingly factory-like, and its managers tend to talk in production-line terminology. Work tasks are fragmented until they become little more than keying an account number and a dollar amount onto a card.

Quite often knowledge of the total job is the prerogative of the computer analysts and programmers. So the computer fundamentally alters management structure in the administrative segments of business. It imposes a new level of functional management in the office that shatters traditional career paths. As John Diebold has recently commented:

> Automation's greatest consequence to business will be the enormous social change resulting from it. The entire role of business, its relation to human wants and its way of satisfying those wants depends upon society. Fundamental changes in society fundamentally change the role of business. Buying patterns, consumption habits, and other social attitudes will be radically affected by the technology, and they, in turn, will produce decisive changes in business operations and methods.

It is the effect of computers on the social and economic life of the business process and nation that results in profound and unforseeable consequences for the next decade.

Often, business management conceives of computer data processing in restrictive mechanistic terms. Management places too much emphasis upon visualizing the computer as merely a superior accounting machine for handling functions previously performed manually. As important as such contributions are, they fall short of realizing the considerable potential inherent in present computer technology for management decision-making in a rapidly and radically changing business and social environment. Many economists believe that technology fosters not only changes in the manner in which business is conducted, but that in so doing, it also creates new business opportunities in turn.

It is necessary to differentiate between the business system itself and the data processing operation of the business. Most businesses are processing matter and energy in order to produce a saleable product. The business brings in raw materials and reorders them into a product. A business data processing system, by contrast, translates data both from the environment and from within the firm for use by the firm. From 2000 B. C., when the Code of Hammurabi was drawn up, to the present, businessmen have been interested in obtaining information on the status of their businesses. Regardless of whether it has been called accounting or a code, it still constitutes a business data processing system. Hammruabi said, "If the merchant has given to the agent corn, wool, oil or any sort of goods to traffic with, the agent shall write down the price and hand over to the merchant; the agent shall take a sealed memorandum of the price which he shall give to the merchant."

The business data processing systems of the period from the times of the Babylonian merchants to the last part of the 19th century were manual systems. The main tools of data processing were pencils, rulers, worksheets, journals and ledgers. Toward the last portion of the 19th century, typewriters and desk calculators became available for business data processing. Machines which could calculate and print the results were produced in 1890.[3] After World War I, accounting machines designed for billing, sales and other purposes began to appear. Punched card business equipment became readily available in the 1930's and dominated the field of business data processing until the late 1950's. The first digital computer acquired for business data processing was a UNIVAC-1, installed in 1954 at General Electric's Appliance Park in Louisville, Kentucky.

The most widely used computer language for business applications is COBOL, which stands for COmmon Business Oriented Language. COBOL was first introduced in 1959 to become a self-documenting business data processing language. The word "common" in the name indicates that the language should be as compatible as possible among a large variety of computers. The important benefit of COBOL is the quantity and quality of documentation produced by the use of the language. However, the documenting quality does cause a program to be wordy compared to other languages. Data names of up to 30 characters permit the wide use of descriptive names for variables. The organization of the COBOL program is logical, but is somewhat more difficult to learn than FORTRAN. Consider the following two sentences from a hypothetical COBOL program written for the purpose of calculating a salary check:

MULTIPLY RATE-OF-PAY BY HOURS-WORKED GIVING GROSS-PAY ROUNDED. COMPUTE EXCESS = (HOURS-WORKED − 40)*1.5

In the first sentence the result of the multiplication of data found at storage locations identified with RATE-OF-PAY and HOURS-WORKED will be stored at a location identified as GROSS-PAY. The result will be rounded before being stored. If the COMPUTE verb had been used, the statement would read COMPUTE GROSS-PAY = RATE-OF-PAY * HOURS-WORKED. In other words, the COMPUTE verb is an alternative which is most suitable for formula-type computations. It is easy to notice the advantageous documentation feature of a data processing operation using the COBOL language. COBOL is a business-oriented, procedure-oriented language which is widely taught in college courses on business data processing.

The digital computer is a useful tool for both large and small business organizations. The current costs of business data processing run from 0.5% to 3% of the gross revenue, depending upon the industry. Computer programs and data processing techniques created by companies with large resources can be utilized by small business. Several computer firms have introduced small computers which rent for a relatively low monthly amount and are suitable for use in small businesses. These small computers can be utilized for accounting functions, including the processing of standard ledger cards. About 25 percent of U.S. small businesses now own small or medium sized computers. Their primary use is for inventory control and business accounting.

Computers are increasingly being used in the business offices for processing messages. Computer systems constructed for the purpose of increasing the ease, reliability and number of messages processed per period of time are called *word processors*. These systems permit letters, memos and reports to be stored, edited and transmitted effectively. Sales of office-automation equipment in 1980 amounted to approximately $6 billion.

Business data processing is particularly useful for retail sales companies such as department stores and grocery supermarkets. In one supermarket in Los Angeles, a computer terminal replaces the usual cash register at the check-out counter. The computer records accounts for the sales and inventory of the store. The computer retains the sale prices of each item in the store and helps the checkout person avoid incorrectly charging the customer. The large savings to the store is in the up-to-the-minute inventory information. The computer keeps continuous records of stock movement at the store, warehouse, and chain headquarters levels and when inventories fall to a predetermined point, it prints out a reorder automatically. This can eliminate the need for backroom storage, overstocking that causes price-cut sales, and extra delivery charges.

Many large companies and store chains now have point-of-sale (POS) terminals for checkout, inventory and credit and for recording of sales. Sears, Roebuck and Co. has installed about 10,000 electronic POS terminals. Each terminal, under computer control, reads merchandise tickets or labels and charge cards. Then it performs all register calculations. The same program can verify credit transactions and produce an immediate review of sales and merchandise. A department store POS terminal is shown in Figure 7–2. Supermarket POS systems use an automatic scanner to input the Universal Product Code (a bar code), which is printed on all merchandise labels.[17] Customers get a fully-itemized receipt; checker errors are almost eliminated. In some states consumers have demanded that hand-pricing be retained, although the POS system does away with need for it.

Computers are used extensively in financial businesses, particularly by the stock market firms. One world-wide data network offers brokers up-to-the-minute information on 9500 stocks, bonds and commodities traded on the world's major exchanges. On this system, the data displayed on the mass terminal includes current stock price, high and low, bid and asked, dividends, earnings and price-to-earnings ratios.

It has been proposed that the menu-sized (8″ × 12″) stock certificates be replaced by punch card certificates. The objective of the proposal is to reduce the large staffs of stock broker firms which simply handle the clerical functions associated with stock certificates. The punch card would include provisions for optical character recognition for high volume processors.

The manager of a business firm must have accurate, up-to-date information on his firm. One of the most effective modes of presenting business information is graphically. A computer can be used to perform the required calculations and produce the required charts and graphs by means of a plotter or a visual display

FIGURE 7–2 The NCR 280 retail point-of-sale terminal checks a purchaser's credit, completes charge sales, updates the store inventory file and keeps a printed record of each transaction. The salesperson uses a wand reader to input barcode information to the store's central computer. *Courtesy NCR Corp.*

device. The computer is able to process large amounts of business data and present the results to the manager. If the results are presented in a printed form, it is often difficult to assimilate them readily. A computer plotter or graphical device can present the results in a clear, concise graphic summary of computer results that ordinarily would fill dozens of pages of printout. With the aid of a recently available graphic plotter program, a businessman can obtain, within an hour of initiating the request, a complete set of graphs showing nine key financial ratios as illustrated in Figure 7–3.[8] Computer-generated charts are also used to show the performance of hundreds of common stocks each day. Graphical results of financial analysis, market research, sales forecasting and monitoring, project management, production inventory and control and personnel management are used extensively in business. Figures can be drawn at computer command and scaled automatically to correct proportions for showing numbers of employees of a firm in each selected business category, as illustrated in Figure 7–4. Computer graphics for business are an important management tool. They effectively extend the ability of the manager in a business enterprise.

Computers can improve the ability of management to guide and control a business enterprise significantly. However, the effective use of a digital computer for business data processing requires proper management of the data processing operation. Several recent reports of a study of business data processing departments indicated that computers were not being properly managed and they were not paying their way. A large proportion of companies use their computers only in routine clerical tasks—payroll, customer orders, inventory control, for instance—where the leverage upon profits is relatively small. Many critics contend

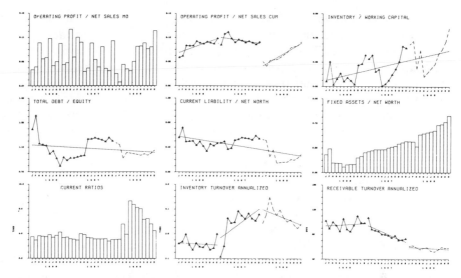

FIGURE 7–3 A single plotter chart for a hypothetical case shows nine key financial ratios covering a three-year period. Such charts are concise and easy to read. They indicate trends and relationships that would be difficult or impossible to obtain from conventional printout. *Photo courtesy of California Computer Products, Inc., and William O'Neil & Company, Beverly Hills, California.*

FIGURE 7–4 Figures can be drawn at computer command and scaled automatically to correct proportions for showing number of employees in each business category. Similar graphics can be produced for formalized business presentation. *Photo courtesy of California Computer Products, Inc.*

that the machines should be unleashed upon more sophisticated activities: for instance, controlling manufacturing operations, optimizing transportation flows, and most important of all, improving the quality of managerial decisions.[6, 7] In many cases the computers have not reduced the cost of operations, even in routine clerical work. What they have accomplished is mainly to enable companies to speed up operations and thereby to provide better service or handle larger volumes. With any phase of a business, if the function is operated effectively and efficiently, the financial return of the operation is attractive. Conversely, if a department (even business data processing) is poorly operated, there will be financial losses. Many firms are using faster, costlier, more sophisticated computers and larger and more costly computer staffs growing along with increasingly complex and ingenious applications. As the applications grow in number, the evidence of profitable results has not increased. One of the problems that has arisen in the past few years is the fact that the environment of business data processing has been changing, but management strategies have not. Management has tended to leave the direction of the corporate computer effort up to the technical staff persons who operate and program the computer. Computers are increasingly being used by small businesses. The small-business computer generally costs between $15,000 and $100,000. These computer systems are usually based on a minicomputer; they use disk files for auxiliary storage. Most recent applications use cathode-ray tube terminals for data entry rather than keypunch machines.[16] A modern small-business computer system is shown in Figure 7−5. Some complicated compromises for a business system computer involve:

1. Local minicomputer *vs.* terminal to a central system
2. Batch mode *vs.* interactive mode
3. Local data validation *vs.* central control
4. Specificity and compactness *vs.* generality and modularity of programs
5. Modification capacity of computer and its programs *vs.* reliability

The following poem, "The Information System," succinctly and clearly outlines the failure of business data processing systems that are not carefully designed to meet clear and specific objectives.

THE INFORMATION SYSTEM*

Marilyn Driscoll

Canto the First: Proposal

*Reprinted, by permission, from *The Arthur Young Journal*, Winter, 1968. Copyright © 1968 by Arthur Young & Company. Marilyn Driscoll is a member of the Communications Department of Arthur Young & Company, certified public accountants.

FIGURE 7–5   The Burroughs B 80, a relatively small general purpose computer system. This system is particularly suitable for business applications. The cost is about $100,000. The system is used by businesses that have branches, warehouses, or other remote facilities. It uses COBOL or RPG languages. The computer itself is shown in the center, with its three associated dual-drive disk storage devices in the rear. The B 80 can simultaneously drive two line printers, shown in the left background. Input data and inquiry can be received from the input and display terminal shown on the right. The remote-entry device on the left is able to store data on tape cartridges for later verification and entry. *Courtesy Burroughs Corporation.*

"An information system," said the president, J. B.,
"Is what this company sorely needs, or so it seems to me:
An automated, integrated system that embraces
All the proper people, in all the proper places,
So that the proper people, by communications linked,
Can manage by exception, instead of by instinct."

Canto the Second: Feasibility Study

They called in the consultants then, to see what they could see,
And to tell them how to optimize their use of EDP.
The consultants studied hard and long (their fee for this was sizable)
And concluded that an information system was quite feasible.
"Such a system," they reported, "will not only give you speed,
It will give you whole new kinds of information that you need."

Canto the Third: Installation

So an information system was developed and installed
And all the proper people were properly enthralled.
They thought of all the many kinds of facts it could transmit
And predicted higher profits would indeed result from it;
They agreed the information that it would communicate
Would never be too little, and would never be too late.

Canto the Last: Output

Yet when the system went on line, there was no great hurrah,
For it soon became apparent that it had one fatal flaw:
Though the system functioned perfectly, it couldn't quite atone
For the information it revealed—which was better left unknown.

There are four ways in which the profits of a firm can be improved by means
of business data processing:

Purpose	*Application*
1. To reduce general and administrative expenses	1. Administrative and accounting uses
2. To reduce cost of goods sold	2. Operations control systems
3. To increase revenues	3. Product innovation and improved customer service
4. To improve staff work and management decisions	4. Information systems and simulation models

Because of the rising cost of clerical operations and the history of the development of computers and business machines, business has concentrated on the first of these purposes. The next important application of the computer is toward the reduction of the cost of goods sold.

The authors of the report believe that it will require a team of top management committed to active leadership and working with the professional computer staffs in order for significant economic gains. As stated by Robert Townsend in his popular book, *Up the Organization*:[18]

COMPUTERS AND THEIR PRIESTS

First get it through your head that computers are big, expensive,
fast, dumb adding-machine-typewriters. Then realize that most
of the computer technicians that you're likely to meet or hire are
complicators, not simplifiers. They're trying to make it look
tough. Not easy. They're building a mystique, a priesthood,

their own mumbo-jumbo ritual to keep you from knowing what they—and you—are doing. Here are some rules of thumb:

1. At this state of the art, keep decisions on computers at the highest level. Make sure the climate is ruthlessly hard-nosed about the practicality of every system, every program, and every report. "What are you going to do with that report?" "What would you do if you didn't have it?" Otherwise your programmers will be writing their doctoral papers on your machines, and your managers will be drowning in ho-hum reports they've been conned into asking for and are ashamed to admit are of no value.

2. Make sure your present report system is reasonably clean and effective before you automate. Otherwise your new computer will just speed up the mess.

Management must not abdicate the responsibility of sound management of computer operations to the computer operating staff. Rather, the managers of the future must be continually involved in assessing and controlling the operation of the data processing function. It is clear that future managers must be well-educated about computers, data processing and computer science.

7.2 BUSINESS DATA PROCESSING FOR BANKS AND CREDIT

A primary application of computers in business data processing has been in banking and credit institutions. This section describes some of the characteristics of business data processing in these related fields. Bank operations are essentially data and information processing activities, including not only internal recording of customers' transactions—deposit accounting, trust, loan, and investment administration, corporate income and expense accounting—but also management information processing, cost controls, portfolio analysis, credit analysis, economic and financial research, plus business and financial information processing services for customers. The character of the devices for performing these operations has changed in the past 30 years from mechanical, manually-operated bookkeeping and proof machines, through semi-automatic bookkeeping machines, tabulating and calculating equipment activated by punched cards or punched paper tape, to electronic computers and data processing equipment and the third generation central processing units and peripherals for information processing, operations research, management science and telecommunications. These changes overlapped the twilight of mechanical technology.

The computer was introduced to banks at a time when the volume of paper flowing through the banks had vastly increased. The volume of checks cleared by the banking system increased 1100 percent during the past 30 years. At the Philadelphia National Bank, for example, over 900,000 items are processed each day by the bank's computer.

While in general banks are concerned with information processing, their specific purpose is to serve their customers. Therefore we can say that banking is a growth service industry, orienting goals and operations toward the customer, and harnessing information and technology to create new customer services. Most business transactions and information are financially oriented. Banking operations' role is that of a vital support element for financial service to the economy and the community.

Commercial banking's unique service function is to facilitate money payments and transfer of funds in the economy through checks—a product of its demand deposit accounts. Checks issued in settling 90 percent or more of money transactions aggregated nearly 35 billion items in 1980, growing at an annual rate of seven percent. The banking system has handled this volume by applying computer automation and adopting the MICR (magnetic ink character recognition) common machine-language program. Its acceptance by the public has also been necessary. The development of MICR-encoded checks made feasible the use of high-speed electronic computer oriented reader-sorters for processing MICR-qualified paper documents, and postponed the paper-handling crisis by increasing many times the check-handling capacity of the bank check collection system. Figure 7-6 shows a magnetically-encoded check being read by a magnetic character reader.

Magnetic character sensing, developed by computer manufacturers in cooperation with the American Bankers Association, permits data to be read directly by both man and machine. By agreement among computer manufacturers, check printers, and the ABA, such banking documents as checks, deposit slips, and debit and credit memos can be printed in magnetic ink. Printed information about the bank of origin, depositor's account number, and other essential data can be read directly by the machine. Only the specific amount of each check or deposit slip need be recorded on the document in magnetic print, and this need be done only once by an operator to process the document through its entire routine.

It is estimated that banks and financial institutions own approximately ten percent of all the computers in the United States and twenty percent of the computer capacity. Banks have gradually automated their operations since 1920. In 1933 the announcement of punch card equipment that could operate with alphabetical characters as well as numbers initiated the era of punched card auto mation. After World War II, mechanized procedures began to include the controlled processing of several stages of work in one operation. The tabulator, calculator, and the summary punch worked in unison as a team. A devoted group of bank systems people became attracted to the science of punch card systems and by 1950, 17 years from the introduction of the alphabetical tabulator, a con-

FIGURE 7–6   A magnetically-encoded check passing by the reading wheel of an IBM
1419 magnetic character reader. *Courtesy of IBM Corporation.*

siderable number of banks could take pride in extremely high-standard installations. The data on the checks and documents was converted to punch cards by
keypunch operators. In the 1960s the magnetic ink character-recognition scheme
was adopted by the banks. Bank checks are precoded, before being issued, with
account numbers in magnetic ink. When the checks are returned to the banks the
account numbers can be read directly by recognition devices that sense the
magnetic ink. The next step in the processing of financial documents is the
availability and use of an input device that is capable of reading a variety of
typewritten or handwritten documents. Optical document readers are available,
but these devices tend to be expensive as well as sensitive to the uniformity and
quality of the documents fed to them. The Bank of America has installed an optical page-scanning system at its San Francisco headquarters. It can read six standard type styles at the rate of 14,000 characters per second. The scanner can
finish in 10 seconds the work once performed by a keypunch operator in one day.
This page reader processes transaction documents from all 950 California branches of the Bank of America.

On-line data processing services have now been developed for connection to branch banks via telephone lines. Transaction data are entered through a teller console at a remote on-line branch. Such data are prefaced with teller, bank, and branch identification and then transmitted over telephone lines to the data center. The data are then processed according to the requirements of the sending institution, and the results are transmitted back via the telephone lines to member banks. An example of an on-line teller terminal in a bank is shown in Figure 7–7.

Many banks have developed a central file concept, which involves collecting in one place all the information about a customer's complete relationship with his bank by means of computers. The biggest problem seems to be economic feasibility. When such systems are successful, the dollars saved through elimination of duplicate records is an advantage. However, the primary advantages are in the intangible services such as customer service, market research, advertising direction, and account profitability.

A computer time-sharing service is being developed to enable small banks to connect with and to utilize large storages of financial management data. By operating a special electric typewriter connected by telephone line to a computer center, a small-town banker can get a print-out of information about conditions in distant bond and money markets, as well as economic forecasts for the nation or his region, and other data. If he is thinking of buying bonds, the computer system will provide quote prices and yields of issues. If he wants to sell, the computer can tell him the market value of his own bank's portfolio. The computer service also advises what investment shifts to make, depending on the bank's tax situation, assets, liabilities and flow of business. Should the bank experience an unexpected drop in deposits, the computer can recommend steps to be taken by the bank.

The banking system as it is now constituted involves the need to process and transport physically the continually increasing volume of paper checks over a vast

FIGURE 7–7   An NCR financial modular terminal system. A passbook-and-document printer is shown in the foreground. In the background is a journal-and-validation printer and a keyboard and display module. This banking terminal system interconnects to a central computer. *Courtesy NCR Corp.*

geographic area within time schedules and other limitations, frequently resulting in delays in collection and availability of fund or credit. The solution to these problems may be the development in the 1980s of a paperless payments or transfer of funds alternative or addition to checks as a payments mechanism. The real question to be explored and answered is: To what extent and for what transactions are checks or similar paper documents *essential*? By 1990, it is anticipated that each year there will be 3.4×10^{11} transactions of checks and credit documents. On the average, each transaction document consists of 50 characters or 400 bits. Thus, the data transferred in 1990 for checks and credit documents would be 10^{14} bits.

Paper money once represented an equivalent amount of gold stored in some banker's vault, but gradually that ceased to be the case. The currency note is no longer convertible into gold. Canada's dollar bill states that the Bank of Canada "will pay to the bearer on demand" one dollar. What it does not say is that it has nothing to pay with, except more dollar bills. Certainly, there is no gold for this purpose. Money—the paper which passes from pocket to pocket—has become merely a demonstration of a man's ability to pay. The same information could be passed with a check. The checking system, one of the great inventions of commerce, gradually gained acceptance by the "man in the street." Although the process of eliminating tangible currency is still incomplete, we are heading in that general direction: a person can now use a credit card, and we hear talk of a "checkless society." Money, in a sense, is information. In making a payment, two forms of information are required: a record of the transaction; and certification that the payer has the requisite wealth to make the transaction. Since money is in one sense information, then it is suitable for the use of computers and automatic systems. Credit cards issued by banks permit cashless transactions and afford credit to holders of the cards. VISA has about 75 million cardholders.[24] This card system relies totally on a computer system.

In the future, the computer may be used to record most of the financial transactions of American citizens. Several systems of eliminating checks and money from most financial transactions have been proposed. One, called the Electronic Fund Transfer System (EFTS), replaces paper whenever practical. This approach conceives of universal credit cards. Several banks are studying the required standardized formats and procedures for the paperless exchange of credits and debits and for the exchange of magnetic tapes for the major clearing magnetic tapes for the major clearing of banks' commercial checks.[9, 10]

In the case of a retail sale, a computer financial system involves communicating with a financial computer utility via a store's terminal to transfer the amount of the sale from the buyer's to the store's account. If the purchaser's balance will not cover the cost, the financial utility extends him credit (if his credit rating is good). At the present time, for regular payments of a fixed amount, such as mortgage and insurance premiums or utility bills up to a given amount, the bill can be sent directly to the person's bank for payment. Such arrangements are naturally well-adapted to computer applications. Other schemes involve using slightly augmented home telephones to instruct banks to transfer funds to another account.

A computer financial utility could develop a complete credit-deposit-loan history for each customer. This history could also enable the financial utility to be a more effective financial adviser to the customer, pointing out his (often unrecognized) spending habits, making analyses, and helping with better planning. Tax returns could also be turned out semiautomatically. Also, "money" could be transferred from account to account or the transaction could involve the extension of credit. The credit could be extended by the seller, based on an indication from the financial utility that the buyer was a good credit risk, or the credit could be extended by the financial utility.

Most credit companies presently utilize computers to record and monitor the transactions of the patrons of the credit company. A credit verification can be initiated by a terminal such as that shown in Figure 7−8. The primary benefits of a computer credit authorization system are: more rapid response to credit inquiries; the authorization of more credit through the availability of immediate credit in-

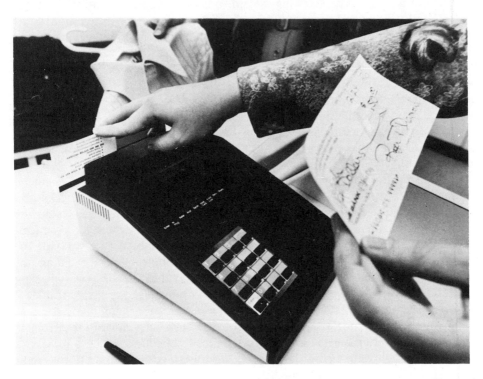

FIGURE 7−8   The IBM 3604 financial terminal is used in stores and other places of business for sales, payment, and credit verification. Using this equipment, a clerk can enter charges for a purchase and receive credit verification. *Courtesy IBM Corporation.*

formation; the reduction of financial losses due to credit card misuses. Under the system, an employee contacts the computer in New York by means of a special telephone. He first inserts dialing cards that signal the computer and identify the employee's establishment. Then, with pushbuttons, he transmits the credit card account number and amount of transaction. Upon receipt of this data, the computer checks its files to determine if the card represents a valid account with a satisfactory credit standing. Another check by the computer reveals any unusual spending pattern that may be developing (a major factor in fraud detection). The computer either gives credit approval immediately, or in doubtful cases, transfers the call to a credit authorizer, at the same time displaying the account record on a display screen, as in Figure 7–9.

Currently, Americans write over 100 million checks each day in addition to 17 million charge slips.[9, 10] Eventually, checks and perhaps most cash will drop

FIGURE 7–9   A credit authorizer at American Express headquarters here reviews a cardmember's account record shown on the screen of an IBM 2260 display station. He is responding to a telephone request for credit authorization from a business establishment which accepts American Express credit cards. Such requests are either approved through an automatic spoken response from the computer or—as shown here—are referred to credit department personnel for special handling. *Courtesy of IBM Corporation.*

from use and all purchases will be on universal credit cards. Each transaction will be recorded in a computer network that will maintain a continuous account of everyone's financial activities. If businesses of all sizes have simple terminals linked to a central computer utility over a communications network, a universal credit-card system is entirely practical. Various schemes could be used to make it difficult for someone to use another person's card. For example, a combination key number known only to the holder of the card on recognition by voice or thumbprint is possible.

The future paperless electronic clearing house banking will handle the settlement, payment, accounting and credit extension functions and will probably consist of a number of commercial banks and other financial institutions grouped into a series of local financial data and information centers and linked together into regional networks. The networks will have central-file storage of information pertinent to the financial profiles of customers, plus payments data and information. The regional centers, in turn, may be interconnected with other regional networks to form an integrated national system to serve all financial institutions and businesses desiring on-line, real-time money payment service. Extension of this computerized telecommunication banking service to the home would seem to be a reasonable, realistic addition. To remain viable, commercial banking must change functionally from a volume handler of paper to a processor of data and information in serving the needs of the community in the computer era.

One universal credit card currently used is a "money key" or card key which is inserted into a terminal. After insertion, the amount of purchase is keyed into the terminal, called an *automated teller*. Positive credits to the customer's account, such as payroll payments, benefits, dividends, and gifts are entered in a similar way. *Giro* payment systems, widely used in other parts of the world, work in an opposite manner to the American check payment system. The Austrians first introduced a Giro in 1883. Basically, it is a system of circular credit, in which money circulates from one holder's account to another. The word is derived from the Greek *guros*, meaning "ring." However, to be of any use, money must also pass into and out of the Giro system in cash, and to and from the other banking systems.

The various Electronic Funds Transfer Systems (EFTS) under development support such sources as automatically clearing checks and debiting and crediting individual accounts, as well as providing cash and banking transactions on demand 24 hours a day through automated tellers. A schematic diagram of an EFTS for banks is shown in Figure 7–10. About 12,000 automated-teller terminals were in operation in 1980. One such terminal is shown in Figure 7–11.

Several savings and loan associations have installed automatic tellers, to dispense cash, in supermarkets. At issue is a question: What constitutes branch banking? Is an automated teller capable of most banking operations the same thing as a branch of a bank?

The benefits from EFTS include convenience for the consumer and reduced cost to the banks. The disadvantages include loss of control over disbursement by the consumer and possible invasion of individual privacy. If every purchase a person makes is recorded, a form of surveillance can be readily instituted.

7.3   COMPUTER CRIME

If the United States moves to a checkless, document-free financial system, new means of protection against fraud must be developed. As legitimate paying through computer networks increases, the power and leverage of fraudulent users increases as well.[10] At present, a transfer of property, such as writing a check, requires a signature, which is a very distinct action by the owner showing his willingness to transfer some of his property. In contrast, the mere pushing of a button or the insertion of a key does not constitute an equally distinct intent of the owner to transfer property. It can easily be claimed that a wrong button was pushed or a wrong number inserted, whereas the signing of one's name on a

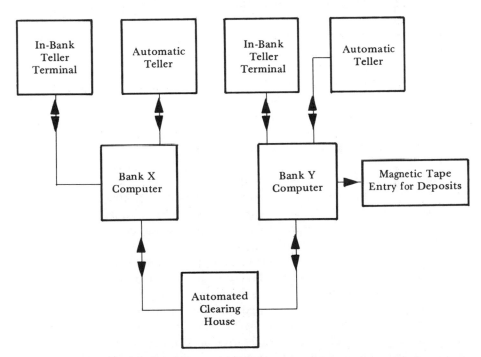

FIGURE 7-10   A schematic diagram of an Electronic Funds Transfer System for banks. A transaction can be carried out through a teller terminal or by means of an automated teller. The credit or debit information is switched from Bank X to Bank Y by means of an automated clearing house.

FIGURE 7–11 An automated teller terminal installed in a supermarket. These terminals can be used to make deposits, withdrawals, and transfers of funds between accounts. *Courtesy NCR Corporation.*

check is an action that cannot readily be renounced as having been committed accidentally.

Prevention of fraud is sought by such means as the user entering a secret code number or using an encoded card in order to gain access to an account. Perhaps a fingerprint or voice identification will serve the purpose of the signature in the future. Several security problems will have to be solved before a completely paperless financial system would be possible or acceptable to the users. Nevertheless, the banking and credit institutions will be significantly altered by the extension of computer automation in industry.

The wide use of computers in business and industry provides opportunites for embezzlement, fraud, and other criminal acts. Criminals can now manipulate the data that represent assets and liabilities in a computer. It is estimated that computer crime costs business $300 million annually.[19]

One individual, Jerry Schneider, applied his own knowledge of the Pacific Telephone Company's computer system to gain access to the Pacific computers from his own terminal. He then "ordered" delivery of telephone equipment after hours to specified remote spots. When the delivery van had left, Schneider had the equipment picked up. He was able to relieve Pacific Telephone Company of $800,000 worth of equipment.

Another individual, an accountant, embezzled a million dollars from various companies. He set up dummy vendor companies in a branch bank and then developed computer programs for his employer's computer. Through these arrangements he was able to claim inflated expenses and to pocket the money when it came in. A wire-transfer fraud used a bank computer to transfer $10.2 million from Los Angeles to Geneva, Switzerland. The criminal obtained the secret transfer codes from the wall (bulletin board) of the wire transfer room.[13]

The largest known computer crime, up to early 1977, was the Equity Funding Life Insurance Company scandal. Of the 97,000 policies that made up $3 billion of business in 1973, over 63,000 were bogus. Officials in Equity had falsified policies in company's computer records. Then they sold reinsurance worth about $2 billion. No auditors caught the embezzlers.

Mr. Parker points out that every large computer operations system is, in his words, a "Swiss cheese." Because computer operating systems are so full of holes, they must be watched and audited constantly. Thus computer auditing has become vital to the business community.

The proposed Federal Computer Systems Protection Act, which attempts to define computer crime, is under debate in Congress.[25] The bill, sponsored by Senator Abraham Ribicoff, claims federal jurisdiction over any criminal misuse of computer systems owned by or doing contract work for the United States government, financial institutions or "any entity operating in or affecting interstate commerce." Bank computers transfer funds across state lines in the normal course of operations.

7.4 COMPUTERS AND MANAGEMENT

The implications of computers for the practice of business management are significant. In the following article, Professor Peter Drucker outlines the opportunites and problems for business managers as computers are increasingly utilized in business.[11]

MANAGING THE INFORMATION EXPLOSION

Peter F. Drucker

Whether and when the "office of the future" will become reality, and what it will actually look like, are still largely conjecture. But other impacts of the new miniprocessor-based information technology are already predictable—and in some cases already with us.

The first impact will probably be a sharp drop in business travel. Few businessmen traveled before 1950 or so, and none, except salesmen, traveled a great deal. But as soon as the jet appeared, two decades ago, hopping a plane for a two-day meeting in Paris, Rio or Tokyo became commonplace for senior executives and even more so for their immediate subordinates.

Whether this is the most effective way to get things done or get to know people is debatable. But the advantage of direct access, face-to-face, to associates, partners and customers in faraway places, so greatly outweighed the fatigue and cost of air travel as to encourage gross overindulgence in it.

Alternative Ways

Now increasingly there will be alternative ways to meet and "share a common experience." No matter how far from each other, executives will more and more be able to "meet in the same room," see each other eye to eye, talk to each other face to face, and exchange reports and graphs, all without physically leaving their own offices. Several satellites, now under construction and expected to begin operations within year or two, will transmit pictures, voices and graphics simultaneously to earth stations that are linked with business subscribers—and thus be able to simulate the three-dimensional space of a "real" conference room in a subscriber's office.

Executives will therefore have to think more carefully about what to use physical travel for; to truly get to know another person, for example, will probably always require a real, rather than a simulated, presence. But at the same time, executives will have to learn what very few of them know so far: how to prepare, organize, run and follow up a short meeting for both achievement and mutual understanding.

For the last 25 years or so, management scientists and computer specialists have been talking a great deal about "total information systems." Now the hardware is available. A good many managers, especially in large companies, already have on their desk a miniprocessor, which combines a small computer for their own use with a terminal for the company's large computer system, complete with a small display screen and increasingly with printout for durable copy. Within a few years, this will become standard equipment, like the telephone on the desk or the hand-held calculator—and the executive miniprocessor may well be no larger than a telephone is today.

With the advent of the desktop miniprocessor, the manager risks being overloaded with paper and data. Indeed the critical problem will not be how to get or how to "process" information, but rather to define what information really is. This is a task that cannot be left to that mythical creature, the "information specialist." Information is the manager's main tool, indeed the manager's "capital," and it is he who must decide what information he needs and how to use it.

Managers will also have to come to grips with some critical questions about the role of information in their organizations. Who shall have access to what information? How can information be protected against fraud, industrial espionage, or prying and gossip-mongering? How can personal privacy be guarded?

How can confidential information be confined to those who are legitimately entitled to it, without a secretiveness which encourages scuttlebutt and demoralizes?

Over the last hundred years, armies have worked out useful rules to deal with these problems: A manager needs to know everything that pertains to his own work and to that of the level immediately above him. Information beyond this may be of "interest" to him, but has little relevance and should basically be restricted. Almost no one, outside of the military, has tried to convert this rule into policy so far; even the military still has a long way to go. Yet without such a policy the new information capacity can only endanger both performance and organization morale.

The greatest impact of the new information technology, however, will not be on the human organization but on the production process. Miniprocessors are beginning to regulate the operation of machines and tools, a process that is already far advanced in numerically controlled machine tools, medical instruments, all kinds of testing equipment and increasingly in aircraft and automobile engines.

This integration of information processing with productive machinery amounts to a "third industrial revolution." The second one began roughly a century ago, when machines were first combined directly with fractional horsepower motors. Until then, power—whether produced by water, steam engine or dynamo—had to be transmitted to machines by belts or pulleys, which in turn meant that power-driven equipment had to be very close to the source of power. A few hundred yards was the limit of distance.

The fractional horsepower motor made possible the central power station. It made possible the modern factory. It gave both flexibility and economy. By 1920 or so, the transmission belt had become obsolete and modern industrial production had emerged. Ten years later, the fractional horsepower motor had taken over the oldest domestic appliance around, the sewing machine. And by 1950, it had been integrated with the typewriter, the toothbrush and the carving knife. The fractional horsepower motor, in effect, took heavy manual work out of the productive process.

The third industrial revolution, in which information processing is becoming part of the machine or the tool, will shift production from being "manual" to being "knowledge-based." Before the second industrial revolution, there were "journeymen" and "laborers." Afterwards, the greatest expansion was in the number of "semi-skilled machine-tenders" and, more important, of "skilled workers." Within the next 20 years, the center of gravity is likely to shift to "technologists"—people whose contributions are based more on formal schooling and theory than on apprenticeship and skill.

There is a good deal of talk today about the need to "reindustrialize" America, to restore the country's capacity to manufacture capital goods productively and competitively. To do this, however, will require a shift to the "third industrial revolution"—that is, to the integration of information processing and production in machines and tools.

Highly Schooled People

Only such integration can make productive the one resource where this country and indeed all industrially developed countries have an advantage, namely, highly schooled people. From now on, in all developed countries, there will be an increasing shortage of young people available for traditional manual work, skilled or unskilled. Tremendously large populations in the developing countries will be available for traditional manual work, and will be willing, or forced, to work for very low wages, even as they rapidly improve their productivity. In such a world, only the integration of information processing and production can maintain and improve the standard of living for workers in the already developed countries.

The miniprocessor will thus provide tremendous opportunites for the industrial economies. But it will also impose tremendous demands on businessmen and on the economy—demands on capital equipment, demands on substantial shifts in productive organization and above all demands on the management of people at work.

7.5 COMPUTERS AND MANAGEMENT SCIENCE

With the increased use of computers in business during the past decade, the new field of management science has grown in importance. During that period the amount of data for a business enterprise has significantly increased and the computer has often been used to provide assistance in the area of business data processing. The use of the data available and the calculating power of the computers available to many firms has led to a mathematical approach to the management of business enterprises, often called *management science*.

MANAGEMENT SCIENCE   A mathematical or quantitative study of the management of resources of business, usually with the aid of a computer.

In management science, solution sequences begin with the identification of a problem and its verbal statement. The problem is then formulated in mathematical terms and analyzed. Usually a computer is used for calculation. A management decision is finally reached.[20]

Management science is closely related to the field of operations research. Operations research is concerned with the allocation of resources to an organization's various activities in a way that is most effective for the organization as a whole. The active beginnings of operations research have been attributed to the military services of the United States and the United Kingdom early in World War II.[20] Because of the war effort, there was need to allocate scarce resources to the many military operations in an effective manner. The various methods of operations research depend greatly upon the completion of a large number of calculations. Thus, the increasing availability of the digital computer after 1950 was a supporting factor in the development of operations research. A definition of operations research is:[21]

OPERATIONS RESEARCH   A scientific approach to decision making that involves the operations of organizational systems.

As the business organization is concerned with the allocation of resources, the field of management science and operations research have many common characteristics and objectives. For the outline in this section, we consider the purposes of operations research and management science to be similar for a business firm; we do not differentiate between them in the following paragraphs.

One of the objectives of a management science approach to a problem is the aim of finding the best or *optimal* solution to the problem under consideration. Thus, rather than being content with improvement, the goal is to identify the best possible course of action. The sequence followed in a management science approach to a problem is illustrated in Figure 7–12.

After formulating the problem in a verbal or written form, often the next step is developing a mathematical model of the problem in a form convenient for analysis. The mathematical model is an idealized representation of the important characteristics of the problem—in mathematical terms. The mathematical model includes *decision variables* whose values are to be determined. An example of a decision variable is the size of the labor force at a plant. Any restrictions assigned to these decision variables are called *constraints*. For example, the maximum size of the work force permitted in a specific plant due to space limitations and safety regulations would be limited or constrained. A model is necessarily an abstract idealization of the problem, and approximations and simplifying assumptions generally are required if the model is not to be unnecessarily complex. Therefore, care must be taken to insure that the model remains a valid representation of the problem. The proper criterion for judging the validity of a model is whether or

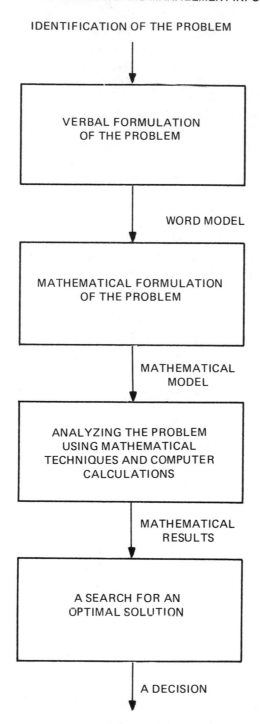

FIGURE 7–12   The management science approach to a problem.

not it predicts the relative effects of the alternative courses of action with sufficient accuracy to permit a sound decision.

In order to determine the optimal or best decision to adopt, one must formulate an objective, or aim, against which the many courses of action may be measured. Many people believe that most firms adopt the objective of maximization of profit as the sole aim of the company. A number of studies have found that, instead of profit maximization, the goal of satisfactory profits combined with other objectives is characteristic of American corporations. In particular, typical objectives might be to maintain stable profits, increase (or maintain) one's share of the market, diversify products, maintain stable prices, improve worker morale, maintain family control of the business, and increase company prestige. These objectives might be compatible with long-run profit maximization, but the relationship is sufficiently obscure that it may not be convenient to incorporate them into this one objective. Furthermore, there are additional considerations involving social responsibilities that are distinct from the profit motive and should be included in the objective of the firm.[5] The objective of the firm must be constructed in a quantitative or mathematical form in order to use the computer and the management science approaches.

The solution to the problem is then calculated as an optimal or best solution based on the examination of the objective in mathematical terms. The objective in mathematical form is called the *objective function*. Often a series of optimal solutions are obtained as a result of improving the model, the data, and the objective function. An analysis of the sensitivity of the model and objective function also may be conducted to determine which input parameters are most critical in determining the solution and therefore require more careful estimation.

Let us consider an example of a business decision which can utilize the methods of management science and the computer.

EXAMPLE 7-1

The bookstore at a college sells one kind of dictionary. The size of the student body is known and it is known that the demand in the coming year is for 1,000 dictionaries. The number of orders placed with the publisher of the dictionary is in control of the bookstore manager and he can place an order for one dictionary (called a unit), or any number up to 1,000 units. The decision variable, X, is the number of orders placed per year. X must be between 1 and 1,000.

The two costs to the bookstore are the ordering cost of each order and the carrying cost of storing the dictionaries while waiting for their sale. If the manager ordered 1,000 dictionaries on one order, the ordering cost would be minimized, but it would lead to high inventory-carrying costs. Similarly, 1,000 orders of one dictionary would minimize the inventory-carrying costs but would increase the ordering costs.

The objective of the manager is to minimize the costs of operating. An objective function to represent this objective would be

$$\text{Total Cost} = \text{Ordering Cost} + \text{Inventory Carrying Cost}$$

or
$$T = O + I \qquad (7-1)$$

After examination and study the manager finds that the ordering cost is a linear function of the number of orders placed. It is modeled as follows:

$$O = 2X \text{ (dollars)} \qquad (7-2)$$

Equation 11−2 states that the ordering cost expressed in dollars is equal to two multiplied by the number of orders placed, X. In other words, it costs 2 dollars per order. The inventory carrying cost may be represented by

$$I = 7200/X \text{ (dollars)} \qquad (7-3)$$

Equation 11−3 states that the inventory carrying cost decreases as the number of orders increases and equals 72 dollars if one hundred separate orders are placed.

A graphic solution of the problem may be obtained by plotting the two costs versus the number of orders placed; see Figure 7−13. Also shown is the total cost, which is the objective function as given by Equation 7−1. The minimum value of the total cost is found graphically to be $240. It is obtained when the manager places 60 orders per year. For this number of orders the cost of ordering would be $120 and the inventory-carrying cost would also be $120. One could readily use a computer to calculate the total costs for various numbers of orders and provide the data for the chart shown in Figure 7−13.

The main advantage of graphic presentation over the presentation of the results in a table printed out by the computer is that over-all relationships can be seen at a glance. More information can be presented on a graph than in a table. An additional factor to be noted from Figure 7−13 is that there is little difference in cost between 50 and 70 orders per year, but that total cost increases sharply when fewer than 20 orders per year are placed. The major limitation of this method is that graphs are two-dimensional, and when more than two variables are involved, graphs become difficult to prepare and interpret.

Another important technique of management science is that of *linear programming*, which deals with getting optimum value from limited resources which are used by competing activities. Use of the adjective *linear* implies that the objective function (or judgment) must be directly related to each of the various costs or factors. The theory of linear programming was developed by John von Neumann, G. B. Dantzig, T. C. Koopmans and a few others. It was applied to the problems of the Berlin air lift in the late 1940s, when all supplies had to be flown into the city because the Russians had cut off ground transport.

The objective function is written as

$$O = c_1 x_1 + c_2 x_2 + \ldots \qquad (7-4)$$

where x_1, x_2, . . . are decision variables and c_1, c_2,. . . are constants. The restrictions or constraints are also written in equation form. Linear programming problems may often be solved using *the simplex method*, which utilizes the digital

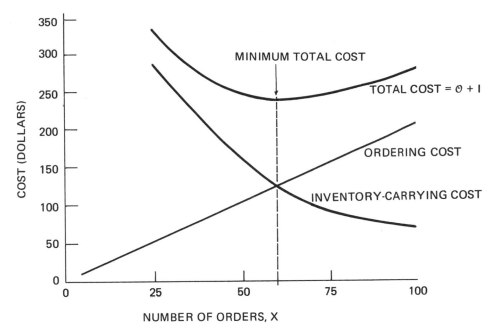

FIGURE 7–13   Costs as a function of the numbers of orders placed during the year.

computer.[21] An example of a linear programming problem is provided in the following paragraphs.

EXAMPLE 7–2

A steel mill produces two grades of steel: grade A and grade B. The mill can produce a maximum of 40 tons of grade A in a month and a maximum of 60 tons of grade B in a month. It requires three hours to produce one ton of grade A and it requires two hours to produce one ton of grade B. There are 180 production hours available each month. The decision variable for the number of tons of grade A and grade B produced per month will be x_1, and x_2 respectively. Thus, the constraints on the decision variables are

$$x_1 \leqslant 40 \qquad (7-5)$$
$$x_2 \leqslant 60 \qquad (7-6)$$
$$3x_1 + 2x_2 \leqslant 180 \qquad (7-7)$$

Equations 7–5, 7–6 and 7–7 can be represented graphically as shown in Figure 7–14a. The shaded area shows the permissible values of x_1 and x_2.

The profit is $30 for each ton of grade A produced and $50 for each ton of grade B produced. The total profit or objective function is then

$$O = 30x_1 + 50x_2 \qquad (7\text{--}8)$$

This objective function is a straight line, shown on Figure 7–14b for several cases. The maximum profit is achieved when $x_1 = 20$ tons and $x_2 = 60$ tons, for which case the profit is $3600 for the month.

Unfortunately, the graphic method cannot be used with more than two decision variables. However, it does help to illustrate the method for which the computer is used for more difficult problems.

Another management science technique is called Program Evaluation and Review Technique (PERT). It is a method of planning, replanning and progress evaluation in order to better control a major operational program. The PERT

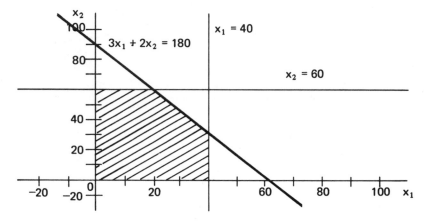

FIGURE 7–14a   The shaded area represents the permissible region for x_1 and x_2.

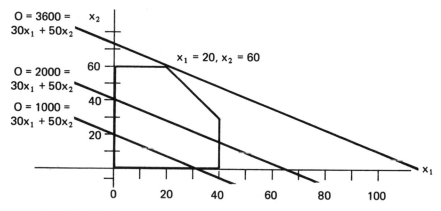

FIGURE 7–14b   The line $O = 30x_1 + 50x_2$ is shown for several values of O. The maximum value of the objective function, $3600, occurs when $x_1 = 20$ and $x_2 = 60$.

technique was developed during 1958 at the Navy Special Projects Office by a project team which studied the application of statistical and mathematical methods to the planning, evaluation, and control of research and development effort. PERT is used to define what must be done in order to accomplish program objectives on time. Through its use, areas of a project that require remedial decisions can be detected and the effect of trade-offs among the three basic factors—time, resources, and technical performance—can be determined. One of the major advantages of PERT is that it provides a method for the diagramming (establishing a network) of a program. Each event is depicted and its relationship to the others expressed. PERT uses time as the common denominator to reflect planned resource application and performance specifications.

Using a computer to develop and monitor a project with PERT, one obtains the following advantages: (1) aid in planning and scheduling a program; (2) continuous, timely progress reports, identifying potential problem areas where action may be required; (3) a simulation of the effects of alternate decisions under consideration and an opportunity to study their effect upon the program deadlines prior to implementation; (4) probability of successfully meeting deadlines.

The computer is used to produce the printed output results of an analysis based on the network representation of the project plan. The network or graph depicts the flow of events and activities in the program.[20]

(The simulation of business processes enables a manager to evaluate the results of various alternatives. Simulation as a general approach to business problems and problems from other fields is discussed fully in Chapter 9.)

One problem in computer simulation and modeling is the necessity of finding the simplest model that nevertheless captures the essence of the problem at hand. Also, quite often a manager may be less interested in obtaining the optimum solution from a model, which is only an approximation in any case, than he is in gaining some insight into the effect on the objective function of changes in the model. A sensitivity study is aimed at providing a measure of the incremental effect (*i.e.*, the sensitivity) of changes in the model. The simplest type of change is to modify the value of a parameter. For example, one may wish to study the effects of a change in sales forecasts in an inventory model.[20]

A simulation model duplicates, more or less faithfully, the actual events that occur over time in the real world for a given set of parameters and decision variables. Certain consequences stem from the events that take place during the course of the simulation. The consequences are then presented to a decision maker, usually in summarized form, to aid him in predicting the consequences of implementing the specified alternative in the real world.

We have briefly treated some of the methods of management science. The computer is able to provide results rapidly from simulations, linear programming, optimization problems, PERT problems, and other problems of managers in business and industry. As the managers of business enterprises become more familiar with these methods they will be utilized more commonly in practice.

7.6   MANAGEMENT INFORMATION SYSTEMS

Perhaps no other concept of computer data processing for business is discussed more than that of management information systems. Yet management information systems, which are often simply labeled MIS, have not been fully constructed, developed or implemented as an actual system for management use.[4]

A definition of a management information system is difficult to formulate since the field is newly developing and in a state of transition. MIS use computers to provide managers with the information they need for making decisions regarding their company's business. Two definitions of MIS are:

MANAGEMENT INFORMATION SYSTEM   (1) A computer system integrating equipment, people and procedures to deliver analysis-supporting and analytical information pertinent to management decisions. (2) A system of people, equipment, procedures, documents and communications that collects, validates, operates on, transforms, stores, retrieves and presents data for use by various top executives of a firm in planning, budgeting, accounting, controlling and other management processes.

At present, top managers in industry resort directly to their computer systems only occasionally. They usually rely on department managers to interpret computer results to them. With a new generation of managers and equipment which provides visual displays such as graphs and figures, the top manager is more able to obtain his information directly from the data processing system. Thus, the trend is toward computer applications which are involved in the daily operation of the business organization. In American business and industry, the percentage of computer resources allocated to produce output for top management averaged only 18 percent of the total during 1970, 38 percent going to middle management and 44 percent to operating supervisors. This 18 percent figure is up only slightly from 14 percent in 1965. It increased to about 25 percent in 1976. Also, as many persons have pointed out, top executives of industry do not often receive the most significant computer output. Usually, they receive information from accounting-oriented data systems, such as sales summaries, product cost reports and other after-the-fact information. What a top executive needs is a decision-oriented data base that can be used, for example, to identify potential market demands; to indicate improvements in operating costs, or to show profit profiles of alternative investment plans.

MIS are most useful to the top-management functions of formulating corporate strategy, designing overall planning and control systems, and setting investment and growth policies. As systems are developed which encompass a greater share of the day-to-day administrative chores of a business, the manager will become free to reflect on the company's investment and program policies and think of new opportunities for the firm.

Information processing systems tend toward management information systems as their purpose transcends a transactions processing orientation in favor of a top management decision-making orientation.[4, 6] In order to understand the information flow in a normal business organization, examine Figure 7—15. The horizontal reporting patterns shown in Figure 7—15a tend to follow horizontal department lines. The vertical divisions shown in Figure 7—15b represent general information such as payroll. By superimposing the vertical patterns over the horizontal, these diagrams attempt to show how management information flows through all levels of a company's operation. MIS is a system of integrated information flow through the company. The concept of integration of information in a MIS is succinctly summarized in an interesting statement by Marshall McLuhan in his recent book:[22]

> It may be simplest to say at once that the real use of the computer is not to reduce staff or costs, or to speed up or smooth out anything that has been going on. Its true function is to program and orchestrate terrestrial and galactic environments and energies in a harmonious way. For centuries the lack of symmetry and proportion in all these areas has created a sort of universal spastic condition for lack of inter-relation among them.

Managers can use MIS to help them orchestrate the operations of their companies.

Often we talk about the value of information and the profit obtained by using MIS. But the plant in a literal sense generates the profit, and the information system helps in managing the operation. Data are collected on the plant operation and information is generated. The data record the level of operation while information results from an analysis of the data. Relevant information is then extracted from the total information and used for management decisions. The underlying concept is that information about a business enterprise is a resource analogous to labor and capital. Management of the business information resource is a function of corporate management, requiring highly integrated information for the sake of efficiency.

A fully integrated MIS may be a competitive necessity for many industries in the near future. A business has an external environment and many internal related environments. The external environment of a business includes the government, industry, financial, and competitive environments. The sales environment is also important to record in the data systems. In Figure 7—16, a business management system is shown which illustrates the flow of information, goods and prediction. The information flow may be integrated in a management information system. Also, the computer which provides the MIS can be used to provide predictions of the market, sales, inventory and production. The predictions are used in conjunction with the available information to make management decisions.

Gould, Inc. has combined a 4 ft. by 5.5 ft. visual display board with a computer MIS to provide a corporate boardroom display. Information on everything from inventories to cash flow can be readily displayed as numbers or in chart form. When the MIS system is connected to a simulator model, the display board can depict the potential consequences of contemplated actions.[32]

An operational system which is a reduced version of an MIS exists at North American Rockwell Corporation. It is said to realize a net annual savings of $150,000, reducing inventory in one of the company's divisions by $2 million. This saving results from sharply lowered labor costs for inventory control and scheduling, reduced clerical effort in labor and job status reporting and less physical inventory. The MIS performs two basic control functions: production control of work-in-progress and inventory control of manufacturing requirements and materials. The system uses on-line computing equipment and remote input terminals at work stations.

A study of more than 50 MIS systems confirmed the view that very few management functions have been automated to date.[4] The MIS is used to support rather than replace the manager. A humanized MIS should be easy to understand, responsive to users, private, and easy to use.[6, 30] A computer system for MIS is shown in Figure 7–17.

Management information systems are becoming increasingly important to business firms. Competition will encourage the development of integrated MIS. Use and development of management information systems during the next decade could lead to major changes in the management function in business enterprises. The manager of the future will be required to know the capabilities of the computer and its integrated use in his enterprise.

7.7   DISTRIBUTED PROCESSING

The declining costs of small minicomputers has reduced the need to centralize a company's computers in many cases. One can now match job requirements to machine capability and location of need. On the other hand, decentralization of the business firms and government agencies has not matched the decentralization of data-processing facilities (which have typically been highly centralized in the past).

The concept of *distributed data processing* is to place computer power where the data is generated or where the data is needed for management. One form of distributed processing system is shown in Figure 7–18.[37] The corporate headquarters has a large host computer, and the dispersed division offices have medium or small computers operating as satellites to the large computer. One of

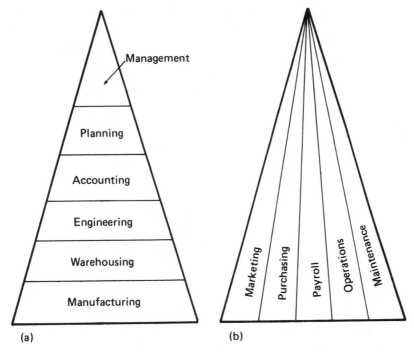

FIGURE 7–15   Horizontal and vertical information flow in a typical firm.

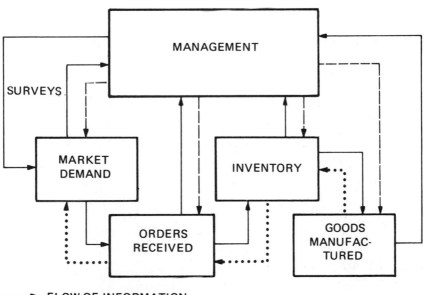

FIGURE 7–16   A business management system illustrating the flow of information, goods and prediction.

FIGURE 7–17   The Burroughs 92 utilizes a flexible disk storage system and provides a business computer for middle size businesses. *Courtesy of Burroughs Corporation.*

the primary characteristics of distributed processing is shared control of data.[38, 39]

The communication of information in business traditionally occupies many people and much financial commitment. Insurance companies, for instance, move mountains of paper forms back and forth. In some insurance firms, claims and policy records are converted to machine-readable cards, but even those cards require keypunch operators, equipment, and tens of thousands of cards. When direct data communication is substituted for paperwork and mailing, enormous savings can result. Major changes can take place in management systems.[42] The dispersion of the work force and the operating units can be more effectively controlled and utilized when distributed processing assists managers. The logistic decisions move to headquarters, but the tactical decisions move out to the satellites.[4] A distributed processing computer system is shown in Figure 7–19.

7.8 OFFICE AUTOMATION

Computers are being actively used in the office in the form of business computers, intelligent terminals and word processing devices. It is estimated that the

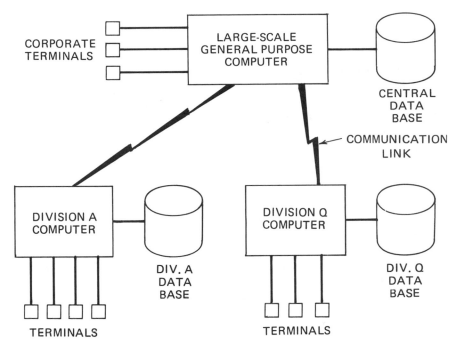

FIGURE 7–18   A distributed data processing system. The corporate headquarters has a large-scale general purpose computer, and the division offices have medium or small computers. Decentralizing data processing can make the company flexible; it requires new management strategies.

FIGURE 7–19   The HP 3000 Series III computer system, which is used as a business system for distributed data processing. This system can use BASIC, FORTRAN or COBOL. The system can support up to 16 terminals. *Courtesy of Hewlett-Packard Corporation.*

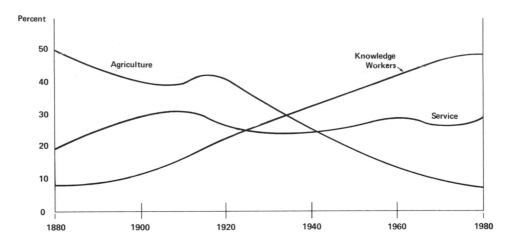

FIGURE 7-20   Since 1960 more workers in the US have been involved in manipulating information than in the food, manufacturing or service industries.

office automation market was $2 billion in 1980 and will grow to $7 billion by 1985.[15]

Businesses in the United States spend over $800 billion dollars on office operations annually. Clerical costs are only 27% of this expenditure. The remainder consists of managers, professionals and other knowledge workers. The cost is expected to grow to $1.6 trillion by 1989 if new office productivity is not achieved. While the average farm worker is supported by $70,000 worth of capital equipment and the average factory worker by $35,000 of capital equipment, the average office worker has only $4000 worth of capital investment supporting his or her efforts.

In order to increase the productivity of the knowledge worker, the functions occurring in the office must be supported with automated equipment. These automated functions are a combination of data processing, word processing, electronic mail, tracking and scheduling, text management, and interoffice conferencing.

The information society, with its increasing number of knowledge workers, requires the support necessary to improve productivity, reduce unneeded travel and improve communication. The shift to a society dependent on knowledge workers is shown by Figure 7-20.[14]

The idea of using a display terminal to transmit messages, review data and prepare reports is relatively new to most professionals and managers.[15] Computer-assisted conferences will assist the manager and a conference will oc-

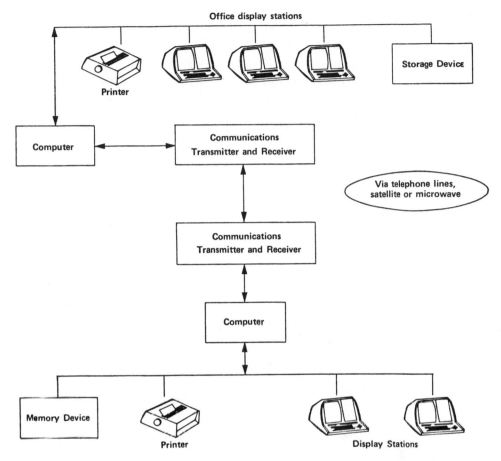

FIGURE 7–21   This electronic office network serves several branch offices of a national firm or is able to connect one firm to another via the communications and computer systems.

cur via a communications network, resulting in a greatly reduced need for travel.[31]

It is expected that office automation will

1. Enhance decision making
2. Raise managerial productivity
3. Reduce clerical costs

In order to achieve these gains, improved links between business and computer system planning will be required. The electronic communication and computer system for a national company will appear in a form as shown in Figure 7–21. A commercial office automation system is shown in Figure 7–22.

SUMMARY

Business data processing is the storage, processing and reporting of data for business purposes. Business data processing can significantly affect the cost structure of a company, when volume production is the rule, by reducing the time taken to produce records and reports. Also, business data processing can be used to reduce the clerical work force required to handle the business data. Business data processing is most efficient when a computer is used to perform repetitious tasks with large masses of data at rapid speeds.

The basic organization of a business is often altered by the introduction of a computer. Quite often, business firms use COBOL, a programming language oriented to business applications. The computer can be used to aid in the reduction of general and administrative expenses; to reduce the cost of goods sold; to increase revenues; and to improve management decisions. Thus far, the primary concentration has been on the first of these purposes.

FIGURE 7–22   An office automation system, the WANG office information system 130. The system supports up to 14 peripheral devices, including workstations. It uses 32,000 bytes of memory. *Courtesy of Wang Laboratories, Inc.*

Computers are effectively utilized for data processing in the fields of banking and credit institutions. Computers process the checks and documents passing through most banks. Also, on-line teller systems have been developed and installed. As the computer systems for banks and credit institutions evolve, our nation may move toward a financial system which does not utilize paper money as it does now.

The fields of management science and operations research have developed during the past two decades due in great measure to the availability of the computer. Management science is a mathematical or quantitative study of the management of resources of a business, usually with the aid of a computer. Among these resources is information, which provides the basis for decisions. Management science incorporates the techniques of linear programming, PERT, system optimization, and simulation, among others.

Management information systems (MIS) are computer systems integrating equipment, people, and procedures in such a way as to deliver analysis-supporting and analytical information pertinent to management decisions. MIS are useful to the top management functions of formulating corporate strategy, designing overall planning and control systems and setting investment and growth plans.[41]

The computer and its use in business data processing, management science and management information systems will result in profound changes in the structure, organization, and function of a business enterprise. The manager of the future must be prepared for the changes and able to incorporate them in his enterprise.

We close this summary with the oft-told story of the computer owned by the Gas Company. One of the customers was away for several months and he duly recieved a bill for $0.00. He ignored it, but the machine expected a reply. It sent another bill and, when that was ignored, it sent a final demand note which included a threat to cut off supplies from the customer's house. The customer thereupon sent his check—which pacified the computer. After a few days his bank manager asked to see him urgently. Why had he written such a peculiar check? "To pacify the Gas Company's computer." "Damn the Gas Company's computer! Do you realize that you have driven *our* computer crazy?"

CHAPTER 11 PROBLEMS

P7–1. List three or four advantages of the use of a computer in the data processing operation of the business operations listed below.
   1. The payroll department of the city
   2. The accounting department of your college
   3. The production department of a toy manufacturer

P7–2. Outline the steps necessary in the processing of data at the accounting office of your college. Draw a chart similar to Figure 7–1 to illustrate the sequence of steps.

P7–3. List the leading applications of computers in business data processing in industry.

P7–4. Investigate and draft a brief report on one of the following business data processing operations in your own town which utilizes a computer in its operation.

1. A retail point-of-sale system in a store
2. A bank accounting system
3. A credit company system
4. A bank check processing system

P7–5. A store sells one item, automobile tires. The total cost is the sum of the carrying cost and the ordering cost. The annual sales are 800 tires and the reordering cost is $10 per order. The average carrying cost is $.20 per tire. Show that the minimum total cost is $80 when four orders of 200 units are processed by the store to the manufacturer.

P7–6. A company produces two grades, x and y, of paper on a paper machine. Here are some of the restrictions under which we must plan production.

Capacity per week: Not more than 400 tons of grade x.
Not more than 300 tons of grade y.

Time: It requires 0.2 and 0.4 hours to produce a ton of products x and y respectively.

There are 160 production hours available each week.

Profit: A profit of $20 and $50 per ton of x and y respectively can be realized per week.

The problem is to determine how much of each paper shall the company make to maximize the profit. Use linear programming and obtain a graphic solution.

P7–7. An industry produces two products, A and B, on which the profit per unit is $50 for either product. There are two processes of manufacture operating in the plant. Under the first process, it requires 10 hours to manufacture each item A and 5 hours to manufacture each unit of item B. With the second process it requires 5 hours/unit for item A and 6 hours/unit for item B. There are 3500 hours of manufacturing time available for each process. Using a graphic solution to the linear programming problem, show that the optimum profit is $30,000.

P7–8. A student has a family car which he can drive to the beach, or he can take the bus. The bus ride costs $3 for a round trip and the auto costs

$2 for a round trip. The student can go to the beach at the most four times each week. Also, due to his family schedule, he can use either form of transportation a maximum of three times per week. His family has set rules on the use of the car by all the members of the family so that for every three times they use the car they must use the bus at least once. Using the linear programming approach, determine the number of times the student should use each form of transportation if he wished to minimize his expenses over a ten-week period.

P7-9.   A firm is interested in scheduling the production of two hand-made products, rugs and blankets. The profit for each rug is $6, and for each blanket it is $9. The problem is to determine the schedule that maximizes profit. The decision variables are thus the quantities to produce each of the products. Let x_1 represent the number of rugs scheduled, and x_2 the number of blankets. The objective function is therefore Profit = $6x_1 + 9x_2$.

The production of the rugs and blankets requires the skills of weavers and spinners. For a given scheduling period (a week, say) they have 1800 hours of weavers' time and 300 hours of spinners' time. Each product requires 2 hours per unit of weaving; while a rug or blanket requires .2 and .5 hours, respectively, of spinning. Use the

FIGURE P7-12   The NCR Criterion 8550 computer uses Metal Oxide Silicon (MOS) memory. This computer functions with COBOL for business applications. On the operator's front desk are shown a video display and a punched-card reader. The man is shown inserting a flexible disk. Directly behind the operator's display are the two disk-pack storage units. *Courtesy NCR Corporation.*

linear programming approach to show that the optimal schedule is to produce 500 rugs and 400 blankets. This will result in the optimum profit of $6,600.

P7–10.   Five questions are provided below. Write a brief statement on each of these questions and add your conclusions after completing the five questions.

1. Are organizational structures of business firms becoming more centralized as a result of computers?
2. Are these organizational changes a *result* of computer technology, or are other factors *causing* the changes?
3. What is the significance of the centralization of the data-processing, or information-technology, function?
4. How has the nature of managerial work changed? Will it change further as certain types or levels of management work are subject to computer systems and management science becomes better-known?
5. How will higher levels of management be affected?

P7–11.   Devise a management information system in graphic form similar to Figure 7–13 for your college bookstore.

P7–12.   Most business data processing computer systems use COBOL. A modern business computer is shown in Figure P7–12. Contact a local business and your college computer data center and determine from them the characteristics and qualities of COBOL. Explain why COBOL is widely used in business.

P7–13.   A firm is producing a product, P, and the annual fixed costs are $300,000. The variable cost is $.80 per unit. The price is related to the overall demand (estimated) as follows:

Price	Demand over Product Life (Units)
$ 2.00	200,000
4.00	150,000
6.00	100,000
8.00	50,000
10.00	0

Using an algorithm and a model for this production, calculate the selling price for maximizing the firm's profit.

NOTE: Problems P7–14 through P7–16 are multiple-choice questions taken from computer-assisted instructional materials. Choose the correct answer and be prepared to defend your choice in each case.

P7–14.   Computerization of the company payroll is recommended because

A. There results a savings of 95 percent in cost of preparing the payroll

    B. There results a savings of 80 percent in cost

    C. There results a savings of 30 percent in cost

    D. There results some savings in cost

    E. The payroll can be produced more quickly and accurately, thus providing better service to employees.

P7–15. Historically, the greatest impetus to business record-keeping resulted from

    A. Income tax legislation

    B. Regulations of the Securities and Exchange Commission

    C. Social security legislation

    D. The need for better business management

    E. The profit motive

FIGURE P7–17   The Bunker-Ramo Telequote III terminal provides prices for securities and commodities traded on more than twenty exchanges. Over 20,000 Telequotes have been installed. They are used to request bid/ask, volume, dividend, Dow-Jones average, and other stock market facts. *Courtesy Bunker-Ramo Corporation.*

P7–16.   A management information system provides information for the purpose of
       A. Meeting management's objectives
       B. Efficient business management
       C. Control of the business operation
       D. Economy
       E. Modernization of the enterprise

P7–17.   Computer systems are used to give quotations for stock market prices. A quotation terminal used by stockbrokers is shown in Figure P7–17. The terminal connects to a central computer which provides instantaneous nationwide quotations. Visit a local stock brokerage firm and examine the quotation terminal used there. Determine from the stockbrokers what they consider to be the advantages and disadvantages of the terminals.

P7–18.   The present (or current) value of income received at a future time (F) should be discounted in value by the interest rate, I, that one could earn on an investment over the period. Therefore the prevent value (PV) is

$$PV = F(1 + I)^{-n}$$

where n is the number of periods in the future that the income is earned. For example, the present value of $1,000 earned two years from now is $841.68 when I is nine percent per year. If a project would yield $1,000 in the first year, $2,000 in the second, and $3,000 for every year after that for another five years, calculate the present value. Prepare a computer program in BASIC, FORTRAN, or PASCAL to calculate the present value. Assume the interest rate is nine percent.

P7–19.   Messages are often sent electronically by businesses, in contrast to paper letters. Electronic messages sent via satellite and flashed onto display screens can be received in less than one second. Contact a local firm using a computer communication system for electronic messages and arrange a visit to observe it.

CHAPTER 7 REFERENCES

1. D. H. Sanders, *Computers in Business: An Introduction*, 4th Edition, McGraw-Hill, New York, 1979.
2. J. A. O'Brien, *Computers in Business Management*, Irwin, Inc., Homewood, Illinois, 1979.
3. R. J. Thierauf and J. F. Niehaus, *An Introduction to Data Processing for Business*, Wiley and Sons, Inc., New York, 1980.

4. R. McLeod, *Management Information Systems*, SRA Inc., Palo Alto, California, 1979.
5. D. H. Sanders and S. J. Birkin, *Computers and Management*, 3rd Edition, McGraw-Hill Book Co., New York, 1980.
6. G. J. Brabb, *Computers and Information Systems in Business*, 2nd Edition, Houghton Mifflin Co., Boston, 1980.
7. P. Edwards and B. Broadwell, *Data Processing*, Wadsworth Publishing Co., Belmont, California, 1980.
8. H. J. Watson, *Computers For Business*, Business Publications, Inc., Dallas, Texas, 1980.
9. S. D. Kaplan, "EFT: How the Public Views It," *Administrative Management*, October 1979, pp. 35–46.
10. D. Waldron and L. D. Ball, "The Bottom Line on Checkless Banking," *Technology Review*, February 1980, pp. 44–52.
11. P. F. Drucker, "Managing the Information Explosion," *Wall Street Journal*, April 10, 1980, p. 21.
12. L. I. Krauss and A. MacGahan, *Computer Fraud and Countermeasures*, Prentice-Hall Inc., Englewood Cliffs, New Jersey, 1979.
13. L. L. Goldberg, "Computers and Crime," *Telecommunications*, May, 1980, pp. 19–26.
14. P. A. Strassmann, "The Office of the Future: Information Management for the New Age," *Technology Review*, January 1980, pp. 56–65.
15. A. Wohl, "A Review of Office Automation," *Datamation*, February 1980, pp. 117–121.
16. V. T. Dock and E. Essick, *Principles of Business Data Processing*, Science Research Associates, Inc., Chicago, Illinois, 1978.
17. W. R. Iversen, "Supermarket Scanners Start to Move," *Electronics*, May 22, 1980, pp. 110–112.
18. R. Townsend, *Up The Organization*, Alfred Knopf, Inc., New York, 1970.
19. D. J. Parker, *Crime by Computer*, Scribners and Sons, New York, 1976.
20. T. M. Cook and R. A. Russell, *Introduction to Management Science*, Prentice-Hall Inc., Englewood Cliffs, New Jersey, 1978.
21. R. J. Thierauf, *An Introductory Approach to Operations Research*, Wiley and Sons, Inc., New York, 1978.
22. M. McLuhan and Q. Fiore, *War and Peace in the Global Village*, Bantam Books, Inc., New York, 1968, p. 89.
23. W. Myers, "Computer Graphics: A Two-Way Street," *IEEE Computer*, July 1980, pp. 49–58.
24. E. Myers, "Shiny Plastic Cards," *Datamation*, October 1979, pp. 52–53.
25. "Crime Bill Revised," *Datamation*, February 1980, pp. 88–89.
26. G. B. Kolata, "New Codes Coming Into Use," *Science*, May 1980, pp. 694–695.
27. M. L. Dertouzos and J. Moses, *The Computer Age*, MIT Press, Inc., Cam-

bridge, Massachusetts, 1980, Chapter 11.

28. M. Murack, *Business Data Processing*, Science Research Associates, Chicago, 1980.

29. C. Evans, *The Micro Millennium*, The Viking Press, New York, 1980, Chapter 10.

30. W. S. Anderson, "The Expectation Gap," *Journal of Systems Management*, June 1978, pp. 6–10.

31. S. R. Hiltz and M. Turoff, *The Network Nation: Human Communication Via Computer*, Addison-Wesley Publishing Co., Reading, Massachusetts, 1978.

32. J. Kelly, "Mapping Out Strategies in a Corporate War Room," *Output*, April 1980, pp. 43–50.

33. E. Colton, *Computers and Banking*, Plenum Publishers, New York, 1980.

34. C. L. Biggs, *Managing the Systems Development Process*, Prentice-Hall, Englewood Cliffs, New Jersey, 1980.

35. R. G. Murdick, *MIS: Concepts and Design*, Prentice-Hall Inc., Englewood Cliffs, New Jersey, 1980.

36. E. M. Awad, *Business Data Processing*, 5th Edition, Prentice-Hall Inc., Englewood Cliffs, New Jersey, 1980.

37. L. I. Krauss and A. MacGahan, *Computer Fraud and Countermeasures*, Prentice-Hall Inc., Englewood Cliffs, New Jersey, 1979.

38. T. Whiteside, *Computer Capers*, Crowell Publishing Co., New York, 1978.

39. R. P. Uhlig *et. al.*, *The Office of the Future*, North Holland/Elsevier, New York, 1979.

40. R. Kling and K. Lundegaard, "Passing the Digital Buck," *Society*, February 1980, pp. 42–49.

41. A. Vinberg and J. E. George, "Computer Graphics and the Business Executive—The New Management Team," *IEEE Computer Graphics*, Vol. 1, No. 1, January 1981, pp. 22–30.

8

DATA BANKS, INFORMATION RETRIEVAL AND LIBRARIES

8.1 DATA BANKS

More than five centuries have passed since Gutenberg invented printing with movable type. Today we have available a wide variety of printed material such as books, newspapers, catalogs and magazines. In addition, we use the typed and written word to record information. All this printed and written material aids in the storage and retention of data, information, and knowledge. One of the purposes of any library is to store printed materials which contain the information and knowledge of previous generations. If we did not store this knowledge, each generation would have to pass on the information orally or constantly rediscover it. The limited information available to generations prior to the ready availability of the printed media hindered the advancement of knowledge and the development of science and technology. Knowledge today is readily available to any literate person in the libraries and the printed material of our western society. New developments in collecting and distributing information, which utilize the computer, will provide additional advantages and challenges to society in the future.

The digital computer has been commercially available for two decades. It has been viewed primarily as a *calculating* machine. However, within the last few years, with the ready availability of low-cost storage, users have started to con-

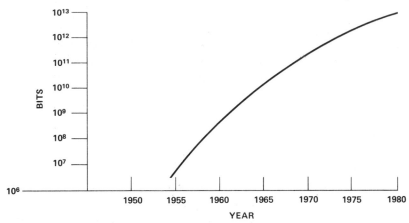

FIGURE 8–1   The capacity of on-line directly accessible storage of large computer systems during the years 1955–1980.

ceive of the computer as an *information storage, processing* and *retrieval* machine. The evolution of large and powerful computer systems developed primarily for storing and retrieving data will rapidly accelerate during the next decade.

The evolution of large-capacity, directly accessible storage of computer systems is shown in Figure 8–1. In 1980, storage units with capacities greater than 10^{13} bits were available. On-line directly accessible storage enables the computer to read stored data without human intervention. Computers can read a piece of data from a large on-line disk storage unit at random in less than one second. Off-line storage, by contrast, refers to a storage medium, such as magnetic tape, to which the machine does not have ready access but which requires the intervention of the operator.

As the capacities of the storage devices have increased, the cost per bit stored has decreased. Figure 8–2 illustrates the estimated numbers of bits stored per dollar of cost during the period 1950–1980. The cost of storing all the information in the pages of this book in a computer device might have been $750 in 1955. It would be about $2 in 1980 (excluding the illustrations). It is the ready availability of low-cost storage units that has fostered the development of data banks and information retrieval systems.

The storage of large amounts of data in readily accessible storage units is useful in business, government, and education, among other applications. A *data bank* is an on-line storage unit retaining large masses of data. In many cases, the kinds of material stored in a data bank resemble lists, directions, tabulations or similar material that has been otherwise available in the printed form. Data banks presently serve the following, among others:

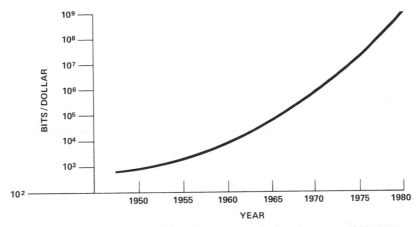

FIGURE 8-2   The cost of on-line storage during the years 1955–1980.

- Transportation reservations
- U.S. economy
- Real estate
- Municipal bond bidding
- Theatre tickets
- Shipping rates
- Stock market prices
- Agriculture
- Medical literature

Many functions can be achieved with data stored in data banks by using the great speed of the computer. Data bank information can be:[1]

(1) Added to or deleted from as desired
(2) Retrieved
(3) Manipulated
(4) Combined with data from other sources
(5) Displayed in graphic form
(6) Transmitted over long distances

Data from data banks is available through terminals in printed form or by computer-generated voice output. (See Chapter 6.) Such services, supplied by large computer organizations, comprise what has been called a *computer utility*.

An example of a data bank is the storage of data on the economy of the United States. Economists and planners in many organizations repeatedly use such data as the Gross National Product (GNP), percentage of unemployment and price index. In 1967, a group of 23 large firms in New York City, primarily banks and insurance companies, formed a cooperative experimental data bank called Project Economics. Since then, several commercial firms have developed

FIGURE 8–3　Old-fashioned mechanical coin banks symbolizing each of the areas or enterprises for which data banks are available. From *Computer Decisions*, a Hayden publication.

data banks available for a service fee. Another example of a data bank is the storage of data on the status of the stock market. This system, which provides up-to-the-minute quotes on each stock covered by the stock exchange, may be seen in action at a local stock broker's office. Data banks are also used to store information on availability of real estate, used automobiles, employment and theatre tickets, among others. Once one of the items described in this type of bank is used, it is noted as unavailable. Once an entire event has occurred, the entire set of data is removed from the system. A partial list of United States Government data banks is given in Table 8–1.

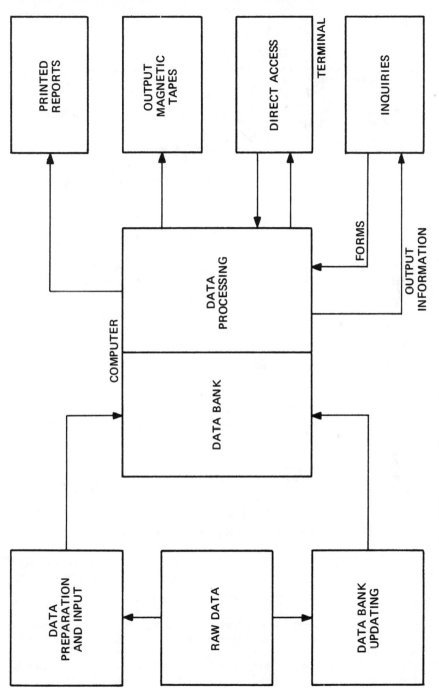

FIGURE 8–4   The operations involved in various types of data banks.

TABLE 8-1

Federal Data Banks

1. Treasury Department	910 data banks with 853 million records
2. Justice Department	175 data banks with 181 million records
3. Defense Department	2,219 data banks with 321 million records
4. Department of Commerce	95 data banks with 447 million records
5. Civil Service	14 data banks with 23 million records

The operations involved in the various types of data banks are shown in Figure 8-4. Data banks may be established to provide printed reports, or magnetic tapes with the output stored on the tape. Also, some data banks are used for inquiry such as reservation systems. Many data banks are connected directly to terminals which provide direct access for the user.

The development of computer data banks has occurred when enormous quantities of data are being generated. Man is experiencing what is often called an information explosion. It has been estimated that knowledge was doubling every 50 years by 1800 and by 1950 it was doubling every 10 years. In 1982, one may estimate that knowledge is doubling every five years. This knowledge must be recorded if it is to be valuable to the members of the future generations. The data banks serve this purpose. They are automated storehouses of data that can be searched as desired; they are technological solutions to the problem of the overabundance of information. The annual transactions in selected industries are shown in Table 8-2.

TABLE 8-2

Annual Transactions in Selected Industries

Type of Transaction	1940	1955	1970	1940-1970 Increase (Percent)
Social Security Payments	222,000	8 million	26 million	11,700%
Airline Passengers	3 million	42 million	171 million	5,600%
Motor Vehicle Registrations	32.5 million	62.7 million	108.4 million	230%
New York Stock Exchange Trans- actions	283 million	821 million	3.2 billion	1,032%

About 100,000 technical reports, 10 million articles in journals, and 30,000 books are published each year. A library of books and reports is a data bank with inexpensive storage and random access. It is available at slow speed via a series of indexes, and it is not automated. A computerized data bank is automated and of high speed and it usually operates at a reasonable cost per item stored. The computer stores the index to the data bank and provides a ready means of updating the index and the stored data.

8.2 INFORMATION STORAGE AND RETRIEVAL

The availability of data in data banks can be overwhelming to the potential user. The user desires to extract information from the myriads of data. The real need of the user of a data bank is information, and he does not care about the data form or structure of the computer that stores the data. The information the user desires is a particular meaning implied by the data in an aggregate or summated form. The definition we use for information in this context is:

INFORMATION   (1) The meaning assigned to data by some agreed upon convention. (2) The aggregation of data that are presented in various forms.

The basic problem of obtaining the information from a data base is that of meaning. A user doesn't ordinarily seek a document or report for its own sake, but for the ideas it contains. Therefore, the seeking of information in a data bank is called *information retrieval*. Thus data becomes information within a framework of relevance. The problem of information retrieval becomes one of classifying and characterizing the information and making it accessible to the user. It is here that the dilemma of retrieval emerges. There is an inverse relation between retrievability and ambiguity, but a direct one between ambiguity and new knowledge (that is, new systems or generalizations into which information is organized). The less ambiguous the information, the more thoroughly it is structured and the easier it is of access. One has only to thread his way through the hierarchy of concepts and categories to the fact or idea he wants.

Efforts to handle information more readily date at least from Aristotle, whose starting point was the way we discourse about things. There are, he postulated, ten ways in which we do so, and he proposed ten categories to comprehend them: substance, quality, quantity, relation, determination in time and space, action, passivity, position, condition. In one way or another, all statements, he held, conform to these categories. Another approach was that of Peter Mark Roget, who sought to deal not with how we discourse, nor what we *seem* to be saying, but with the words we use to say what we say. In his thesaurus he tried to map the senses in which words are used. His framework consists of six basic classes of sense: abstract relations, space, matter, intellect, volition and affections, each divided into sections and subdivided into topics, together amounting to a framework like Aristotle's, though more explicitly detailed. In one way or another, the schemes of Roget, Aritsotle, Dewey and others are used to organize and classify data.

Extracting information, however, is more than the inverse of classifying it. The two processes together comprise information storage and retrieval:

INFORMATION STORAGE AND RETRIEVAL   The technique and process of accumulating, classifying, storing, and searching large amounts of data, extracting and reproducing or displaying the required information contained within the data.

Information retrieval is not a new concept, but recently several computer-based information retrieval systems have been under development. Some of the prob-

FIGURE 8–5   A large library of magnetic tapes for information retrieval. *Courtesy of Minnesota Mining and Manufacturing Co.*

lems confronted in building a computer-based information retrieval system are:

(1) Those involved in the selection of data which will constitute a request
(2) Ascertaining the relevance of key words which will identify an item
(3) Economics of response time, since a shorter response time increases the cost of retrieving an item.

A large library of magnetic tapes recording a vast amount of data is shown in Figure 8-5. An off-line tape is selected and accessed for information retrieval. (In Chapter 6) we defined *access time* as the time required to locate and read a stored record.) While a tape storage system results in a longer response time, it is a relatively low-cost storage device for an information retrieval system. A floppy disk storage device is capable of storing the text of 200,000 books and can retrieve one book in 10 seconds.

The quality of an information retrieval system is measured by how much relevant information, compared to irrelevant information, is provided in response to a query. One might state this measure of quality as follows:

$$\text{Quality} = \text{Relevant Information}/\text{Irrelevant Information}$$

where a large number for the measure of quality is desired.

An additional characteristic of information retrieval is the task of matching the information that is stored with what is relevant at a particular time. Often the very process of trying to answer a question changes our needs. In a search through categories of references and through possibly relevant data, we discover unforeseen aspects that change our concepts of what we seek. Reference data that so modify the course of our search also become information. The inquiry and answer process is a feedback process; it is the strength of a good information retrieval system when one can obtain rapid access to the information and at the same time can restate the inquiry as a result. This allows the user to search and retrieve information in a dialog process between man and the data bank.

The computer data bank also provides a constantly updated storage of data. As an example, consider the updating of simple facts like telephone numbers. Each day in the U.S. there are 80,000 changes or additions to listed numbers. Each day there are ten million inquiries to information operators; each question and answer now consumes an average of 12 seconds. It is obvious that updating the data bank and speeding up referrals to it can justify a computer even if what is retrieved is a tiny block of data—one phone number for each inquiry. The annual transactions of many industries have grown substantially over the past decades, as is shown in Table 8-2. These transactions are accurately recorded in large data banks.

There are two major classes of information retrieval services. The first provides information of a scientific or technical nature. The second is the information retrieval system for general information, such as real estate information or theatre information. Both types of systems are currently available. We are moving into an age when intelligent persons in all professions will use computer terminals to supplement their personal knowledge. This combination of man and computer will yield an age of *symbiotic man*. Man's abilities will be extended by the aid of the computer information retrieval system.

Information retrieval systems deal with data, records and files. Each piece of raw information the system receives is called a *data item*. A collection of such data items is called a *record*. If a data bank were to store information about an employee, the employee record would contain, for example, the name, city, occupation and age of each person. Records are collected into logical units called *files*. The arrangement and interrelation of records in a file form a *data structure*. The field in computer science concerned with the study and application of data structures, files, records and information retrieval is often called *information science*.

The speed of modern computers allows for a random-search retrieval system and unstructured files that are useful for storing certain data (see Ch. 6). Since

FIGURE 8–6   The HP 1000, Model 80 information storage and retrieval system is capable of maintaining the records for a region or division of a company or all the records for a medium-size company. The central processing unit is located in the desk (lower left), and a display terminal is used for input and inquiry. The data is stored in disk storage units mounted in the cabinet with magnetic tape drives. This system provides interactive real-time multi-terminal access. *Courtesy Hewlett-Packard Company*.

the unstructured file does not require a given piece of data to be stored in a particular location, it is not necessary to predefine and prestructure such a file. As a result, one has the ability to extract and integrate data from unique or nonstandard format documentation, in spite of the fact that most of the data entered into computer storage is repetitive format information from tabulations or standard forms. A medium-sized information storage and retrieval system is shown in Figure 8−6.

One of the most important functions in the input of data is the indexing of the material received. Indexing is the characterization of records (*e.g.*, by descriptive phrases) which permits effective retrieval of the stored data. The most commonly used index schemes are key-word oriented. Important data should be indexed in detail while less important information receives less detailed indexing. No one indexing system is identified as best for all applications.

Typical indexing systems are the key-word in context indexing (KWIC) system and the alphabetical subject indexing system. A key-word is a term selected to describe the subject content of the input material and is usually drawn from the specific text or title. While matching or combining key words to locate stored data is generally not practical or efficient in manual search systems, a computer is ideally suited to this matching process. The use of key-word indexing allows the computer the flexibility of handling inquiries that cannot be predicted during the preparation of the data base. The development of an information system includes people, software, hardware and a data bank as shown in Figure 8−7.

The art and science of developing effective information retrieval systems will be an interesting field of endeavor for the next decade at a minimum.

Information retrieval systems have potential application in many diverse fields. The following various types of data have been stored in data banks:

(1) Abstracts of technical articles
(2) Legal case decisions
(3) Characteristics of equipment in an industry
(4) Physical properties of chemicals
(5) Records of the maintenance of automobiles
(6) Crime records of a municipality.

For example, the International Association of Chiefs of Police established a goal of a national crime information system. In Washington, D. C., a file of 330,000 active criminal records is available for tens of thousands of inquiries each day from anywhere in the nation. The California Highway Patrol has a computer coupled to the computer at the Federal Bureau of Investigation. A centralized file for stolen autos and porperty and a file for over 100,000 wanted persons comprise part of the national system. This system aids in the pursuit of wanted criminals and the recovery of stolen property in the U. S. and Canada. The FBI National Crime Information Center handles over 100,000 transactions per day.

Several computer information retrieval systems are being developed for

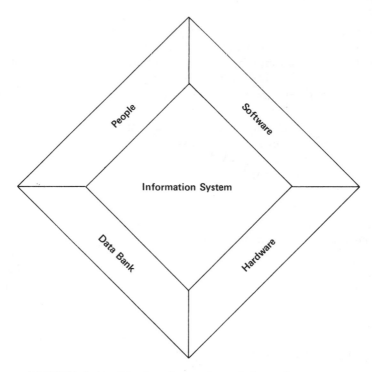

FIGURE 8–7   The four factors in an information system.

aiding the legal system. A large number of civil suits reach the United States courts. One result is a flood of legal precedents which may or may not be significant to a particular case and which may make achieving a rapid and just settlement difficult.

The computer is an ideal tool for assisting lawyers in their search for precedents. The lawyer of the future may well use the terminal in his office to instruct distant computers to carry out a search for him and to display legal information. One lawyer might use the computer to search fo a statute related to a particular case. Setting up the necessary files for such a system, however, will take a vast amount of work and time.

A computer information retrieval system for the U. S. laws has been developed.[3] If an attorney needs to examine the laws of all states, a requirement that occurs often, this effort can require the perusal of 26,000 law tomes. The company which is developing the computer system has stored in the data bank all the statutes of the 50 states, the U. S. Code and 14 volumes of U. S. Supreme Court decisions.[3] The service, now available, is invaluable to legislators who need to research all the existing codes in force. Depending on the difficulty of the search, the length of time for a search can vary from a minute to eight hours. The

FIGURE 8–8   The Dow Jones News/Recall information terminal System 7. This system
also provides data on stocks, bonds, options and commodities. *Courtesy
Bunker-Ramo Corporation.*

system currently used requires about eight hours for a search of statues in all 50
states. The LEXIS computer system incorporates most corporate law decisions. It
contains 1.25 billion words of legal data. The legal system of the United States
should be aided in the future by the availability of legal-inquiry systems for
researching legal statutes and precedents. This system will enable the country to
provide the ready access to a trial and justice our democracy requires for the individual.

Information concerning 6,000 companies is stored in the Dow Jones
News/Recall (DJN/R) system. Using the stock symbol, one can display all
reports on any recorded company. Quotations of prices, volumes, revenues and
other vital statistics are available for the 6,000 companies. Information about industries, stocks, government commissions, and other economic statistics are all
held in the DJN/R data bank. The terminal for the system is shown in Figure
8–8.

The U. S. Patent Office has 3.5 million U. S. patents and 7 million non-U. S.

patents stored in its manual files. In an ideal system all the patent data items would be converted to computer data and stored in a data bank. The total amount of patent data is approximately 600 billion characters, which exceeds the current on-line capability of computer information retrieval systems. However, an on-line storage of patent abstracts is feasible and is currently being planned by the U. S. Patent Office.

Of course, these are many applications of data banks and information retrieval systems to industry, government, and education. One of the most important applications of information retrieval systems is to libraries. This application is examined in the following section.

8.3   INFORMATION RETRIEVAL AND LIBRARIES

The rate at which man has been accumulating and storing useful knowledge has been growing for several thousand years. The invention of writing and the invention of movable type in the 15th century are two landmarks in the history of recorded knowledge. Prior to 1500, Europe was producing approximately 1000 new books per year. By 1950, the rate had increased so that Europe was producing 120,000 titles per year. By the end of the 1960's the output of books in the world had approached the rate of 1000 titles per day.[6, 14] The number of journals and articles is also rapidly growing. On a worldwide basis, scientific and technical literature is produced at a rate of 60 million pages a year. Is is the computer which has assisted the recent acceleration of the growth of knowledge, and the computer will assist in the storage and retrieval of this vast amount of new knowledge.

A library is a repository of books, journals, newspapers, and other printed material which can be used for reading and examination. The word library comes from the Latin word *liber*, which means "book." Traditionally, the library has been a storehouse of books. With the increasing number of books and journals and the increased literacy of our population, the need for automation in the libraries has grown.

There are three main types of libraries: the public library, usually a general collection with emphasis on current publications; the special library, with mostly current material focused on one or more fairly narrow areas of interest; and the academic library, with both current and historical material in all the fields covered by the educational and research programs, plus some coverage of the intellectual life of the world at large.

The academic library must have both depth and breadth, which explains why Harvard University has eight million volumes and why there are nearly a hundred other universities in this country with over a million. Each of these hundred annually buys more than 5% of the titles published in the world. (Each library with a million titles holds half of 1% of all the titles published since Gutenberg.)

At the IBM Advanced Systems Development Division library in Los Gatos, California, an on-line, totally integrated system has been in operation for several years. It establishes continuity and consistency among the basic library procedures, beginning from a single bibliographic input. Each of the library functions—acquisition, receiving, cataloging and circulation—has been automated. Each is an individual module.

The system now in operation utilizes direct on-line communication with a computer to capture bibliographic data correctly and completely. This input is then processed to provide the computer printouts for the record-keeping functions of the library. Twice a week, an updated listing of all items in circulation is printed. The computer also issues a statistical report of how many items have been borrowed, how many requested and how many reserved. Moreover, a complete list of reserve requests is issued, indicating the names of people requesting each item. All this information provides the librarian with precise knowledge of what books are in circulation and who has them. It also suggests titles in demand, for which the library should consider purchasing additional copies.

In general, libraries will be utilizing computers increasingly, along with the associated peripheral computer technology in the future decade. For example, microform and microfilm techniques, computer indexing, and automated abstracting and extracting will be a few among the many new aids to libraries. One possible consequence of automation in libraries is that of libraries becoming elements of one or more integrated networks.[9] Through a computer network, the availability of materials could be increased in libraries of all kinds and sizes in the nation. System Development Corporation, in a recent study of libraries and the use of computers, recommended the following five projects:

(1) A prototype network of regional libraries
(2) An expanded, computer-based National Union Catalog
(3) A national bibiography
(4) A national referral and loan network
(5) A national library storage and microform depository system

Some of the possible consequences of the introduction of computer automated libraries are:

(1) Use of microforms, microfilms and digital information for storage of information (supplementing or replacing storage methods now in use)
(2) A shift of operation from *circulation* to outright *distribution*
(3) Providing users with a high order of ready access to reference materials

We have already mentioned the use of microforms and microfilms. In terms of storage, 10,000 pages can be recorded on an area the size of one page of this book. Also, microforms and microfilm can be located, retrieved, and read by means of computer-controlled peripheral equipment such as computer microfilm readers. Distribution of printed materials has been largely by means of quick copying machines placed in libraries. Over a billion pages of copies of articles or pages of a book are made each year in libraries in the U.S.

The costs of providing access to all materials in a library are significantly higher as one increases the automation of libraries and attempts to decrease the response time for a request. However, the development of systems for ready access will provide computer-aided reference services in the future. For example, computer automation of the library card catalog still is not economically feasible, but should become feasible as new developments occur.

Four areas of automated library activities have been attempted: bookkeeping operations connected with ordering and receiving departments; handling catalog data for books, sometimes accompanied by book catalogs printed by computer; circulation control; and information retrieval of technical data, law citations and bibliographical citations.

The Library of Congress is the library of the United States whose first obligation is to meet the information needs of the Congress, but in many ways it also serves as a national library. The Library of Congress has about 60 million items and the official catalog contains some 16.5 million records.[8] The library collects material from all over the world and receives material written in 125 languages. It houses the largest and most varied collection of any library in this country and also provides a national bibliographic service. The United States, unlike most other countries, does not have an organized national bibliography to announce materials published in the country. Through its printed-card service and book catalogs, the Library of Congress has assumed these functions. The library also maintains the National Union Catalog (NUC), which contains records of approximately 12.8 million titles, each record having posted to it the names of the libraries holding any particular title. Project MARC (for MAchine Readable Cataloging) is a series of ambitious experiments in computerized library processes, concentrated at present on the handling of catalog data. Since the Library of Congress is pivotal, to the degree that these experiments are successful they will affect the entire library world.

Index Medicus of the U. S. National Library of Medicine indexes more than 20,000 articles a month from approximately 3,000 journals selected from more than 20,000 received.[6]

Project INTREX (INformation TRansfer EXperiments) is a program of research directed toward the functional design of new library services at the Massachusetts Institute of Technology. One of the concerns of Project INTREX is to conduct a series of experiments to determine how the traditional library catalog can be effectively augmented and combined with on-line computer operation to provide users with a more powerful, comprehensive and useful guide to library resources. Present plans call for augmenting the traditional catalog in scope, depth and search means. For example, the augmented catalog will contain entries for reports and individual journal articles as well as the traditional entries for books. Furthermore, in addition to the title and author of each item, such things as the bibliography, an abstract, key words and key phrases of each item will be included as part of its catalog entry. A user will be able to conduct searches on nearly any combination of the data contained in a catalog entry. Present plans also call for providing alphanumeric communication between user and computer by means of a high-speed, flexible display console.

The advancing technology coupled with the computer will alter the use of libraries in the future. Trips to the library may become unnecessary. With the use of still-experimental display devices, the reader may be able to request the printed material of interest to him and view it on a screen in his home or office.

8.4   DATA BANKS, INFORMATION RETRIEVAL AND PRIVACY

Computer information systems containing data about individuals are needed increasingly in the public sector to record such items as census data, medical statistics and Social Security records. Governments need these records to carry out their responsibilities; planners and social scientists need them to understand society and to suggest measures to take it in the directions considered desirable; business need the records for effective operations, service and management.

These systems which contain the information are increasingly being integrated within larger networks of data banks. Integrated systems provide accurate, consistent data at lower costs and with greater coverage than do isolated data banks. The availability of computer terminals and the ease of communication also increase the tendency to integrate and interconnect data banks.

The ready availability of information about persons stored in data banks leads to a concern in our nation about the privacy and security of information and the possible misuse of such information. Privacy and security are in many ways different issues. Security relates to the safeguarding of the information stored within a computer data bank. Privacy means the protection of the individual from (1) unreasonable observation; (2) unreasonable usurpation of his name or likeness; and (3) unauthorized access to personal or confidential information. Privacy is a social question, while security is largely a technical question. The development of technical systems to provide secure data banks is currently being accomplished. A secure system is one that will not allow entry by unauthorized individuals. Security checks such as codes, passwords and guards will help to insure that the data stored within a machine is secure. To protect computer-stored information from unauthorized use or modification, elaborate mechanisms such as encipherment of information, authentication procedures, and devices by which users can be identified by voice or handprints are used.[12]

Privacy is the more difficult problem to solve. This problem requires legislation as well as responsibility on the part of the individual who is seeking information to limit his searching and his questions to that information for which he has immediate need and which he is qualified to know.[12, 14]

Untold amounts of information about individuals have existed heretofore. However, the mechanical means for retaining and disseminating this information have been sufficiently difficult to limit use of that information. The citizen's records with selective service, the military, the Veterans' Administration, the Internal Revenue Service, the FBI and any number of other agencies remained just that: a record of past activities on file with the respective agencies. The computer, however, has made possible the exchange of such information to an instantaneous basis so that, if necessary, all such information can be brought together.

The question of privacy is not limited to the citizen's dealings with his government. In business, particularly in the business of retail credit information, great danger for the individual exists. Here, there is an established practice of collecting all derogatory information about individuals from whatever sources may be available and holding such information for call from respective member businesses (primarily retailers and banks) who want to know the individual's credit record before extending him credit.[14]

There are some 2500 credit-reporting agencies which collect and store this information in data banks.

The conflict between the state's need for information and individual freedom has long been a social issue. The computer not only has intensified this conflict; it has also changed its character, which is as much political and social as it is technical. The balance is between the values of civil liberties against those of efficiency and secrecy in government operations. For example, several social scientists and statisticians have suggested the creation and maintenance of a national data bank. Its use would remedy many defects of current records and procedures which result in information unresponsive to the needs of vital policy decisions. A lucid and helpful discussion of the necessary legal safeguards to insure privacy in a computer society is provided in an article by Alan F. Westin, a noted legal scholar and professor of law and government. The article is abstracted below.[12]

It has always been American political policy to limit the surveillance of citizens. This is one principle of the Constitution. However, when the Constitution was written, there were only two main ways to observe the citizenry: physical and psychological-judicial. Without electronic listening devices, the only way surveillance could be conducted was by entering places to listen and observe. Citizens might be tortured to give information. They could also be forced by the courts to testify against themselves. This primitive form of surveillance, common in the 18th century, was specifically forbidden by the American Constitution.

By the end of the 19th century, however, the technology that makes it possible for a man to talk to another miles away also raised the possiblity of invasion of privacy. Even early telephones were tapped, and the invention of the microphone made it possible to plant "bugs" for surveillance work as early as the 1890's. Fortunately it was early established that evidence from such surveillance was not admissible in court.

As the country became fully industrialized, and as income taxes were instituted, record-keeping increased on a massive scale. This was particularly true in the period between the World Wars. Still the citizen was protected from invasion of his privacy by the inability of the government to process, organize, and put to use the great amounts of raw data it collected on most citizens.

Now, as we suggest above, the development of data banks and retrieval procedures makes it possible to know and use many different kinds of information. The citizen stands alone; in fact, he is more than alone. His very integrity can be dismantled. He may be made the subject of psychological inquiries, the results of which can be made part of his permanent "Record" and ultimately used against him. Such inquiries can be made through tests administered directly or indirectly, or through devices like the so-called "Lie Detector," or polygraph, which themselves can be administered without the knowledge of the subject.

Information-gathering, and to some extent information-sharing as well, is not restricted to government agencies, of course. Private clubs, schools and even churches are all joining a general movement toward amassing more and more information about their membership.

In addition, the economy has been moving toward a no-cash method of operation, as described previously. In order for the banks and charge plans to function they must collect and share information about individual card-holders.

One might wish for a government that could ignore this potentially enormous base for surveillance. However, under the most benign conditions any government would be tempted to take and to use information about individuals for such otherwise worthy projects as statistical analyses of labor force, minimum wages, welfare, and even highway and utility planning. Even if this information were to be used in an aggregate, in the beginning it "belongs" to the citizen, and putting it to use without his knowledge or his ability to disagree with it is an invasion of his privacy.

Well-meaning citizens may set about to remedy this situation, but the problem has many components. American law does not define personal information as having value, although ironically it does assign value to business information, patents, and the like.

Another problem we face in ensuring privacy for the individual is that there is no way for the citizen to talk back if information about him has been falsely stated. This area of potential conflict is most prone to violation of the due process provisions of the Constitution. If you have ever had a bank error reported as an overdraft in your checking account, and you have tried to get the error corrected, you can easily imagine what would happen if your record with the IRS were similarly first damaged, then used against you.

Finally, the very impartiality of data information banks may work to the disadvantage of the individuals reported in them. It is possible to ask for important information about either a large or a small population. The small population could be a single citizen. It must be arranged, therefore, to bar operators from extracting any given single data files.

What all this suggests is first that the citizen should have the right to refuse to report or to have circulated information about himself. The key to this conception is in the First Amendment to the Constitution. Possibly information could be divided into classes or types, ranging from harmless information open to everybody (*e.g.*, birth date) to highly limited and confidential information. It is also obvious that laws must be made which would allow only restricted use for any given kind of information.

All that has been said about the inherent dangers of information processing on a national scale can also be said about intelligence procedures.

Although we do not now have the legal machinery to ensure that the individual's privacy can be protected while stores of information are amassed and used, we do have historical precedents for arranging such legal devices. Naturally it is to be hoped that our elected officials will work out the proper protections within these traditions, and in time and in such a way that the many benefits from use of computers will be accompanied by means of oppression or violation of individual rights.

Professor Westin described the need for a new legal approach to the computer storage and processing of personal information. Recently Westin has suggested that a "writ of habeas data" should be required to justify the use of computerized information against and individual just as a writ of habeas corpus requires that the state justify an individual's imprisonment.

California has recently passed into law legislation which (1) recognizes an individual's right of privacy, and (2) designates computerized data in state files as "public records." This legislation may well prove to be a landmark in the fight to establish a right to privacy and would seem to guarantee the right of an individual to read his own file.[15]

It has been recommended that the nation draft model statutes and develop ethical guidelines which would permit data to be disseminated without violating due process—*e.g.*, the individual's right to defend himself against punitive action taken by the data recipient; the individual's right to protection against self-incrimination, and his right of appeal to a higher authority when an administrative agency controlling a data bank takes an action which he opposes concerning his file. Also, a public review committee might be established for the purpose of an annual audit of each data bank's operation in terms of civil liberties. The committee could be made up of representatives from various legal, professional and occupational groups, and should include some persons experienced in the particular field of policy of the data system.

Several recent books have listed possible legal actions to account for the new forces in society due to the impact of the computer.[11, 15] Some of the suggested legal actions include:

1. The establishment of a Privacy Commission with the authority to license and to require an impact statement for each operating or proposed data bank.

2. A register of data banks should be established, including the following information:
   a. The name and address of the person responsible for the operation of the data bank
   b. The nature of the data stored or to be stored therein
   c. The purpose for which data is stored therein
   d. The class of persons authorized to extract data therefrom
3. As far as possible, facts, not opinions, should be stored.
4. All interrogations of data banks should be automatically logged.
5. The public should have the right to inspect records stored in the data banks.
6. The individual should have the right to take issue with personal data stored about him.
7. Aged data should be removed.
8. Security procedures should be registered with a national auditing agency.

In a sense, what has been proposed in many instances is the development of an Information Bill of Rights, which would guarantee the right of access by a citizen to his data file, the right to review it and correct it, and the right to appeal its use to an ombudsman.

Since the United States has become a records-oriented society, the capacity of the computer has led government and organizations to collect and to store more detailed and intrusive personal information about individuals than had ever been possible before. Abuses of record-keeping existed in previous manual systems; they have been carried over to computer systems.[11] For example, Social-security numbers are increasingly being used as the connecting link by which computer data banks can exchange confidential information.

Because of the citizens' Constitutionally-derived rights to know what evidence is being used against them, and to cross-examine their accusers, there has been a movement toward legislation for privacy. President Ford signed Public Law 93–579, the Privacy Act of 1974, into being on December 14, 1974. This law applies to all federal information systems. It requires standards of accuracy, relevance, timeliness, and completeness in using or transferring data to agencies.[14, 15] Each federal agency is required to publish a description of all its data banks annually; all agencies are also required to permit persons to inspect records about them personally.

Sweden has enacted legislation establishing a Data Inspection Board which screens applications from public and private agencies or firms to establish data banks. The Data Inspection Board may grant or revoke permission to keep data banks. No data bank may list criminal records or psychiatric treatment except with the permission of the Board. Individuals listed in a data bank are entitled to free printouts of their files. Every Swede gets a number at birth to be used for the data banks. Sweden has established an elaborate system of protection for its citizens.

"Privacy can be expensive in dollars, efficiency and organizational rationality, and not every measure that promises to increase our right to be let alone may seem justified when balanced against these expenses for consumers, managers and taxpayers," comments Professor Westin.[20] The proper balance will be achieved during the 1980s.

SUMMARY

The computer is a useful device for information storage, processing and retrieval. With the advent of relatively low cost storage the computer lends itself to the development of data banks. A data bank is an on-line storage unit retaining

FIGURE 8–9   © Sidney Harris. Used with permission.

large masses of data. Data banks are used to retain economic, social and industrial data among others. A terminal is one possible access connection for the potential user. A computer data bank is automated, of high speed, and it usually operates at a reasonable cost per item stored.

Information is the meaning assigned to the data or an aggregate representation of the data. It is the desired output of an information retrieval system. Information retrieval is the process of accumulating, classifying, storing and searching large amounts of data and extracting the required information from it. The quality of an information retrieval system is measured by how much relevant information, in comparison to how much irrelevant information, is provided in response to a query. Information retrieval systems have been developed for airlines, government functions, and the legal profession among others.

Computer information retrieval systems will aid in the operation of the libraries of the future. Computers are being used for automated acquisitions, receiving, cataloging and circulation. The primary items of cost for automated libraries will be the amount of information stored and the response time required as a result of an inquiry. In the future, a device in the home or the office may display information upon request.

Computer information systems containing information about individuals are increasingly necessary to govern and manage our complex society. However, the ready availability of information about persons leads to a concern about the privacy of information. Privacy, in this context, is primarily concerned with unauthorized access to personal or confidential information. The conflict between the need for accumulating information in a data bank, and the protection of an individual's freedom, must be reconciled. An illustration of this conflict is shown in Figure 8-9. What may be required in the future is an Information Bill of Rights for the citizen.

CHAPTER 8 PROBLEMS

P8-1. Differentiate between the concepts of *data* and *information*.

P8-2. Discuss the difference between a data bank and an information retrieval system.

P8-3. Determine if the storage and retrieval of the students' academic records at your college would be appropriate for a computer information retrieval system.

P8-4. If an information retrieval system were developed as proposed in Problem 8-3, would a problem arise concerning the privacy of the students' confidential records?

P8-5. A measure of information might be, in a particular case, a student's grade point average up-to-date, or the balance in his checking account. If possible, establish a query for this piece of information and determine the quality of relevant information received. (Refer to Section 8–2.)

P8–6. A medical information network provides a user access to data stored in Bethesda, Maryland. The user may access the computer from terminals located throughout the United States.[6] Obtain information about the National Library of Medicine from your local user center, if possible. Determine the annual usage of the network. Discuss the advantages of the system.

P8–7. The over-the-counter securities market has an on-line national network for prices and quotations (NASDAQ). Visit a local stockbroker and watch the system in action. How many stocks are maintained in the data bank?

P8–8. A typical rent-a-car agency has over 1,000 terminals connected to its reservation computer. Determine for a large auto rental agency (a) the size of its computer; (b) the number of transactions completed each year.

P8–9. There are about 5,000 government data banks in the United States. What are the possible implications of this large number of data banks and their potential interconnection?

P8–10. Approximately one-half of the 17,000 travel agents in the United States use a computer reservation and ticket system that connects directly to the airline computers.[5] Visit a local travel agent and investigate the system in use.

P8–11. Control Data Corporation offers a solar energy technology data bank called *Technotec*. Contact your local CDC office and inquire about the data bank and its characteristics.

CHAPTER 8 REFERENCES

1. C. J. Date, *An Introduction to Database Systems*, 2nd Edition, Addison-Wesley Publishing Co., Reading, Massachusetts, 1979.
2. O. H. Bray and H. A. Freeman, *Data Base Computers*, Lexington Books, Lexington, Massachusetts, 1979.
3. L. M. Bronscomb, "Computing and Communications—A Perspective of the Evolving Environment," *IBM Systems Journal*, Vol. 18, No. 2, 1979, pp. 189–201.
4. F. W. Hondius, "Computers: Data Privacy," *IEEE Spectrum*, March 1980, pp. 67–70.
5. "Computer Rescue for Travel Agents," *Business Week*, April 7, 1980, pp. 81–82.
6. T. E. Doszkocs *et. al.*, "Automated Information Retrieval in Science and Technology," *Science*, April 4, 1980, pp. 25–30.

7. "A Computer Watchdog for Securities Trading," *Business Week*, May 5, 1980, p. 42.
8. F. G. Withington, "Coping With Computer Proliferation," *Harvard Business Review*, June 1980, pp. 152–164.
9. D. S. Stein, "Data Banks: How to Know Everything," *Output*, June 1980, pp. 36–41.
10. D. C. Tsichritzis and F. H. Lochovsky, *Data Base Management Systems*, Academic Press, Inc., New York, 1977.
11. D. B. Parker, *Crime by Computer*, Scribner's Sons, New York, 1976, pp. 242–246.
12. A. F. Westin, "Legal Safeguards to Insure Privacy in a Computer Society," *Communications of the Association for Computing Machinery, Vol. 10, No. 9, 1967.*
13. *J. A. Sproul, "Computer Assisted Legal Research," American Bar Foundation Research Journal*, 1976, No. 1, pp. 175–226.
14. M. L. Dertouzos and J. Moses, *The Computer Age*, MIT Press, Cambridge, Massachusetts, 1980, Chapter 12.
15. L. J. Hoffman, *Modern Methods for Computer Security and Privacy*, Prentice-Hall, Inc., Englewood Cliffs, New Jersey, 1977.
16. H. J. Watson and A. B. Carroll, *Computers for Business*, Business Publications, Inc., Dallas, Texas, 1980, Chapter 16.
17. A. T. F. Hutt, *The Design of a Relational Data Base Management System*, Wiley and Sons, Inc., New York, 1980.
18. M. Vetter, *Data Base Design Methodology*, Prentice-Hall, Inc., Englewood Cliffs, New Jersey, 1980.
19. J. G. Burch *et. al.*, *Information Systems: Theory and Practice*, Wilcy and Sons, Inc., New York, 1979.
20. D. Whieldon, "How Much Will Privacy Cost?" *Computer Decisions*, August 1979, pp. 54–62.
21. A. F. Westin, "The Impacts on Privacy," *Datamation*, December 1979, pp. 190–194.
22. R. E. Smith, *Privacy: How to Protect It*, Anchor/Doubleday Inc., Garden City, New York, 1979.
23. K. C. Landon, "Privacy and Federal Data Banks," *Society*, February 1980, pp. 50–56.
24. W. Kiechel, "Everything You Wanted to Know May Soon Be on Line," *Fortune*, May 5, 1980, pp. 226–8.
25. G. Salton, "Automatic Information Retrieval," *IEEE Computer*, September 1980, pp. 41–55.

9

SIMULATION AND GAMES

9.1 COMPUTER MODELING AND SIMULATION

Modeling and simulation are of great value to business, industry and government because they permit one to study the effects of various decisions or choices without going through the complete process of the phenomenon being considered. In a sense, the computer is cast in the role of an actor. By lowering the effective cost of calculating compared with experimenting, the computer induced a shift toward calculation in many fields where once only experimentation and measurement were practical.[1] In some cases, such as that of the Apollo spacecraft, a simulation of the phenomenon is necessary prior to the actual experiment. In this section we consider the development and use of computer models which aid in the evaluation of ideas and the study of real or hypothetical situations. This use of computer models is called *computer simulation*.

A model is a qualitative or quantitative representation of a process, showing the effects of those factors which are significant for the purposes being considered.[2] Models exist in most sciences and many businesses. When a computer is applied to this service, we have a *computer model*, defined as:

COMPUTER MODEL   A representation of a system or phenomenon in a mathematical or symbolic form suitable for demonstrating the behavior of the system or phenomenon.

Modeling is the process of making a model. The model may not represent the actual phenomenon in all respects, but it should adequately describe the essential characteristics.

Simulation involves subjecting models to various stimuli or situations in such a way as to explore the nature of the results which might be obtained by the real system:[2]

> SIMULATION   The use of models and the actual conditions of either the thing being modeled or the environment in which it operates, with the models or conditions in physical, mathematical, or some other form.

Simulation is used to explore the results which might be obtained from the real system by subjecting the model to representative environments which are equivalent to, or in some way representative of, the situations the investigator wants to understand. Simulation allows the investigator to obtain the essence of a phenomenon or system without requiring all of the reality to be duplicated.

Through abstraction of pertinent information from the real world, we attempt to reproduce, in the computer, all conditions important to the entity he wishes to explore. Once these conditions have been incorporated into a computer simulation, the computer can be used to change, rearrange or improve upon the information it has been given.

In many ways, simulation is an art as well as a science. The effectiveness of any computer simulation rests on the user's ability to abstract only those factors that affect the system or process he wishes to duplicate. Reality is simulation's starting point, but not its boundary; simulation experts can mold the starting situation into uncounted situations and thereby can also predict future consequences. These facts are suggested by the composite Möbius Strip in Figure 9–1, which relates the moonscape to equations for celestial navigation and to human physiology.

Although in this chapter we limit our discussion to computer simulation, simulation using physical equivalents has had an interesting history. Some very useful early simulations were a simulation of muscle fascicle using ropes; a simulation of electric eels using pewter, wood, glass and leather, and a simulation of electric potentials in nerve and muscle, using zinc and copper. The modelers were Alfonso Borelli, who made one of the first convincing attempts to reduce a physiological phenomenon to purely mechanical principles; Lord Henry Cavendish, who used simulation to establish the argument that electrical phenomena could occur in animals; and Emil duBois-Reymond, who is often said to have founded modern electro-physiology and who used a simulation to help derive his most famous theory, the Peripolar Molecular Theory.

Prior to 1940, the then relatively low-performance aircraft could be flight-tested by skilled pilots with an acceptable risk. However, the high-performance aircraft and spacecraft designed during the past three decades required preflight test by simulation. Furthermore, as flight simulators became available it became

FIGURE 9–1 Möbius strip suggesting simulation
of lunar landing.
*Courtesy of SDC
Corporation.*

economically feasible to use them for flight training. During World War II, the
Link Trainer was used to train many pilots. Currently, simulators which provide
realistic mockup cockputs with motion and out-the-window visual cues simulate
actual flying conditions so accurately that it is quite easy for a pilot to become ab-
sorbed in his duties to such an extent that he forgets he is not actually flying.[3]

In 1969, the United States landed the first men on the moon and brought
them back safely. This task would have been very costly in lives and expense
without simulation of the flight for testing and training purposes. The only alternative to simulation, in this case, would have been trial-and-error flights. The
importance of simulation is highlighted by Walter Schirra's remark from Apollo
7 in space, when ground control suggested that he try something new: "Uh-uh.
Not till I've tried it in the simulator first."

Figure 9–2 shows a training device based upon simulation. It is in operation
as scientists at the Langley Research Center of the National Aeronautics and
Space Administration (NASA) conduct simulation tests to determine human
ability to control braking maneuvers for lunar landings. These tests are part of an
extensive NASA program at Langley for guidance and control of spacecraft for
landing upon the moon's surface. The initial condition for these simulations is
assumed to be the point of horizontal braking from a lunar orbit at a moon
altitude of about 25 miles. The pilot operates a hydraulic analog simulator as

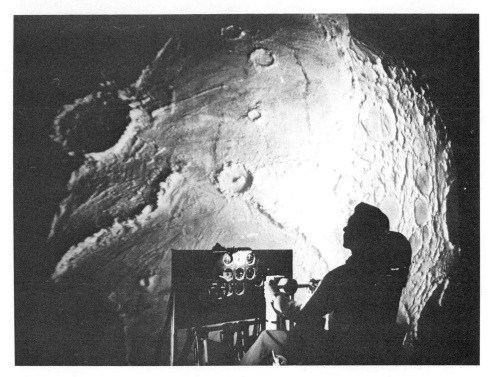

FIGURE 9–2   Simulation test equipment for lunar landings. *Courtesy of NASA.*

though it were a vertical-landing spaceship. A stand at the pilot's right holds a
slide projector for projection of the lunar surface upon a curved background.

When an explosion crippled Apollo 13, the crisis was resolved by using the
simulator at Cape Kennedy—while Apollo 13 drifted along its course without its
normal cabin oxygen supply. The Command Module Simulator was built to provide astronaut training. It consists of a digital computer complex that provides
dynamic representations of spacecraft systems, a complete and accurate presentation of exterior visual scenes, and an exact replica of the spacecraft interior.[3]
This simulator is used to conduct tests to determine human ability to control
braking maneuvers for lunar landings. An external view of the Command
Module Simulator is shown in Figure 9–3. The simulated vehicle is an exact
replica of the interior of the Apollo spacecraft as shown in Figure 9–4. All the
switches, instruments and other details are exact. The views out the windows and
telescope are simulated optically. The computation needed to drive the simulation
is done by a complex of four digital computers acting as a single unit to provide
real-time simulations of all Command Module subsystems throughout the mission. Furthermore, by simulating the Saturn subsystems, a realistic enactment of

FIGURE 9–3   External view of the command module simulator, completely surrounded
by the out-the-window visual display system. The instructor-operator station is shown in the foreground. *Courtesy of NASA.*

the launch-booster and translunar injection portions of the mission is provided.
The computers also generate telemetry information in actual format for transmission to ground station equipment. Changes in routines caused by malfunctions
and other special inputs are also simulated.[4]

Simulation techniques are not limited to the aerospace and aeronautics
fields. They are being applied with great success to the design of large office
buildings by architects, who find the reduction of complex, interrelated design
elements to accurate visual displays invaluable. Designers can now project, with
the computer, precisely how a building or landscape will look in ten or twenty
years, given a particular set of circumstances. They can also pretest their building
plans for maximum effectiveness before the cornerstone is laid.

A major airline created a computer model to study its proposed computerized
ticket-reservation system. The model used in this study projected that the reservation system would not work as designed unless larger computers were used. The
airline didn't believe it, and was later forced almost to double its computer
capacity.[6]

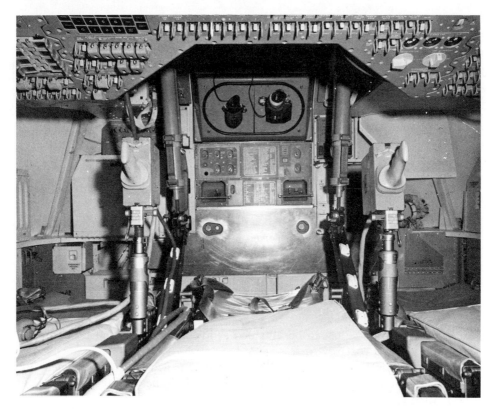

FIGURE 9–4 Internal view of command module simulator showing instruments and controls which duplicate exactly the details of the Apollo spacecraft. *Courtesy of NASA.*

We can trace the history of mathematical models from the beginnings of mathematics. One early example of a mathematical model is the Pythagorean theorem, which dates from the sixth century B.C. in Greece. Besides mathematical models we note the early existence of analog models such as world globes, relief maps and wind tunnels. An early use of simulation was developed hundreds of years ago when leaders of opposing armies would study military tactics by moving miniature soldiers around on a scale model of a battlefield. This concept is still with us, except that the "war games" are simulated on a digital computer.[5]

There is an increasingly large class of systems and problems which cannot easily be modeled by using mathematical techniques. Such systems as an airline ticket-reservation network, movement of a tank-car fleet, complex manufacturing systems, transportation networks, military logistics systems and capital investment are examples. These systems are complex and difficult to define. Simulation of these systems can be achieved by building a simulation of symbolic processes which are equivalent to those that occur in the actual system. In developing the digital computer simulation, the analyst describes the system structure and logic (or operating rules) to the computer by means of a program. Simpler simulations of this nature, and simulations where efficient use of computer time is a prime consideration, may be written in a language such as FORTRAN. The price for this efficiency, however, is substantially increased programming time and skills. As a result, specially developed simulation languages have been developed.[5,6]

Assuming that the model and the simulation are reliably accurate, the advantages of computer simulation are:

1. System performance can be observed under all conceivable conditions.
2. Results of field-system performance can be extrapolated with a simulation model for prediction purposes.
3. Decisions concerning future systems presently in a conceptual stage can be examined.
4. Trials of systems under test can be accomplished in a much-reduced period of time.
5. Simulation results can be obtained at lower cost than real experimentation would cost.
6. Study of hypothetical situations can be achieved even when the hypothetical situation would be unrealizable in actual life at the present time.
7. Computer modeling and simulation is often the only feasible or safe technique to analyze and evaluate a system.

A computer simulation may be developed in FORTRAN, BASIC or a language specifically developed for simulation. Three widely-used simulation languages are GPSS (General Purpose Simulation System), SIMSCRIPT, which is an ALGOL-based language and GASP IV.

In constructing a model with GPSS, the analyst uses special-purpose blocks which serve as the language's instructions, and then constructs a flow chart incorporating the system structure and the decision rules. SIMSCRIPT, on the other hand, is statement-oriented, rather than block-oriented. In using this language the analyst describes the system by means of English-like statements resembling those in FORTRAN and PL/1. The first step in the analysis of any particular system is to isolate the system's elements and formulate the logical rules governing their interaction. This yields a model.

Let us consider a system of ship docking which can be simulated using GPSS.[6] Cargo ships arrive at a small port with a known arrival pattern. While in port, the ships unload some of their cargo, taking a certain amount of time, and then proceed on their voyages. There is only one pier, and if a ship arrives while another is unloading, it must wait. If several ships are waiting, the one that arrived first will be unloaded first. Of interest here is the total amount of time that a ship will spend in port, including the time spent waiting for the pier to become available.

This process is illustrated graphically in Figure 9–5. The dynamic transactions are simulated in GPSS using a block notation. To provide input for the simulation, program cards are prepared from a block diagram flow chart of the system under study. The flow chart for the ship arrival system is shown in Figure 9–6. Once the system model is loaded, the GPSS program generates and moves transactions from block to block according to timing information and logical rules incorporated in the blocks. The program executes the movements and maintains a record of the time sequence. The program executes the movements and maintains a record of the time sequence. The program also maintains a record of the status of delays and the time consumed by the process. The output of the program will be:

1. The amount of ship traffic flowing through the complete system and its parts.
2. The average time for ships to pass through the system and portions of the system.

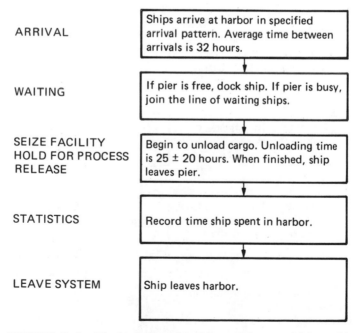

FIGURE 9–5   The logic flow for ships arriving at a harbor with one unloading dock.

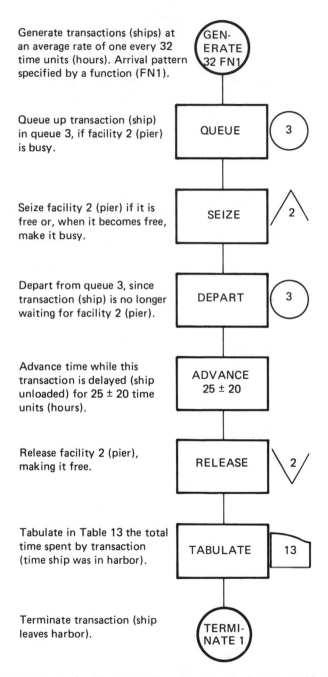

Generate transactions (ships) at an average rate of one every 32 time units (hours). Arrival pattern specified by a function (FN1).

Queue up transaction (ship) in queue 3, if facility 2 (pier) is busy.

Seize facility 2 (pier) if it is free or, when it becomes free, make it busy.

Depart from queue 3, since transaction (ship) is no longer waiting for facility 2 (pier).

Advance time while this transaction is delayed (ship unloaded) for 25 ± 20 time units (hours).

Release facility 2 (pier), making it free.

Tabulate in Table 13 the total time spent by transaction (time ship was in harbor).

Terminate transaction (ship leaves harbor).

FIGURE 9–6   The GPSS flow chart for the harbor problem.

3. The amount of use of each portion of the system.
4. The maximum and average lengths of queues occurring at various points in the system.

The simulation language GPSS can be used to solve a variety of problems. In general, these problems have one characteristic in common: they involve transactions in which people or equipment are competing for services of other people or equipment. It is of interest how well the service organization will respond to the demands. For instance, GPSS may be used for the design of a telephone system to intercept and service telephone calls automatically when the calls cannot be put through because new numbers have been assigned, or because units have been disconnected. It could also help with simulation of automobile flow patterns along roads and through intersections and toll gates to determine properly-sequenced lane segments.[6]

The simulation language GASP IV is designed to model a system involving both discrete and continuous processes.[14] In discrete simulation, for example using GPSS, the dependent variables of the model can change values only at specified times. For example, inventory levels can change only when items are received or sold. In continuous simulation models, the dependent variables may change continuously over time. GASP IV has been used to simulate global climate, insect growth in agricultural systems and insurance-company operations.[34]

The use of other simulation languages as well as FORTRAN and BASIC for the simulation of biological and chemical systems has developed during the past few years.[8] The principle of *change through time* is a basic pattern in many of life's processes. A study of evolutionary processes using simulation has many appealing facets. Recently, a simulation of a biological system was accomplished using FORTRAN. The system studied was the variation of the population of the hare (*Lepus Americanus*) over hundreds of years. It had been noted, using data from the records of the fur-trading Hudson's Bay Company dating back to 1790 and from other observations, that the sizes of various populations of the hares in eastern Canada followed a fairly regular cyclic pattern of alternating abundance and depletion. Highs of abundance occurred about every ten years. It has also been noted that the population of the Bay Lynx (*Lynx Rufus*) also had ten-year cycles and that they correlated very well with the fluctuations in the hare populations. It has been determined that 89 percent of the lynx's diet consisted of the varying hares and also that when the hares were at a population low, lynxes were often found dead of starvation or in emaciated and starving condition.

This example of the close correlation between the lynx and hare populations in Canada has been used for many years in ecological studies and biology textbooks as a classic example of a predator-prey relationship. The model chosen by the authors of the study is illustrated graphically in Figure 9–7. The seven variables identified for inclusion are:

1. Hare birth rate   HBR
2. Hare death rate   HDR
3. Lynx birth rate   LBR
4. Lynx death rate   LDR
5. Lynx kill ratio   LKR
6. Lynx-hare population ratio   LXH
7. Resource level R_h

A population block is shown for both the lynx and hare populations. The hare population increase is generated by a birth rate block which adds to the hare population block. Similarly, the natural hare decrease is generated by a hare death rate block which subtracts from the hare population block. This is equivalent to saying that the population of hares at generation (i + 1) is equal to the population at generation i plus the hares born minus the hares that died. The hare population is further reduced by the number of hares killed by lynx predation, as represented in the kill ratio block. A similar feedback relationship was established for the lynx population.

Also, the functions of the hare birth rate and death was rate versus the hare population were developed from recorded data. A similar set of functions was

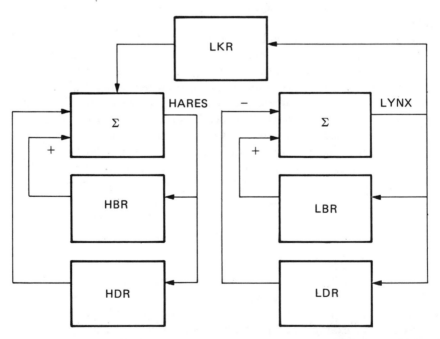

FIGURE 9–7   The functional model of the lynx-hare system. *Copyright 1970 by Simulation Councils, Inc. P.O. Box 2228, La Jolla, Cal. Reprinted by permission.*

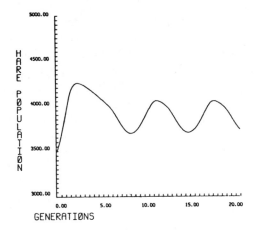

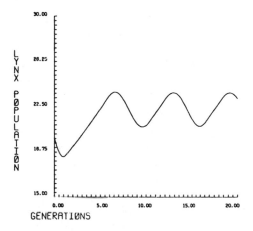

HBR = 100%
HDR = 25%
LBR = 25%
LDR = 15%
LKR = 200/1
R_h = 4000
HAREIC = 3500 (initial population)
LYNXIC = 20   (initial population)

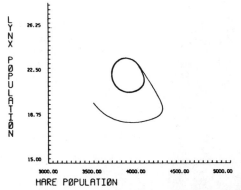

FIGURE 9–8   The variations of the lynx and hare population shown for one set of parameters over 20 generations. The lynx and hare populations are plotted together in (c). *Copyright 1970 by Simulation Councils, Inc. P.O. Box 2228, La Jolla, Cal. Reprinted by permission.*

developed for the lynx population. The parameter values of the simulated system could be entered by the user. Figure 9–8 shows the variation of the populations for a specific set of parameters. For the given set of parameters, the system is oscillatory, exhibiting the expected periodic variations in the populations. One can easily alter the parameters and establish new population variations. Thus, one could study the effects of various ecological changes.

The study of chemistry and molecular structure can be carried out by computer simulation. The graphic representation of a molecular structure is shown in Figure 9–9. The computer can be used to generate various new molecular structures as the investigator varies the parameters. In this manner the structure may be studied visually and various desirable structures may be chosen for laboratory experimentation. The human researcher, from his intuitive vantage point, guides the machine, each partner doing what he is best fitted for. The computer simulates the molecule according to the rules of physical and chemical theory. The computer represents the molecule with enough structural detail to make plausible a metaphorical identification of the computer with the molecule. The computer model used in this way, far from reducing the scientist to a passive bystander, reinforces the need for the creative human element in experimental science, if only because witless calculation is likely to be so voluminous as to be beyond the power of even the fastest computer. Human judgment and intuition must be injected at every stage to guide the computer in its search for a solution. Painstaking routine work will be less and less useful for making a scientific reputation, because such efforts can be reduced to a computer program. All that is left for the scientist to contribute is a creative imagination.[1,2]

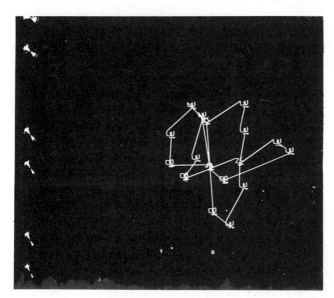

FIGURE 9–9 Graphic representation of a molecular structure. In chemical research new compounds are studied visually and molecular structures are generated by the computer as the investigator varies the parameters of the structure. *Courtesy of Adage, Inc.*

The simulated fall of water spilling over a cliff and splashing into a pool is shown in Figure 9–10. This figure is part of a series of computer simulations used for the study of the dynamic behavior of fluids accomplished by John P. Shannon of Los Alamos Scientific Laboratory. The dynamics of a liquid drop splashing into a pool have also been studied by Shannon and Francis Harlow.[17] One series of photos, obtained from a computer simulation, is shown in Figure 9–11. This series of photos shows the behavior of the free surface through the following sequence of events:

1. A crater is formed and fluid splashes to the side.
2. Fluid rushes back to fill the crater.
3. A jet column is formed along the collapse axis.
4. The jet column rises will above the initial pool surface and may break into several droplets.
5. The jet column falls back, creating a second crater and lateral wave.

The drop shown in Figure 9–11 is relatively fast-falling, with an initial speed, U_o, of 4.0 where

$$U_o = (R/2H)^{1/2}$$

and R = radius of the drop and H = the height from which the drop freely falls. This simulation results is not only dramatic, but also revealing of the dynamics of fluid movement.

The digital computer has recently been introduced as a general purpose simulator in the highschool classroom.[9] The idea is to expose students to experimentation which would not normally be available in the school laboratory. Simulation is particularly apropos for students when the experiment is too complex, expensive or dangerous to carry out in the laboratory. A computer simulation program entitled EVOLU permits the user to explore some of the factors which affect evolutionary changes. The user studies a population of pepper moths, which normally are light in color, but which produce a small percentage of

  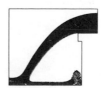 

FIGURE 9–10 Simulated waterfalls spills over the edge of a cliff and splashes into a pool in this computer experiment performed by John P. Shannon at the Los Alamos Scientific Laboratory as part of a general study of dynamic behavior of fluids with the aid of numerical models. *Courtesy of John P. Shannon.*

dark-colored mutants. He specifies the rate of production of mutants, the number of light-colored moths in the initial population, the time (in a 30-year span) at which an environmental change occurs, and whether that change is beneficial to light-colored or dark-colored, moths. This simulation parallels an occurrence in Great Britain, where, before the Industrial Revolution, the environment favored light-colored moths, but, where, since the Industrial Revolution with its concomitant air pollution, dark-colored moths are favored. A computer run of the program EVOLU is shown in Figure 9–12. The initial population is 10,000 moths, the evolutionary change occurs in the fifth year and the mutation rate is 5%.

In addition, a program entitled POLUT, which is an elementary simulation of a water-pollution situation, has been developed.

In this simulation, the user is permitted to choose the type of body of water, the water temperature, the type of waste being discharged, the rate at which it is discharged, and the type of waste treatment. Two computer results of this program are shown in Figure 9–13 and 9–14. In Figure 9–13, the results of dumping untreated sewage waste into a fast-moving stream are shown. The waste

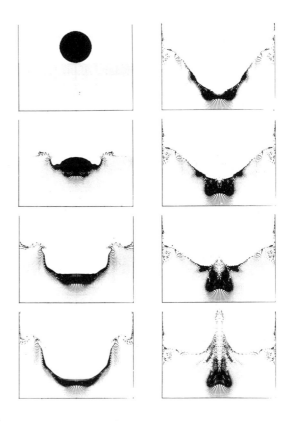

FIGURE 9–11 The cross-section of a splashing drop with an impact speed of 4.0 Photographs shown (read left, down; right, down) are t = 0, 5, 10, 15, 25, 28, 30 and 35 units of time. *Courtesy of John P. Shannon.*

WITHIN A LARGE POPULATION OF PEPPER MOTHS, THERE ARE A FEW
INDIVIDUALS WHICH SHOW UP DARKER IN COLOR THAN THE NORMAL
LIGHT COLORED MOTHS BECAUSE OF MUTATIONS.

YOU ARE GOING TO STUDY THIS POPULATION OF PEPPER MOTHS FOR 30
YEARS AND SEE WHAT HAPPENS TO THE NUMBER OF DARK AND
LIGHT MOTHS WHEN YOU ALTER ENVIRONMENTAL CONDITIONS.

SELECT A MUTATION RATE VALUE FROM 1 TO 10, WHEREIN THE HIGHER THE
NUMBER, THE HIGHER THE MUTATION RATE AND THUS THE GREATER THE
PERCENTAGE OF DARK MOTHS PRODUCED.
? 5

HOW MANY LIGHT COLORED MOTHS ARE THERE IN THE AREA? SELECT A
NUMBER FROM 1000 to 1000000? 1E4

YOU HAVE THE POWER TO CHANGE THE ENVIRONMENT.
AT WHAT POINT IN OUR THIRTY YEAR PERIOD DO YOU WANT
TO IMPLEMENT YOUR POWER? SELECT A YEAR FROM 3 THROUGH 10.
? 5

IS THE ENVIRONMENTAL CHANGE GOING TO FAVOR LIGHT MOTHS (TYPE 1)
OR DARK MOTHS (TYPE 2)? 2

IN TABLE FORM HERE IS WHAT HAPPENS TO THE POPULATIONS.

YEAR	MUTATION RATE	NUMBER OF DARK MOTHS (ADULTS)	NUMBER OF LIGHT MOTHS (ADULTS)
1	5	0	10000
2	5	0	10000
3	5	0	10000
4	5	0	10000
5	5	500	9500
6	5	975	9025
7	5	1426	8574
8	6	1855	8145
9	5	2262	7738
10	5	2649	7351
11	5	3017	6983
12	5	3366	6634
13	5	3698	6302
14	5	4013	5987
15	5	4312	5688
16	5	4596	5404
17	5	4866	5134
18	5	5123	4877
19	5	5367	4633
20	5	5599	4401
21	5	5819	4181
22	5	6028	3972
23	5	6227	3773
24	5	6416	3584
25	5	6595	3405
26	5	6765	3285
27	5	6927	3073
28	5	7081	2919
29	5	7227	2773
30	5	7366	2634

FIGURE 9–12   The printout of the program EVOLU when an environmental change occurs in the fifth year and the mutation rate is 5 percent.

```
                      WATER POLLUTION STUDY
        DO YOU WANT INSTRUCTIONS(YES=1 , NO=0)? 1

          IN THIS STUDY YOU CAN SPECIFY THE FOLLOWING CHARACTERISTICS:

        A.THE KIND OF BODY OF WATER:
            1. LARGE POND
            2. LARGE LAKE
            3. SLOW-MOVING STREAM
            4. FAST-MOVING STREAM

        B.THE WATER TEMPERATURE IN DEGREES FAHRENHEIT:

        C.THE KIND OF WASTE DUMPED INTO THE WATER:
            1. INDUSTRIAL
            2. SEWAGE

        D.THE RATE OF DUMPING OF WASTE, IN PARTS PER MILLION(PPM)/DAY:

        E.THE TYPE OF TREATMENT OF THE WASTE:
            0. NONE
            1. PRIMARY (SEDIMENTATION OR PASSAGE THROUGH FINE SCREENS
                        TO REMOVE GROSS SOLIDS)
            2. SECONDARY (SAND FILTERS OR THE ACTIVATED SLUDGE METHOD
                        TO REMOVE DISSOLVED AND COLLOIDAL ORGANIC MATTERS)

        ##########

        BODY OF WATER? 4
        WATER TEMPERATURE? 60
        KIND OF WASTE? 2
        DUMPING RATE? 10
        TYPE OF TREATMENT? 0
        DO YOU WANT:  1. A GRAPH; 2. A TABLE? 3. BOTH? 1
```

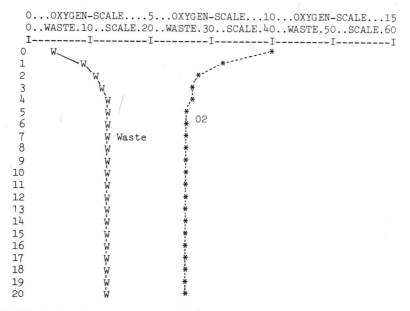

FIGURE 9–13 The printout of a program for a water pollution study, showing the effects of dumping untreated sewage into a fast-moving stream.

in the stream builds up to a constant level and is carried away by the stream. In Figure 9–14, the effects of dumping untreated industrial waste into a slow-moving stream are exhibited. The waste continues to build up and the oxygen content drops to a level where the fish begin to die. The effects of the use of waste-treatment techniques and the temperature of the water can also be studied using this program. Such uses of simulation in the schools clearly affords opportunities for students to experience certain phenomena rather than to learn about them vicariously from teachers.

The simulation of biological systems has been pursued for the past twenty years. However, recently, with increased emphasis on the environment, the simulation and study of the ecological processes in our environment have increased in importance. Professor Kenneth Watt has worked for several years with a team of scientists to develop models of various ecosystems for computer simulation.

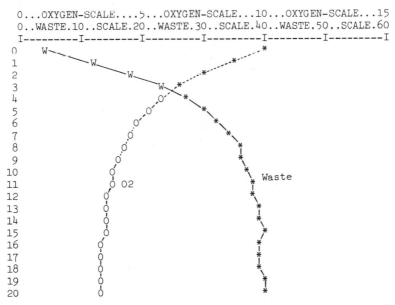

FIGURE 9–14   The printout of a program showing the effects of dumping untreated industrial waste into a slow-moving stream.

They have developed operating models of a sample county in California and selected state phenomena: crime, education, farm production, taxation, transportation and population growth. Using computer simulation, Watt's projections indicate that the world's estimated 2,100 billion barrels of oil reserves will be depleted around the year 2000. In response to intense demands for more energy, the coal reserves will be used up next. By then, atomic energy may or may not take up the slack. "If it turns out there isn't enough atomic power," says Watt, "the carrying capacity of the world will suddenly drop from somewhere between 10 billion and 20 billion people to something between 1 billion and 4 billion. This simply means starvation and perhaps violent wars between the haves and have-nots."

Professor Watt and his colleagues have also developed a simulation model for the United States called SPECULATER. A summary diagram of the model is shown in Figure 9–15. The model incorporates the transportation, economic, and agricultural sectors; it accounts for the population characteristics of the nation. Watt concludes, "agricultural exports will increase to offset the unfavorable

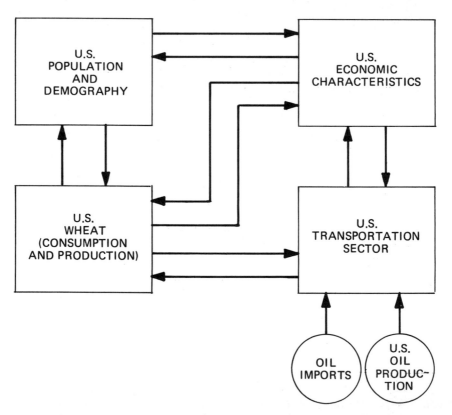

FIGURE 9–15   The basic SPECULATER model for the United States.

trade balance due to increased fuel imports.''[18] The simulation causes Watt to favor policy that would increase energy prices and to lower population-growth rates.

The study of international and national conflicts and politics has been developing using simulation as one method of study. A simulation study of inter-nation response entitled *Inter-Nation Simulation* (INS), has been used for several years. During a simulation run the international system is imitated realistically; states engage in trade and aid, hold world conferences, etc., and a world newspaper is published. Wars, however, are bloodless and formalized, with their outcome decided by computer. The simulation is a simplification of the actual process, but it aids in understanding international politics and conflicts. This simulation has been used both for experimental and instructional purposes. The research uses of simulation are concerned with the development and testing of hypotheses and theory in international relations. One particularly interesting ex-ample of the use of INS for instructional purposes is the simulation at Essex University in England of the Arab-Israeli conflict.

Several persons at Rensselaer Polytechnic Institute are working on the development of a multinational political-economic decision-making simulation-called PSW−1. This latter simulation, which is computer-controlled, provides for the generation of machine-readable records of role-player decisions for subse-quent analysis. In the political science classroom or research center, a major ad-vantage of the utilization of simulation techniques is that the participant can learn from his mistakes without suffering the real-life consequences when mistakes are made while learning. The simulation exercises are useful in teaching political and diplomatic skills when the consequences of error in the real-life con-text are so costly as to effectively prohibit trial-and-error learning. The PSW1 (Politically Simulated World, Model 1) simulation is a computer-assisted simula-tion exercise which makes it possible for students to learn some of the lessions in politics through participation. The developers of the simulation model also foresee PSW−1 proving useful as a research tool by means of which further in-sights into the relations of men and governments can be obtained. The par-ticipants in the simulation play the roles of decision-makers and the decisions are recorded on IBM punched cards. The cards themselves are the run through the computer and the simulation control program to provide the new balances for the participants for the next round. Simultaneously, the computer is also recording on a separate computer tape the complete record of these interactions for later analysis by the simulation directors. The PSW−1 simulation operates within a number of economic, political and sociological constraints and dynamic relation-ships. At the end of each simulation round, the computer generates measures of the effectiveness of the decisions of the role players.

Another example of a computer-based international relations simulation is called POLIS. This interactive simulation is based at the University of California, Santa Barbara. It involves political interaction among nine nations represented by nine colleges and universities which communicate through a computer network.

A simulation model for allocating urban activities in a state has recently been prepared. In recent times, there has been a prodigious and continuing increase in the demand for various public facility investments in urban areas, stemming from the sheer increase in population, higher incomes, greater mobility and expanding leisure. This escalation in demand has placed acute pressures on the current supply of various public facilities and has brought about continuing problems of planning and resource allocations. For many of these public facilities the requirement for long lead-time planning suggests that plans will have to be worked out and reliably implemented so that the urban areas can evolve systematically, consistent with desired human activity patterns and a spectrum of public tastes. With the desire to have the state governments play a more central role in guiding development patterns within their boundaries, the anticipation and planning of future growth and development in a state is necessary. The elements of a state's plan should encompass the economy, land development patterns, transportation facilities, open space and outdoor recreation. A simulation model has been developed for allocating land-using activities in a state to various uses in a politically sensitive framework. The model incorporates and accounts for shifts in economic activities and social impacts.

The model for Connecticut incorporates nine simultaneous equations involving the following activities:

Construction Employment
Retail and Wholesale Employment
Business and Professional Services Employment
Personal Services Employment
Manufacturing Employment
Other Employment
Population in Low Income Tertile
Population in Middle Income Tertile
Population in High Income Tertile

The land-use model was used to develop projections of population and employment for the 169 towns in Connecticut in 1970, 1980 and 2000. The economic, transportation and industrial consequences of these land-use estimates may then be examined for planning implications. The simulation of land use in a state may assist the planner in preparing meaningful and useful plans which have been experimentally tested using the simulation model.

Professor Jay Forrester of the Massachusetts Institute of Technology has used simulation to model the characteristics of industrial and managerial systems[19] In management systems, the simulation is based on the component structure and informatin flow in an industry and the policies are used within the industry to show how the resulting dynamic behavior is produced. In a recent book entitled *Urban Dynamics*, Forrester simulates the city as an interacting system of industry, housing and people.[20] The book presents a theory, in the form of a computer model, that interrelates the components of a city. It shows how the interacting processes produce urban growth and cause growth to give way to stagnation. Various changes in policies are examined within the simulation model to show their effect on an urban area. A simulation of a hypothetical urban area over a 250-year period is considered.The criterion used in evaluating in the performance of the city and the efficacy of the alternative public policies is the minimization of taxes per capita. A number of proposals are tested using the simulation model, among which are the following: a job training program; job creation by bussing to suburban industries or by the government as employer of last resort; financial subsidies to the city, and low-cost housing programs. Figure 9-16a illustrates the behavior of the simulation model of an urban area. It presents the nine system-level variables over 250 years. The first 100 years is a period of exponential growth, but then the land area becomes filled, growth ceases, and the aging process begins. At year 100, near the end of the growth phase, the labor population is almost double the underemployed population. This is a healthy distribution of the labor resource; it results in economic mobility for the underemployed population. Underemployed labor, in Forrester's terms, includes unemployed and unskilled workers. By the year 150, the labor population has fallen and the underemployed population has risen until these two groups are almost equal. Business activity has declined and the area has taken on the characteristics of a depressed city. Figure 9-16b shows the related variables during the same 250 years resulting from the simulation. During the first 100 years of growth the underemployed-to-job ratio and the unemployed-to-housing ratio remain almost constant. During the period 90 to 140 years, these curves reverse and the underemployed have increased while available jobs decreased; the result is a precipitous rise in unemployment. But in this same period the housing that is aging and becoming available to the underemployed is rising even more rapidly. The model shows the behavior of some cities. The evolution of an urban area, according to this model, creates a condition of excess housing at the stagnation point of the city.

Forrester attempts to include the political and social effects in his computer model. He states:

> We find it relatively straightforward to include the so-called intangible factors relating to psychological variables, attitudes, and human reactions. Again, if the influences can be discussed and described, they can be inserted in the policy structure of a model. Any person who discusses why people act the way they do, or explains a past decision, or anticipates a future action is relating the surrounding circumstances to the corresponding human response. Any such discussion is a description of decision-making policy. Any such policy statement can be put into a system model.

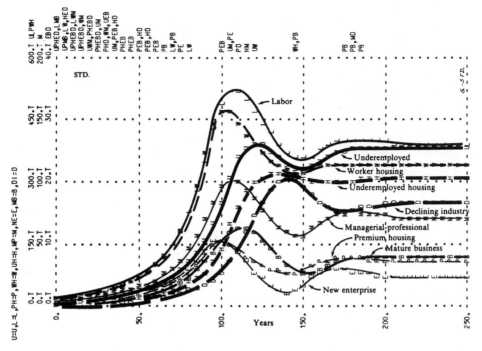

FIGURE 9–16a   A 250-year simulation of an urban area through the periods of develop-
ment, maturity and stagnation. Reprinted from *Urban Dynamics* by J.
W. Forrester, by permission of the M.I.T. Press, Cambridge, Mass.
Copyright © 1969 by the Massachusetts Institute of Technology.

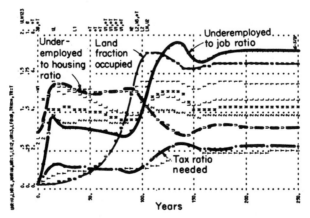

FIGURE 9–16b   Compensating changes in housing and employment. Reprinted from
Urban Dynamics by J. W. Forrester, by permission of the M.I.T.
Press, Cambridge, Mass. Copyright © by the Massachusetts Institute
of Technology.

The result of a governmental policy is shown in Figure 9–17. In this example a slum housing demolition program of 5 percent per year and a two percent
new-construction program is initiated. The result is a 44% decrease in underemployed housing. Also skilled labor grows 62% while new enterprise increases
75%. The net flow of people from underemployed to labor has increased
114%.[20] According to this simulation model, it seems that in order to
reestablish a healthy economic balance and a continuous process of internal
renewal, it appears necessary to reduce the inherent excess housing of depressed
areas and to encourage the conversion of part of the land to industrial use.

One criticism of the computer model is that the suburbs never explicitly appear in it. However, the simulation model does illustrate the following attributes
of large interconnected systems:

1. Complex systems often do not behave in a fashion consistent with intuition.
2. Complex systems are strongly resistant to most policy changes.
3. Many complex systems tend to counteract most programs aimed at
   alleviating the symptoms.
4. In complex systems, the short-term response to a policy change is apt to
   be in the opposite direction from the long-term effect.

Computer simulation models are especially helpful in predicting and understanding the effect of urban management policies on the urban area under study.
Much research work remains to be accomplished in this area.

In a recent study of a city as a system, another computer model with a purpose similar to Forrester's is used to analyze the planning and decision making
process in a city. The application of a computer-based simulation in an urban
planning and decision process is illustrated in Figure 9–18. The use of a simulation in city planning and management is expected to grow in the next decade.

Simulation of business and economic systems has been used for over a
decade to analyze the effect of various strategies. Economists who specialize in
the mathematical description of economic principles have used computers to construct and analyze complex mathematical models of the U.S. economy. This effort has assisted somewhat in synthesizing large amounts of economic information. The effort has also led to a consistent view of the economy. Certain assumptions about the future of the economy as a whole can be programmed into a
model and individual users adjust the parameters of the model to deal with their
own particular industry or market. One model of the economy uses 242 equations
to incorporate many variables. The well-known Wharton Model is based on
research at the Wharton School of Business at the University of Pennsylvania. It
provides short-term forecasts, and it is the only U.S. model. It has been operated
publicly for forecasting for some years. This model is basically a quarterly model
of the Keynesian type. It has grown out of earlier experimental models pioneered
by Professor Lawrence Klein over the last 25 years.

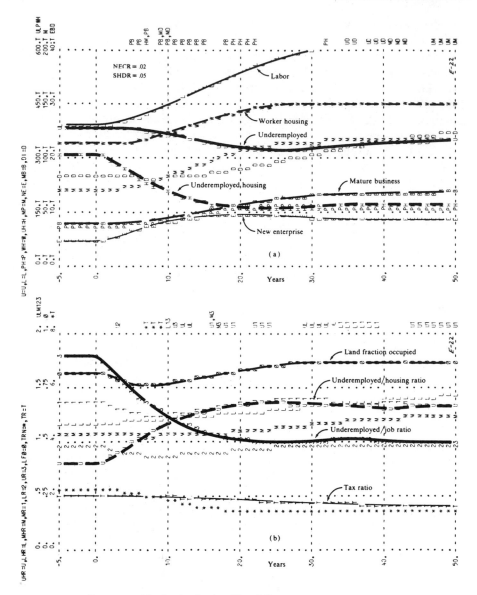

Changes caused by slum-housing demolition of 5% per year and new-enterprise construction of about 2% per year started at time = 0. In 1-3a note the rise in labor, mature business, and new enterprise; the decrease in underemployed housing; and the upward economic movement of underemployed into the labor class. In 1-3b see the decrease in the underemployed/underemployed-jobs ratio. The underemployed/underemployed-housing ratio necessarily rises to more crowded conditions as the job ratio improves.

FIGURE 9–17   Relationships among housing, employment, taxation and other factors. Reprinted from *Urban Dynamics* by J. W. Forrester by permission of the M.I.T. Press, Cambridge, Mass. Copyright © 1969 by The Massachusetts Institute of Technology.

During the past several years, investigators have developed computer models of the dynamics of the world's resources, population, capital investment, and economics. Professor Forrester, in his book *World Dynamics*, discusses a model that interrelates population, capital investment, geographical space, natural resources, pollution, and food production. Forrester's model states that to bring the world system into equilibrium by 1980 would require the reduction of pollution generation, capital investment, the birth rate, and natural-resource usage by more than 30%.

In an important book, *Limits to Growth,* Meadows uses Forrester's computer model to investigate the effects of various policies on world population and natural resources.[21] Meadows concludes that the world cannot sustain the exponential growth of population and resource usage. Critics of the Meadows study maintain that the conclusions resulting from the use of the model are not surprising, but rather must lead us to reexamine our political processes, priorities, and values.

A group of international business leaders called The Club of Rome sponsored the Meadows study and then subsequently sponsored a further use of the world computer model by Professors Mesarovic and Pestel.[22] The Mesarovic study extends over a period of fifty years; attempts to include a simulation accounting for all realistic variables. The study interconnects models of the following systems or influences:

1. Individual
2. Socio-political
3. Population
4. Economics
5. Agrotechnology
6. Ecology

Mesarovic and Pestel conclude from their simulation studies that catastrophe can be avoided only by global cooperation guided by a rational master plan for long-term growth. The Club of Rome has also published a study of a model of the world and of interaction among nations.

9.2 MANAGING BUSINESS WITH COMPUTERS AND SIMULATION

A recent article by Leo Gainen presents the thesis that businesses will be managed in the future by application of system analysis, implemented through the use of computer simulation. Significant portions of this article are given below.*

> This article develops a thesis that businesses will be better managed in the future by application of system analysis implemented through judicious

Leon Gainen, "Computer-Aided Business Management through Simulation," *Proceedings of the Second Hawaii Conference on System Sciences*, Hawaii, 1969. With the permission of McDonnell-Douglas Corp. and the author.

use of computer simulation. In 20 years, simulation information centers (SIC's) will be as commonplace in business operations as scientific and business data processing centers are today. This development is inevitable if one assumes the continued current rate of progress in computer simulation application, computer hardware and software technology, and formalization of theory and invention of techniques to make computers more available to the manager. The acceptance of systems analysis, control theory, operations research, model building, computer technology, and simulation in engineering, business administration, and social and physical science college curricula supports this projection. Future collegians will accept the requirement to learn these technologies as they now do basic economic theory.

BACKGROUND AND RATIONALE

If the historical trend continues of a 10- to 12-year period being necessary for management to keep informed of computer developments and effectively use computers in scientific computation centers (SCC's) and management information centers (MIC's), it can be projected that 10 to 15 years hence, SIC's will be common in industry.* (See Figure 9-19.) Furthermore, the company that leads the way in establishing information processing systems tying MIC's and SCC's to the SIC's on a simulation-by-exception basis will gain a sizeable competitive advantage in its industry.

. . .

We are now in an era of expanding simulation use. But simulation is rarely the regularly accepted means of analytical support for management decisions. It is an exploratory toy rather than an operational tool. We know of business simulation applications for task and resource analysis, job shop balancing, and production scheduling. Other simulation applications are as well-publicized, but are considered strictly scientific (for example, analysis of space vehicle flight dynamics and trajectory determination). Still others cross the line between resource analysis and scientific simulations, such as simulation to rationalize space flight mission control and military systems command and control. PERT network analysis and its derivatives are other well-known, widely-used approaches to activity simulation.

*References to "centers" are merely descriptive. Conceptually (and feasibly), a single physical location could accomplish all of the centers' functions. Also feasible today is a single computer that is properly organized in terms of software, peripheral equipment, and communications channels.

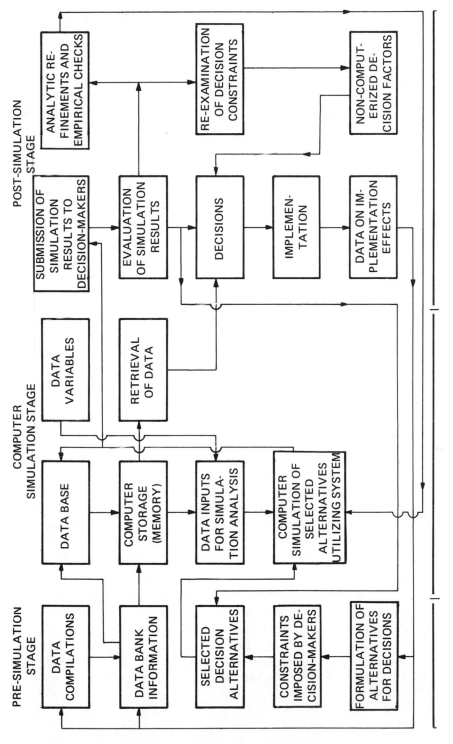

FIGURE 9–18   The application of the computer-based system to urban planning and decision process.

There are, however, more important indicators. Our great universities have begun to formalize the theory and demonstrate the practicality of simulation. Many large universities are equipped with remote terminals for on-line simulation computation as a classroom tool. Hardware manufacturers are combining the speed and flexibility of analog devices with the accuracy and scope of digital computers so that hybrid computation systems are organized as system simulators. New computer simulation languages have been developed to ease the simulation problem solver's burden, after he selects a simulation technique. See Table 9–1.

MANAGEMENT IMPACT OF SIMULATION

Today's managers have been weaned of earlier conservative attitudes regarding scientific computing and business data processing. However, the question remains as to whether they will be more receptive in the future when their subordinates conceive, formulate, and propose simulation solutions to management problems. It is believed that they will be more receptive. More importantly, tomorrow's managers will better understand the context of simulation in the spectrum of analytical tools at their disposal. They will have used these techniques and found them successful during their own career development. Thus, the climate is slowly changing both for worthwhile simulation programs to be incorporated into business operations and for the emergence of SIC's.

Simulation takes many forms. In general, simulations are recognized as having come about because other analytical techniques are either nonexistent (for the situation to be studied) or too expensive (for the amount of confidence in the expected result). Perturbing a live system to try out unusual situations is too disruptive and provides little analytical data for confident predictions about behavior; therefore, the system is modeled and simulated on a computer. Often, dynamic system interactions are not computationally tractable, so the system is formulated as a series of discrete input/output relationships between and among subsystems and examined in a computer simulation over a finite range of system states.

How will simulation contribute to better management? To answer this question requires examination of some simulation activities that are now aiding management. Three basic forms of simulation, each with a variety of applications, have evolved for management exploitation: business games, resource analyses, and system effectiveness simulations. Businesses of the future will encounter variations of these forms, used with an advanced computer hardware system and harnessed as management tools.

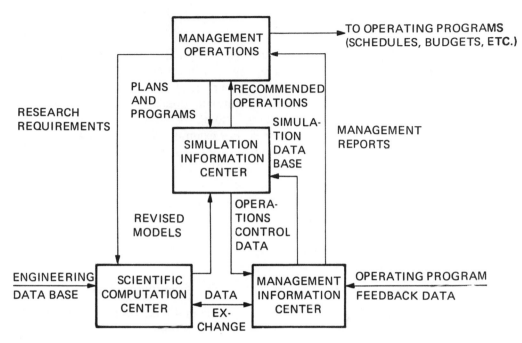

FIGURE 9–19   Future computer center organization.

TABLE 9–1
Current Simulation Languages

Discrete, Recursive Systems		Parallel, Continuous Systems	
Name	*Year Released*	*Name*	*Year Released*
SIMSCRIPT	1961	DYNAMO	1962
GPSS	1961	DES-1	1963
SIMTRAN	1963	MIDAS	1963
CSL	1963	HYBLOC	1964
SIMULA	1963	PACTOLUS	1964
CLP	1964	DSL/90	1965
ESP	1964	SPLASH	1965
MILITRAN	1964	UNITRAC	1965
SOL	1964	EASL	1965
OPS-3	1966	CSMP	1966
GASP IV	1970	GASP IV	1970

BUSINESS GAMES

In management games, realistic business situations are enacted requiring decisions by people playing managers' roles. Realistic information, such as reports, trend curves and two-way plots of key variables is provided to the player; his decision actions stimulate a reaction in the business process being simulated, according to some statistical expectation modeled from historical or research data. For example, if a marketing decision is being enacted and the alternatives are to spend resources either (1) for research to develop new products of (2) for expanded production of today's product line, the manager (that is, the game participant) uses historical data and makes his decision. The short- and long-term effects are computed and reported to the player for his iterative reaction. In structure, these games are like the household game *Monopoly*; however, the plays are measured and the consequences evaluated with more realistic business decision factors.

The following are three values to such a situation enactment:

1. It permits observation of people in lifelike situations without interfering with actual business operations.
2. It demonstrates to functionally oriented management personnel, in clearcut, amply qualified terms, the interactions between their function and others that exist, sometimes subtly, sometimes probabalistically, in any enterprise.
3. It enhances learning of a management enterprise.

This is the way management games are used today. Future use will emphasize the management and not the game. With multiprocessing and direct-access mass data storage used in time-shared computing systems, computation time, space requirements, and costs are being steadily reduced. With better display equipment and better communications, management data presented for "game" decision-making could be the real facts of today's business operation. The SIC will support a management decision room where alternative decisions are tried and observed in simulation exercises to predict the consequence of each. A second role of the simulation is as an exercise for trainees and managers who are not normally required to make specific functional decisions will be an added bonus for the firm.

RESOURCE ANALYSIS

Resource analysis simulations today are used to accomplish research in product management areas as diverse as make-or-buy policies, plant layout inventory-level analysis, and policy-making for product processing through an assembly line.

Consider the future use of this form of resource analysis simulation. For example, when problems of inventory control are being simulated, the model on which inventory predictions are predicated must be established and validated. Thereafter, the future manager can use this model to call the SIC for (or to be called by the SIC about) a specific item. The simulation will consist of extracting from data files current item status data, up-to-date parameter values of demand, holding cost data, depletion charges, and other model input values necessary to perform an analysis. The SIC could be continually performing, on a time-shared basis, necessary statistical and logical computations to prepare preselected data for simulation on demand. As a routine operation, selected critical items might be subjected to status prediction without management intervention by means of elapsed time or specific condition triggers. Thus, the present research nature of such simulations will become that of evaluating models and revising their structure; what is today considered advanced research simulation could become almost a continuously operating business procedure.

Other present-day simulation applications now treated as policy-making research will become management decision-making simulations. For example, shop resource allocation decisions can be evaluated daily before a work shift starts on the basis of current data on machine conditions (real-time links to SIC), personnel availability (time-clock sensors), spare parts and work-in-progress status (inventory data files), and production objectives (delivery schedules). Last-minute shifts in shop operation can be scheduled by shop orders relayed to each work center. The manager's role would be to approve actions derived from simulation analysis, to make revisions based on the latest information, or to initiate a new analysis if system transients could affect predicted results.

SYSTEM PERFORMANCE-SYSTEM EFFECTIVENESS

In the process of hardware design, such as in major space programs, availability and reliability evaluations are continually performed to estimate system worth. Often, system performance is simulated to derive probabilities of achieving desired levels of operation, with parameters such as component failures and severe stress conditions, being explicitly considered.

Two approaches to reliability estimation are appropriate. The first involves building and field- or bench-testing a relatively small number of subsystems to derive estimates of life, maintainability, mean times to failure, and other important measures of overall system reliability. The second does not use field test data of actual hardware, but estimates the measures of reliabiltiy either from known subsystem values (where operating environments are similar to present system operational requirements) or from engineering data describing similar systems.

Unfortunately, for many new system developments, little experience exists from which to estimate subsystem reliability values. . . . A means of capturing and using experience data is a simulation model. The problem of keeping model development current if system structure changes during system development is severe. One technique is based on knowledge of both scope and detail of particular kinds of system organization. First, there must be a canonical system structure, such as a job-shop operation or a space-vehicle design program. For these types of systems, component subsystems are well-understood. [Then, reduction of the system to a computer simulation requires either selection of particular submodels and their parameters or optional configurations of subsystems. Thereafter, well-defined program generators can be built to construct specific simulation models for analyzing different constructs of these systems within the bounds of current system knowledge.]

9.3 SEVERAL EXAMPLES OF COMPUTER SIMULATIONS

Computer simulation of color-forming patterns in shells is an interesting example of a simulation which provides the quality of an excellent simulation, and also provides insight into the physiological principles of the pattern-forming process.[24] The formal characteristics of a pattern of complex appearance on a molluscan shell were studied by developing a simulation of the pattern formation. The pattern involves a random factor determining starting points of diverging lines of pigment. The simulation program attempts to answer the question: What are the rules controlling the deposition of pigment? Professor C. H. Waddington has argued that there are several types of morphogenetic processes, among which are forms produced according to algorithms; template-generated forms, and forms arising from the interaction of spatially-distributed reactants. The shell studied is shown in Figure 9–20a. The physiological model for the simulation was based on an algorithm which generated random numbers. The algorithm is basically as follows:

> Let the computer display trace out the distribution of pigment
> along a series of vertical lines, starting on the right and adding
> more and more to the left.

Let "pigment deposition initiation" occur on any line by a random process. Once it has begun at a certain point, suppose that (i) the process of pigment deposition spreads laterally along the later lines at some specified rate, and (ii) increases in intensity until it reaches some upper threshold, at which it cuts out and pigment deposition does not occur. Suppose further that when two lines of pigment deposition meet they add together to surpass the upper threshold, and deposition ceases.

A rather successful pattern resulting from this simulation is shown in Figure 9–20b. When the investigator wrote his algorithm, he was postulating an explanation for the pigmentation of this species. He based his algorithm on what he was and how he thought it came about. The similarity between the natural pattern and the one generated from the scientist's algorithm is so striking that one is tempted to infer that the algorithm is, in fact, a reasonable explanation for the phenomenon. Whether this inference is sound or not, the acceptance of the algorithm rested on simulation by a computer.

Computer simulation systems can provide as output a picture or representation of the result of an experiment. For example, a laboratory simulation of an electronics experiment is shown in Figure 9–21.

The computer has been successfully used to model human behavior and personality. Ordinarily, we consider the computer a manipulator of numbers, when in fact it is a manipulator of symbols, of which numbers are but one class of symbols. In recent years, psychologists have shown a great deal of interest in the information processing capabilities of the human being—for example, how the human stores information, how he responds to information and what his various reaction times are. A large share of this interest in human information processing has come about because of the need for studies of the human factors involved in the integration of people into large man-machine systems, especially where the machines are information processing machines. One goal of this work is the simulation of valid theories of human mental function.

A model is an abstraction of a reality under study.[12] Good model builders are usually good question seekers. The right question will result in the correct model. The concepts of good model building include:

1. Objectivity
2. Consistency
3. Availability of data
4. Applicability

The models must be explicit, consistent and able to aggregate the variables fairly.

Possibly the most important of all tests to which any model must be subjected is sensitivity analysis. How sensitive is the model to slight changes in parameters, to variations in initial conditions or modifications in the interrela-

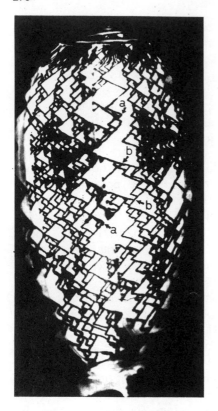

FIGURE 9–20a   A shell (*Conus* sp.)
showing patterns
of pigmentation.
Growth is from
right to left.

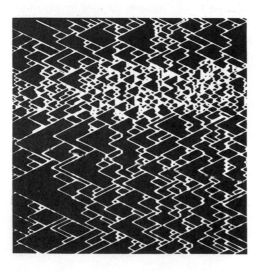

FIGURE 9–20b   A computer simulation of the growth
of a molluscan shell
pigmentation pat-
tern.

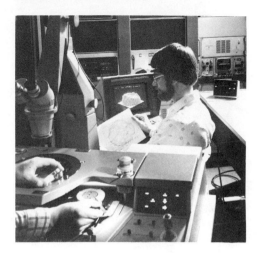

FIGURE 9–21 A pictorial computer output from a laboratory simulation of an electronics experiment. The graphics terminal is used to display profiles of the characteristics of semiconductor materials. A hard copy of the computer plot is shown in the operator's hand. A Tektronix 4010 terminal and plotter are used. *Courtesy Tekronix, Inc.*

tionships? Usually a modeler has a mental model (or image) of his model. He knows how sensitive it is to change, and he is aware of the underlying behavior.

The use of computer simulation will continue to grow at an even greater rate, proportionally, than the increase in the number of computers. Simulation is useful in many fields.[14,15]

Because of the complex nature of modern business systems, data processing aids (including simulation) are increasingly required to assist the intuition and judgment of management in the evaluation of new methods, concepts, and designs. The practice of experimenting directly on a business and implementing a system before it is fully understood inevitably causes disruptions of normal operations, hasty last-minute corrections, and often personnel or customer resentment. To avoid costly mistakes, the consequences of change must be anticipated before actually implementing a program, and all alternatives should be thoroughly explored.[10]

Computer simulation provides an effective means of testing and evaluating a proposed system under various conditions in a laboratory environment. The system's behavior is modeled by a computer program, which reacts to various operating conditions in a manner both qualitatively and quantitatively similar to that of the system itself. Several hours or weeks, or sometimes even years, of simulated activity can be examined on a computer in a matter of minutes. Results help to gain insights, test hypotheses, demonstrate or verify new ideas and establish feasibility. Computer simulation is expected to grow in importance and use during the next decade. Disciplines not formerly using simulation techniques may find new frontiers opening to the researcher, student and practitioner.

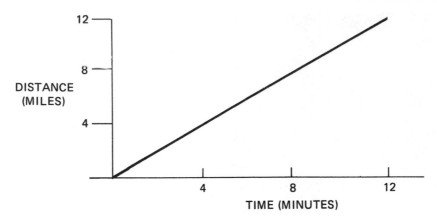

FIGURE 9–22   Distance *versus* time performance of a racing car with a constant speed.

9.4   EXAMPLES OF COMPUTER SIMULATION USING BASIC MATHEMATICS

Simulation is a study of the performance of a system, through the use of a model in which performance is a function of time. In this section we discuss several examples of computer simulation.

First, consider the simulation of a racing car traveling along a straight track. The speed of the automobile S is related to the distance traveled by the equation

$$d = S \cdot t \qquad (9\text{–}1)$$

where t is the time of travel from the starting point. Now, if the auto travels along the straight track at a constant speed S_c, we can calculate the distance traveled during an increment in time Δt as

$$\Delta d = S_c \cdot \Delta t \qquad (9\text{–}2)$$

where Δd is the incremental distance. If the incremental time Δt is one minute in each case and the speed is $S_c = 1$ mile per minute, we obtain the distance versus time performance, as shown in Figure 9–22.

We are aware that the model of a racing car must account for the fact that the driver will change the speed of the vehicle as the engine and the wind will allow; thus, the model must actually accommodate changes in the speed S as time varies. We then choose a small period of time Δt and assume the speed is constant during the period Δt. Let us assume the car will require at least one-half minute to change speed, and the speed during that period of time is essentially constant. Then we are able to state

$$\Delta d = S \cdot \Delta t \qquad (9\text{–}3)$$

where $\Delta t = .5$ minute, and where S is the average speed during the inverval of time. A racing car might experience a speed change as listed in Table 9–2

TABLE 9-2

Time (minutes)	0	0.5	1.0	15.	2.0	2.5
Speed (miles/minute)	0	.20	.30	.40	.50	.50
Average Speed		.100	.250	.35	.45	.50
		←Δt→	Δt	Δt	Δt	Δt
Incremental Distance Δd (miles)		.05	.125	.175	.225	.25
Total Distance (miles)			.05	.175	.35	.575	.825

resulting in the average speeds as listed in the same table. The average speed is represented by the equation

$$S = \frac{S_e + S_b}{2} \qquad (9\text{–}4)$$

where S_e = speed at the end of Δt and S_b = speed at the beginning of Δt.
The incremental distance and total distance traveled are also given in Table 9–2. The results are graphically illustrated in Figure 9–23. The algorithm for the simulation is deduced from the equations. The average speed is

$$S = \frac{S_e + S_b}{2} \qquad (9\text{–}5)$$

or it may be written as

$$S = \frac{S_{n+1} + S_n}{2} \qquad (9\text{–}6)$$

where n = the counter. The distance traveled during the nth interval is

$$\Delta d_n = S \cdot \Delta t \qquad (9\text{–}7)$$

where Δt is a constant. Then the algorithm for the total distance traveled is

$$d_{n+1} = d_n + \frac{S_{n+1} + S_n}{2} \cdot \Delta t \qquad (9\text{–}8)$$

where n varies from 0 to a preselected value. For example, the total distance d_1 is

$$d_1 = \frac{.20 + 0}{2} \cdot 0.5 \qquad (9\text{–}9)$$

since $d_0 = 0$. Then, we have

$$d_2 = 0.5 + \frac{.30 + .20}{2} .5 \qquad (9\text{–}10)$$

The computer is able to store the past value of d_n and all previous values of the speed. It can thus calculate the incremental distance traveled. While this simulation is fairly simple, it is illustrative of the process.

Let us develop a simulation model of the interaction of rabbits and foxes in Australia. The number of rabbits is r. If left alone, this number would grow indefinitely until the food supply was exhausted. However, the foxes (f) present on

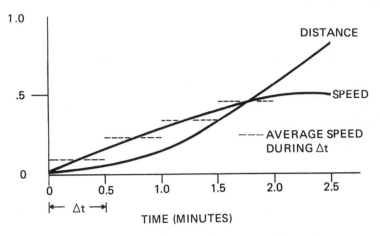

FIGURE 9–23   A simulation of an automobile road race.

the continent are predators which control the growth in the number of rabbits. Finally, the effect of the available food on the rabbit population is represented by the variation of the variable x. Thus, the three simulation variables are:

$$r = \text{number of rabbits}$$
$$f = \text{number of foxes}$$
$$x = \text{quantity of food}$$
available to the rabbits

The equation representing the number of rabbits is:

$$r_{n+1} = kr_n - af_n + bx_n \qquad (9\text{–}11)$$

This equation states that the number of rabbits at the time $t = t_{n+1}$ is related to the number of rabbits, r_n; the number of foxes, f_n; and the food x_n; at the time $t = t_n$.* Recall from the preceding discussion that the increment of time is $\Delta t = t_{n+1} = t_n$ and it is assumed that $\Delta t = $ one unit of time, such as a week. In a similar manner, the other two equations are:

$$f_{n+1} = df_n + gr_n \qquad (9\text{–}12)$$
$$x_{n+1} = hx_n - mr_n \qquad (9\text{–}13)$$

The parameters of the simulation model as k, a, b, d, g, h and m. These parameters are selected to cause the model to fit the actual change in the populations. Equation 9–11 states that the rabbit population would increase if f and x were ignored. Equation 9–12 states that the number of foxes would decrease if there were no rabbits; that is, r equal to zero. Equation 9–13 states that the food

---

*The number of rabbits this month depends on how many rabbits and foxes, and how much food, there was last month.

TABLE 9-3

n	o	1	2	3	4
r	100	90	69	44.1	21.1
f	10	15	16.5	15.2	12
x	100	90	81	74.1	69.7

increases with time and the rabbits decrease the food supply proportionally to their number.

Let us consider the case where $k = 1$, $d = .5$, $a = 2$, $g = .1$, $h = 1$, $b = .1$ and $m = .1$. Then the series of equations is:

$$r_{n+1} = r_n - 2f_n + .1x_n$$
$$f_{n+1} = .5f_n + .1r_n$$
$$x_{n+1} = x_n - .1r_n$$

These equations may be programmed for a computer, assuming an initial value for r_0, f_0 and x_0. If $r_0 = 100$, $f_0 = 10$, and $x_0 = 100$, we can calculate the next incremental value of the variables as:

$$r_1 = 100 - 2(10) + .1(100) = 90$$
$$f_1 = .5(10) + .1(100) = 15$$
$$x_1 = 100 = .1(100) = 90$$

If the calculations proceed for several periods of time Δt, we obtain the response listed in Table 9–3. This series of calculations is easily obtained from a computer simulation and the result can be provided in a plotted format.

The calculations result in numbers which are not integers, but rather are decimal numbers. Of course, the actual number of rabbits, for example, is an integer and the decimal portion of the number should be rounded according to the rule that the number is increased to the next higher integer if the decimal portion is one-half or greater, and conversely if the decimal portion is less.

Notice that in Figure 9–24 the number of foxes increases but then decreases again as the number of rabbits continually drops. The simulation could be carried out for several more periods. This type of simulation is quite revealing of the nature of the process. The parameters of the process can be altered in order to try another set of conditions.

A computer simulation will provide more accurate solutions as the increment of time, Δt, is decreased. As the increment of time is decreased, the number of increments required to simulate a total time period T is proportionally increased. For example, in the case of the speed-simulation example discussed earlier, we use $\Delta t = 0.5$ minute. If the total period of interest is 10 minutes, the simulation requires a series of 20 calculations. If, in order to improve the accuracy and closeness of approximation, we let $\Delta t = 0.5$ minutes, then a sequence of 200 calculations would be required to yield the results for a 10-minute period. Nevertheless,

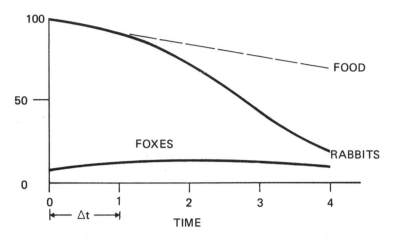

FIGURE 9-24   The rabbits and foxes in Australia.

the computer can easily provide hundreds of calculations rapidly and with a computer simulation, one can readily use the increment required to provide reasonable accuracy.

9.5   COMPUTER GAMES

The use of computers to aid in the playing of games has grown in recent years. Until the last few decades, game playing was primarily restricted to humans or special-purpose machines. Today, however, computer scientists are dedicating a considerable amount of effort toward programming digital computers to play games. A game, which is a common activity, is a closed system with a set of explicitly stated rules and a fixed goal. A formal definition of a game may be stated as follows:

GAME   (1) An activity among two or more independent decision makers seeking to achieve their objectives in some limiting context. (2) A contest with rules among several adversaries who are attempting to win specified objectives.

Many activities in life involve the characteristics of game playing. Such activities involve decision makers seeking to achieve objectives in some limiting context. The autonomy of human wills and the diversity of human motives result in gamelike forms in all human interactions, and in this sense all human history can be regarded as gamelike in nature. The word "game" signifies the richest and most diverse of human activities. The dictionary suggests the range: diversion, sport, fun, competition and play among others. The wide use of "game" as a metaphor for many social, political, economic activities indicates the similarity which, we assume, exists between games and lifelike activities. It is this very similarity that causes us to consider the use of computers for game playing.

The analogy between games of strategy and economic, social and political behavior is fairly obvious. Perhaps most of us are familiar with the game Monopoly, which is modeled on a theory of economic life. Game playing is not limited by geographical boundaries; it has a rich history. It is a common experience for an individual to strive to learn how to achieve maximum advantages, and most games are models of common situations. Thus the game-player may be considered one who is learning how to gain advantages in models of real situations. Of course, some games involve the action of the players to achieve a common goal against an obstructing force or natural situation which is not itself a player.

Games may have originated in the playing out of tribal life, war or commerce. They permitted the player to try out a role within the game without the cost of the real situation. The creative aspect of the game combines the luck of the player and a respect for the realities of life. A game has a rational, analytic component and an emotional, creative component. The game's analytic dimension includes the strategic and structural characteristics experienced in life. The emotional aspect of the game includes chance and a realization that often the action of the game is as important as the outcome. One interesting example of a game that has been played using a computer is the well-known game of Monopoly.

Some political and social activities can be viewed as games. Warfare can be imagined as a form of a game. Real wars are painful, expensive, unfortunate and not practical for actual experimentation. However, for centuries people have been using war games, mock battles, maneuvers and other forms of simulated contests to prepare for war. Perhaps you are familiar with the saying "The wars of Britain have been won on the playing fields of Eton." Eton is a private school in England which produced a large percentage of the officers of the British army during the height of the British Empire. Presumably they learned the skills that made them superior fighters as they simulated war in their intermural sports.

The analysis and learning of processes in the form of games is present in a contest such as an election. A game in economics, politics, or war involves several players utilizing the resources of skill, knowledge, and luck and always involves a contest of individuals making conflicting decisions and holding conflicting objectives. Thus, we find that many processes can be viewed as games. What cannot be viewed as a game are those processes which have predetermined procedures or results, such as those processes we considered as candidates for simulation in the preceding sections of this chapter. Games are simulations of the real world, but not all simulations are games. The computer simulation of the evolution of dark moths is not a game since the results are predetermined by an algorithm and there is no winning or losing outcome.

Game playing is being applied to business management. Business executives are playing games which simulate the operation of their businesses. One such game permits several teams of players to compete for a market. The teams allocate their capital to sales effort, research and development and production each month. They select certain sales options and research options. Periodically, these options are entered into a computer as data and the teams compete, on the basis of their decisions, for the available market for the item the companies are producing. The players receive a computer output at the end of each period and thus are able to learn about the process of allocating resources and managing a business enterprise.

The rules and the goals of a game are usually well known by all the players. The strategy—the method of choosing the most desirable move or series of moves—is not known. It is the strategy involved in playing the game that varies and allows the player to learn from his mistakes and successes.

The goal in playing a game is to obtain the objectives by using a suitable strategy. A single individual, playing alone, faces the simplest problem; his best strategy is the one that brings him the predetermined maximum gain. In two-person games, each player wishes to win a maximum amount of score, but he can do this only at the expense of the other. This situation results in what is termed a zero-sum game, since the sum of one player's gains and the other's losses (a negative number) is zero. One player has to design a strategy that will assure him of the maximum advantage. But the same is true of the other, who naturally wishes to minimize the first player's gain, thereby maximizing his own. This clear-cut opposition of interest introduces an entirely new concept, the so-called "minimax" problem. Examples of two-person, zero-sum games are Chess, Bridge, Poker, Rummy, and Checkers. These games can be played with a digital computer as one of the players. Computer programs are available for playing these and other games with individuals. An example of a computer game is shown in Figure 9–25.

A non-zero-sum game is one in which the winner's gain is not necessarily at the cost of the loser. All players can win, as in peace-keeping, or all can lose, as in nuclear war. Non-zero-sum games are more complex than zero-sum games but more like life in that while encompassing the purely competitive aspects they also include the preservation of that game itself, which is the social objective of the players. The best strategy in such games is one that maximizes the total wins of all players. This is sometimes called the Pareto optimum, after the great mathematical economist, Wilfredo Pareto, who first expressed this concept.

As an example of a recent computer game, consider *Grand Strategy*, which is a game of international conflict developed by Raytheon Company for the U.S. Department of Defense. The global cold war conflict incorporates three power alliances of 39 nations with conflicting interests. The action takes place over a simulated ten-year period, divided into weekly events. The game is a non-zero-sum game in that all nations can win peace and prosperity. The roles of the players are as political, military and economic leaders of the nations.

Another example of a computer game developed for the U.S. Government is called *Corridor*. This game incorporates the political and economic factors which come into play in the formulation and implementation of regional transportation policy. The game decisions are made by the players, but in areas of complex calculations, such as economic consequences of moves, the computer assists in processing the data resulting from these decisions. The area simulated in the exercise is the Northeast Corridor, incorporating the area from Boston to Washington, D.C. For simulation purposes, the Corridor was divided into major urban centers, the states they were located in, and several multistate superstructures. The players assume the roles of federal and state officials, representatives of the transportation industry and representatives of the consumer.

The transportation industry is subdivided into its rail, air, road, and water modes, each represented by a single player controlling the full resources of his particular mode throughout the Corridor. In addition, each mode was also represented by a labor union. The simulation consists of an economic submodel and a political submodel: the economic submodel concerned with the operation of the transportation industry and the intercity flow of goods within the Corridor; the political one with all other factors affecting the planning and implementation of regional transportation policy. The objective of the game is to maximize the profits of the individual player.

A popular example of a computer game that has increased in use over the past several years is the game of LIFE. It is a kind of solitaire played by one person on a checkerboard which is displayed on a computer video terminal.[28] The rules of the game are programmed within a computer, and the result is a continually-evolving set of graphs.

The design of computer games is an interesting and important activity. An elementary situation in business competition will serve to illustrate the design of a game. Let us design a competitive two-person, zero-sum game. An established firm, Mature Industries, is being challenged by Newcomer, Inc. an aggressive new firm. The management of Mature Industries guides their policies by their balance statement (that is, their budget and the sales projections of one year ahead). The management of Newcomer, Inc. also uses Mature Industries' balance sheet as their guide, since their aim is to put Mature out of business. They consider Mature's losses their gains and *vice versa*, regardless of what their own balance shows. Both are faced with a decision, namely whether or not to undertake an extensive advertising campaign. The outcome depends on what both firms do, each having control over only its own decision. We assume, however, that both firms have enough information to know what the outcomes will be, given both decisions. The Table in Figure 9–26 shows the payoff the Mature Industries of various decisions of the two companies. The effect, in millions of dollars, of each set of decisions is shown. For example, if Mature and Newcomer both advertise, the loss to Mature Industries is one million dollars. Now, consider yourself as the manager of Mature faced with the avowed strategy of Newcomer.

FIGURE 9–25   The TRS-80 color computer, which is useful for games and simulation
Courtesy of Radio Shack, A Division of Tandy Corporation.

	NEWCOMER ADVERTISES	NEWCOMER DOES NOT ADVERTISE
MATURE ADVERTISES	−1	+1
MATURE DOES NOT ADVERTISE	−2	+2

FIGURE 9–26   The payoff matrix for Mature Industires for a two-person, zero-sum
game with two firms making a decision about advertising.

If the aim of Newcomer, Inc. is to drive Mature out of business, what do you decide as the manager of Mature? The decision of Mature to advertise is the best of the alternatives assuming that Newcomer, Inc. will try to maximize Mature's loss. In setting this game up, you would not tell the player who assumes the role of Mature about the strategy of Newcomer. Rather, the manager of Mature should learn the stragety of Newcomer by experience, thus gaining valuable insight into one strategy of the business world.

The sequence of steps in designing a game is similar to the sequence of steps in ordinary problem solving. One method of developing a game in which the computer assumes the role of one player is to use rote learning. The computer amasses a dictionary of moves by trial and error; reenforcing the successful moves and deleting the unsuccessful moves. Thus, the moves of a single game are stored as they are chosen by the computer. If the game is lost, the final losing move is eliminated. If the game is won, these moves are retained as options. This method of machine learning is depicted in Figure 9–27. The algorithm for the computer program deletes the choice in the last situation where a decision was possible from the repertoire of future possible moves.

Nim, a game thought to be of Chinese origin, lends itself to programming for a digital computer. In one version, each player has 10 coins set in a pile. Each player in turn takes one, two or three coins from the pile, and he must take at least one coin. The player who takes the last coin from his pile loses. The computer can be programmed to play according to the algorithm shown in Figure 9–27. Prior to 1945, several machines were built to play Nim. Since then, several programs have been written to play this game with a human player opposing the computer.

In 1901, Charles Bouton, a professor of mathematics at Harvard University, completed an analysis of the game and developed an algorithm for game play. A player knowing the algorithm can always improve his chances of winning the game. Likewise, a computer program designed to play Nim properly can usually win against a player not knowing the algorithm. The winning approach to playing Nim is always to present your opponent with an even position. An even position is determined by (1) writing the number of objects in each pile in binary notation; (2) obtaining the sum of the digits of every column of the binary numbers; and (3) dividing the obtained sum by 2. The position is even if no remainder resulted from the division. A program can be readily written to follow this algorithm and to play a good game of Nim with a human opponent.

The idea of playing Tic-Tac-Toe on a machine was conceived as far back as the 1800s. Charles Babbage, the English mathematician, wanted to build a machine to play Chess and Tic-Tac-Toe, to help finance his efforts to build his Analytical Engine. Today, Tic-Tac-Toe programs have been written for many digital computers.

The game of Checkers can be played between a human player and a computer. The checkerboard is divided into 64 squares, colored alternately light and

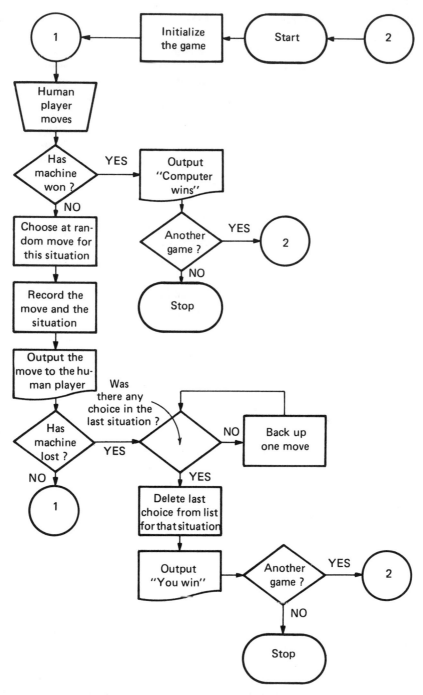

FIGURE 9–27   A flow chart of a rote method for a computer to learn to play a winning
game.

dark, and each side is provided with twelve men, known as white and black. At the beginning of the game the twelve men are placed on alternate squares on the opposite side of the board from the opposing men. The men never leave the color upon which they are first placed, and all moves must be diagonal. The object of the game is to capture all the opponent's men and remove them from the board, or else pen them up in such a manner that they cannot move. Checkers involves a set of 10^{40} possible moves in an average game. Dr. Arthur Samuel of Stanford University has written a checker-playing program which is based on the rote method of learning as illustrated in Figure 9-26; Samuel's checker-playing program plays a good game and is capable of beating most amateurs.

Chess is a highly-valued game of intellectual skill. Computer scientists have been working on several versions of computer programs for playing a skillful version of Chess with a human opponent. Such programs have been written at Northwestern University and Carnegie-Mellon University.[16] The top chess program, Chess 4.9, written at Northwestern University, can beat the typical tournament player. A program at Carnegie-Mellon defeated the world champion backgammon player.

Electronic games using microcomputers are available to play chess, bridge, checkers and backgammon. Sales of these games reached $1 billion in 1980.[16] The Sargon chess game can be entered into a personal computer for a first-class challenge.[23]

The use of computers in the playing of games is an exciting and interesting aspect of computer simulation. A game is an activity among two or more decision makers seeking to achieve their objectives within the limits of the rules of the game. This activity has great interest to computer scientists, since computers can help to play games and aid in the training of business managers, legislators and city officials, among others. In addition, computer games are of interest as exercises in computer programming. It is quite a challenge to program a computer to play a game of skill with a human opponent. Computer games can be serious training exercises as well as of intellectual interest to a computer scientist.

SUMMARY

The modeling and simulation of real processes is of great assistance to business, industry and government because they permit one to study the effects of various decisions or choices without going through the complete process of actually constructing and testing the phenomenon being considered. A model is a representation of a system or phenomenon in mathematical or symbolic form suitable for simulation is to explore the various results which might be obtained from the real system by subjecting the model to representative situations and inputs that are equivalent to those occurring in actual life.

In the use of simulation models, one should avoid the use of only one variable. For example, a highway might be investigated with respect to traffic patterns only. But pollution, urban blight etc. must also be considered. All simulations must include the effects of many parameters and inputs if the results are to be considered realistic. A simulation is an abstraction of reality, and caution must be exerted to include the pertinent effects of the environment. Simulation is an art as well as a science. The effectiveness of a simulation rests on the simulator's ability to abstract only those factors that affect the process he wishes to duplicate.

Some examples of useful computer simulations are in aeronautics; ticket reservation systems; logistics systems; economic systems, and political situations. Simulation is also useful for teaching the effects of various decisions on the environment, economics, politics, and business.

The use of computers to play games is an important dimension of computer simulation. A game is an activity among two or more decision makers seeking to achieve their objectives within the limits of the rules of the game. A game does not have predetermined strategies or results and is to be contrasted with a computer simulation model for which the results can be predetermined. A game involves several decisions throughout the course of a game and a strategy of play which is not predetermined. Games are quite useful in training students, managers and public officials to make wise decisions and to experience of the resulting consequences. Also, computer games are of interest to computer scientists since the programming and development of algorithms of games is a challenge in itself. Simulation and games are an important aspect of computer science and it is expected that the field will grow in importance in the next decade.

CHAPTER 9 PROBLEMS

P9—1.   Distinguish between a model and a simulation.

P9—2.   Describe a model of the process of registering at your college. What are the essential characteristics?

P9—3.   List several advantages of computer simulation.

P9—4.   Name several systems or phenomena for which you could develop a model and a computer simulation

P9—5.   Develop a simplified model of the population growth of your town. Using data available from the town's records, obtain parameters that fit the data. Predict the population of your town during the next 20 years using a computer simulation.

P9—6.   Develop a game of three firms competing for a market for widgets. The three variables to be considered are: (1) advertising expenditures; (2) production expenditures; (3) research and development expenditures. Use simple relationships such as the linear relationship of the proportional expenditures for each of the three variables.

P9—7. Describe some of the advantages and uses of the simulation of business activities.

P9—8. Program and run the computer simulation of the rabbits and foxes problem described in the chapter. Run the simulation with an increment of time Δt equal to 1 unit. Examine the results of the simulation for correctness and give the time required to complete the run on the computer.

P9—9. Program the game of Nim for the computer. Record the winning record of the computer.

P9—10. Develop a computer program for playing Nim by learning a strategy via the method illustrated in **Figure 9—26**.

P9—11. Develop a computer program for the two-person, zero-sum game of the two firms deciding to advertise as illustrated by Figure 9—25. Let several persons assume the role of Mature Industries and find if they can determine the strategy of Newcomer, Inc.

P9—12. Obtain the rules for the game of LIFE and program them for the computer.[28] It will be necessary to have a video display terminal available.

P9—13. Prepare a BASIC program for a time-sharing system that enables interaction between the player and the computer. The purpose of the game is for the player to guess in a limited number of moves (say, seven moves) a number selected by the computer and lying between 1 and 100. The computer should give a hint after each guess by printing out one asterisk for "far away from the correct answer" and up to seven stars for "close" and progressively "closer."

P9—14. The cyclical character of undergraduate engineering-college enrollments may be related to the number of available jobs. One equation representing engineering enrollment is:

$$ENR(N) = 40,000 - 0.50ENR(N-5) + 0.60ENR(N-1) + 0.5SLE(N-4)$$

where ENR = freshman engineering enrollments and SLE = salary level for graduating engineers. Prepare a computer simulation for the period 1980 to 1990. Set ENR(1975) = 42,000, ENR(1979) = 50,000 and SLE(1976) = 16,000. Assume that salaries grow by $1,000 each year after 1976.

NOTE: Make the correct choice for each, problems 9—15 and 9—16. Be prepared to defend your answer.

P9—15. A discrete simulation is characterized by
        A. A clock mechanism

      B. Queue data
      C. Non-continuous state changes
      D. Two of A, B, C
      E. All of A, B, C

P9–16.   A management game is an example of
      A. Numerical analysis
      B. Artificial intelligence
      C. Regression
      D. Simulation

CHAPTER 9 REFERENCES

1. G. Gordon. *System Simulation*, 2nd Edition, Prentice-Hall Inc., Englewood Cliffs, New Jersey, 1978.
2. S. Jacoby and J. D. Kowalik, *Mathematical Modeling with Computers*, Prentice Hall Inc., Englewood Cliffs, New Jersey, 1980.
3. J. Rhea, "Flight Simulation Techniques," *Electronic Design News*, March 1980, pp. 7–10.
4. G. A. Korn and J. V. Wait, *Digital Continuous System Simulation*, Prentice-Hall, Englewood Cliffs, New Jersey, 1978.
5. W. G. Lehnert, *The Process of Question Answering: A Computer Simulation of Cognition*, Wiley and Sons, New York, 1978.
6. T. M. O'Donovan, *GPSS: Simulation Made Simple*, Wiley and Sons, Inc., New York, 1980.
7. J. W. Harbaugh and G. B. Carter, *Computer Simulation in Geology*, Kreiger Publishers, New York, 1980.
8. N. R. Brockington, *Computer Modeling in Agriculture*, Oxford University Press, New York, 1979.
9. C. R. Scott and A. J. Strickland, *Tempomatic IV: A Management Simulation*, 2nd Edition, Houghton-Mifflin, Boston, 1980.
10. B. B. Jackson, *Computer Models in Management*, Irwin, Inc., Homewood, Illinois, 1979.
11. D. S. Spencer, *Game Playing With BASIC*, Hayden Book Co., Rochelle Park, New Jersey, 1978.
12. M. L. Dertouzos and J. Moses, *The Computer Age*, MIT Press, Cambridge, Massachusetts, 1980, Chapter 13.
13. S. P. Ladany, *Optimal Strategies in Sports*, North-Holland Publishing Co., New York, 1977.
14. A. Bork, "Learning With Computer Simulations," *IEEE Computer*, Oct. 1979, pp. 75–84.

15. J. Randers, *Elements of the System Dynamics Method*, MIT Press, Cambridge, Massachusetts, 1980.
16. R. A. Shaffer, "Electronic Games Get Smarter," *Wall Street Journal,* Aug. 15, 1980, p. 17.
17. F. H. Harlow and J. P. Shannon, "Distortion of a Splashing Liquid Drop," *Science,* Aug. 4, 1970, pp. 547—550.
18. J. W. Brewer and K. Watt, "Simulation of Energy Flow and Land Use," *Simulation,* February, 1976, pp. 157—160.
19. J. W. Forrester, *World Dynamics.* Wright-Allen Publishing Co., Cambridge, Masschuetts, 1971.
20. J. W. Forrester, *Urban Dynamics*, MIT Press, Cambridge, Masschuetts, 1969.
21. D. H. Meadows, D. L. Meadows, J. Randers and W. W. Behrens, *The Limits to Growth*, Universe Books, New York, 1972.
22. M. Mersarovic and E. Pestel, *Mankind at the Turning Point,* E. P. Dutton and Co., Inc., New York, 1974.
23. D. Spracklen, *Sargon: A Computer Chess Program,* Hayden Publishing Co., Rochelle Park, New Jersey, 1978.
24. C. H. Waddington and R. J. Cowe, "Computer Simulation of a Molluscan Pigmentation Pattern," *Journal of Theoretical Biology,* Volume 25, 1969, pp. 219—225.
25. G. D. Brewer and M. Shubik, *The War Game: A Critique of Military Problem Solving,* Harvard University Press, Cambridge, Masschuetts, 1979.
26. D. C. Montgomery and R. G. Conrad, "Comparison of Simulation and Flight Data for Missile Systems," *Simulation,* February 1980, pp. 63—71.
27. J. Darzentas, "Simulation of Road Traffic," *Simulation,* May 1980, pp. 155—164.
28. *Simulation of Ecological Processes,* Second Edition, Unipub Inc., New York, 1979.
29. I. Hodder, *Simulation Studies*, Cambridge University Press, New York, 1979.
30. U. Poch and W. Graybeal, *Simulations: Principles and Methods*, Winthrop, Englewood Cliffs, New Jersey, 1980.
31. N. R. Adam and A. Dogramac, *Current Issues in Simulation,* Academic Press, New York, 1979.
32. R. R. Drersch, "Using a Computer Model to Evaluate Business Operating Plans," *Simulation,* April 1980, pp. 109—116.
33. D. Ahl and S. North, *More Basic Computer Games,* Creative Computing, Morristown, New Jersey, 1980.

10

COMPUTERS AROUND THE WORLD

10.1 INTRODUCTION

The digital computer was developed primarily in the United States, but other countries have developed their own computers as well as purchased American computers. Countries which were once dubious about the economic role of computers now are attempting to introduce computers extensively into business and government.*

As Schreiber points out in his book *The American Challenge*, application of management techniques, including information processing, has constituted the technological challenge which the U.S. has presented to Europe and the rest of the industrialized world.[1] He says:

> In the industrial war, the major battle is in the field of computing. This battle is very much in doubt, but it has not yet been lost. "Between 1970 and 1980," according to Jacques Maisonrouge, "the most important industry in the world, after oil and automobiles, will be computers."

*Here are some expressions for "Computer" from other languages: *Computador, Rechenmaschine, Mahashev, Chotnik, Machina per calcoli, Rekenmachine, Elektronno-vychislitel'naya mashina, Calculateur.*

Approximately one-half of the world's computers are in the United States. This country has about 54% of the value of installed computers in the world, as is shown in Table 10–1.[3] Many nations expect to double the value of their installed computers during the last years of this decade.

The United States manufacturers that sell computers worldwide are led by IBM, Burroughs, Honeywell, Univac and Control Data Corporation.[4] These multinational computer companies together control approximately 80% of the world market. Honeywell and IBM generated more than one-half of the 1980 revenues from overseas business.

IBM has factories in most major European countries. It sold $9 billion worth of computers and computer services outside the United States in 1980. IBM is an integrated multinational company, with plants in Great Britain, West Germany, Italy, France and Sweden. IBM holds about 60% of the market worldwide.

The United Nations has studied the potential for international cooperation in the field of computer science. The transfer of computer technology from the developed nations to the developing nations is under study. In order for nations to develop industrially, they need knowledge and technical ability with computer applications. There is a worldwide consciousness of a need for some type of inter- and intra-country plan for technological cooperation if overseas computer industries are to develop as quickly as those in the US did. If these plans embrace both computing hardware and programs such action could have far reaching effects throughout the world in the very near future.[3]

Computer companies based in the United States dominate the international computer market. The US companies produce 80 percent of the computer hard-

TABLE 10–1
Worldwide Computer Industry Installed Value

	1976 ($ billions)	1980 ($ billions)
United States	39.8	62.7
Western Europe	22.0	38.8
Japan	7.2	18.2
Others	4.4	4.9
Total	73.4	124.6

TABLE 10–2
United States Exports of Electronic Computers and Parts
Source: U S. Bureau of the Census

	1967	1969	1972	1973	1979
Amount (millions)	$432	$636	$1,800	$2,300	$5,100

ware sold in the world. The value of exported US computers and parts for the years 1967 to 1979 is shown in Table 10–2. Although production by subsidiaries of US computer corporations is not included, the US exported $5.1 billion worth of computer equipment during 1979. West Germany, the United Kingdom, Japan and France were the leading markets for United States computer equipment in 1973–1979.

Despite an increase in the production of computers in foreign countries, notably in Britain, France and the USSR, it is said that a "technology gap" exists. However, beyond the existence of a technology gap, the most limiting factor preventing users in Europe and Asia from realizing the full potential of the computer is the scarcity of qualified personnel at all levels: programmers, operators, technicians, etc. Among the top countries importing computers, related equipment and office equipment, four were over $1 billion markets in 1978. The top ten importers of computers and related equipment are listed in Table 10–4.[2] However, in 1979, the United States trade balance in computers and related equipment exceeded $4 billion (that is, exports exceeded imports by $4 billion).

The top ten foreign firms in the computer industry are listed in Table 10–3.[3] Note for comparison that IBM revenues exceeded $81 billion in 1978.

The global minicomputer market is increasing rapidly from $310 million sales in 1971 to $6 billion in 1980. In 1980 the Unites States had more minicomputers installed than the rest of the world combined.[4] While the United States had 500,000 minicomputers in 1980, West Germany had 130,000 and Japan 60,000.

The needs for computers in business, industry and government are great everywhere in the world. However, computers require capital for purchase and construction, and qualified personnel to operate and use them. As a nation is able, it will increase its use of computers in order to maintain and improve its competitive world economic position.

TABLE 10-3
Foreign Firms in the Computer Industry in 1978

Rank	Name	Country	Computer Revenues ($ millions)
1	Hitachi	Japan	1,830
2	Toshiba	Japan	1,633
3	Fujitsu	Japan	1,248
4	CII—Honeywell	France	1,061
5	ICL	Great Britain	1,019
6	Olivetti	Italy	789
7	Siemens	Germany	703
8	Nippon Electric	Japan	672
9	Philips	Netherlands	602
10	Nixdorf	Germany	554

TABLE 10-4
The Top Ten Computer Import Markets

Rank		1977 Imports (millions of dollars)
1	West Germany	1,383
2	United States	1,370
3	France	1,335
4	United Kingdom	1,159
5	Canada	669
6	Italy	620
7	Japan	500
8	Netherlands	483
9	Belgium	342
10	Sweden	303
	World Total	10,521

NOTE: The import market is recorded for computers and office equipment.

10.2 COMPUTERS IN LATIN AMERICA, WESTERN EUROPE, AND JAPAN

There is a strong interest in learning and applying the latest techniques to computer use in South America. But the primary problem is a shortage of trained personnel and the lack of contact with the centers of computer development, primarily the US. Computers will become more rapidly used in South America and other developing regions of the world as computer science education becomes available in the colleges and schools. Also, an important step will be the centralization of regional computer centers and the training of computer technicians, operators and programmers. Another possiblity is to develop a program to transfer US experience in computer science and management to developing countries by means of assistance programs. When we analyze the situation with respect to the use and availability of computers in South America, we can learn quite a bit about the situation in other regions of the world with equivalent conditions. While we must not overextend the analogy, the problems and potential of South America resemble those of Africa, the Middle East and parts of Asia to a great extent.

Japan is a highly industrialized nation with one of the highest annual percentage increases in Gross National Product. The computer field is growing rapidly in Japan. In 1971 the total of computers in use in Japan was 7,900. This number grew to 34,000 in 1976 and 100,000 in 1980. The Japanese computer industry is well-developed. About 40% of the computers purchased in Japan in 1980 were imported. The remaining 60% were manufactured by several large Japanese computer manufacturers. Nippon Electric and Toshiba have merged their computer efforts. Other joint efforts are Mitsubishi Electric and Oki Electric, which produce a COSMO computer, and Fujitsu and Hitachi, which jointly produce a series of computers. Future computer developments will be led by the triumvirate Fujitsu, Hitachi and Mitsubishi and the pair Nippon and Toshiba.[5, 6] Obviously, in order to compete worldwide, Japanese computer manufacturers have been forced to merge their computer divisions. This development is similar to what has occurred in the United States and Western Europe. The annual Japanese market is $4.5 billion; it is growing at 15% per year.

In terms of installed value, IBM has supplied 26% of the computers in Japan, while Fujitsu has supplied 16%. The total value of installed computers in Japan was $18.2 billion, as shown in Table 10—1. Fujitsu holds a large share of the stock of Amdahl Corporation, an American company, and thus is becoming active in the United States market. Japan is supplying subsidies to its two computer combines in order to make them competitive worldwide. Japan's computer companies hope to become a computer utility serving all of Southeast Asia. Already, Japan itself uses computers for business purposes and is approaching a cashless society with billing, paychecks and purchase data transferred from one computer to another. Japan had more than 7,000 automated teller terminals in use in 1977.

Japan has an ambitious program for computer research and development, with a cumulative cost of $65 billion. This program (Japan Computer Usage Development Institute) calls for an annual expenditure of approximately 0.5% of the Japanese GNP in contrast to the estimated expenditure for computer research and development of about 0.1% of the United States annual GNP. One unique factor in the Japanese market is the use of Kanji (Japanese character) input/output devices.

Western Europe had $39 billion worth of computers installed in 1980, in contrast to Japan, which had an installed base worth $18.2 billion. With about the same population as the United States, Western Europe contains about one-half the computer base installed in the United States, as shown in Table 10—1.[2] In terms of computers installed, the U. S. has supplied about 80% of the computers. IBM currently holds about 60% of the Western European market, and other American companies account for 20% of the market. Total expenditures for computers, peripherals, software and services was approximately $20 billion in Western Europe in 1979. The rate of growth of revenues in the Western European computer market is estimated to be 20% for the next several years.[8]

There were about 40,000 computers installed in the United Kingdom in 1980, in contrast to only 5,000 installed in 1971. The value of installed computers in the United Kingdom is $8 billion. The primary British computer company is International Computers Ltd. (ICL), which had revenues of $1 billion in 1979.

France has about 40,000 computers installed, with a value of about $9.0 billion. The primary computer company in France is a result of a merger in 1976 of Compagnie Internationale pour L'Informatique (CII) and Compagnie Honeywell Bull (CHB). The resulting company (CII-CHB) receives subsidies from the French government. It is partially owned by Honeywell Corporation of the United States. It is estimated that CII-CHB accounts for about 27% of the installed value of computers in France, with IBM accounting for 54%.[3, 16] CII-CHB had revenues in 1979 of about $1.2 billion.

West Germany has about 25,000 computers in an installed base worth $5.7 billion. The largest German manufacturer is Siemens. However, IBM accounts for more than 60% of the West German market. Siemens has revenues of about 18% of the West German market.

One of the major problems of the computer manufacturers in Western Europe has been the fragmentation of the computer market among a large number of competitors. Ten years ago, there were more computer companies in Western Europe than in the United States, but the output of each company was small compared to that of their American competitors. During the past eight years, mergers of many smaller computer companies in Western Europe have led to a significant reduction in the number of European suppliers of computer systems.

For example, in France, Compagnie des Machines Bull was merged with General Electric of America. This company was then merged with Honeywell to form Compagnie Honcywell Bull (CHB). Eventually CHB joined with CII to form the relatively large—and now competitive—firm mentioned above.

An attempted marketing merger of CII, Siemens, and Philips of the Netherlands endured only two years before CII left that combination to join with CHB.

Originally Great Britain had eight computer manufacturers, including Ferranti and Elliott Automation. After a series of mergers, ICL emerged as a relatively strong competitor and the United Kingdom's only computer manufacturer.

Minicomputers are becoming an important computer sales item in Western Europe. Digital Equipment Corporation of the United States holds about 50% of the Western European market, while other American firms hold about 25%. There are about 300,000 minicomputers installed in Western Europe, and the

TABLE 10-5
Comparison of Three Nations' Use of Computers in 1979

	U. S.	*W. Germany*	*U. S. S. R.*
Population	220.6	61.4	263.8
Gross National Product ($ billions)	2,368.5	760.5	1,500
Number of Computers (excluding microcomputers)	500,000	100,000	40,000
Computers/million persons	2,270	1,630	151
Computers/GNP ($ billion)	211	131	27

market is growing rapidly, at about 30% per year.[4] Minicomputers are made in Europe by Siemens, Nixdorf, Philips, and CII.

An estimate of the number of installed computers in several nations in 1975 is summarized in Table 10—5. These are approximate figures only and do not fully illustrate the computer power of a nation, since there is no differentiation between large and small computers and their speed of operation, etc. The gross national product of each country is also given and the ratio of the number of computers to the GNP in billions of dollars is determined. This ratio takes into account the variation in the wealth of the nations. It is interesting to note that this ratio varies from approximately 100 to 211 for Western Europe, Japan and the United States. The industrialized nations appear to fit within this range and 150 computers per billion dollars of GNP appears to be an average standard for the industrialized nations. One might consider a threshold indicating computer capabilities of a nation as 60 computers per billion of GNP. It is also interesting to note that the ratio of computers per million persons is highest in the United States, with 2,270 computers per million persons. Most Western European nations have a ratio of about 800:1,000,000, while the less-developed nations have a ratio of about 50 computers per million persons.

10.3 COMPUTERS IN THE USSR AND EASTERN EUROPE

Computing in the Soviet Union has made great advances during the past decade, particularly in application to numerical methods for airframe design, rocketry, mathematical modeling and machine tool control. Business data processing has been slower to develop but it promises to be an area of opportunity for the future. There have been some recent attempts to utilize computers in industry and commerce. However, it has been estimated that the Soviets are still some four to five years behind in the design of digital devices and there appears to be a significant shortage of trained personnel.[10, 11] Of course, the Russians are aware of the latest methods of management and scientific applications used in the West. In the use of digital computers for scientific purposes, the Soviets have shown their prowess in using computers in the launching of Sputniks, Luniks and other spacecraft. However, it is only recently that attention has been focused on economic applications of computers, with the purpose of optimizing production, distribution, planning and administration.

The COMECON countries (USSR, East Germany, Poland, Bulgaria, Romania, Czechoslovakia, Hungary and Cuba) which now account for about one-third of the world's industrial output, embarked during their 1971—1975 Five Year Plan upon a rapid expansion of their computer industries. The COMECON nations trade among themselves to a great extent. For example, 60% of Czechoslovak computer equipment exports go to the USSR. During 1973, twelve western computer manufacturing countries shipped only $120 million worth of computer equipment to COMECON. During the same year, East Germany shipped $155 million worth of computers to the Soviet Union.[12]

The Soviet Union had about 40,000 computers installed in 1979. Second-generation computers using transistors have been available in the USSR for a decade. The primary computers in use are the Minsk and BESM series. These are primarily used for scientific and management applications. About 4,000 Minsk computers are operating in the COMECON countries. The Minsk-32 is the primary machine for management information systems (MIS). The BESM-6 is one of the Soviet Union's most powerful computers; it carries out one million operations per second. The BESM-6 uses a 48-bit word and has a 64,000 word main storage unit capable of operating with an access time of two microseconds. The BESM-6 uses a Soviet computer language called ALPHA. Other Soviet computers use ALGOL as well as ALPHA.

A computer using integrated circuits, called the NAIRI-3, became available in 1970. This small and popular computer is capable of performing 20,000 operations per second.

Since 1972, the new COMECON computer series is called RYAD; it is produced as a joint venture of seven socialist countries. This series of computers is designed for applications that include process control systems, plant automated management systems, and regional management systems (or Management Information Systems). The RYAD computer is similar to the IBM 360. The largest RYAD, Model 1040, is competitive with a large IBM 360 in terms of computing power. The main memory uses magnetic cores; it has an access time of 450 nanoseconds. The technology of this machine lags behind that of the United States by about six years. The RYAD series includes models that operate in the range of 30,000 operations per second up to 1.5 million operations per second.

The Soviet Union has about 150 computers per million persons compared with 1600 computers per million persons for France and West Germany. Poland has about 60 computers per million inhabitants. The COMECON nations are now experiencing a lack of trained computer personnel as they attempt to increase their use of computers rapidly.

It is interesting to note that a nation with a centrally administered economy such as the USSR apparently does not have a central agency in charge of computer production and use. This fragmentation of computer development and production is similar to that which occurred in Western Europe during the past decade and which brought forth the large number of mergers of computer companies in the period 1968–1976.]11]

The computer equipment in the USSR primarily consists of equipment constructed with transistors; it would be considered second-generation equipment in the United States. However, work is underway on the development of third-generation computers using integrated circuits.

A computer commonly utilized in the USSR is the Minsk-22, which has been installed in a new computer center for the state department store in Moscow.

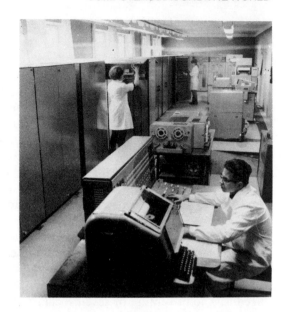

FIGURE 10–1   The MINSK-22
Computer at the Institute of
High Energy Physics, Moscow,
USSR. *Courtesy of TASS from
SOVFOTO.*

More than 200,000 shoppers daily produce 160,000 transactions. A staff of 8,000 mans 128 warehouses stocking 330,000 different types of goods. The computer center performs warehouse management and prints daily reports of trade. In the future, the center will also handle forecasting and inventory management at the point of sale.

A photo of the Minsk-22 computer at the Institute of High Energy Physics in Moscow is shown in Figure 10–1. The Minsk-22 is a medium scale transistorized computer capable of 6000 operations per second.

In Eastern Europe, the pattern of computer usage appears to be set by Russia. Several of the Eastern European countries manufacture computer peripheral equipment. The United Kingdom has been particularly successful at selling computer equipment to Eastern Europe, particularly through the International Computers, Ltd. group of merged companies. However, IBM, through its European subsidiaries, has sold computer equipment to Eastern Europe, particularly to Yugoslavia. Also, Compagnie Honeywell-Bull of France has sold a significant number of computers to Eastern Europe, particularly to Czechoslovakia. It has been reported that Eastern European countries in COMECON assigned top priority to large hard-currency investments in Western-made computers and peripheral gear for the next five-year plan, running from 1975 through 1979. The Eastern European countries have been reported to be shopping openly for Western European and US computers.[10]

Computer sales to Eastern Europe from the US and Britain would be higher if they did not have to contend with the strategic trade controls agreed upon by NATO countries. The list of strategic goods that are not to be sold to Communist nations presently includes large third-generation computers with a capacity greater than the IBM 360/40. The United States banned computer exports to the USSR in 1980 in retaliation for the Soviet invasion of Afghanistan.[12]

10.4   COMPUTERS IN CHINA

The Chinese computer industry started with aid from the Soviet Union in the late 1950s. The first computer using transistors in China was introduced in Peking in 1964. Known as the DJS-21, it is believed to be in use today.[15] There are several computer manufacturing facilities in China now. The weakest link in Chinese computer technology appears to be lack of a range of useful peripheral equipment.

The latest series of computers in China includes the DJS-6, completed in 1968, the DJS-18, first displayed at the Canton Trade Fair in 1974, and the DJS-220, introduced in 1979. The DJS-18 has a speed of 150,000 operations per second. It has a memory of 65,000 48-bit words and a core memory with an access time of two microseconds. The largest Chinese computers are 48-bit word machines with speeds of one million operations per second. The new DJS-11, for example, became available in 1976. It is capable of one million operations per second. The DJS-11 has 130,000 words of 48-bit memory, and it is capable of multiprogramming. A comparison of the fastest computers in the United States, Soviet Russia and China is given in Table 10–6.

It is estimated that there were about 1000 computers available in China in 1979. China has recently purchased computers from Compagnie Honeywell Bull of France and ICL of Great Britain. The demand for computers in China is likely to absorb all of its domestic production for the remainder of this decade.

10.5   BARRIERS TO THE FLOW OF COMPUTER DATA

One of the potential barriers to international use of computers is the regulation of computer data by many nations.[15, 16] As a result of the fear of unauthorized use of personal data by the police, government agencies and private en-

TABLE 10-6

Comparison of the Fastest Computers—1980

Nation	Computer	Speed (Operations/second)
U. S.	ILLIAC IV	200 million
U. S. S. R.	BESM-X	15 million
China	DJS-11	1 million

terprise, many nations have instituted laws and regulations on computer data and its flow. Also, many nations fear that the free flow of information will increase their dependence on telecommunications technology and the multinational companies that lead in this area.

In many ways information is a commodity and therefore open to control, taxation, and tariffs at national borders. Since data flow from computer to computer via satellite and microwave links is central to credit systems and international firms, the free flow across borders is greatly desired. All this issue is clouded by the fact that economic rivalry underlies much of the controversy.

CHAPTER 10 REFERENCES

1. J. Schreiber, *The American Challenge*, Atheneum House, Inc., New York, 1969.
2. B. O. Szuprowicz, "The World's Top 50 Computer Import Markets," *Datamation*, December 1979, pp. 125–127.
3. L. P. Solomon, "The Top Foreign Contenders," *Datamation*, May 25, 1979, pp. 79–81.
4. B. O. Szuprowicz, "Minicomputer Markets Around the World," Mini-Micro Systems, May 1978, pp. 60–63.
5. "Doing Business in Japan," *Electronic Business*, June 1980, pp. 128–132.
6. A. Durniak, "U. S. Beachhead for Japanese Computers is Only the Start," *Electronics*, March 27, 1980, pp. 113–136.
7. G. Gregory, "Japan Turns Its Ingenuity to the World Computer Market," *IEEE Spectrum*, April 1979, pp. 69–71.
8. "European Strategies to Fight IBM," *Business Week*, December 17, 1979, pp. 73–76.
9. "Comparing Superpowers—The Way U. S.—Soviet Economies Stack Up," *U. S. News and World Report*, February 11, 1980, pp. 26–27.
10. D. J. Reifer, "Snapshots of Soviet Computing," *Datamation*, February 1978, pp. 133–138.
11. J. E. Austin, "Computer Aided Planning and Decision Making in the USSR," *Datamation*, December 1977, pp. 71–74.
12. T. G. Donlan, "Technology Ban," *Barrons*, February 4, 1980, pp. 11–12.
13. I. L. Auerbach, "Computing In China, 1979," *IEEE Computer*, November 1979, pp. 52–60.
14. D. J. Reifer, "Snapshots of Computing in China," *Datamation*, March 1979, pp. 125–131.
15. J. Walsh, "There's Trouble in the Air over Transborder Data Flow," *Science*, October 6, 1978, pp. 29–32.
16. A. Pantages, "Is the World Building Data Barriers?" *Datamation*, December 1977, pp. 90–103.

17. T. A. Dolotta, *et. al.*, *Data Processing in 1980–1985*, Wiley and Sons, Inc., New York, 1976, Chapter 2.

18. "World Electronic Markets: Computers," *Electronics*, January 6, 1977, pp. 82–83; 101.

11

COMPUTERS IN URBAN AND GOVERNMENT SYSTEMS

11.1 INTRODUCTION

The United States Government is the world's largest single computer user. Some 12,000 computers are now being operated by the Federal Government.[3] In addition, the state and municipal governments make extensive use of computers. The US Government has approximately nine percent of all the machines in the United States and seven percent of the computers in the world. The purchase cost of Federally-owned computers was $5 billion in 1979, and it has increased continually since then.

Computers are used in the Federal Government to accomplish worthwhile tasks not otherwise feasible and to improve and reduce the cost of government operations. Also, computers are used for management activities that contribute to more efficient and economical procurement and utilization of computers. Some examples of applications of computers in the Federal Government are:[1]

- Congressional investigators used a computer to keep track of information gathered and used in the Watergate probe. Information was stored and retrieved by alphabetical, chronological order, and by name and subject.
- Weather forecasts up to 30 days in the future are being made with more reliability.

TABLE 11-1
Computers in the Federal Government

Year	1960	1970	1975	1980
Number of Computers	300	4500	7200	12,000

- Refunds due a taxpayer are now being offset against back taxes owed by the same taxpayer.
- Essential information for solving crimes is becoming available on a nationwide scale. (The National Crime Information Center is operational. It links state and metropolitan area police systems through a computerized central index of documented law enforcement information.)
- The time required for processing new drug applications was reduced from one year to six months, partially as the result of the availability of computer-produced periodic status reports. An 18-month backlog has been virtually eliminated.

The growth of the number of computers used by the Federal Government is shown in Table 11-1. Immediately following World War II, the government

FIGURE 11-1 The SEAC computer, the first computer at the National Bureau of Standards, was completed in 1950. For the fourteen years of its useful life, SEAC was used by dozens of other government agencies; portions of this computer are now preserved in the Smithsonian Institution. This computer was one of the first general purpose, internally-sequenced, electronic computers. *Courtesy of the National Bureau of Standards.*

ordered two computers, one for the Census Bureau and one for the Pentagon. However, the Bureau of Standards built a computer for its own use which was completed and operating late in 1950. This computer was named SEAC (Standards Eastern Automatic Computer.) The SEAC was one of the first, if not the first, general purpose internally-sequenced electronic computer in operation in the US. It is shown in Figure 11-1.

By 1980, the Federal Government spent $1.4 billion for the use of commercial data processing services. It also purchased $600 million worth of computer equipment during fiscal year 1980. The Federal government purchases about 1500 mid-sized or large computers annually.

The state governments in the US have also purchased and used computers for the various functions of state government. California's state agencies have more computer power at their disposal than do those of any other state. California has 250 digital computers and employs about 5,000 persons to operate and program them. The state spent approximately $200 million on computers and computer use during the 1979–1980 fiscal year.

The applications of computers in urban and Federal government are diverse and far reaching. McLuhan says, "The extreme decentralizing power of the computer in eliminating cities and all concentrations of population whatever is as nothing compared to its power to translate hardware into software and capital goods into information."[4]

While the computer may not have yet eliminated cities, it has aided in the process of suburbanization and diffusion of population. This has necessitated the use of computers to assist with the problems arising from suburbanization. In London, England, and San Jose, California, a computer traffic control system is used to improve the utility of the highway system. In London, the 1.4 million dollar system operates 100 traffic signals in a 6.5 square mile section of London. The British Ministry of Transportation maintains that a 5 percent reduction in journey times will be attained as a minimum.

The computer is used in many localities to count votes at election time. One simple scheme which uses computers and a punched card is the IBM Votomatic system. A voter at a poll is given an unpunched card which may be punched with a sharp stylus. The unperforated card is placed in a bed or holder, and a mask is laid over the card. The overlay mask indicates the voter options and various candidates' names. Then the voter can punch the holes and mark his vote. The card is then placed in a ballot box and all the cards are run at a computer center. Using this procedure, Los Angeles County is able to tally over a million votes for a variety of candidates and provide early counts by 10:00 p.m. on election night.*

*Los Angeles suffered unfavorable nationwide publicity in 1970 when tardy vote counting and vote-count irregularities were charged to computer vote tabulation in a primary election. Eleven states, in a (possibly) shortsighted step, have already forbidden the use of computers in election tabulations. However, it is specifically permitted by law in 38 states and 16 million ballots were counted by computer in the 1976 November election.

Only 7% of the nation's counties use computer-counted punch card ballots. This fact is due to concern over the security, reliability, and cost of the computerized systems.

The use of computers by the Internal Revenue Service has resulted in greater tax returns to the government as well as more efficient processing of the taxpayer's forms. Probably the IRS could not be able to process the individual forms without the aid of computers. In 1930 the IRS processed six million tax returns. In 1980, it processed 140 million. In addition to individual returns, there were approximately 400 million information returns, including W−2 forms, reports on interest paid by banks, stock dividends, and similar data to process. The IRS began a program of computer automation in 1961 when it set up a nationwide computer network centered in Martinsburg, Virginia. Now all individual and corporate tax returns are being processed by computers. The IRS runs nine full scale computer centers located in regional offices throughout the country.[8] In 1980, computer operations at IRS added $140 million to federal tax collections. This brings the total additional revenues from IRS's use of computers to $800 million since 1962. In addition, EDP has resulted in quicker and more efficient processing operations. Also, large-scale, direct data entry terminals have been developed for IRS. The use of terminals eliminates the use of punched cards, since the data is entered directly from the tax return to magnetic tape storage. This system eliminates the punching and verification of 400 million cards per year by IRS. The IRS computer system provides a rapid, efficient, auditing system which should reduce the number of errors and evasions in the tax process.

A program of magnitude similar to that of the Internal Revenue Service is that of the US Census Bureau. Every ten years, the US Census Bureau accumulates the facts on the population. As a result of the 1980 census, the headquarters of the Bureau received four billion facts concerning 220 million Americans. This data was processed by four large computers. Analysis of the data relates parameters such as income, housing, sex, occupation, marital status, education and age. The study determines trends in large areas such as congressional districts, states, and even the nation as well as in small areas such as neighborhoods. The completed questionnaires are photographed and scanned by a computer reader converting the data to 6500 reels of magnetic tape. Since the census reports, which are required by an Act of Congress, are confidential, all names are dropped from the questionnaires before the information is coded on magnetic tape.[9]

The automation of census data was begun by Hollerith in the 1880 census and has proceeded since under the pressure of increasing population. In 1790, when the United States took its first decennial population census, each person was asked five questions and the statistical summaries for the whole country were printed on a total of 56 pages. In 1980, the four billion facts obtained from the 220 million Americans were used to allocate Federal funds for highways and to realign the boundaries of congressional districts. Business also makes use of the census data for marketing and manufacturing location purposes. The US census is an important statistical tool for government and business. However, security of each individual's data must be assured. The question of the legitimacy of the 68 census questions is a matter of concern, and this will certainly be a question to be considered in preparation for the 1990 census.

Computers will be used extensively by the US Postal Service during the 1980s. The Service has 32,000 offices, which process nearly 90 billion pieces of mail each year. The New York City Post Office alone deals with 35 million pieces of mail daily. Since the late 1970s, new methods of automation utilizing computers have been developed; plans were made, for instance, to install 210 computers and sorting machines in 136 cities. One computer system under development will enable a postal operator to sort mail merely by glancing at the zip code on a letter as it flashes by and pressing a zip-coded keyboard. The keyboard will feed the information to a computer, which will tell a sorting machine to which of 277 destination bins the letter goes. Twelve operators will be able to sort up to 36,000 letters an hour at an estimated savings of $13.5 million a year in labor.

Computers, automation and new methods may enable the Postal Service to avoid collapsing under the burden of an ever-increasing volume of mail and increasing costs of processing. The USPS ran a deficit of $1.5 billion in 1976. The Service committed $300 million to automated processing equipment in 1980. Now about 60% of the mail is sorted mechanically. The USPS has spent $50 million for computers over the past several years. Computer-controlled optical character recognition for sorting mail has not yet achieved reliable service. Nevertheless, it is anticipated that computers will aid the Postal Service in overcoming its deficits, reducing the troubles that have plagued its operation in the past.

The USPS has approved the installation of an Electronic-computer-originated mail (ECOM) service.[12] This electronic mail service serves large volume mailers through 25 post offices. The system will use computers interconnected by cable; it should be operational in 1982.

The US Labor Department is using computers to assist in the placing of job seekers in suitable employment. A job bank using a daily computer output list of available jobs is used to help place the unemployed in more than 20 cities. The job banks are used by the various state employment agencies. Some agencies use interviews to match the individual with the job, while others use the computer. In these latter cases, the applicant's characteristics and qualifications are also put into a computer and then matched by the computer with the job specifications given by the employer. Proposals have been made to investigate the feasibility of a national job bank. If a national employment system with computer-aided man and job matching does eventuate, the mobility and employability of the worker could be greatly improved.

The Social Security Administration of the US uses 27 computers in the largest commercial computer installation in the world. The volume of data is awesome. It requires 165,000 reels of tape for storage. Every day one million earnings entries are processed and the system accounts for 197 million citizens. In addition, the Social Security Administration administrates the Medicare and Medicaid systems for some 21 million persons. The Administration uses computers effectively to accomplish the overwhelming task of collecting $301 billion in deductions and paying out $2.9 billion in benefits every month.[3] The Social Security system sends sixteen million recurring federal payments directly to the recipients' accounts. The transactions are sent as computer messages from the Social Security computer to the computers of the recipients' banks. The Social Security data bank can be accessed by any one of 3700 terminals located in 1300 regional and district offices.

Computers are widely used by the Federal and state governments in diverse applications. In the next section we consider the use of computers for urban planning and municipal information systems.

11.2 URBAN PLANNING AND MUNICIPAL INFORMATION SYSTEMS

Computer systems are in various stages of adoption and use within the urban and metropolitan governments. There are many urban problems, but finding solutions for urban problems and fitting computer technology into those solutions requires careful definitions of problems and alternative solutions. The problems of congestion, pollution, urban education, poverty, housing and race relations are difficult to attack using the computer as an aid. One view is that of urban problems as productivity problems. Public sector activities, many of them in cities, have had alarmingly small productivity increases while productivity has been increasing in most other sectors of society. Services are becoming more and more important (especially public services) in our national economy; increased productivity is necessary to continuing development of the national economy. The question remains: how can computer systems help increase the productivity of urban services?

Planners are also concerned by the distribution of the services rather than the amount of service. How can we distribute the services more evenly and insure the equality of services to all groups? Of what value is it to solve the financial problem of the transit system of a city, if the system does not serve all residential areas efficiently?

The functions of urban planning are currently being revitalized by modern computer-oriented management science techniques. As we found in Chapter 7, management science can be used to understand and control complex systems consisting of interrelated components which evolve with time. Underlying all management science techniques is the rigor of quantification: the planner asks how much each alternative will cost and what the benefits will be. Often simulation techniques are used to analyze the various courses of action.

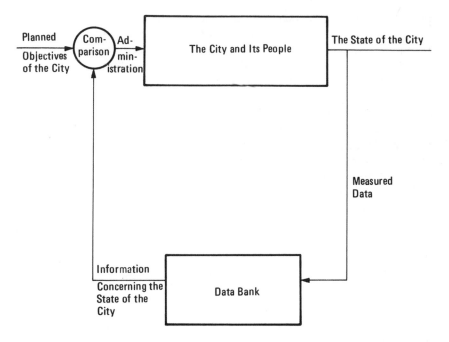

FIGURE 11–2   A conceptual model of a municipal management information system.

The intended solutions to interrelated systems often result in unforeseen consequences. A new highway, for example, built to provide faster access between the city and its suburbs, also radically affects the living patterns of the area it passes through, dominating the area and often causing the original residents to move to the suburbs. In such a case, the new highway, by responding to one need, introduces several others.

The need for complete and up-to-date information about an urban region's condition leads to the concept of a central data bank. The United States Census can provide more than ten million pieces of data to describe the characteristics of an urban region containing 100,000 people. Other state and federal agencies can add fifty million data items. This data can be looked on as a data bank to be drawn on by all the municpal planners and managers. Ideally information would not be fragmented among many agencies, but would appear in one central computer file. A conceptual model of a city and the management of the city using an information system is shown in Figure 11–2. The data bank is used to provide information for management purposes. There is currently a significant amount of activity toward the development of municipal data banks and municipal information systems.

The urban planner wishes to use information systems for such activities as planning sites for public facilities such as schools, police stations, firehouses, roads and hospitals. The city executives wish to use the information systems to manage and allocate the resources of the city to the various functions.

For example, one urban systems group, in New York City, plans to attack the problem of air pollution with the assistance of a computer information system. Such an approach includes developing mathematical models and statistical analyses and designing on-line processing systems which include remote terminals and sensors. The Location and Mapping Program (LAMP) installed in Nashville, Tennessee in 1975 offers maps and location information for streets, school districts, zoning and building lots.[7,9] The system is used for locating stoplights, sewer lines, utilities, streets and all zoning boundaries.

The computer could project air quality (for each segment of the city) from six to 48 hours in advance by processing information on current air quality together with an emission model (amount and type of pollutant, by location, based on weather forecasts and daily, weekly and seasonal variations) and a dissipation model (cleansing of air, by location, based on wind direction and velocity and atmospheric conditions). The computer can compare this predicted air quality with accepted clean-air standards, and recommend control actions necessary to prevent the development of hazardous pollution levels in any part of the city.

The wealth of detailed information about the city required by advanced planning techniques is not to be had from the traditional systems of record-keeping. Thus, additional sensors and measurement systems will be required to complete the system.

An example of the components of a comprehensive municipal management information system is given in Figure 11−3.

In the past the use of information systems by municipalities has been quite limited. Only a portion of the available data was collected or recorded and the municipality was managed on a short-range basis. Recently the US Department of Housing and Urban Development has initiated a program for developing municipal information systems. The information system is to be composed of four subsystems—dedicated to public safety, public finance and related book-keeping chores, human resources (health, education, welfare, etc.) and physical development (urban planning, public works, facilities maintenance.) For example, such municipal information systems will assist in the prevention and control of crime and fire, speed traffic flow and detect sources of pollution. With an adequate data base, the population shifts within an urban area can be accurately measured and used for purposes of urban planning for schools, roads and other public services. One potential advantage of a municipal information system is the ability provided the user to investigate the relationship among various factors affecting the municipality.

Computers can be used by public safety agencies to increase their productivity.[2, 11] In the recent notorious case of the "Los Angeles Hillside Strangler,"

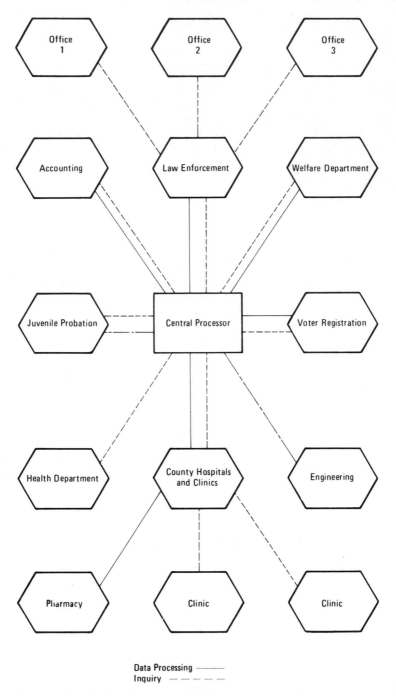

Data Processing ——————
Inquiry — — — —

FIGURE 11–3   An example of the components of a comprehensive municipal management information system. *Courtesy of IBM Corporation*.

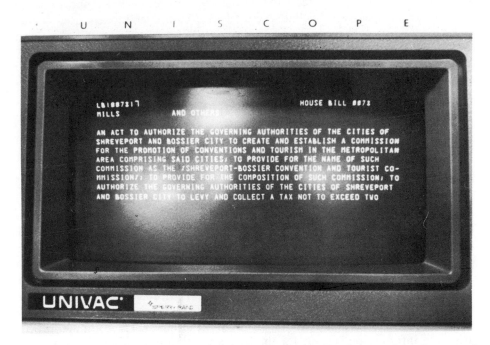

FIGURE 11–4   Louisiana legislators utilize a computer retrieval system for new or pend-
ing legislation by means of terminals connected to the state's data processing system. Retrieval of the title, status and bill sponsor is possible
within three seconds of inquiry. A close-up view of an actual bill is shown
as one might view it from one of the terminals installed in the House,
Senate, Legislative Council's office, or Lieutenant Governor's office. In
addition, lawmakers can order a printout each morning to learn of all
bills introduced the previous day. *Courtesy of UNIVAC Division of
Sperry Rand Corp.*

computers were used to isolate and correlate clues. Los Angeles had 130 detec-
tives working on the case, with 10,000 clues recorded in the largest law enforcement computer in the western US.[11] A case was slowly built when one likely
suspect was listed in the computer under clue numbers 6111, 6458, 7598, and
7745. The task force had a lead which resulted eventually in an arrest.

Computer information systems may be used to assess the future consequences of public decisions. With the aid of urban simulation models, which were
discussed in Chapter 9, the effects of various public actions may be assessed.
Forrester's recent book, *Urban Dynamics*, attempts to use this approach for a
model city.[10] For example, one simulation assesses the consequence of the
Federal Government's providing new city housing for low income persons. Ac-

cording to the model, an increase in housing and jobs results in the short run, but over the years, both will decline. Nevertheless, computer models used for the public policy process have not yet lived up to expectations. Computer models for urban planning purposes have been limited in quality, applicability, and utility. The use of simulation and models of urban regions will be a valuable approach for urban planning in the coming years.

11.3 COMPUTERS AND THE LEGISLATURES

Computers can be used to assist the functions of the legislative as well as the executive branch of sate and federal government. For example, the Pennsylvania Legislature provides its members with up-to-date computer reports on bills that are working their way through the legislative process. Members of the Pennsylvania General Assembly who desire to know the status of a key bill in the number of the proposed law at computer terminals situated at various points in the capitol. The current information is provided on the visual display at the terminal and the information is also typed out at the terminal. The computer process keeps the information current for the legislators. An illustration of a computer legislative retrieval system is shown in Figure 11–4.

The US Congress has initiated several studies and discussions concerning the use of the computer in assisting Congress. A congressional computer information system, if adopted, would give every one of the 535 representatives and senators access to the tons of information that now can be tapped easily only by the senior committee chairmen. A congressional computer system would be helpful, if only to keep track of the 12,000 pieces of legislation introduced annually. During the 96th Congress (1975–1976), members were called upon to consider 40,000 bills and resolutions; of this total, 4,000 became law. Not only must the senator or representative respond to the pressures of daily legislative operations, but he must also respond to the needs of his constituents, who now average 450,000 per member. With the demands on each legislator growing each year, the assistance of automatic data processing in the decision-making process is desirable. Representative Jack Brooks of Texas introduced a bill (H.R. 404) into the Congress in January 3, 1969, which called for the development and establishment of an information system for the Congress. This bill was subsequently passed as Public Law 89–306. In addition, a bill, H.R. 17654, was introduced into the House of Representatives on May 18, 1970, concerned with the reorganization of the legislative process; it included recommended action toward the development of a data processing service for the legislative branch of the Federal Government. Portions of H.R. 17654 are reprinted below.

TITLE IV—CONGRESS AS AN INSTITUTION
Part 1—Joint Committee on Data Processing

Congressional Findings and Policy

SEC. 401. (a) It is the sense of the Congress that there is an urgent, critical, and continuing need on the part of the Congress and the legislative branch generally for a modern, effective, and coordinated automatic data processing and information storage and retrieval system—

(1) to assist the Congress, its committees and Members, its officers and employees, and its offices and other organizational units, and the respective agencies, offices, and other organizational units in the legislative branch generally, in obtaining and analyzing information;

(2) to expedite their operations and activities; and

(3) to facilitate and improve the performance of the legislative and representative functions of the Congress.

(b) It is, therefore, the policy of the Congress, in view of this need—

(1) that the Congress and the legislative branch shall be provided with, and shall acquire, establish, and maintain, by purchase, lease, or otherwise, the most modern, up-to-date, efficient, effective and coordinated automatic data processing and information storage and retrieval equipment and facilities which are appropriate to the needs and requirements of the Congress and the legislative branch generally;

(2) that a method of continuous, coordinated, comprehensive, and efficient planning and review shall be established and maintained by the Congress for the continuing development and improvement of such equipment and facilities and the use thereof . . .

The United States Congress uses computers to increase the quality and efficiency of the legislative process.[5] The Congress employs computers for:

1. Administrative systems
2. The Legislative Calendar system
3. The Committee Calendar system
4. A bill-status system

There is also an electronic voting system using two computers and 48 terminals. The members of Congress each insert their identification cards into a terminal and push a button. The representative may vote by punching one of three keys: "Aye," "Nay," and "Present." A running total of the vote as well as each member's vote are displayed on the walls of the chamber. The voting system also keeps a record for each member.

The use of computers in the legislative branches of the Federal and state governments is growing and will enable the legislators to keep pace with the ever-increasing complexity of government.

11.4   COMPUTERS AND THE MILITARY

In addition to the 12,000 computers used by the Federal government, there are thousands of special purpose computers used by the US military. Since 1971, the Department of Defense has spent more than $8 billion for a computer network for gathering intelligence and controlling US military forces anywhere in the world. This whole network is known as the World Wide Military Command and Control System (WIMEX). In emergencies the President and the Joint Chiefs of Staff rely on WIMEX computers to warn of attacks and to coordinate and control all activity by US military organizations. The action room of the Pentagon is one of the 27 major command posts relying on WIMEX.[12]

One command post located inside Cheyenne Mountain in Colorado incurred a false war alert on November 9, 1979 which resulted in a state of alert and a flight of ten jet aircraft interceptors. The system is often faulty. Another example of crisis was the Guyana incident in November 1978 when the Joint Chiefs of Staff turned to WIMEX for details on what planes, troops and medical aid were available. At the height of the crisis a power outage interrupted the link between the system computers. The system serves well, but at times it fails in its performance.

11.5   COMPUTERS, GOVERNMENT AND THE FUTURE

The pervasive use of computers in government has resulted in many concerns about government computer data banks, computer networks and their consequences. Has the computer contributed, or is it contributing, to the movement toward centralization in American government? Can citizens be confident that private information concerning their Social Security or prior military status is not wrongly accessed or released?

The use of computers by government in the future can be portrayed in a narrative or scenario form. J. C. R. Licklider has provided one scenario in a recent book; it is reprinted below.[1]

> On the whole, computer technology continues to advance along
> the curve it has followed in its three decades of history since
> World War II. The amount of information that can be stored

for a given period or processed in a given way at unit cost doubles every two years. (The twenty-one years from 1979 to 2000 yield ten doublings, for a factor of about 1,000.) Waveguides, optical fibers, rooftop satellite antennae, and coaxial cables provide abundant bandwidth and inexpensive digital transmission both locally and over long distances. Computer consoles with good graphic display and speech input and output have become almost as common as television sets. Some pocket computers are fully programmable, as powerful as IBM 360/40s used to be, and are equipped with both metallic and radio connectors to computer communication networks.

An international network of digital computer communication networks serves as the main and essential medium of informational interaction for governments, institutions, corporations, and individuals. The Multinet, as it is called, is hierarchical—some of the component networks are themselves networks of networks—and many of the top-level networks are national networks. The many subnetworks that comprise this network of networks are electronically compatible and physically interconnected. Most of them handle real-time speech as well as computer messages, and some handle video.

The Multinet has supplanted the postal system for letters, the dial telephone system for conversations and teleconferences, stand-alone batch-processing and time-sharing systems for computation, and most filing cabinets, microfilm repositories, document rooms, and libraries for information storage and retrieval. Many people work at home, interacting with coworkers and clients through the Multinet, and many business offices (and some classrooms) are little more than organized interconnections of such home workers and their computers. People shop through the Multinet, using its cable television and electronic funds transfer functions, and a few receive delivery of small items through adjunct pneumatic tube networks. Routine shopping and appointment scheduling are generally handled by private-secretary-like programs called OLIVERs which know their masters' needs. Indeed, the Multinet handles scheduling of almost everything schedulable. For example, it eliminates waiting to be seated at restaurants and if you place your order through it can eliminate waiting to be served.

Governments do their "paperwork" in subnetworks of the Multinet. In the process, they generate huge data bases, but the fact that they are computer-processable keeps their sheer volume from limiting their usefulness. Task-control programs know, for example, who has to sign off on, coordinate on, or simply read each item, and by what date. They regulate the flow of information through the offices and agencies, preventing the accumulation of backlogs and keeping track of productivity. They also enforce rules of access and dissemination that have been painfully worked out over the years, ensuring executive privilege to working papers and at the same time making available to Congress, for example, data that the rules say Congress ought to have.

The security features of the Multinet make it possible to control access selectively at any level, from the basic item of information to the highest-level subnetwork. Some of the functions of the defense and law enforcement sectors of government are carried out in subnetworks to which other, ordinary subnetworks have no access at all. Other sensitive functions, such as proprietary commercial functions and funds transfers, are protected at lower levels so that the government can monitor them selectively. The security rules and procedures have been developed with such exquisite care and so fully tested, proven, demonstrated, and explained that almost everyone accepts their validity and effectiveness. They are regarded as essential parts of the networks; indeed, they have been more difficult to realize than the hardware and transmission-level software.

Once in a while there is a flurry of rumors about international espionage within the Multinet, but widespread belief in them is precluded by the fact that entrances to and exits from national networks are under national control, access control is so highly developed, and complete audit trails are recorded. More frequently, a national government is accused of monitoring more assiduously than the law allows, but in the United States, at least, no one has yet come up with audit trails to prove it.

Networking has greatly increased the effectiveness as well as the efficiency of many of the functions of defense. Command and control are based upon on-line, interactive data management, modeling, problem solving, and communication. The command and control function is very closely coupled to intelligence analysis and dissemination (which embraces the same kinds of activity) and even to some components of intelligence acquisition. That is, many intelligence functions can be carried out within the span of a single command decision process. State, Defense, the CIA, and other departments and agencies are interconnected so effectively that organization charts do not seriously interfere with teamwork. Indeed, the network protocol graph has largely displaced the organization chart. The FBI and state and local law enforcement agencies are internetted* in protocol-controlled patterns, of course, with one another and with offices in the defense complex.

The government uses the Multinet to monitor and regulate the day-to-day operations of business and industry. Stock markets, for example, operate within the Multinet, as do stockbrokers and buyers and sellers and the financial departments of corporations, and the government monitors and records every transaction. Government access—indeed, all access—to the data pertinent to regulation is controlled by the already mentioned security rules and procedures. Many government services are executed in or delivered through the Multinet. Weather forecasting, market reporting, the census, and the modernized post, telephone, and telegraph services are obvious examples, but there are many others, such as mediation, licensing, insurance, statistics and indicators, and library services. Much of the function of revenue collection is part and parcel of computerized commerce and electronic funds transfer, which are of course carried on within the Multinet. Advisory polls and formal elections have been carried out through the Multinet since 1990, when the universal ID system, based on computer recording and identification of fingerprints, was set up on a nationwide basis.

SUMMARY

The United States Government is the world's largest single computer user. The computer is used by the Federal government for functions in the Bureau of the Budget, the Internal Revenue Service, the Weather Bureau and the Census Bureau—among others. The computer is also used in state and municipal government functions. The computer is used, for example, to count votes and to provide a job bank for those seeking available employment.

Computers are being used in municipal information systems and for urban planning. With the aid of computer information systems and management techniques, the cities are attempting to solve the problems of traffic, crime, housing and schools. In addition, simulation techniques enable the planner to assess the consequences of various public policies and alternatives.

Computers are being used by the legislative as well as the executive branch of

*Connected via computer communications networks.

government. Computer systems assist the legislator by maintaining information on all the legislation under consideration and related data. The computer is indeed a useful tool for governmental activities.

CHAPTER 11 PROBLEMS

P11—1. Inquire at the city hall of your town about the use of computers to aid the government of the city. List several uses of computers that are presently accomplished.

P11—2. List several uses of computers that could be added to aid the government of your city.

P11—3. Design a voting system for your campus government which utilizes punched cards and requires the voter to punch holes in his card in order to register his vote.

P11—4. State governments account for about $500 million worth of spending on computers and their software. Contact your state government and determine what the computer expenditures were for your state last year. What is this percentage of the total state budget? What agency of your state government is the largest user of computers?

P11—5. Computers are used extensively in law enforcement. Visit your city or county law-enforcement agency and determine its use of computers for storing and retrieving information about crime.

P11—6. The computer industry itself is affected by government regulation. Investigate government control of the computer industry and list all the federal and state agencies that regulate, in part, the computer industry.

P11—7. While it is critical that government use computers to store data regarding the citizens it serves, it also arouses fear of unauthorized use of private information by others. Conduct a survey of some of the citizens of your community regarding governments' uses of computers, the fear of centralization and invasion of privacy.

CHAPTER 11 REFERENCES

1. M. L. Dertouzos and J. Moses, *The Computer Age*, MIT Press, Cambridge, Massachusetts, 1980, Chapter 6.

2. B. Niblett, *Computer Science and the Law*, Cambridge University Press, New York, 1980.

3. "Uncle Sam's Computer Has Got You," *US News and World Report*, April 10, 1978, pp. 44–48.
4. M. McLuhan, *War and Peace in a Global Village*, Bantam Books, Inc., New York, 1968, pp. 88–89.
5. N. Gregory, "Congress—The Politics of Information," *Data Management*, November 1978, pp. 10–18.
6. N. Simon and A. Minc, *The Computerization of Society: A Report to the President of France*, The MIT Press, Cambridge, Massachusetts, 1980.
7. M. Stephens, *Three Mile Island*, Random House, New York, 1981.
8. J. Kirchner, "IRS Center Ready—Are You?" *Computerworld*, April 14, 1980, pp. 1–2.
9. "Counting On Minis, Micros for the 1980 Census," *Mini-Micro Systems*, November 1979, pp. 39–40.
10. J. W. Forrester, *Urban Dynamics*, M.I.T. Press, Cambridge, Mass., 1969.
11. B. Farrell, "Stalking the Hillside Strangler," *New West*, March 10, 1980, pp. 19–24.
12. W. J. Broad, "Computers and the US Military Don't Mix," *Science*, March 14, 1980, pp. 1183–1187.
13. B. Wilkins, "P. O. Readies Electronic Mail," *MIS Week*, August 27, 1980, pp. 1–2.
14. "Clogged Courts Try the Electronic Cure," *US News and World Report*, April 28, 1980, pg. 96.
15. W. H. Dutton, "Automating Bias," *Society*, February 1980, pp. 36–41.
16. F. Halpern, "Current Trends in the European Computer Market," *Datamation*, September 1980, pp. 157–160.

12

COMPUTERS AND THE ARTS

12.1 INTRODUCTION

Digital computers are machines, and the notion of machines creating works of art has nearly always been rejected by man. Creativity and the creation of art has heretofore been reserved for the human. What can an unfeeling, intelligent, but unemotional machine do in the world of art? As Geoffrey Jefferson said in 1949, in his *Lister Oration*, "Not until a machine can write a sonnet or compose a concerto because of thoughts and emotions felt, and not by the chance fall of symbols, could we agree that machine equals brains—that is, not only write it but know that it had written it. No mechanism could feel (and not merely signal, an easy contrivance) pleasure at its successes, grief when its valves fuse, be warmed by flattery, be made miserable by its mistakes, be charmed by sex, be angry or depressed when it cannot get what it wants."

During the past few years, the use of the computer to generate poetry, music, dance, choreography and graphic art has increased significantly. However, it is the symbiosis of computer and man that provides the world with the works of art. That is, man, using the computer as a tool, creates the works. The following poem was produced by the Manchester University computer under the *instructions* and *guidance* of a man.

```
You will see the
                   weeping
Lord Now Maybe     Time
And Mr. Mendel
                   All in A
    Solarhythm          Cloak.
```

Although most philosophers will agree that creativity is a function of mankind alone, the computer has extensive capabilities for carrying out elaborate and precise instructions. It is the combination of man and his "personal" computer, somewhat like his "personal" piano—a machine after all—that creates the work of art. As Don Fabun recently stated:[1] "Someday—not too far from now—people will "ride" their personal computers with all the excitement that the motorcycle rider feels when he storms down the long tunnel of the night. We will, with computers, explore our mental world with something that shares, amplifies and defines our experience. In doing so, it will help us define ourselves as human personalities."

While the computer can do only what it has been programmed to do, perhaps it provides a source of creative amplification through its rapid, untiring attempts. Certainly, the results have not been tallied yet and we shall learn in this decade if the man-computer partnership leads to new lights, new forms of art and most of all to beauty.

The existence of the new creations, strikingly beautiful or absurdly comic, like the computer itself, seem to many people to have no ancestors or origins. The scores of drawings, films and musical compositions resulting from the artist/computer partnership are admired or attacked, but hardly understood because they are a new and little-understood challenge to our cultural perspective.

In a sense the computers will challenge the very capacity that man has regarded as making him supreme and unique: his ability to think—his brain-power. One can say that the computer has transcended its original purpose, quick mathematical calculation, and is now reaching toward the ability to simulate Descartes' irreducible requirement for humanity.* Whether that simulation will ever become a reality is another question, but the very attempt places the old *New Yorker* cartoon, in which a huge computer types a message to its white-smocked attendant, reading *Cogito, ergo sum*, in a new perspective.

The computer provides a high-speed information processor for the artist, who can now use the computer to enter the world of the scientist and examine those laws which describe physical reality. "The artist," as Professor Csuri, of Ohio State University, has said, "may alter the parameters to create a different kind of artistic world. In a highly systematic and disciplined manner he can deal with fantasy and imagination. One example [of this] . . . is the well-known

*Descartes, a seventeenth century mathematician and philosopher (See Chapter 2), stated his fundamental truth as *Cogito, ergo sum*, or "I think, therefore I am."

Lorentz transformation . . . a theory of special relativity [explaining] the apparent distortion of a form as it approaches the speed of light. It would be interesting to see what happens graphically to a drawing of a turtle or a hummingbird as it approaches the speed of light. The artist may be interested in the absurdity of such an idea and it may give him a different kind of form. He may enjoy the contradiction of a turtle traveling near the speed of light.''

Some of the relevant uses of the computer in the arts are listed below:

- Detecting the influence of one poet on the works of another
- Creating motion pictures
- Deciphering ancient languages
- Choreographing a ballet
- Analyzing the vocabulary of eighteenth century French political writers
- Composing a symphony

The inspiration of the artist, combined with the capabilities of the computer, will undoubtedly bring forth new artistic forms. Although this evolution is in a primitive stage now, the computer is an instrument with great potential. The instrument will come alive in the hands of a great artist.

In this chapter, we consider the application of the computer to the various arts. In the next section, we examine the use of the computer in the creation of paintings, drawings, films and graphic design. In the following section we consider the use of the computer in the world of music and dance. Finally, in Section 16-4, we examine the application of the computer to the study of literature and other subjects of the humanities.

12.2 COMPUTERS AND THE VISUAL ARTS

The techniques and concepts which have been developed during the past decade for generating visual displays of the results of computer problem-solving can be used to make artistic visual displays.

Art has always depended upon science and technology to supply both the medium in which the work is done and the tools for doing it. The techniques are common whether the computer is used to generate visual displays of scientific data (e.g., shapes and motions of mechanical systems, mathematical rotations of n-dimensional objects, motions of atoms in a fluid) or shapes and motions which may be important in design or as an artistic medium.[3]

The computer and the current conceptional basis of the arts are reflections of the era in which we live. Our environment is structured in technology, and the machine in some ways exemplifies the spirit of the times. Just as the painting and poetry of earlier times reflected the living fabric of those times, the art of our time will reflect the technology available to the artist. Computer art is, at least in part, a bridge between the artistic realm and the scientific-technical realm.

Computer art, which uses the computer as the medium, is a relatively new art form. The artist has long recognized that repetition and proportion contribute to a good effect in a drawing or painting. The computer can readily repeat a line or shape and calculate, with the proper program, the proper perspective for an object. Perspective is essentially geometric and can be included in computer art. Impressionism, which developed during the last half of the 19th century, has a partially mathematical basis and included an aspect called substitution, which suggests the notion that separate representations in space provide different subjective impressions. Substitution is also a major component of computer art and is quite mathematical in its precision and its technique.

The work of the school of the Futurists during the 20th century also contributed to computer art. The Futurists included conceptions and impressions of machines and motion in their art. Artists such as Klee, Feininger and Duchamp concerned themselves with mathematics and optical illusions. Feininger's subjects, for example, have cubical and trapezoidal shapes and the relationship is of a mathematical nature.

Algorithms and mathematics are equally important to the modern artist, and he finds a new tool in the computer. A computer can take a mathematical figure and repeat it continually with great precision. An algorithm can cause the computer to distort or permute the figure as well as to repeat a pattern with slight permutations randomly about a prescribed area. Guided by a relatively simple program, it can substitute one figure for another or produce a complicated figure for each point on a line. In addition, a computer can expand, contract, reshape, multiply or transform a figure or a series of lines. Combinations of all these functions drive all computer art. [4,30,31]

In the following article, A. M. Noll of Bell Telephone Laboratories explores the possibilities of the computer as an artistic medium.[5]

THE DIGITAL COMPUTER AS A CREATIVE MEDIUM*

A. Michael Noll

Bell Telephone Laboratories

The notion of creating art works through the medium of machines may seem a little strange. Most people who have heard about the experimental use of digital computers in creative endeavors have probably shrugged them off as being of no consequence. On the one hand, creativity has universally been regarded as the personal and somewhat mysterious domain of man; and, on the one hand, as every engineer knows, the computer can only do what it has been programmed to do—which hardly anyone would be generous enough to call creative.

*Reprinted with the permission of the Institute of Electrical and Electronic Engineers and the author.

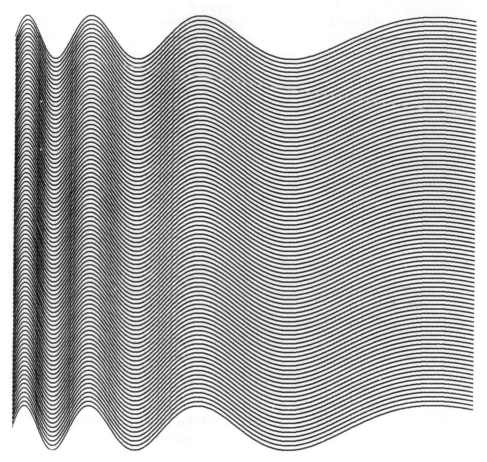

FIGURE 12–1   "Ninety computer-generated sinusoids with linearly increasing period."
The top line of this picture was mathematically expressed as a sinusoid
curve. The computer was then instructed to repeat the line 90 times. The
result approximates closely Bridget Riley's painting "Current." *Courtesy
of A. M. Noll and Bell Telephone Laboratories.*

Nonetheless, artists have usually been responsive to experimenting with and even adopting certain concepts and devices
resulting from new scientific and technological developments.
Computers are no exception. Composers, film animators, and
graphic artists have become interested in the application of computers in their creative endeavors. Moreover, recent artistic experiments with computers have produced results that should
make us reexamine our preconceptions about creativity and
machines. Some of the experiments, described in this article,
suggest, in fact, that tight interaction between artist and com-

puter constitutes a totally new, active, and exciting artistic medium.

How does an artist work?

There is an anecdote attributed to Henri Matisse about how to approach the creative act of painting. You take a blank white canvas, the French artist said, and after gazing at it for a while, you paint on it a bright red disk. Thereafter, you do nothing further until something occurs to you that will be just as exciting as the original red disk. You proceed in this way, always sustaining, through each new gambit with the paint and brush, the initial high visual excitement of the red disk.

The anecdote is a somewhat simplified version of Matisse's idea, but even if we take it lightly, it can do a number of things for us. For one thing, it dispels some of the sense of mystery that hovers over the procedures of the creative person. It tells us something concrete and easily visualized about the creative process while emphasizing the role of the unexpected ideas for which the artist lies in wait and for which he sets a formal "trap" in his medium.

Even a relatively "passive" medium—paint, brushes, canvas—will suggest new ideas to the artist as he becomes engaged. The resistance of the canvas or its elastic give to the paint-loaded brush, the visual shock of real color and line, the smell of the paint, will all work on the artist's sensibilities. The running of the paint, or seemingly "random" strokes of the brush, may be accepted by him as corporate elements of the finished work. So it is that an artist explores, discovers, and masters the possibilities of the medium. His art work is a form of play, but it is serious play.

Most of all, the Matisse anecdote suggests that the artistic process involves some form of "program," one certainly more complex than the anecdote admits, but a definite program of step-by-step action. Without doing too much violence to our sense of what is appropriate, we might compare it to a computational hill-climbing technique in which the artist is trying to optimize or stabilize at a high level the parameter "excitement."

Once we have swallowed this metaphor, it becomes less improbable to imagine that computers might be used, in varying depths of engagement, as active partners in the artistic process. But computers are a *new* medium. They do not have the characteristics of paints, brushes, and canvas. Nor are the "statements" that grow out of the artist's engagement with them likely to be similar to the statements of, for example, oil paintings. An interesting question to explore, then, is how computers might be used as a creative medium. What kinds of artistic potentials can be evolved through the use of computers, which themselves are continually being evolved to possess more sophisticated and intelligent characteristics?

The character of the computer medium

In the present state of computer usage, artists are certainly having their problems in understanding engineering descriptions and in learning how to program computers in order to explore what might be done with them. However, they *are* learning, and they have already used digital computers and associated equipment to produce musical sounds and artistic visual images.

The visual images are generated by an automatic plotter under the control of the digital computer. The plotter consists of a cathode-ray tube and a camera for photographing the images "drawn" on the tube face by deflections of the electron beam. The digital computer produces the instructions for operating the automatic plotter so that the picture-drawing capability is under program control. Musical sounds are produced by the computer by means of a digital sampled version of the sounds that must then be converted to analog form by a conventional digital-to-analog converter.

For both of these artistic applications, a challenging problem is the composition of special-purpose programming languages and subroutines so that the artist can communicate with the computer by using terminology reasonably similar to his particular art. For example, a special music compiler has been written so that the composer can specify complex algorithms for producing a single sound and then pyramid these basic sounds into a whole composition. A similar philosophy has been used in a special language developed for computer animation called Beflix. Both applications share the drawback that the artist must wait a number of hours between the actual running of the computer program and the final generation of pictorial output or musical sounds when he can see or hear the results.

Since the scientific community currently is the biggest user of computers, most descriptions and ideas about the artistic possibilities for computers have been understandably written by scientists and engineers. This situation will undoubtedly change as computers become more accessible to artists who obviously are more qualified to explore and evolve the artistic potentials of the computer medium. Unfortunately, scientists and engineers are usually all too familiar with the inner working of computers, and this knowledge has a tendency to produce very conservative ideas about the possibilities for computers in the arts. Most certainly the computer is an electronic device capable of performing only those operations that it has been explicitly instructed to perform. And this usually leads to the portrayal of the computer as a powerful tool but one incapable of any true creativity. However, if creativity is restricted to mean the production of the unconventional or the unpredicted, then the computer should instead be portrayed as a creative medium—an active and creative collaborator with the artist.

Computers and creativity

Digital computers are constructed from a myriad of electronic components whose purpose is to switch minute electric currents nearly instantaneously. The innermost workings of the computer are controlled by a set of instructions called a program. Although computers must be explicitly instructed to perform each operation, higher-level programming languages enable pyramiding of programming statements that are later expanded into the basic computer instructions by special compiler programs. These programming languages are usually designed so that the human user can write his computer program using words and symbols similar to those of his own particular field. All of this leads to the portrayal of the computer as a tool capable of performing tasks exactly as programmed.

However, the computer is such an extremely powerful tool that artistic effects can sometimes be easily accomplished that would be virtually impossible by conventional artistic techniques. For example, by calculating and drawing on the automatic plotter the perspective projections from two slightly different directions of some three-dimensional object, the computer can generate three-dimensional movies of novel shapes and forms. Such three-dimensional animation, or kinetic sculpture, is far too tedious to perform by any other method. The computer's ability to handle small details has made possible intriguing dissolves and stretches, such as those executed by Stan Vanderbeek, without the tedium of conventional hand animation. Mathematical equations with certain specified variables under the control of the artist have also been used by John Whitney to achieve completely new animation effects. Much of "op art" uses repetitive patterns that usually can be expressed very simply in mathematical terms. The waveforms shown in Figure 12—1, which are like Bridget Riley's painting "Currents," were generated as parallel sinusoids with linearly increasing period. Thus, computer and automatic plotter can eliminate the tedious part of producing "op" effects.

Computers most certainly are only machines, but they are capable of performing millions of operations in a fraction of a second and with incredible accuracy. They can be programmed to weigh carefully, according to specified criteria, the results of different alternatives and act accordingly; thus, in a rudimentary sense, computers can appear to show intelligence. They might assess the results of past actions and modify their programmed algorithms to improve previous results; computers potentially could be programmed to learn. And series of numbers can be calculated by the computer that are so complicatedly related that they appear to us as random.

Of course, everything the machine does must be programmed, but because of the computer's great speed, freedom from error, and vast abilities for assessment and subsequent modification of programs, it appears to us to act unpredictably and to produce the unexpected. In this sense, the computer actively takes over some of the artist's creative search. It suggests to him syntheses that he may or may not accept. It possesses at least some of the external attributes of creativity.

The Mondrian experiment

How reasonable is it to attribute even these rudimentary qualities of creativity to an inaminate machine? Is creativity something that should only be associated with the products of humans? Not long ago, in 1950, A. M. Turing expressed the belief that at the end of the century "one will be able to speak of machines thinking without expecting to be contradicted." Turing proposed the now well-known experiment consisting of an interrogator, a man, and a machine, in which the interrogator had to identify the man by asking the man and the machine to answer questions or to perform simple tasks.

A crude approximation of Turing's experiment was performed using Piet Mondrian's "Composition With Lines" (1917) and a computer-generated picture composed of pseudorandom elements but similar in overall composition to the Mondrian painting as shown in Figs. 12—2 and 12—3 respectively. Although Mondrian apparently placed the vertical and horizontal bars in his painting in a careful and orderly manner,

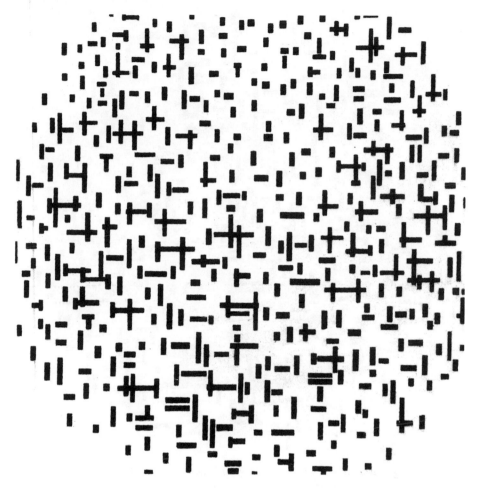

FIGURE 12–2   "Composition With Lines" (1917) by Piet Mondrian. (Reproduced with permission of Rijkmuseum Kröller-Müller, Otterlo, the Netherlands, © Rijkmuseum Kröller-Müller.)

the bars in the computer-generated picture were placed according to a pseudorandom number generator with statistics chosen to approximate the bar density, lengths, and widths in the Mondrian painting. Xerographic copies of the two pictures were presented, side by side, to 100 subjects with educations ranging from high school to postdoctoral; the subjects represented a reasonably good sampling of the population at a large scientific research laboratory. They were asked which picture they preferred and also which picture of the pair they thought was pro-

FIGURE 12–3 "Computer Composition with Lines" (1964) © A. Michael Noll, 1965.

duced by Mondrain. Fifty-nine percent of the subjects preferred the computer-generated picture; only 28 percent were able to identify correctly the picture produced by Mondrian.

In general, these people seemed to associate the randomness of the computer-generated picture with human creativity whereas the orderly bar placement of the Mondrian painting seemed to them machinelike. This finding does not, of course, detract from Mondrian's artistic abilities. His painting was, after all, the inspiration for the algorithms used to produce the computer-generated picture, and since computers were nonexistent 50 years ago, Mondrian could not have had a computer at his disposal. Furthermore, we must admit that the reduction in size of the original painting and its xerographic reproduction degrades its unique aesthetic qualities. Nevertheless, the results of the experiment in light of Turing's proposed experiment do raise questions on the meaning of creativity and the role of randomness in artistic creation. In a sense, the computer with its program could be considered creative, although it can be argued that human creativity was involved in the original program with the computer performing only as an obedient tool.

These questions should perhaps be examined more deeply by more ambitious psychological experiments using computer-generated pictures as stimuli.

Toward real-time interaction

Although the experiments described show that the computer has creative potentialities beyond those of just a simple tool, the computer medium is still restrictive in that there is a rather long time delay between the running of the computer program and the production of the final graphical or acoustic output. However, recent technological developments have greatly reduced this time delay through special interactive hardware facilities and programming languages. This tightening of the man-machine feedback loop is particularly important for the artist who needs a nearly instantaneous response.

For example, in the field of music an electronic graphic console has been used to specify pictorially sequences of sounds that were then synthesized by the computer. Functions for amplitude, frequency, and duration of a sequence of notes were drawn on the face of a cathode-ray tube with a light pen. If desired, the computer combined specified functions according to transparently simple algorithms. Thus, the fine details of the composition were calculated by the computer and the overall structure was precisely specified by the graphical score. The feedback loop was completed by the computer-generated sounds heard almost immediately by the composer, who could then make any desired changes in the score.

A similar man-machine interactive system has been proposed for choreography. In this system, the choreographer would be shown a computer-generated three-dimensional display of complicated stick figures moving about on a stage, as shown in Figure 12−8 below. The choreographer interacts with the computer by indicating the spatial trajectories and movements of the figures. Random and mathematical algorithms might be introduced by the computer to fill in certain fine details, or even to give the choreographer new ideas to evaluate and explore.

A new active medium

The beginnings of a new creative partnership and collaboration between the artist and the computer clearly emerge from these most recent efforts and proposals. Their common denominator is the close man-machine interaction using the computer to generate either musical sounds or visual displays. The computer acquires a creative role by introducing randomness or by using mathematical algorithms to control certain aspects of the artistic creation. The overall control and direction of the creative process is very definitely the artist's task. Thus, the computer is used as a medium by the artist, but the great technical powers and creative potentialities of the computer result in a totally new kind of creative medium. This is an *active* medium with which the artist can interact on a new level, freed from many of the physical limitations of all other previous media. The artistic potentialities of such a creative medium as a collaborator with an artist are truly exciting and challenging.

Interactive aesthetic experiences

In the previous examples the artist sat at the console of the computer and indicated his desires to the computer by manually using push buttons or by drawing patterns on an electronic visual display. These are probably efficient ways of communicating certain types of instructions to the computer; however, the communication of the actual subconscious emotional state of the artist could lead to a new aesthetic experience. Although this might seem somewhat exotic and conjectural, the artist's emotional state might conceivably be determined by computer processing of physical and electrical signals from the artist (for example, pulse rate and electrical activity of the brain). Then, by changing the artist's environment through such external stimuli as sound, color, and visual patterns, the computer would seek to optimize the aesthetic effect of all these stimuli upon the artist according to some specified criterion.

This interactive feedback situation with controlled environment would be completely dynamic. The emotional reaction of the artist would continually change, and the computer would react accordingly either to stabilize the artist's emotional state or to steer it through some preprogrammed course. Here then is a completely new aesthetic experience utilizing man-machine communication on the highest (or lowest, if you will) subconscious levels and computer processing and optimization of emotional responses. Only a digital computer could perform all the information processing and generate the sights and sounds of the controlled environment required for such a scheme. One is strongly tempted to describe these ideas as a consciousness-expanding experience in association with a psychedelic computer!

Although such an artistic feedback scheme is still far in the future, current technological and psychological investigations would seem to aim in such a direction. For example, three-dimensional computer-generated color displays that seem to surround the individual are certainly already within the state of the art. Electroencephalograms are being scrutinized and studied in great detail, using advanced signal analysis techniques; it is not inconceivable that some day their relation to emotional state might be determined.

Artistic consequences

Predictions of the future are risky in that they may be really nothing more than what the person predicting would like to see occur. Although the particulars should be viewed skeptically, they actually might be unimportant; if the art of the future follows the directions outlined here, then some general conclusions and statements can be made that should be independent of the actual particulars.

The aesthetic experience will be highly individualistic, involving only the individual artist and his interactions with the computer. This type of participation in the creative and aesthetic experience can be experienced by artist and nonartist alike. Because of the great technical and creative power of the computer, both the artist and nonartist are freed from the necessity of strong technical competence in the use of different media. The artist's "ideas" and not his technical ability in manipulating media could be the important factor in determining artistic merit. Conceivably, a form of "citizen-artist" could emerge, as envisoned by Allon Schoener. The interactive aesthetic experience with computers might fill a substantial portion of that great leisure time predicted for the man of the future.

The artist's role as master creator will remain, however, because even though the physical limitations of the medium will be different from traditional media, his training, devotion, and visualization will give him a higher degree of control of the artistic experience. As an example, the artist's particular interactions with the computer might be recorded and played back by the public on their own computers. Specified amounts of interaction and modification might be introduced by the individual, but the overall course of the interactive experience would still follow the artist's model. In this way, and for the first time, the artist would be able to specify and control with certainty the emotional state of each individual participant. Only those aspects deliberately specified by the artist might be left to chance or to the whims of the participant. All this would be possible because the computer could monitor the participant's emotional state and change it according to the artist's specifications. The artist's interaction with the computer would be of a new order because the physical restrictions of the older media would be eliminated.

This is not to say that the traditional artistic media will be swept away; but they will undoubtedly be influenced by this new active medium. The introduction of photography—the new medium of the last century—helped to drive painting away from representation, but it did not drive out painting. What the new creative computer medium will do to all of the art forms—painting, writing, dance, music, movies—should be exciting to observe. We might even be tempted to say that the current developments and devices in the field of man-machine communication, which were primarily intended to give insight into scientific problems, might in the end prove to be far more fruitful, or at least equally fruitful, in the arts.

Computer graphics range from familiar line drawings through images redrawn by a computer to the artist's desires, to randomly-produced shapes. As Harold Rosenberg, art critic of *The New Yorker*, has written, "The inspiration of machine art is problem-solving; its chief aesthetic principle is the logical adjustment of means to end."

The latest computer-graphics development is the computer-processing of scanned photographs. In this technique, the individual dots that make up an image can be transformed by the computer to numbers or symbols (a kind of "computer pointillism"), or a symbolic variation of the photograph can be programmed. This technique is based on reproducing an object rather than creating a new one. H. P. Peterson of Honeywell, Inc. recently scanned a reproduction of the Mona Lisa with a computer and reconstructed it entirely of minute, two-digit numbers based on a scale of 100 increments between black and white. It required a scanning time of four minutes and a plotting time of 16 hours.

Also, a reproduction by K. C. Knowlton and L. D. Harmon of Bell Telephone Laboratories is shown in Figure 12—4. They have divided the shades of gray into 14 different tones. For each tone, they program the computer to

FIGURE 12–4 "Gargoyles in Paris," by Ken C. Knowlton and Leon D. Harmon.

substitute tiny hieroglyphic symbols—faces, airplanes, animals, musical notes, telephones and automobiles. The effect is not unlike a Seurat painting. Held close up, the hieroglyphs are seen separately. When it is held at arm's length, a whole painting can be seen. This is simple substitution.

The same techniques that are used for computer graphics can be used for generating computer-animated films. The artist and the computer work with freely invented forms, shapes and dynamic rhythms. The art form used by John Whitney, one of the leading artists working with computer films, is often called Constructivism.[6,19] It is abstract art without the illusion of a subject. Constructivism originated in Europe toward the end of the last century. It has offered creative inspiration to some of the 20th century's leading architects and artists, including Walter Gropius, Paul Klee, Wassily Kandinsky, and Piet Mondrian. In the 1920s, the new movement provided the impetus for the great Bauhaus school in Germany.

Whitney calls his films visual music since he uses the computer to orchestrate motion. He describes his films as "a compositional language of graphics in motion" paralleled by musical counterpoint, or "patterns graphically superimposed over themselves forward and backward in many ways." He uses an algorithm and suitable shapes to generate the motion. The algorithm allows for accelerations, decelerations and oscillations of the figures. Whitney's computer-generated color

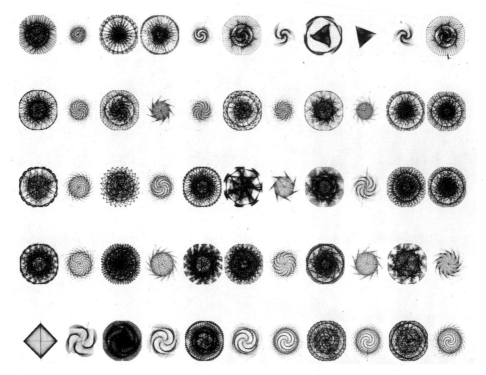

FIGURE 12–5   Some figures from a computer-animated film by John Whitney. *Courtesy of John Whitney and Computing Report.*

film, *Permutations*, was shown at the 1968 Lincoln Center Film Festival in New York.* Some figures from Whitney's films are shown in Figure 12–5.

Charles Csuri of Ohio State University is an American artist who has used computers as a means of extending his art. An illustration of his computer-aided art is shown in Figure 12–6. The four faces of an old man were generated by a computer and use selected symbols to develop the figure. A realistic line drawing of an old man was used as the data check and the line drawing was transformed into a shaded image using a computer algorithm.[7]

A recent exhibition in London entitled "Cybernetic Serendipity" explored and demonstrated the relationships between technology and creativity.[8] *Cybernetics*, which we explore further in Section 13–7 and Chapter 14, is defined as follows:

> *Cybernetics* The science of control and communication in complex electronics machines such as computers, control systems and the human nervous system.

*Permutations is distributed by the Film Library of the New York Museum of Modern Art for non-profit showings.

FIGURE 12–6   Four computer-generated drawings of an old man. A spiral, rectangle, triangle and star are used as the symbols. *Courtesy of C. Csuri.*

FIGURE 12–7 "The Friendly Grey Computer–Star Gauge Model #54" (1965), by Edward Kienholz. Motorized construction as a rocking chair. Collection, the Museum of Modern Art, New York. Gift of Jean and Howard Lipman.

By the title "Cybernetic Serendipity," the sponsors of the exhibition mean the faculty of happy chance discoveries through the means of complex machines, especially computers. Hundreds of items illustrating the discoveries of art through the use of the computer were exhibited.

The computer has inspired the artist to create objects of art.

Edward Kienholz's construction entitled "The Friendly Grey Computer" is shown in Figure 12—7. This construction is in the collection of the Museum of Modern Art in New York and the catalog describing the piece states:

> A folklore has rapidly developed about the computer. It has become a wonder child, capable of answering any question, solving any problem. As he does so frequently, Kienholz here makes use of modern folklore. His mood, though still sardonic, is gentler than in the grim *Back Seat Dodge—'38*. His directions for operating *The Friendly Grey Computer* advise us:
>
> *Flashing yellow bulb indicates positive answer. Flashing blue bulb indicates negative answer. Green jewel button doesn't light so it will not indicate anything. Computers sometimes get fatigued and have nervous breakdowns, hence the chair for it to rest in. If you know your computer well, you can tell when it's tired and sort of blue and in a funky mood. If such a condition seems imminent, turn rocker switch on for ten or twenty minutes. Your computer will love it and work all the harder for you. Remember that if you treat your computer well it will treat you well.*
>
> Kienholz kindly programmed the computer to give more "yes" than "no" answers. A question random-found on a card: "Will I ever get a boyfriend?"*

The relationship between the graphic artist and the computer is becoming increasingly productive. In the future, programming languages will undoubtedly be developed for helping artists to communicate with the computer. Mr. K. Knowlton of Bell Telephone Laboratories has summarized the relationship:

> The problem of providing an artist with good software involves the search for a comfortable compromise between the extremes of machine autonomy and machine stupidity. In the first case, we have a machine that works almost entirely automatically, producing great volumes of output over which the artist has little control except for culling the results. At the other extreme, the programmer has complete spot-by-spot control, but far too much effort is required for specifying an interesting picture. . . . The outcome of present experimentation ultimately may be a number of relatively suitable languages for artists. Such languages may become sufficiently established and familiar—no

"NOT BAD FOR A COMPUTER, BUT THE
CHIMPANZEE'S WORK HAD MORE FEELING."

FIGURE 12–8   © *1981 by Sidney Harris. Used with permission.*

longer a cute gimmick—that artists can use them to say
something without the medium itself arousing such curiosity, ac-
claim or disdain as to distract severely from the artistic content
of the work.

Computer-generated special effects for motion pictures are a modern example of computer assisted graphic art.[18] Using a set of special cameras, computers and recording devices, a series of space travel scenes were created for *Star
Wars* and *Buck Rogers*. A commentary on computer art is shown in Figure 12–8.
Whether computers will enable the artist to produce great works of visual arts is
an open question. Certainly, the computer is a new and important medium for
some artists to use in the creation and production of visually beautiful art. The
possibilities inherent in the computer as a creative tool will do little to change

those idioms of art which rely primarily on the dialogue among the artist, his ideas and his media. They will, however, increase the scope and diversity of art.

12.3 COMPUTERS AND MUSIC AND DANCE

> To set to work to make music by means of valves, springs, levers, cylinders, or whatever other apparatus you choose to employ, is a senseless attempt to make the means to an end accomplish what can result only when those means are animated and, in their minutest movements, controlled by the mind, the soul, and the heart. The gravest reproach you can make to a musician is that he plays without expression; because, by so doing, he is marring the whole essence of the matter. Yet the coldest and most unfeeling executant will always be far in advance of the most perfect machines. For it is impossible that any impulse whatever from the inner man shall not, even for a moment, animate his rendering; whereas, in the case of a machine, no such impulse can ever do so. The attempts of mechanicians to imitate, with more or less approximation to accuracy, the human organs in the production of musical sounds, or to substitute mechanical appliances for those organs, I consider tantamount to a declaration of war against the spiritual element in music; but the greater the forces they array against it, the more victorious it is. For this very reason, the more perfect that this sort of machinery is, the more I disapprove of it; and I infinitely prefer the commonest barrel-organ, in which the mechanism attempts nothing but to be mechanical, to Vaucanson's flute player, or the harmonica girl.
>
> E. T. A. Hoffmann
> *Automata*, 1816

A computer can produce a numerical description of a sound wave or a combination of sound waves. Thus, the artist interested in music can use a computer to assist in the production of music. A Decca record of 1962, *Music from Mathematics*, shows that the computer can play tunes in a variety of tone qualities, imitating plucked strings, reed instruments and other common effects, and going beyond these to produce shushes, garbles, and clunks that are unknown in conventional music.

The electric signal, which by means of a pickup goes into a sound system, can be specified by a sequence of numbers which give the amplitude of the signal at regularly spaced instants of time. The number of numbers required is about 20,000 per second for high-quality music; and approximately 20,000 three-digit numbers provided each second by a computer is sufficient to describe any music.[16,17] Thus, a computer in conjunction with equipment for turning a sequence of numbers into electronic signals that can excite a loudspeaker is truly a musical instrument.

The development and composition of computer music has taken place during the past decade and is still embryonic. The user of the computer can specify the wave form, the pitch and the amplitude and the relationship of these variables. However, very few people have many years of experience with music composed by means of a computer.

The composer John Cage has successfully used a random process in the selection of notes for computer-generated music. Other composers of computer-assisted music are James C. Tenney of Yale University, Harry F. Olsen of RCA, Gerald Strang of California State University, Long Beach, and J. K. Randall of Princeton University. Using a computer, Lejaren A. Hiller of the University of Illinois produced the famous "Illiac Suite for String Quartet."[9]

It is not easy to use computers to assist in the creation of music. The complexity of music places difficult obstacles in the path of the composer. The composer must develop the music through an elaborate set of instructions which form a program, which in turn determines the composition of the score to be played and all interpretive musical characteristics for each instrument. On the other hand, the composer can, if he likes, allow the computer to choose pitch, loudness or anything else randomly, where and when he pleases.[15,16,29]

The computer doesn't compose the music; the person does, with the assistance of the computer. Most computer music generating programs consist of a large package of computer programs (subroutines) that incorporate basic procedures. The composer adds his or her own specifications to these subroutines to yield a score. The meaning of music provided by the composer is the structure he provides for the collection of sounds. The aesthetic content of music can be analyzed in terms of fluctuations between the two extremes of total randomness and total redundancy. For example, in 1795 Simrock published a system for composing waltzes and contredanses using chance operations which have been attributed to Mozart. Two dice are thrown, and the resulting number is referred to the table to determine the sequence of measures in the composition. A dice-music program has been applied to provide a composition. Two kinds of music that have been generated in this manner are pieces for chimes and for bagpipes.

Computer music, like other branches of machine art, has no body of critical judgment on which an aesthetics can be built. Most critics of computer music use the 19th century criteria, such as:

1. There must be an artist who is the sole creator of a work of art.
2. That work should be judged in the context of the history of its type.
3. It should also be unique and limited in availability.

(Most computer music is the result of effort by many workers who may be artists

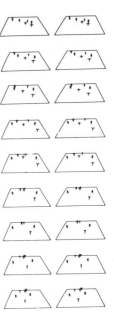

FIGURE 12-9 A choreographed sequence of dance movements obtained with the assistance of a computer. *Courtesy of A. M. Noll and Bell
Telephone Laboratories.*

and computer scientists, and the works of art are often reproducible in large
volume at low cost.)

Computers may be used to compose dance sequences as well as musical compositions. A choreographer plans the sequence of movements in a dance or ballet.
He can use a computer as the musical composer does. In fact, most choreography
is completed with the full dance company present and the finished plans often remain only in the minds of the dancers. Without extensively developed dance nota-
tions and well understood methods for dance choreography, the computer must
be used by experienced choreographers in the composition of dances.

One means of computer choreography proposed by A. M. Noll uses a computer and a visual display.[10] The choreographer interacts with the computer
during the creative process. Stick figure representations of the dancers appear on
some form of three-dimensional display. The choreographer, by manipulating
different buttons on the console, controls the movement and progress of the
work. The different movements of each dancer are stored in the computer
memory and requested by the choreographer and put together as a sequence. An
illustrative sequence of dance movements is shown in Figure 12-9. The
choreographer can easily make corrections and changes in the dance. Also, the
computer could calculate the display for any specified vantage point so that the
choreographer could ascertain the impact of the stage motion as seen from any
location in the theatre.

Since 1964 Professor Jeanne Beaman has been working with Paul Le Vasseur

FIGURE 12–10   Computer-generated choreography at the University of Pittsburgh. *Courtesy of Professor Jeanne Beaman and Lilo Brych, W.Q.E.D., Pittsburgh, Pa.*

at the University of Pittsburgh in the development of computer-programmed dance. Figure 12–10 shows a computer coreographed dance.

The aesthetics of music and dance are difficult to define in terms suitable for use with a computer. Nevertheless, the computer provides the composer or choreographer with a tool which is capable of representing an orchestra or a dance company and storing the composition or dance at every stage of development. The computer is certainly a valuable tool for composers and choreographers to consider using in the development of their art. While computer music and computer dance are embryonic arts at present, they appear likely to grow in importance in the future.

12.4   THE COMPUTER AND THE HUMANITIES

The computer has considerable potential to assist the creative writer, the historian, the archeologist, and the literary scholar. In increasing numbers, archeologists and museum scholars are studying the artifacts of the past with a new tool—the computer. Computer applications are being found in data storage and retrieval for art and archaeological works, in the analysis of artistic content, the execution of aesthetic decisions, detection of art forgeries and in the field of museum education.

At a recent meeting at the Metropolitan Museum of Art in New York, curators, museum directors and teachers exchanged ideas on computers and their potential applications in museums. Mr. Dauterman, Associate Curator at the Metropolitan, told the conference how he is using a computer to classify and catalog Sèvres porcelain. "We found that each piece of Sèvres porcelain had a set of incised marks—initials, symbols, numbers—in various combinations," said Mr. Dauterman. "We decided to use a computer to help determine their significance. At the same time, the computer could produce the first reference list of such markings, which would be a valuable tool for collectors and scholars."

An Egyptian temple built during the period 1367 to 1350 B.C. was later completely dismantled. Computers are now being employed to recreate the building.[12] The temple lies in 30,000 pieces—too many, it is said, for the human brain to assemble without assistance. But by matching photographs of the individual pieces on computers, American and Egyptian archaeologists expect to have the temple reconstructed, at least pictorially.

The computer will be helpful to the historian in the problem of linking individual acts with the historical results. The view of long historical patterns is partial and fragmentary. Theories of history have concentrated on impersonal forces, laws, environment determinants, and the singular effects of local religious, political, and other leaders. Other variables, such as series of individually identifiable decisions leading to changes minor in themselves, but cumulatively effective over long time spans, have been too numerous and complex to account for within the record. The computer will assist the historian in tracing all the human beings and the myriads of relationships that culminate in an historical force or result.

The question of whether a computer can write prose and poetry is an interesting and provocative one. The computer is certainly able to generate surprising combinations of words and phrases. Experiments with random combinations of words have produced several interesting serendipitous products.

The more important current potential of the application computers to literature is in the area of literary scholarship. Professor Louis Milic reviewed the varieties of computer applications to literature in a recent article.[14]

> In 1961 an item appeared in the *New York Times* describing a landmark computer project of James T. McDonough. McDonough for the previous four years had been reducing the *Iliad* of Homer to patterns representing the meter of the Greek epic and encoding these patterns on punched cards. Then he used a computer in an attempt to discover whether the uniformity of the patterns showed that the poem had been written by a

single author, a question about which there had been a discussion during the past century. Since this first use of computers for the solution of literary problems, many other scholars have used computers for various literary projects.

Computers have been widely used in research fields related to literature such as machine translation, the making of concordances, attribution study, editing, and bibliography as well as the study of linguistics. The field of computational linguistics is currently active and a great deal of valuable research is taking place in it which will ultimately be of use in translation and even in literary analysis. Work in automatic syntactic analysis, sentence generation and semantics has implications for all kinds of word-connected activity.

The task of attributing an anonymous or uncertain work to its author requires processing a substantial portion of text for each possible author and comparing its features with those of the work in question. Previously such attributions were made impressionistically on the basis of intuitively-perceived similarities or differences which could only be summarized as a work sounding like the work of a specific author. With the use of a computer, the identification of the authors of such works as "The Federalist Papers" and the Epistles of Saint Paul were made possible. Perhaps we can look forward to a settling of the Bacon-Shakespeare-Marlowe dispute concerning the authorship of the plays of Shakespeare by means of a computer study.

The use of computers in the study of idiosyncratic patterns in individual writing is called computational stylistics. If a text contains a sufficient selection of terms from a given category, it is concluded that the writer was concerned with that theme. Thus it has been concluded, for example, from the number of words about lunacy (mad, madly, madness, insane, disease) in the first act of *Hamlet* that Shakespeare had this in mind when he wrote the play. Many conclusions can be reached by studying word-clusters and word-associations. This approach has the virtue of attacking the semantic component of language, which has been a great problem to all literary users of computers.

The computer is utilized by the literary scholar to assist in distinguishing between the aesthetic and commonplace, good literature and bad, poetry and mere verse. These questions become specific as the person studies words, phrases, themes, plots, symbols, stylistic devices, meaning and value. The computer will increasingly become a tool of great value to the literary scholar within the next decade.*

*Surveys and articles on the progress of research in the humanities which utilize computers appear in the monthly journal *Computers and the Humanities*.

The recent prize-winning book *Godel, Escher, Bach: An Eternal Golden Braid* by Douglas R. Hofstadter treats art, music and computer science.[19] It draws analogies among mathematics, music, and art, among other subjects. The book is a modern treatise of the philosophical bases of art coupled with an understanding of science.

"I SIT HERE AND SOLVE MATHEMATICAL PROBLEMS, PROGRAM ELECTRONIC MUSIC, ANALYZE ARCHITECTURAL POSSIBILITIES...BUT SOMEHOW BEING A RENAISSANCE MAN ISN'T WHAT IT USED TO BE."

FIGURE 12–11   *Courtesy of Sidney Harris, New York* and *Saturday Review, Inc.* From *Saturday Review*, Feb. 15, 1969.

SUMMARY

The possibilities and opportunities for artistic creation and scholarship by utilizing the digital computer are numerous. Several opportunities will undoubtedly occur to the reader in his studies. In a few years, we may be able to hear in our living room, with the aid of computer-synthesized music, a musical composition completely indistinguishable from what we might hear in a concert hall. We may hear a poem written by a computer, sung in a computer voice, to an accompaniment of computer-generated and computer-played music. Perhaps we will see a ballet of persons dancing in patterns generated by computer-aided choreography. The artist and the computer will work together in a partnership to provide man with new works of art. Undoubtedly, a large portion of the products will be of little lasting value, but we can expect much of value from this new tool. In some sense, the computer provides a source of creative amplification. (One man's view of the new artist-machine partnership is illustrated in Figure 12–11.) While the new partnership will not be necessary for all artists, those who explore the potential of the computer in the creative arts will probably find new media, new modes of expression and new sources of beauty. Certainly, many artists will welcome the chance to explore the new arts just as Stravinsky, Feininger, and Balanchine did in the past.

CHAPTER 12 PROBLEMS

P12–1. List several applications of computers to the arts.

P12–2. Reexamine Figure 12–4 and discuss the effects of substitution utilizing various tiny hieroglyphic symbols. What would be the effect on using a set of symbols different than that used in Figure 12–4?

P12–3. Describe your response to viewing the photo of the Friendly Grey Computer which appears in Figure 12–9.

P12–4. Programming a computer to compose a musical work or choreograph a dance sequence is a difficult project. Design an algorithm for composing a simple musical piece.

P12–5. Develop a computer program for the algorithm of Problem 12–4.

P12–6. Two famous electronic music equipment manufacturers are (1) Moog Music, Inc. of Williamsville, New York, and (2) Buchla Associates of Berkeley, California. Contact one of these manufacturers and determine the specifications of a computer system for electronic music.

P12–7. A reproduction of computer art by Grace Hertlein is shown in Figure P12–7. Prepare a brief analysis of the technique used to yield this drawing.[4]

FIGURE P12–7 "Beasts in the Field" by Grace Hertlein. The original work is 26"
× 30". It is executed on a tan pastel paper. The animal forms are Picasso
derivations. This is one of thirty works from the Creation Series.

P12–8. Research in the classics that once took two months can now be accomplished in minutes with the help of a computerized data bank of the
classical Greek language. The system will eventually store 90 million
words to form a thesaurus.[27] List several possible scholarly uses for
such a data bank.

CHAPTER 12 REFERENCES

1. D. Fabun, *The Dynamics of Change*, Prentice-Hall Book Co., Englewood
   Cliffs, N. J., 1967.
2. "Computer Art," *Datamation*, August, 1976, pp. 124–126.
3. M. L. Dertouzos and J. Moses, *The Computer Age*, MIT Press, Cambridge,
   Massachusetts, 1980, Chapter 2.
4. G. G. Hertlein, "Computer Art: Steps Toward a Measurable Analysis,"
   Computers and People, May, 1974, pp. 13–17.

5. A. M. Noll, "The Digital Computer as a Creative Medium," *IEEE Spectrum*, October, 1967, pp. 89–95.

6. Y. Sting and J. Gips, *Algorithmic Aesthetics*, University of California Press, Berkeley, California 1979.

7. C. Csuri and J. Shaffer, "Art, Computers and Mathematics," *Proceed. of the Fall Joint Computer Conference*, 1968, Thompson Book Co., Washington, D.C., 1968, pp. 1293–1298.

8. J. Reichardt, "Cybernetic Serendipity," *Studio International*, London, England, 1968.

9. L. Hiller, Computer Music: "Illiac Suite for String Quartet and Computer Cantata," Heliodor-MGM Records, New York, 1973.

10. A. M. Noll, "Choreography and Computers," *Dance Magazine*, Jan., 1967.

11. S. Aaronson, "With a Song in His Digital Computer," *The Sciences*, May, 1974, pp. 13–16.

12. "Computing the Temple," *Science News*, Vol. 94, Oct. 12, 1968, pg. 361.

13. W. Willson, "The Computer as an Art Connoisseur," *Los Angeles Times*, April 10, 1978, pg. 1, 6.

14. L. T. Milic, "Winged words—varieties of computer applications to literature," *Proceedings of the Fall Joint Computer Conference*, 1967, Thompson Book Co., Washington, D.C., 1967, pp. 321–326.

15. *The BYTE Book of Computer Music*, BYTE Publishers, Peterborough, New Hampshire, 1978.

16. "First Philadelphia Computer Music Festival," *Creative Computing*, Morristown, New Jersey, 1979.

17. R. L. Oakman, *Computer Methods for Literary Research*, University of South Carolina Press, Columbia, 1980.

18. "Turned to Bits," *Optical Spectra*, April 1980, pp. 80–83.

19. D. R. Hofstadter, *Godel, Escher, Bach: An Eternal Golden Braid*, Basic Books, New York, 1979.

20. P. Boulez, "Maestro Computer," *Unesco Courier*, April 1980, pp. 28–33.

21. H. Kenner, "Computerized Ulysses: Establishing the Text J. Joyce Intended," *Harpers*, April 1980, pp. 89–95.

22. P. Mackay, "Computers in the Performing Arts," *Theatre Crafts*, April 1980, pp. 26–41.

23. M. Lyon, "Third Medium for the Music Composer: Computers," *Technology Review*, November 1979, pp. 86–87.

24. S. Mcngelberg, "Computer Implemented Music Analysis and the Copyright Law," *Computers and the Humanities*, June 1980, pp. 1–20.

25. J. Raben, *Data Bases in the Humanities and Social Sciences*, North Holland, New York, 1980.

26. W. Buxton *et. al.*, "The Evolution of the SSSP Score Editing Tools," *Computer Music Journal*, Vol. 3, No. 4, 1979, pp. 14–25.

27. J. A. Moorer, "How Does a Computer Make Music?" *Computer Music Journal*, Vol. 2, No. 2, 1978, pp. 32–37.
28. L. Hiller and L. M. Isaacson, "Experimental Music: Composition with an Electronic Computer," *Greenwood Press*, Westport, Connecticut, 1979.
29. W. Bateman, *Introduction to Computer Music*, Wiley and Sons, New York, 1980.

13

APPLICATIONS OF COMPUTERS

13.1 INTRODUCTION

Computers have influenced our way of conducting business, our industry, our schools and the services provided by our government. In this chapter, we consider the applications of computers in various selected fields in industry, education, and government.

13.2 THE APPLICATION OF COMPUTERS IN THE MEDICAL SCIENCES

A significant part of medical practice involves processing information about symptoms, tests and diseases. As physicians are able to formalize the relationships among symptoms, diseases and treatment, they will be able to utilize computers increasingly to help deliver medical services to people who need and desire them. Expenditures for health and medical purposes are the third largest total in the United States, behind only food, which is first, and national defense, which is second. Approximately $210 billion were spent for health care services of all kinds in 1980, for instance.

We live in a time of rising expectations for health services, but the delivery of health services is inadequate. In the future computers and the information systems built around them will be directed toward developing improved methods for the prevention, diagnosis, treatment and management of disease. More satisfactory forms of health-oriented instrumentation, automation, computation, communications, systems engineering and operations research techniques must be developed to aid in this endeavor.

The essence of medical practice is to collect information about a patient, evaluate it in light of knowledge and experience, and then make decisions about the action to be taken to cure the patient. Only after information is processed can the doctor treat the disease actively. The computer may assist the medical practitioner by storing and making accessible the important facts. Computers can speed communications, distill information from data, and safeguard against human errors. Also, computers can reduce the time a patient must spend in the hospital by helping with the data-collecting routine even prior to his entry.

Computers are currently screening vast numbers of patients' electrocardiograms, with each individual screening requiring 15 seconds. They are also used to supervise post-operative care of open-heart surgery patients. For example, a computer has monitored approximately 400 patients following open-heart surgery at one large hospital. It maintains records and monitors on the patient's heart rate, blood pressure, fluid drainage, and temperature. The computer controls the monitoring devices and determines whether the patient needs infusions of blood or other special solutions or medications; then it automatically starts the infusion and stops it when it should. Already entrusted with the management of patients who have undergone the most complex open-heart surgery (multiple valve replacement, artery and heart repairs), it can also be applied following other forms of surgery and for serious medical conditions.[1]

When a patient is seriously ill or has received extensive surgical treatment, the delicate balance of salts and chemicals (especially sodium, potassium, and chloride ion) in the blood may be altered. Serious destructive changes occur in the cells of the brain and the muscles, among them the heart, if the chemical imbalance continues. An automatic monitoring device can make the difference between chemical death and survival. Here the computer can be of great value, for not only can it monitor blood serum chemical levels—in fact, it can also be attached to devices which supply missing chemcials intravenously *as they are needed*.

The computer will increasingly be used to assist physicians, nurses and hospitals to provide medical services. The primary areas of application of computers in the field of medicine and health services are (1) monitoring a patient's condition; (2) storing a patient's medical records; (3) assisting in the diagnosis of diseases; and (4) maintaining central information systems, as in hospitals.

We have briefly mentioned the advantage of a computer monitoring system for patient care. Several on-line monitoring techniques to improve the care of patients have been developed.[2,3] Automated techniques for the collection and rapid retrieval of readings of the physiological performance of a patient have been developed which utilize a computer. The aim of the computer system is to aid in the identification of potentially dangerous conditions early enough in their development in order to correct them easily and minimize their effect on the patient. At the end of each day, the computer can produce a 24-hour log of all activity, including the results of the analyses performed. The doctors can also obtain a graphic record of the results for each patient that plots the behavior of the variables against time. The variables monitored by one system are, among others, (1) temperature; (2) heart rate; (3) premature ventricular contractions; (4) respiratory flow and pressure, and (5) circulatory system blood pressures.

The number of tests that are typically performed on a hospitalized person number from 50 to 350. Laboratories are called on to perform over half a billion of these tests annually. The increasing number and complexity of these tests are generating serious problems with respect to their performance and the handling and storage of the data from individual patients. The reproducibility and reliability of the tests and the incidence of errors are often unacceptable. The one method of producing faster, cheaper, more reliable, and more accurate tests is the automation of the entire clinical laboratory process, from sample acquisition to computer print-out of final results on the patient's chart.[6]

The logical combination of a computer, a clinical laboratory and an intensive care unit for the monitoring and management of the critically ill has resulted in several special-purpose hospital care units. These units, which include coronary and intensive care facilities, trauma, renal dialysis and post-surgery recovery wards, now provide up to five percent of beds in community hospitals. A computer patient monitoring system provides real-time acquisition and display of data, analysis of clinical tests, and management of the data of the patient. The availability of such information has been life saving, particularly in coronary care units, where mortality has been reduced from 30 percent to less than 15 percent.[3] Computer monitoring and automated clinical systems are expensive, but they enable a hospital to reduce the staff which must monitor the condition of the critically ill and to provide improved care for the critically ill.

Computers can be utilized to automate the process of collecting data from the patient. This process, usually performed by a physician, is called the development of a patient's medical history. One automated medical data collection system developed at the Mayo Clinic uses a display terminal to present a series of questions. Patient responses are entered on the display terminal with an electronic light pen. Computer-administered questioning permits the effective use of question branching. This means a questionnaire can be tailored to the individual patient, so that factors such as sex, age, education, and ability to understand questions can be accounted for. Moreover, the patient answers only those questions which pertain to his own medical problems.[1] Pictorial techniques also allow the patient more freedom of expression. For example, the illustration shown in Figure 13-1 permits him to specify the location of abdominal pain. The patient responses are condensed into a concise summary statement for the examining

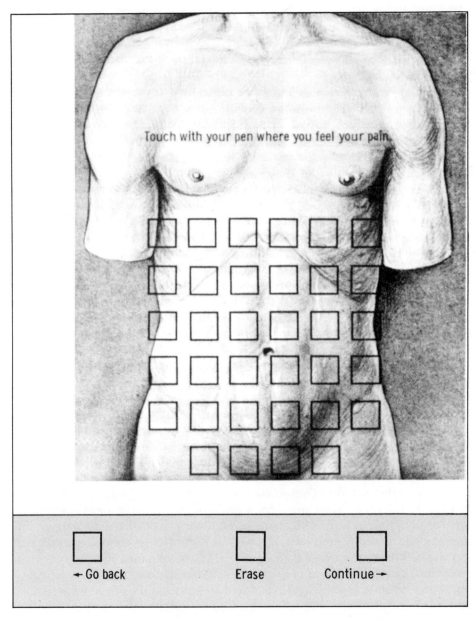

FIGURE 13–1   A pictorial question for the patient to answer in the development of an automated medical history. *Courtesy of IBM Corporation* and *the Mayo Clinic.*

physician. In one test, the automated medical history system obtained approximately 95 percent of the information normally recorded by the physician.[5]

The purpose of screening for disease is to discover people who appear to be well but who are in fact suffering from disease. Such people can then be given treatment, and steps can be taken to prevent spread of the disease. Thus, screening is a way of combatting disease because it can help detect disease in its early stages and allow it to be treated adequately before it secures a firm hold. The health screening center at Kaiser-Permanente in California uses a set of cards with a single question on each. The patients are asked to sort the cards into piles containing questions to which they have answered "no" and those to which they have answered "yes." The patient's responses are then entered directly into the computer using a card reader. Another computer system uses a terminal to display 320 different sequences of questions to develop a medical history. The time spent by patients at the terminal has varied from 12 to over 60 minutes with an average of 25 minutes. Patient response to automated medical history-taking has been quite favorable. In the case of the experimental systems the patients were routinely asked whether they would prefer to give the history to the machine as they have done; to a physician; to a nurse; or whether they have no preference. They are also asked to indicate whether they think the history was complete, incomplete, interesting, dull, or difficult to understand. Although over half the patients expressed no preference, it is of interest to note that of those who did express a preference, the machine was favored over the physician by a margin of approximately three to one. Also, almost all the patients stated that they found the automated history interesting.

After information about a patient is developed and recorded in an automated medical history system, it is used to provide a printed summary output for the physician. The information can also be retained in the computer storage for subsequent retrieval. The accumulation of large masses of medical data has led to the development of medical data banks. In Sweden, the medical records of one and a half million persons in the Stockholm region are recorded in a data bank. The information is filed in the memory bank in layers, each with more detailed information. There are three levels now, but this can be expanded. The first level has basic identification; the second, such critical medical data as drug allergies, vaccinations, and past illnesses. The third layer covers hospital visits and X-ray information. A person's records can be obtained by reference to an identification number, his name, or just his physical description in an emergency. Only hospital staff members with a "need-to-know" status have keys that can turn on the display terminals which in turn are coded to the computer by locations. The X-ray department, for example, can get only X-ray information.

In addition, such personal information as psychiatric treatment can be obtained by certain physicians, who must insert a special code number into the machine. The computer also keeps track of those who requested such confidential displays.

In the future, it is possible that a centralized computer data bank will be developed which will contain the medical histories of an entire population of a city, a state or even a nation. Plans are underway to develop such a bank for Jerusalem in Israel. The data bank is being used for individual patient treatment; the development of community health profiles; as a population register, and the study and control of epidemics.

A computer in a hospital can be used for retaining the records of patients and also scheduling for best utilization of clinics and wards; accounting services; automation of the clinical laboratory, and physiological monitoring. It has been estimated that 25 percent of the total operating budget of the average hospital goes to the recording, handling, and sorting of medical information by nurses.[10] A hospital information system using a terminal input to a computer should reduce the cost of information processing and storage. Automated ward record-keeping systems are currently being developed. Automated patient records will some day be available to even the remotest small hospital in the United States on a time-sharing basis. A medical information terminal is shown in Figure 13-2. The terminal shown uses a light pen and typewriter for input. It can be used in a ward for admissions, clinical tests, and retrieval of patient data, drug orders and other functions.

A centralized totally integrated hospital information system would be able to include such functions as accounting, admissions, room scheduling, orders and inventories, scheduling of X-ray and operating room facilities, laboratory report tests, diet planning, and patient information retrieval, among others.[6] The Veterans Administration has been active in developing an automated hospital information system which is comprised of a number of automated subsystems. One of these is the medication subsystem, composed of a number of activities linking those organizational entities of the hospital involved in the ordering, preparation, distribution, administration and use of the medications and supplies issued by the pharmacy. The recent establishment of a national drug code system will provide an identification code in computer language to permit automatic processing of drug data by manufacturers and hospitals.

The development of medical data banks will assist the medical practitioners in the delivery of health services to the citizens of the United States. The delivery of the best attainable health services is a major national concern and a major economic investment. Automation of medical information is necessary to process the information necessary for the task.

Major changes in the delivery of health services arising from the use of computers will occur during the next decade. One of the most significant changes will be in the field of patient diagnosis. Computers augment man's reasoning power and thus can be used to assist the physician in the diagnostic process. For computers to aid such processes, however, a series of systematic algorithms must be developed that correspond in some sense to the reasoning used by the diagnostician.[5] A flow chart of the diagnostic-treatment cycle is shown in Figure 13-3.

FIGURE 13–2　The display terminal of a medical information system. Physicians, nurses, and others requiring information from the system simply insert their ID card (and/or a patient's ID card) into one of the input/output stations located strategically around the hospital. A general index of formats is then called to the screen of the electronic display at that station shown in the figure. The index contains general categories for all the information stored in the system. For example, it may list titles of more specific indices, drug order forms, order forms for treatment and laboratory tests, patient lists, and other basic classes of information. The requesting individual touches an electronic light pen device to the face of the display over the indexed item he wishes to see. This action causes the index to dissolve, and the selected information to appear. The selected information can be updated, modified, or erased by using the typewriter keyboard at the station. It can be proofread on the screen, then automatically returned to system storage with the push of a button. *Courtesy of Sanders Associates, Inc.*

At present, the computer could be used to assist the physician at steps 1, 2, 4, 5, 6 and 9. Steps 3 and 8 are decisions which will be retained by the physician. After the probabilities for the alternative possible diagnoses have been determined, the treatment plan must be made (See Box 5 of Figure 13–3). The computer can help the practitioner choose the alternative treatments and procedures to obtain the best results. Uncertainty implies no knowledge of even the probabilities involved and presents the most difficult treatment-value problem. Progress has been ob-

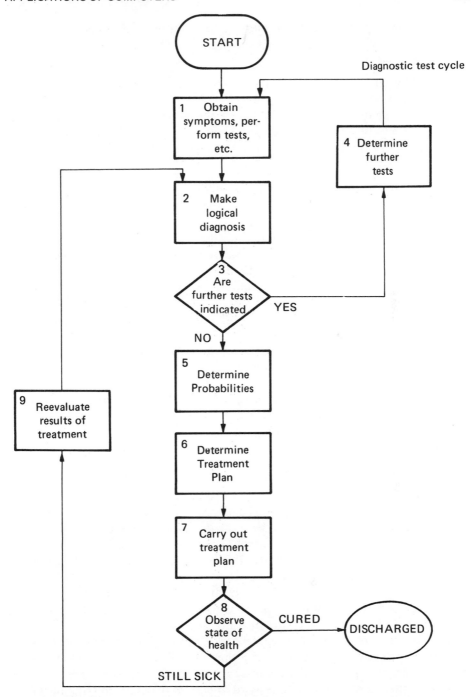

FIGURE 13–3   Flow diagram of the diagnostic, testing and treatment process.

tained in applying linear programming to the treatment decision, particularly where a combination of treatments is required. The process of diagnosis consists of four basic steps:

1. Obtain the case facts from the patient's history, physical examination and laboratory tests.
2. Evaluate the relative importance of the different signs and symptoms.
3. List all diseases which the specific case can resemble and (4) eliminate diseases from the list until a disease category fits or its exact nature cannot be determined.

It is widely believed that errors in differential diagnosis result more frequently from errors of omission from the list than from other sources. The computer can be used to store all the possible diseases in the category list. The diagnosis can be accomplished by the physician with the assistance of the computer, which retains the disease list and assists in the elimination of the diseases that do *not* fit the symptoms of a particular patient. Some experimental computer diagnostic systems use a matrix, or table, of symptoms and the related probability of a specific disease. The data accruing from examination of a new patient are fed into the machine and compared with the data in the probability matrix. The most probable or likely diagnosis is then computed. In continuing studies conducted at the University of Florida College of Medicine, a computer program has been developed which will make a correct assessment of the thyroid function of an individual after his symptoms, signs and laboratory test results have been supplied to the machine. The original probability matrix for this program was constructed from data from 879 patients. A study of this system at the University of Florida showed that only 2.8 percent of the last 500 patients screened had been misdiagnosed by the program.

At Toronto General Hospital, a computer is used to provide physicians with printed information about the volume and width of a patient's left ventricle—the heart pump—much more rapidly than by manual methods. An on-line terminal will provide (in real time) a graph of heart volume versus time as the patient is X-rayed.[12] This system greatly aids in the diagnoses of diseases.

A computer can be used to control and record information from a radio-isotope scanner used to detect tumors. The computer is also used to average the data and printout a graph of the area scanned. In Figure 13-4, the result of a scanning of a human's brain is shown. An isotope is injected into the brain and a nuclear detector connected to a computer are used to provide the diagnostic graph of the brain and the location of a tumor or other lesion.

A new diagnostic tool, Computerized Tomography, is one of the most revolutionary developments in medical technology. The technique makes it possible to obtain a cross-sectioned x-ray image of any body section in order to locate tumors or other diseased tissue. The word *tomography* is derived from the Greek word *tomes*, meaning "a slice or section."[1,2]

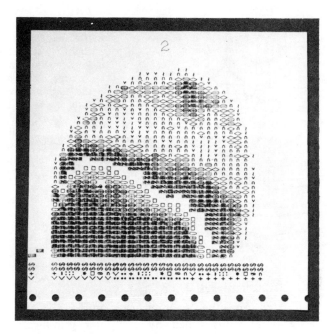

FIGURE 13–4   A computer printout of a brain scanning using an isotope indicator and a
computer algorithm for locating a brain tumor. Note the brain tumor in
the upper right of the photo. *Courtesy of Honeywell, Inc.*

At the 118th annual meeting of the American Medical Association, computers demonstrated their skill at diagnosing some 263 diseases, including 78 mental and emotional disorders. Over 1,750 different symptoms of gastrointestinal, urinary, and emotional diseases were handled by the computer, providing a differential diagnosis, based on the various combinations fed in by the participating physicians, almost instantaneously. The system has been compared to an encyclopedia of medical knowledge which opens itself at the appropriate page.

Computers may be used to simulate the physiological systems of the human body and thus aid in their study. At the University of Pennsylvania, a research study is using a computer model of the human circulatory system that will include the cardiovascular system. The computer model is a mathematical description that includes all the hundreds of variables and the complex relationships that determine their behavior. Investigators are able to conduct experiments in which they can change variables in the system and determine the effects of the changes.

A computer graphics simulation of the human heart has been accomplished using a graphic output.[13] Recent techniques of computer graphics enable investigators to model the complex motions of the heart. Theoretical models of heart muscle contraction and relaxation for normal or diseased states can be

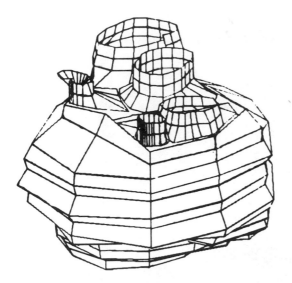

FIGURE 13–5   A computer generated graphical view of the heart from behind and slightly above. The three large, cylindrical openings on its superior surface are, from the top downward, the pulmonary artery, the aorta, and the superior vena cava. The two smaller cylindrical openings represent two pulmonary veins. The surfaces occupying most of the heart proper represent the left and right atrium. The inferior, or lower, portions of the heart represent the ventricular surfaces. *Courtesy of Dr. A. F. Bowyer.*

tested for correspondence, visual subjective data from angiocardiography can be quantitatively evaluated and the teaching of complex heart anatomy and physiology can be significantly aided by computer graphics. A computer-generated graphic model of the heart is shown in Figure 13–5. A computer program can be used to construct heart images at a rate of six drawings per minute and thus simulate heart motion by showing the heart chambers in sequential stages of contraction and relaxation. These models can be used for research and education.

Computers are becoming significantly important to the practice of medicine and the delivery of health services. The need for effective management of health data is important for financial and health-information reasons. Medicare alone will create some half-billion paper documents on prescription drugs in the period 1980–82.[4]The handling and storage of health records must be increasingly automated in order to avoid a paperwork crush. The computer will be able to assist the physician, the nurse, and other health service persons in providing more effective tests, diagnoses of disease, and hospital care, hopefully at reduced costs to the patient. Computers, perhaps on a time-sharing basis, will become part of the equipment necessary for medical practice and hospital operation.

13.3 COMPUTERS, LAW ENFORCEMENT AND THE LEGAL SYSTEM

The application of computers to law enforcement and the legal system is becoming increasingly important. In law enforcement, the computer is used to increase the probability of prevention of crime, or the apprehension of criminals once crimes have been committed. In the legal system, computers help to provide increased means for citizens to obtain rapid and equitable justice.

Because airplanes and superhighways permit easy mobility of criminals, time is an important factor in law enforcement. Thus, the use of a computer information network provides the rapid information necessary for timely law enforcement.

Several programs for the use of computers to aid in the law enforcement process are presently being developed and put into use. The National Crime Information Center of the Federal Bureau of Investigation provides 100 control terminals which serve local, state, and Federal law enforcement agencies in the United States and Canada. Thirty-one regional computer networks are integrated with the National Center. The Center contains over two million records concerning wanted criminals and certain types of unrecovered stolen property, such as guns, vehicles and securities. The average number of transactions handled each day is more than 52,000. Positive responses resulting in an enforcement action average over 500 per day.[16]

California employs a computer information system called California Law Enforcement Telecommunications System (CLETS). This system stores information on criminals and motor vehicles and provides a high-speed message-switching system enabling any urban or rural law enforcement agency to obtain instant information on wanted persons, stolen and lost property, firearms and stolen vehicles. The five-million-dollar network utilizes computerized crime files from the California Highway Patrol, Department of Motor Vehicles and Department of Justice as well as data files from the FBI National Crime Information Center in Washington.[18] The computer system receives a daily flow of 35,000 messages from 1,000 terminals in the state. The system uses two pairs of computers; it can switch 17,000 messages per peak hour, provide a 24-hour retrieval capability, operate 24 hours a day for seven days a week, generate internal messages to send between centers, and accept messages of unlimited size.

A city police department may use a computer to store the data generated as a result of the activities of the department. Reports of incidents and investigations are stored in the computer for detective investigations, juvenile reporting, field investigations, offense and arrest reports, accident reports, traffic citations, narcotics tests, officer activity reports and a daily work report. This information is used to detect crime centers and criminals statistically as well as to achieve the best distribution of police manpower.

A computer system for fingerprint encoding and classification has been proposed.[17] Fingerprints have been used systematically as a means of establishing a personal identification for nearly a hundred years. The ten-finger file has been accepted by almost every country to be the single most reliable and convenient way of general personal identification. However, as populations grow, the task of searching fingerprint files becomes increasingly more difficult. In the United States, the Federal Bureau of Investigation has about 175 million ten-finger cards on file. In addition to the FBI file, almost all police departments maintain their own extensive files. Since file-searching procedures are at present largely manual, obviously a great deal of manpower is involved in searching fingerprint files. It is possible to automate the fingerprint-searching process for the ten-print file and this may be accomplished within the decade. A system for identification by means of a computer stored single-fingerprint file has been demonstrated experimentally.[17] The single fingerprint of the right index finger is encoded by means of an input device and transmitted to the computer. In the experiment a set of 110 individual fingerprints was used. A test of 53 prints against the 110 stored in the computer resulted in an identification of 49 of the 53 prints. This system or one similar in objective may lead to a computer-oriented identification system used for law enforcement as well as identification purposes.

The legal ramifications of the applications of computers are also interesting and important. Computers have brought about significant changes in business accounting and data processing. As business shifts from ledgers to computer accounting systems, the legal system must reconsider the law concerning admissibility and proof of business records. The laws of evidence have generally required that business records be visibly legible. But computer tapes are not legible visibly and the magnetic tape itself cannot be read by a human. A print-out from the tape must first be made, and it has been questioned whether it is admissible evidence. The Nebraska Supreme Court, in the case of *Transport Indemnity vs. Siebe* in 1965, was the first to allow a print-out as evidence. Other courts are following this precedent. The courts of the future may require the availability of a computer to examine the evidence submitted in business cases. In addition, the computer may be used to schedule trials and hearings to provide the speedy access to justice which is promised by the Constitution of the United States.[16]

Computers will provide continuing assistance to the law enforcement agencies and the legal system of the nation. Many applications of computers in law enforcement are as yet unenvisioned. Yet the rapid and completely integrated processing of the information related to crimes and accidents should improve the quality of protection for all citizens significantly.

13.4 COMPUTER APPLICATIONS IN TRANSPORTATION AND AEROSPACE SYSTEMS

The transportation of goods, materials and people is a vital function performed by various companies, public services, and by individuals. A transportation activity can be viewed as part of a transportation system, with the movements of goods and people as objectives. Several trends in the transportation industry will lead to the application of computers to various functions. In this section we limit our discussion of applications to the following modes of transportation: aerospace; airlines; railroads; ships, buses and autos.

While the aerospace transportation system transports very few people, it is important because many computer applications developed for space travel can be transferred and adapted for use by other transportation modes. The aerospace industry uses many computers and has developed many applications which are currently used by airlines, railroads and other segments of the transportation industry.

The National Aeronautics and Space Administration (NASA) is responsible for US efforts in aerospace. The objective of space travel is to transport several astronauts to outer space and the moon for scientific exploration. The space mission of a vehicle with astronauts is a complex, hazardous mission. A reliable guidance and computer-control system is required. Reliability is a primary objective of an aerospace computer. An initially-perfect computer has only a limited lifetime of error-free computation. For protection, the computer uses redundancy in order to achieve the necessary reliability.

The computer on a spacecraft supervises the guidance of the craft. In the Apollo vehicle, a computer built into the craft coordinates the flight. The astronauts let the computer control most of the flight while they check its progress and provide input information. The guidance and control system is illustrated in Figure 13–6. The computer stores information about the spacecraft's position and speed; automatically projects the craft's future course; calculates any needed course corrections and automatically controls the firing of engines to

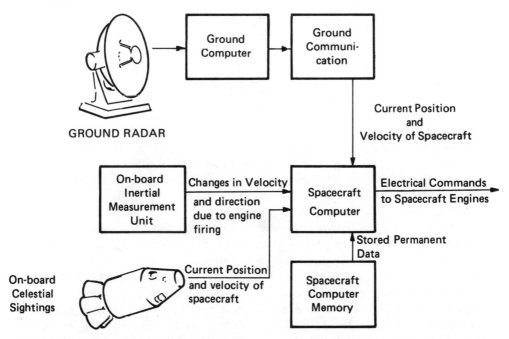

FIGURE 13–6   Guidance and control system of an Apollo spacecraft, using an on-board computer.

move the craft back on course. The inertial measurement unit provides the computer with a fixed reference by which to gauge the spacecraft's attitude, and to sense and relay to the computer any changes in speed and attitude that result from engine firings. Another source of information is the network of radar tracking stations on earth. In both an earth-orbital mission, such as Apollo 9 and a lunar flight, these stations are the computer's main source of data. The radar tracks the spacecraft and, using a computer, calculates the spacecraft's velocity and position. The calculations are then radioed to the spacecraft's computer. The third source of input data is information from the star and landmark sightings made by the astronauts.[21]

The NASA radar tracking stations and associated calculation and communication system utilizes more than 100 computers. In the first Apollo flight that landed on the moon, there were two computers in the lunar module and one computer in the command module. Computers at the Kennedy Space Center monitored the countdown and controlled the lift-off of all Apollo flights. At the Goddard Space Flight Center in Greenbelt, Maryland, computers received data from the worldwide tracking system and, after evaluating it, transmitted it to the Manned Spacecraft Center in Houston. There, computers enabled Mission Control to monitor virtually every aspect of the Apollo 11 mission in real time. The computer complex at the NASA Manned Spacecraft Center is shown in Figure 13-7. This computer system operates so fast that there is virtually no time delay between receiving and solving a computing problem. The reliability of the NASA communications, tracking and data acquisition network, is at this writing, 99.92 percent. Computers are used to calculate liftoff data needed by the astronauts as they leave the moon to rendezvous with the command module. They are also used to calculate the orbit path for the lunar module and the rendezvous calculations. The computers are used from liftoff to splashdown to calculate the path of the spacecraft and to control the steering and firing commands of the craft's engines. A space mission would not be possible without the use of computers for communication and control of the mass of data necessary for a successful mission.

The Viking spacecraft that landed on Mars in 1976 cruised for ten months from Earth to Mars over a distance of 750 million kilometers and arrived on time and on target. The guidance computer on Viking controlled the spacecraft to a safe landing and operated the Viking equipment on Mars for 58 Martian days. The Viking Mission Control and Computing Center used a complex computer system to generate mission plans and to process the data from the spacecraft.[21]

As the complexity of space projects has grown, the amount of data transmitted and recorded has increased significantly, as is shown in Figure 13-8. With increasing complexity of space missions the equipment on a mission has grown more complex and the duration of the mission has increased. The amount of data transmitted had grown in 1967 to 1700×10^6 bits per day. The physical size of the spacecraft computers has been reduced, while reliability and speed have been improved significantly.

The computers and the associated techniques used for aerospace missions are now being used or considered for use in other transportation systems. Many of the applications of computers to aerospace missions can be transferred with little alteration to the monitoring and control of aircraft. Paralleling the trends of larger crews, longer operational times, and greater complexity in future space

FIGURE 13–7   Real time computer complex in NASA's Manned Spacecraft Center uses five powerful computers, IBM System/360 Model 75's. Here in this room operations of the spacecraft and astronauts are monitored, tracking information is analyzed and computations guiding the flight are made for display to mission controllers in the mission control room. Clockwise from foreground are printer, card read punch, printer, tape units, and the Model 75 console with its two typewriter inquiry stations. *Courtesy of IBM Corporation.*

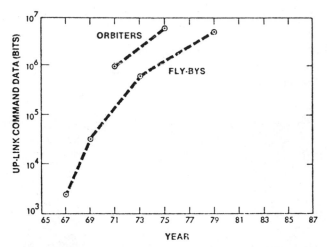

FIGURE 13-8   The total data transmitted to the first six planetary spacecraft missions during the period 1967 to 1979.

missions, the trends in aircraft such as the Boeing 747 are toward greater passenger capacity, more operational aircraft hours and more complex systems. During the past decade the aircraft industry has experienced an increase in the number, variety, and speed of aircraft, in the number of passenger miles flown, and in the complexity of the control systems. Aircraft computers are used for: (1) systems monitoring; (2) full management; (3) guidance and navigation; (4) flight data display; (5) communications; and (6) collision avoidance, among other purposes. It was the navigational function that first brought computers to aircraft. More recent applications, especially for the newer commercial and military planes, include traffic aids for landing, holding and collision avoidance.

Future operations of spacecraft such as the Space Shuttle will require computers that can communicate to and from ground stations to transmit location and environmental atmospheric data so that the true heading and ground speed can be calculated. The computer can in turn relay to the ground station the craft's status. Such information can be relayed to a central control system to help in determining arrival and location/prediction. A reply can than be sent to the craft to adjust its course and speed in order to alter its arrival time and location for landing.

The amount of airline traffic may increase threefold in passenger-miles during the next decade. This increase presents many problems in air and ground logistics. One basic problem is concerned with relating available space to the potential or committed traveler and it will increase the need for more sophisticated reservation and passenger-information systems. New reservation systems and extensions to current ones will include computerized fare computation, schedule generation, ticket generation and accounting to prorate the air fare between involved carriers. A large computer complex used for passenger service and reservations is shown in Figure 13–9.[23] This system is necessary to store the records for the passengers using one airline. It can service one million passengers up to the time of their flight.

According to estimates, the number of aircraft owned by airlines increased from 2,200 in 1967 to an estimated 4,000 in 1980. Over this same period, the number of private aircraft increased from 114,000 to 200,000. While computers alone cannot alleviate the air traffic congestion problem, the proposed National Airspace System, when fully implemented, will provide automated Air Traffic Control Services (see below). The broad objective of the system is to increase traffic-handling capabilities and increase air safety by relieving air traffic controllers of tasks that can be computer-assisted.

Computer control of all air traffic is planned for the near future by the Federal Aviation Administration. The system is planned to control all take-offs, landings, and enroute flight. The purposes of the computer system are to relieve congestion at airports and to provide accurate control of planes in flight in order to avoid collisions. Air flight controllers now rely primarily on manual and visual methods of directing plane movements. A computer system can be used to monitor flights and determine flight paths to avoid collisions.

FIGURE 13–9 Eastern Airlines, whose jets carried more than 30 million passengers in 1979, is operating a powerful computer-based reservations system. Built around three computers, the Passenger Service System serves Eastern's reservations offices. The system can store records for one million passengers at a time, and it can record information on 1,300 daily flight segments, including time of departure and arrival, meals, class of service and fares. As it monitors the preparation of each passenger's itinerary, it assures that all details are in order. The slowest part of the new reservations system is voice communications between the passenger and reservations agent. The agent has nearly instantaneous communication with the computers to retrieve information or make a reservation. *Courtesy IBM Corporation.*

Computers are extensively used for flight-simulation systems. A computer flight simulation system is used to train and upgrade pilots in the operation of an aircraft realistically, safely and economically without ever leaving the ground. For example, a simulator of the Boeing 737 controls all the variables of a flight situation and directs the simulator to recreate the same sensations that would occur in actual flight. Thus, the simulator provides the runway feel and sound the pilot actually would experience during a takeoff. As the plane reaches flying speed and the pilot eases back on the control yoke, the computer sends out the necessary signals to cut off the mechanisms providing the runway sensations. If the pilot tries to take off before the plane has attained flying speed, the simulator creates a stall, with authentic sounds and violent cockpit vibrations. The cockpit in the trainer looks just like the real one, with all the controls and instruments.

Queen Elizabeth 2, a new cruise ship, includes a computer on board for full technical, operational and business-data processing operations. The computer is used for recording the data from the engines and machinery automatically and controlling the fuel use of the engines. The computer is also used to calculate, using weather reports received, the optimum speed and course to minimize fuel consumption without undue delay in the ship's schedule. The computer is also used to monitor and store information about the ship's cargo, supplies, and fresh water.

Computers are being increasingly used by the nation's railroads in an attempt to improve the efficiency of the industry and the attendant profit. Recently, a computer system has been developed to improve the control of the 2.2 million freight cars being used to haul shipments in the US and Canada. The identification system is called Automated Car Identification (ACI); it utilizes trackside scanners to detect color-coded identification panels on the sides of passing cars. All freight cars have been labelled.[20] The system is used to provide status and location information for loaded cars. Also, in the future, computer management systems for both empty and loaded cars are expected to improve railroad car utilization significantly. A coordinated information system for all railroads should help to achieve that objective.

Computer control of railroad yards is expected to occur in the near future. The basic function of a railroad yard is to sort and service freight cars. Often time delays occur in the yards with an attendant loss in the utilization of freight cars. Automated railroad yard control will become a reality as the systems using computers are developed and implemented.

Computers are being in the control of new urban rail transit systems such as the Bay Area Rapid Transit System (BART) in the San Francisco region as well as the new Washington, D. C. Metro system.[25] The BART system, which was the first to be completely automated, began operations in 1972, and the automatic train control system failed to meet specifications. A major accident occurred in the first year.[25] The system was designed for trains running on headways (time between trains) as close as 90 seconds and at speeds of 80 miles per hour. At this writing, headways of six minutes are the best achieved. The computer system supervises scheduling, routing, and train speeds. A display board, shown in Figure 13–10, provides information on the operations of all trains.

Computers can also be applied to the monitoring and control of the movement of buses and automobiles. A computer-assisted scheduling system has been developed to control and coordinate a fleet of small driver-operated buses. The fleet provides a taxi-like service for almost the same low price as that of a bus ride.[23] The would-be rider telephones a central location where the computer, on receiving the request, dispatches a vehicle to the caller's home on a route on which the driver can pick up several passengers. This system, called Dial-a-ride,

FIGURE 13–10   The operator at the train control console can display train operations at the console and on the display board above. The panel next to the telephone displays malfunction alarms. The keyboard can be used to request various data displays on the cathode ray tube above it. It is also used to enter minor program changes, such as a change in the nominal (20 seconds) dwell time at a passenger station. Typers to the left and right of the console make record copies of CRT-displayed information and of all alarms associated with train operations. *Courtesy of Westinghouse Electric Company.*

was operationally successful in Santa Clara County, California, and Haddonfield, New Jersey in 1975, but it was discontinued because it was too costly. The system is being tried in many small American cities. The system's objective is to provide convenient transportation close to that of taxis or personal cars, with cost to the rider about equal to the cost of driving his own car.

Computers are now used in automobiles for engine control, anti-skid braking, service diagnosis, cruise control, and even taxi-fare metering.[26] Small microcomputers, which can be built into cars and trucks, are becoming especially attractive for helping manufacturers meet improved standards for fuel economy. For instance, the 1977 General Motors Toronado incorporated a programmed computer for spark-timing control. Utilizing the variables of engine speed, crankshaft position, manifold vacuum pressure and engine coolant temperature, the computer control achieved 8% fuel economy benefits at 1977 emission levels. The microcomputer comprises two integrated circuit chips and a 10,000-bit read-only memory.[26] Several automobile firms are studying the development of a total automobile computer control system.[27] The value of automobile electronic systems with microprocessors is projected to rise from $1.2 billion in 1980 to $3 billion in 1984. In the 1981 model year, the US automakers used 300 million integrated circuits.[26]

Several computer systems for the control of automobile traffic flow in a city have been implemented. New York City's Department of Traffic has been gradually installing a computer controlled traffic system. In the Borough of Queens, some 500 intersections, on seven major arterial roads, are now under the control of a computer.[23] Eventually the city plans to extend the system to 7500 of the city's 9000 intersections with traffic signals. Computer traffic control systems are also currently working in San Jose, California and Wichita Falls, Texas. The purpose of each system is to coordinate the traffic lights in a city so that the traffic flow is controlled in the best possible manner and the travel time for each individual trip is reduced.

The application of computers to transportation systems is a logical outcome of the ability of computers to monitor and control space vehicles, railroad trains, rapid transit trains, automobile traffic and ship travel. Computer systems are providing vital assistance in the operation and maintenance of the vast and important transportation industry.

13.5 COMPUTERS AND PROCESS CONTROL

The control of industrial processes, such as the production of steel, is an important function of our industrial system. A process control system combines the sensors (for measurement) with a computer to regulate, record and control a process. The basic functions of a process computer are to collect input data from the process and to monitor the use of this information to control the process in a desired manner.

An industrial process is a series of operations which produce a given commodity or product. The operations involve the treatment of energy or matter and its conversion, by chemical or physical means, to produce the products therefrom at a profit. Measuring instruments, or sensors, are used to obtain information about the state of operation of a process. This information is used by the computer in conjunction with information about the desired state of the process in order to determine a control action. A computer process control system may be defined as follows:

COMPUTER PROCESS CONTROL SYSTEM   A system based on a computer connected to sensors which monitor a process for handling matter or energy. The computer output is used to control the process in order to produce a product at a profit.

Modern industrial and laboratory processes are primarily derived from 17th and 18th century investigations in chemistry and physics. Discovery of physical laws, electricity, chemical elements, the steam engine, and the development on all scientific fronts of new industrial devices were put to good use by practical men. Their efforts resulted in the invention of processes on which were founded a number of industries, such as those which today produce chemicals, steel, textiles, electric power and petroleum. The objective of a control system is the achievement of balance among yield, waste, quality, operating expense and profit.

By 1980 more than 25,000 digital process-control computers were installed in the United States. In addition, there were 130,000 microcomputer controllers in use in the United States. The electric power industry used the most computers. The process computer control industry experienced its initial growth during the period 1960–1980. In the electric power industry, it is expected that the capacity delivered by the utilities will double during the next decade. During that period, it is also estimated that three out of four power generators will use process control computers.

The ultimate goal of many industries is to achieve the "automatic factory."[33,34] Sixty-nine percent of the price of all US manufactured goods is attributable to shop and production cost. The computer-controlled manufacturing plant is a possibility for the future as industry strives for increased productivity per worker.

The control of a process is graphically illustrated in Figure 13–11. This form of computer control is called *closed-loop*, since the measurements are used in the computer calculations to compare with the desired objective and ultimately to control the input variables of the process.

As a practical example of a process-control system, consider the steering control of an automobile. The vehicle dynamics and the resulting path along the road together make up the process. The desired objective is the completed path along the right side of the road in the proper direction, as shown in Figure 13–12. The output variable is the actual path of the vehicle which is measured by the

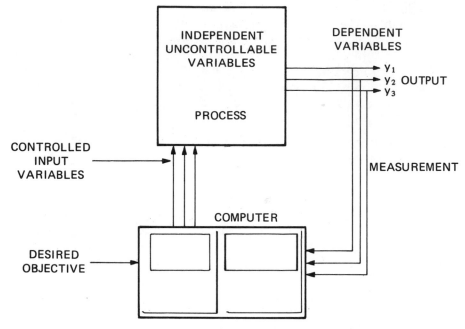

FIGURE 13–11   A computer process control system.

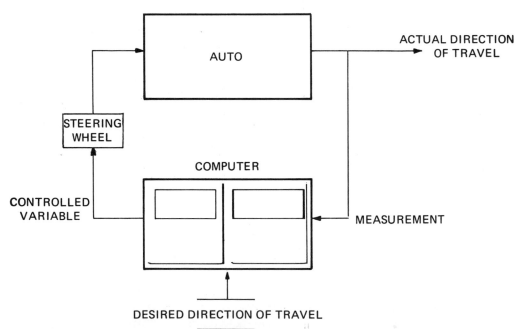

FIGURE 13–12   The steering control of an automobile travelling on a road.

driver's eyes. This information is compared with the desired path stored and generated in the driver's brain (which is like a computer). Then the resulting controlling action is taken to steer the vehicle.

The production and control of paper and paper products is an industry that has experienced increased introduction of computer control. The pulping, bleaching, and production of paper is a large and complex process. Papermaking involves some unique characteristics, such as the large amount of high-speed rotating mechanical equipment required to make paper. The large amount of distributed mechanical equipment and the high-speed nature of the operation has resulted in a difficult process to control. There are 750 mills in the United States and it is estimated that over one hundred paper mills are under the control of a computer. In one newsprint paper mill, a computer is used to monitor and control over 200 variables in the papermaking process. Every hour the paper machine produces a 102-inch diameter reel of paper weighing 29 tons, as shown in Figure 13–13. The machine drives are all computer controlled and the computer collects and analyzes data of interest to the control operator and prepares and prints logs for management in addition to controlling the major functions in the process. The control room of this computer-controlled process is shown in Figure 13–14.

The electric power generation and distribution industry is the largest industry in the United States. Expansion of the generation capability has continued to match the continuing growth of consumer use and demand. The nation's generating capacity exceeded 550 million kilowatts in 1980, and the electric energy used in the United States was 2,750 billion kilowatt-hours during 1980. This figure represents about 37 percent of world total electric energy production. Computers can save two percent of the cost of producing electric power. They can provide more efficient use of facilities and help to avoid the power blackouts which could occur in integrated networks of generating plants. can save two percent of the cost of producing electric power. They can provide more efficient use of facilities and help to avoid the power blackouts which could occur in integrated networks of generating plants.

There are other interesting applications of computers to the control of processes. For example, in a manufacturing plant, material handling accounts for almost 75 percent of plant space, with a good portion used for storage and in-process inventory. Therefore, we can expect increasing computer control of material flow, which is one of the least-automated functions now. A new concept is the use of stacker cranes and high-rise storage areas for maximum space utilization. A computer control is being developed which "knows the address" of each part in storage and directs the stacker crane to any address within the system. The computer control of physical storage and movement of produced goods is a growing industry. Total inventory-carrying units can run to 30 percent of the cost of the goods, thus becoming a primary factor in many industries. A computer-controlled warehouse has been built. It has proved a valuable tool for controlling costs of inventory and materials handling.[36]

FIGURE 13-13   A computer controlled paper machine produces a 102 inch reel of paper every hour. The computer controls and monitors over 200 variables of this production process. *Courtesy of Control Engineering.*

Many manufacturing processes use metal-cutting tools. The productivity of computer-controlled tools is many times that of manual tools. Also, machining accuracies are substantially increased by the use of computer control. In current terminology, *numerical control* refers to the control of machine tools by punched paper or magnetic tapes suitably encoded with directive information. A direct-computer controlled machine tool is a step beyond the numerically controlled tool. The computer machine tool system makes it possible to extend the data loop of a machine beyond the operator's station. The data-manipulating power of the computer can be tapped to make the machine work more efficiently. Data on the machine's output and status can be collected automatically, analyzed, and distributed to manufacturing management, and fed back into machine scheduling.[34] Computer-controlled machine tools will contribute to total factory automation, with attendant reduced costs and reduced raw-material wastage. For instance, Japanese industrial productivity climbed more than 25 percent between 1975 and 1980. This increase can be attributed largely to increased use of computer-controlled machinery.[34]

FIGURE 13–14 The control room of a computer controlled paper mill which oversees all major process functions, from wood grinding to the operation of the paper machine reel. Both the groundwood mill operator and the papermill operator are able to communicate with the computer at any time. *Courtesy of Control Engineering.*

FIGURE 13–15 The nation's first completely computer-controlled hot sheet mill has been put into operation at Bethlehem Steel Corporation's new $400 million plant at Burns Harbor, Indiana. The computer system tracks production from the time the huge slabs enter the mill until the hot rolled sheet coils reach the delivery area. Communications between the computer and the operators are flashed through this control pulpit. As the nation's most powerful hot sheet mill, the facility uses motors totaling 108,000 horsepower. It is capable of speeds of 3,750 feet a minute. The 80-inch mill's own electrical substation could supply the needs of a city of 100,000 persons. *Courtesy of Westinghouse Electric Corporation.*

The control of large steel mills by computers has resulted in improved efficiency and increased production in a given period of time. A computer-controlled steel mill is shown in Figure 13–15. The computer monitors the temperature of the sheet and the thickness of the sheet, among other variables, and generates correction commands that control the speed of movement of the sheets and the distance between the rolls.

A new range of applications of computers to control industrial processes is being opened up with the availability of small computers constructed with integrated circuits and commonly called *minicomputers*. A minicomputer is often the size of a suitcase (16" × 24" × 12"), has a memory of 10,000 to 400,000 bits, and costs $4,000 to $20,000. The minicomputer is small in size and relatively low in cost, but it incorporates significant computer power. Over 20,000 minicomputers have been manufactured each year for the past several years for use in industrial process control systems. The use of low-cost minicomputers for process control systems will accelerate the automation of industry during the next decade.

Microcomputers are also used for process control systems. An automobile computer control system is shown in Figure 13–16.

Computer control systems are not without their failures. Computer equipment problems during the Three Mile Island nuclear plant mishap of 1979 involved a 2 1/2 hour lag in generating data on the overheating reactor plant's status.[29,30]

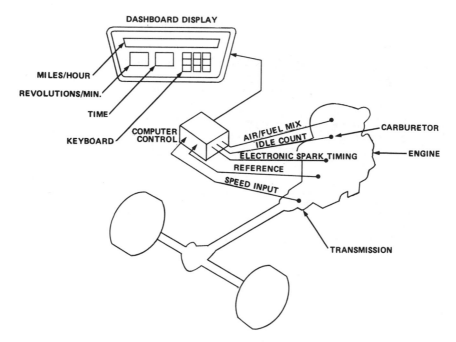

FIGURE 13–16 A schematic drawing of an automobile computer control system.

13.6 THE MAN-COMPUTER PARTNERSHIP

The partnership of man with his assistant, the digital computer, has brought about new opportunities and new applications for computers. The use of a machine such as the computer in cooperation with, and under the control of, a man results in an amplified ability. Thus, rather than taking man out of an automated system, we are suggesting that he be properly employed in terms of his abilities and limitations and that the computer be used to assist the man in completing the necessary calculations and storing information.

A man may interact and communicate directly with a computer by means of a visual display computer terminal such as the one shown in Figure 13−17. The unit shown uses a light pen, as well as a typewriter, for communication with the computer. In the illustration the man is manipulating geological data.[35] The nature of geological studies, for example, requires a visualization of the geological relationships represented by contour maps, perspective displays, cross sections, and other representations of three-dimensional data. Interactive computer graphics is a recent development that enables the geologist to converse with the computer in terms of this graphic language. By using a light pen on a series of graphic displays, the geologist can select and edit data, apply a variety of numerical models, and display results in the form of contour maps, cross sections, and so forth.

The essential feature of the man-computer partnership and the use of a visual display graphics terminal is the immediate interaction between man and machine. Ideas and problems are communicated to the machine and their effects and results are displayed rapidly so that the author can change and improve them gradually to produce the desired results. The user is able to think, experiment, and design with the aid of the computer and so improve his ideas in a dynamic manner not possible when using a computer as a batch processor. The interactive

FIGURE 13−17 A visual display computer terminal, the IBM 2250, with a light pen and a typewriter for input and communication with the computer. A perspective diagram is shown on the display and the man is pointing the light pen to a point on the display. *Courtesy of IBM Computing Report.*

graphics terminal provides two-way, on-line interaction with the computer, usually through the means of time-sharing a large computer among several users. Alternatively, several on-line graphics systems use a computer dedicated to sole use with the graphics terminal. The display terminal typically uses a cathode ray tube (CRT) as the display device as is shown in Figure 13–17. A common means of drawing on the display screen is the light pen, which is a photo-electric device for sensing light shown in Figure 13–17.

By integrating computers and laboratory experiments into closed-loop systems, investigators acquire data at high rates; reduce data in real-time; optimize conditions in the experiments more readily than they could without the help of the computers; and record many variables for later reference. The computer is used to control the laboratory experiment in a manner similar to that shown in Figure 13–11. An example of a computer-controlled laboratory experiment is shown in Figure 13–18.

Interactive computing in which humans work on problems while linked to a

FIGURE 13–18   The HP 1000 computer controls a laboratory experiment. The computer is housed in the desk cabinet with a disk storage on the right side of the desk. A video display and keyboard are used to control the experiment. *Courtesy Hewlett-Packard Corporation.*

powerful computing system is providing new opportunities to designers, architects, cartographers, geologists and businessmen. The computer is adept at calculating rapidly and accurately and storing the results while the person is adept at linking concepts and applying insight and reasoning to a problem. A comparison of the abilities of man and computer is given in Table 13−1.[34] The power resulting from the linking of man and the computer will provide new strengths and opportunities. Interactive graphics offers much in the way of bringing the program user closer to the problem-solving process.

One major use of interactive graphics systems is in the design of machines, buildings, automobiles and other products. General Motors uses a system called DAC (Design Augmented by Computer) and it has been reported that the time-shared DAC system is approximately ten times faster than the batch processing mode of processing computing problems for design purposes. The DAC system is used to design automobile parts within a man-computer partnership.

The computer-man partnership has been used in the design process in textiles, integrated electronic circuits, and architecture, among other applications.[36] Users claim a reduction in the time required to perform certain design functions of up to six to one. Interactive graphics can also be used for management information systems. Primarily, the display allows the manager to ask the question "what if?" in the context of changing inventory levels, changing production levels, and a variety of other factors. Interactive graphic displays can also be used in process computer control. In such systems, the operator can control a process by setting the objectives and monitoring the systems progress while the computer stores and manipulates the data and provides the control signals to the process. The human operator readily detects related events or groups through visual interaction with a graphic display, being able to see relationships instantly that might be extremely time-consuming to find by other means.

The use of computers to assist in design is called computer-aided design (CAD). Many such computer systems also provide assistance in the manufacturing process. They are called computer-aided manufacturing (CAM) systems. The evolution of CAD/CAM technology has emerged for commercial use in the 1980s. The sales of CAD/CAM systems are expected to be $2 billion in 1984, and the market is growing by 25% per year. A CAD/CAM system is shown in Figure 13−19.

The two major categories of CRT displays are alphanumeric and graphic. Alphanumeric displays show only numeric, alphabetic, and special characters, usually on predetermined lines, similar to a typewriter; graphic displays present line drawings, curves, schematics, etc., in addition to presenting alphanumeric information at random positions. A grid of lines provides the ability to display a relationship of three variables in three dimensions as shown in Figure 13−17 and 13−20. A three-dimensional structure created by a computer is illustrated in Figure 13−21. It is desirable to be able to rotate and manipulate an object

TABLE 13-1
A Comparison of the Information Processing and Decision Making
Abilities of Man and the Computer*

MAN	INFORMATION PROCESSING *COMPUTER*
Relatively low-speed information processor. Essentially a single-channel processor at any instant.	High-speed information processor. Can handle many channels simultaneously.
Weak and inaccurate as a computer. Tires quickly; especially in routine, boring jobs.	Tireless and fantastically accurate in comparison to man. Man should never compute if he can get a machine to do it.
Man is easy to program. He does not require extremely precise instructions. He is *flexible*.	Programming machines is time consuming. Each instruction must be detailed and specific.
Man's short-term memory is limited in size, accuracy and permanence. Access time is relatively high.	Machine memory can be almost unlimited. Accuracy and performance are high. Access time is very low.
Man processes information so slowly that he is relatively inefficient in search tasks, although he is good at recognizing and identifying targets once they are located.	Machines can rapidly search hugh quanities of data for well-defined targets, but accuracy suffers as target definition is worsened.
Man has an excellent long-term memory for related events. Generalized relevant patterns of previous experience can be recalled to solve immediate problems.	This property can be built into machines only at great expense.

DECISION MAKING

Man can generalize and employ inductive processes.	Machines have less capability for induction and generalization.
A human being does not always follow an optimal strategy—usually because he cannot perceive or examine all ramifications of a situation and cannot compute all the possible solutions.	Machines always follow built-in strategies, or they can compute optimal strategies given sufficient information.
Decisions can be made despite incomplete information and where the rules are not certain.	A computer usually demands complete information before making a decision.
Human decision-making time is relatively high. Often man wavers between alternatives if the decision is not clear-cut.	Machines are fast and specific.
Man is always needed to set priorities, establish values, set goals, risks.	Machines must be instructed as to priorities, values, goals, etc.
Targets of opportunity are recognized better by man.	Machines are relatively insensitive to unspecified opportunities.
Humans can improvise superbly.	Machines improvise poorly.
Man learns from past experience.	Machines can learn, too, but are not proficient at it yet.

*Courtesy of E. G. Johnsen and NASA.

FIGURE 13–19 A computer aided design and manufacturing system (CAD/CAM). The system uses a raster-scan display terminal, a central processing unit (upper right), a disk storage (upper left) and a work station incorporating a light pen, keypad and printer. *Courtesy of Computervision Corporation.*

displayed on the screen of the display; several display terminals provide this ability. Also several terminals, such as the one shown in Figure 13–22, provide a joystick (control handle) and mouse input devices, as well as a typewriter, in order to move a cursor (arrow) on the screen and thus draw an object or communicate a location to the computer. The mouse input device translates movement of the mouse, or small rolling device, to the cursor movement.

The application of computers to interactive design is illustrated in Figure 13–23, which shows a terminal being used for map-making.[37] Computer graphics have also been applied to the development of a numerical control program for a machine tool. An engineer can design a new part or modify an existing one in one sweep by applying his light pen to a computer display screen. He can then call for display of the image of a cutting tool on the screen and can "lead" cutter along every external or internal surface of the part that is to be machined.

The partnership of man and computer will result in new and improved

FIGURE 13–20   A picture on a CRT of an auto body part composed of 2500 short-line segments. The designer is able to alter and manipulate the auto part. *Courtesy of Adage, Inc.*

FIGURE 13–21   A three-dimensional structure created by a computer illustrates the ability of computer graphics terminals to generate three-dimensional displays. *Courtesy of Professor I. Sutherland and Mr. G. Watkins.*

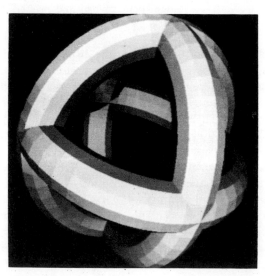

designs in the fields of architecture, electronics, industry, business, and government, among others. Man and computer acting in concert to solve a problem or design a product will be synergistic; that is, the united action of the two agents will produce a greater effect than the sum of the two individual actions. The whole of the man-computer partnership is greater than the sum of the two parts.

Color graphics systems are now available. They expand the use of computer produced graphs instead of long computer printouts. High quality color graphic terminals now sell for less than $10,000. It is expected that color graphics will grow in use in design and management. A color graphics terminal is shown in Figure 13–22.

13.7 COMPUTERS AND EDUCATION

The applications of the computer to the process of education are many and varied. Computers are able to store, manipulate and process information and thus assist in the process of education. In this section we will consider some of the potential and actual applications of computers to education.

Classroom scheduling by computer is an accomplished fact at many colleges and schools.[48] Some computer programs are used for assigning individual students to classroom groups and insuring that the number of groups matches the number of available teachers, and that these groups and teachers fit into available

FIGURE 13–22 A display terminal with a typewriter input option as well as a Joystick and Mosue input option. The mouse shown in the left foreground is two-dimensional, useful for positioning a cursor (arrow) on the screen of the display. The movement of the mouse on wheels causes the cursor to follow in an identical manner. The joystick is another device for positioning a cursor on the screen. *Courtesy of Computer Displays, Inc.*

classrooms. The whole operation typically takes place once a term. Mechanizing this unpleasant and tedious task is clearly worthwhile and useful accomplishment that is receiving wide acceptance. Scheduling classes, however, is less difficult than keeping track of individual students week by week, day by day, hour by hour, or minute by minute, and matching them in turn with resources themselves

FIGURE 13-23   Computer-assisted map making is considered technically feasible through a new method of direct graphic communication between the cartographer and a computer. The method uses an IBM 2250 graphic display unit. It was developed by IBM in cooperation with the U. S. Coast Geodetic Survey.

Among the responsibilities of the Coast and Geodetic Survey are making and updating aeronautical charts, more than 2,500 of which are used in the United States. To meet the demands of constantly increasing air traffic, these charts must be updated monthly or even weekly.

Normally, a cartographer makes changes on such a chart by working with a draftsman at a drawing board. By storing the chart data in a computer, however, the cartographer can reproduce any part of it on the screen of a 2250, as in the photograph above, and make required changes by using a light pen. On the screen he can quickly alter the size or position of symbols, lines, blocks of text, or other data; and, simply by pushing a button on the terminal's keyboard, he can enter the changes into storage. A computer-operated printer can then produce updated master charts for commercial reproduction. *Courtesy of Computing Report.*

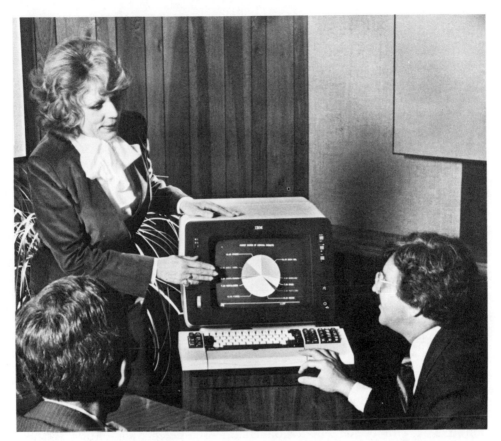

FIGURE 13—24   The IBM 3279 color display station, first delivered in 1980, can display
up to seven colors. It is useful for graphic reports and charts. *Courtesy
of IBM Corporation.*

parceled out in smaller packages than teachers per semester or rooms per
semester. Several programs are currently being developed for the purpose of
recording the progress of individual students by utilizing a computer. Meanwhile,
the use of computers to aid in administrative functions of education, such as
record-keeping, has been accomplished at many colleges and schools.

The use of the computer to assist a student in the learning process is known
by several names, of which the most common is *computer-assisted instruction*
(CAI). The purpose of the use of the computer in CAI is to aid and assist both the
teacher and the student in the educational process. One objective of CAI is to offer the student individualized instruction; it approximates the personal services of
a tutor who tailors the learning experience to the individual learner. It has been
shown that a student receives a more successful learning experience when the

educational curriculum adapts to the individual learners. The computer allows each student to proceed according to his own capability with his performance constantly monitored.[49] A definition of computer-assisted instruction is:

COMPUTER-ASSISTED INSTRUCTION   An interactive system containing a student and a computer and using a natural language such as English to produce long-lasting changes in the intellectual knowledge of a learner.

The computer technology is available to construct CAI systems for students in schools and colleges in the United States. The primary obstacles to the wide use of CAI systems are economic and pedagogical. The pedagogical question is: How may the educational community of teachers and the supporting education industry devise ways of individualizing instruction and of designing a curriculum that is suited to individuals?[51]

The use of CAI programs offers the opportunity to multiply the effect of the best teachers by repetitive use of programs generated by their talents and refined by their experience and that of the students. Also, CAI permits the teaching of material where either no qualified instructors are available, or where students are available only at irregular hours.

The student can interact with the computer in three separate ways. First, the computer can be used for drill and practice sessions which supplement the regular teaching process. This work is particularly suitable for the skill subjects. Second, the computer can be a personal teacher—a tutor—for the student. Here the system has the main responsibility for helping the student understand a concept and develop skill in using it. The aim is to approximate the interaction a patient tutor would have with an individual student. A third possible computer-student system is the dialog system, in which the student can conduct a genuine two-way conversation with the computer. Although drill-and-practice and tutorial systems are already in operation on an experimental basis, the dialog system may be some years away because of several technical problems.

An example of a relatively simple and inexpensive teaching computer is the Texas Instruments Speak and Spell device. It is a one-pound, hand-held device that asks for words to be spelled. Then, after the human punches in the spelling, the device tells the human by voice if the spelling is correct. The device has stored in it 200 words. It sells for under $70.

A variety of modes of interaction can be used in the man-computer interaction of a CAI system. Most CAI systems use a typewriter as the input device and a cathode-ray tube as the display device. The typewriter is usually connected by a telephone line to a time-sharing computer. While most CAI systems use a CRT display, several systems also use a computer-contolled slide projector to allow presentation of any graphic material. It is also possible to include a tape recorder under computer control to supplement the slides and typewriter. Several systems accept inputs from typewriter, light pen, or both. A CAI terminal is shown in Figure 13–25. This terminal uses a typewriter and a light pen for input and a CRT

FIGURE 13–25 A student terminal of a CAI system at Pennsylvania State University, using an IBM 1500 Instructional System. The terminal consists of an image projector to the left of the CRT, a cathode ray tube display, a light pen shown on the right side of the CRT, and a typewriter. *Courtesy of IBM Corporation and Pennsylvania State University.*

and slide projector for display to the student. By means of the terminal, the student is able to engage in a two-way communication with the computer. The student actually communicates with a CAI program stored within the computer and monitored and processed by the computer. The program within the computer was written by an author and then stored for later use. The preparation of useful, effective CAI programs is a costly, difficult task; this factor contributes to the potential high cost of CAI instructions.

Authors of CAI programs often use a branching technique which is very suitable for computer operation. Branching can be used to move the student to remedial or to advanced work. It is through branching, based on the student's prior knowledge and recent history of performance, that the author (via the computer) can fit the course to the student. Most courses are programmed so that the student has no choice in branching, but a few do allow the student to select a course of action.

For example, in one course segment of a CAI program, the student may choose among three alternative routes. He may elect to take a quiz, receive feedback on the adequacy of his knowledge, and then move to the beginning or end of this course. He may also receive instruction, move to a review, and then take the quiz. He may also receive instruction, move to a review, and then take the quiz. His third choice would be to go directly to the review, then to the quiz, instruction, or to another review. If he chose the first alternative and passed the quiz, he would have passed the course within a short period of time.

Branching may be done so subtly by the course author that the student is not aware of it. The author may also give the student the choice of branching and caution him of the consequences. Branching can also be used to take a student through a series of questions as shown in Figure 13–26.

Computer-assisted instruction may be seen as teaching by two methods of instruction: the traditional method, and the self-teaching method. Of course, the dichotomy between these two is not sharp or clear, but it is worth considering in terms of actual practice. The traditional method consists primarily of drill and practice of skill subjects under study. The self-teaching method is a tutorial system with the computer providing the stimulation.[52] Students in the CAI tutorial process find themselves in a new give-and-take situation rather than the passive lecture-listening situation. Most students seem glad to be able to ask questions of the computer which they would not otherwise have the opportunity to have answered in any comparable detail.

Cost affects any decision to implement an operating CAI system. The PLATO project at the University of Illinois has designed its system with the objective that the cost of using the CAI system is comparable with the cost of

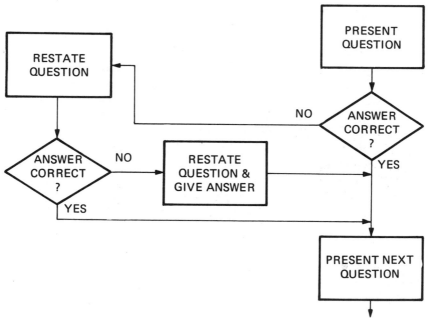

FIGURE 13–26   A flow chart of the branching process followed in one CAI program for drill and practice.

teaching, using conventional methods. The goal is to achieve a cost of thirty cents per terminal-hour for use of the computer and terminal. The University of Illinois PLATO system now has 1,000 terminals located in colleges and schools throughout the United States and Canada. The users have access to more than 3,500 hours of instructional material in more than 100 subject areas.[55,56] One of the major costs of CAI is the cost of lesson preparation.

Control Data Corporation announced the commercial offering of PLATO in 1976; the system was to be used primarily for industrial training centers and local learning centers. The cost of CAI using Control Data Corporation's system may be as high as $12 per terminal-hour.[56] However, the cost of this system is expected to decline over the next several years.

A CAI project in New York City used a computer to serve 192 terminals, similar to the terminal shown in Figure 13−25, located at 15 elementary schools in the city. About 6000 students used the terminals for a drill and practice program in arithmetic. The per terminal cost was $2230 per year, and 25 pupils used the terminal each day. Significant improvement in the students' abilities in arithmetic were measured. The median cost was $89 per student per year to utilize the CAI system.

The Philadelphia School District had 70,000 students using computers in 1976. The computer was used for occupational guidance, CAI, testing, and mathematics tutoring. A sample lesson of a second grade arithmetic drill and practice session is given in Figure 13−27.

The advantage of CAI is the projected ability to offer a learning experience to a student on an individual basis. Thus, the individual learner, using the computer as his tutor, may progress at his own pace and according to his own ability.

The reader should recognize the danger of unrealistic expectations that computers will take over a large portion of the instructional task within the near future. Even accepting the most optimistic estimates of the cost of CAI, the present system of education is cheaper by a factor of ten. Furthermore, the expected savings may be cancelled out by new demands for technical personnel, course preparation, and update costs and revised curriculum materials.

Computers can be used for simulation and can effectively offer the learner simulated experiments at a reasonable cost. Also, computers can be arranged to provide management assistance for courses and curricula. The TICCIT system (Time-Shared Interactive Computer Controlled Information Television) is being tested under the direction of Mitre Corporation. TICCIT uses a minicumputer to service 128 consoles. The TICCIT system is an approach to CAI which combines computer and television technologies.[52] Up to 128 students at a time may receive individualized instruction through the use of computer-generated color television displays, videotapes, and audio. The student uses a typewriter keyboard for input. The system, which was developed by Mitre Corporation, is now marketed by Hazeltine Corporation. It is in use at Phoenix College, Northern Virginia Community College, and Brigham Young University.

PLEASE TYPE YOUR NUMBER. 157
NOW YOUR FIRST NAME.

ROBIN

THIS IS A MIXED LESSON ON COUNTING AND
INEQUALITIES.

24, <u>26</u>, 28, 30

62, 65, 68, <u>71</u>

20, 23, 26, <u>27</u>

NO, TRY AGAIN.

20, 23, 26, <u>28</u>

NO, THE ANSWER IS 29

TRY AGAIN.

20, 23, 26, <u>29</u>

CHOOSE < OR = OR >.

16 <u>></u> 8 + 7

51 <u>=</u> 51

18 <u>≤</u> 9 + 8

NO, TRY AGAIN.

18 <u>></u> 9 + 8

FIGURE 13–27   A sample lesson of a Grade 2 arithmetic drill and practice session. The
student types his or her answer in the blank underlined space provided.
Courtesy RCA Corporation.

In the following article, Professors Alpert and Bitzer examine the potential
of CAI and discuss specifically the projected usage and costs of the Plato system
at the University of Illinois.[54] A basic component of the Plato system is the use
of a flat display device which is inexpensive and reliable. A photo of the experimental display unit is shown in Figure 13–28.

ADVANCES IN COMPUTER-BASED EDUCATION*
D. Alpert and D. L. Bitzer

Since its initiation in 1959, the PLATO program at the University of Illinois has been committed to exploration of the educa-

*From *Science*, Vol. 167, March 20, 1970, pp. 1582–1590, with the permission of *Science* and the
authors. Copyright 1970 by the American Association for the Advancement of Science.

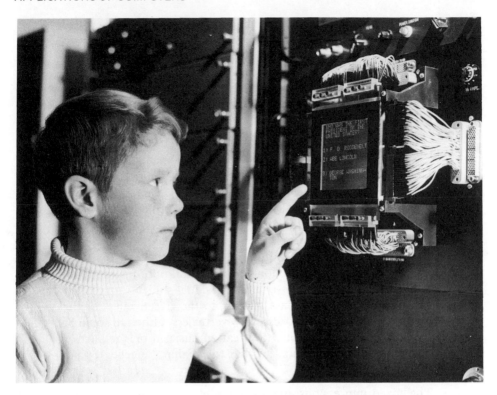

FIGURE 13–28   The Digivue electronic display panel is a flat, glass display device with an inherent memory capable of displaying information. The Digivue has been used in the Plato system at the University of Illinois. The display consists of a sealed assembly of thin parallel glass parts filled with an ionizable gas mixture. *Courtesy of Owens-Illinois, Inc.*

tional possibilities and the engineering and economic problems relating to the introduction of the modern high-speed computer as an active element in the instructional process. During the past decade, numerous other groups at universities, nonprofit institutes, and industrial corporations have also begun to explore the possibility of utilizing modern computer technology for education. A widely varying array of such efforts is encompassed by the term "computer-assisted instruction." (CAI).

The setting for these activities is an overall formal educational process in which the national investment is more than $50 billion annually, a commitment which is expected to increase to well over $100 billion by 1980. Yet, despite this large national commitment, it is commonly agreed that there are vast unmet needs in education, in terms both of quantity and of quality. There are growing demands for more mass education over a larger fraction of the human life-span, and demands for more individualized instruction tailored to the specific preparation and motivation of a given student. However, these expanding educational needs have not been matched by increases in the productivity of the educational process. Rather, the costs per student at all levels and in various types of institutions have been rising so rapidly as to cause serious concern for the future.

Under these circumstances, it is not surprising that many institutions have sought to enhance educational productivity and to enrich the instructional process by the introduction of technology, especially the technology of the modern high-speed computer. The many programs in computer-assisted instruction have been based on recognition of the unique value of the computer in adapting the selection and presentation of instructional materials to the pace and style of individual students and in acquiring and processing data relating to the effectiveness of the teaching and learning processes. Nevertheless, although some of these programs have met with great enthusiasm on the part of highly qualified educators, it is fair to say that the general reaction has been mixed.

The mixed impressions about computer-assisted instruction are due in part to the wide variation in notions as to the types of systems that are feasible and the teaching strategies that are possible. Several recent assessments of the field attest to the wide diversity of the objectives and professional specialization of such programs and to the even greater diversity of technological and educational resources available to them. At one end of the spectrum is the conception of such instruction simply as an automated version of a drill and practice lesson or a programmed textbook; at the opposite end is visualization of a remarkably powerful new medium capable of various instructional modes which can assist the student in becoming an efficient and independent learner in many fields and at all levels of education.

Another source of confusion lies in considerations of the costs of computer-assisted instruction and in mixed perceptions as to the state-of-the-art of available CAI technology. Some proponents of such instruction initiated programs and sought financial support as long ago as 1965, on the premise that significant operational application was feasible with the computer technology then available. Others took it for granted that the prime need was an innovative approach to the preparation of lesson materials, and that the lesson materials developed would be compatible with later systems. Many proceeded on the assumption that economically feasible follow-on systems would somehow inevitably be developed, but they had little insight or evidence concerning what might evolve and when it might happen. The widespread interest of the popular press in the potential promise of such activities heightened the expectations of educators and the general public alike, but did not provide a basis for understanding the key issues.

. . .

Since the economics of computer-based systems was recognized as a central issue at an early stage in the Plato program, we present here an assessment of the problems and potential of computer-assisted instruction from the perspective gained by this experience. In fact, the Plato program has for some time proceeded on the premise that the technology of the 1960s was not capable of making a significant and economically practical contribution to the nation's educational program. As early as 1964, a broad systems approach aimed at a novel and economically sound solution was set in motion. We proceeded to identify the specific systems problems in which technological innovations were called for; furthermore, as new educational ideas or teaching strategies were conceived, the design of hardware and software systems was modified to incorporate them. Although not promising immediate widescale utilization, this approach was in many ways far more ambitious than those built around available commercial systems in its perception of the possible role of the computer in education. To accent and characterize this approach, we have found it useful to describe our activity by a different and perhaps more appropriate term: "computer-based education." We call the laboratory in which the current effort is centered the Computer-based Education Research Laboratory. In this article, however, we use the terms "computer-assisted instruction" and "computer-based education" (CBE) interchangeably.

The Plato program has directed its efforts toward meeting two different, though related, objectives.

1) Investigation of the potential role of the computer in the

instructional process. The major objective of this phase has been to examine the question, What is educationally possible?

2) Design of an economical and educationally viable system incorporating the most valuable approaches to teaching and learning developed in the above investigation.

To achieve the first objective, three successive and increasingly versatile systems (Plato I, II, and III) were designed and built. These systems were intended to explore the educational possibilities without regard to the economic constraints imposed by the technology availabe at the time of their completion. The initial stage of Plato III, a system utilizing a large commercial second-generation computer, was installed in late 1964 and has been in continuous use since then. A network of four associated demonstration centers was added early in 1969. Exploratory educational efforts with Plato systems have now involved experiments in at least 20 fields of study and over 100,000 student-contact hours (much of it for academic credit) in course work at the elementary, secondary, and college undergraduate and graduate levels. Among the results have been the realization of many new teaching strategies, valuable experience in different institutional environments, and an assessment of the attitudes of students, teachers, and authors of lesson materials.

. . .

What is Educationally Possible?

What is the role of the computer as an active element in the educational process? It is now widely accepted that the computer can be a valuable tool in the presentation of drill and practice routines in fields like elementary mathematics and vocabulary development. A capability for such programs was provided by the earliest and most limited system, Plato I. Plato II provided a more expanded tutorial capacity. The most important consequences of these two systems, however, were their simulation of research and development leading to the broader capabilities of Plato III, which was designed for optimum educational versatility without specific concern for costs. In continuing full-time use as an exploratory system, Plato III has provided opportunities for developing many powerful new teaching strategies in fields as diverse as algebra and anatomy, psychology and pharmacology, languages and life sciences.

Without wanting to underrate the usefulness of computer-based systems for such rote learning situations as arithmetic drill and practice, we think it important to dispel the notion that computer-assisted instruction is limited to this type of application or is, in effect, an automated version of the Skinner teaching machine. The teaching strategies developed for Plato III are so far removed from this approach as to represent a totally different concept of the role of computer-based systems in education. To provide insight into the actual possibilities, it is important, first, to correct certain misconceptions about computer-based education. We list some of these, and give a brief commentary on each.

Misconception 1: Computer-based education is synonymous with programmed instruction. Computer-based education makes possible unprogrammed instruction or student-controlled learning by utilizing teaching strategies which differ completely from the basic tutorial logic of most programmed instruction. While of substantial value for the development of certain skills, the interchange of factual information between man and computer is only one mode whereby a teaching strategy may be incorporated into the computer. For example, the information may be stored in the machine in the form of simulated models of an actual system or device; one may simulate such widely differing systems as a biological organism (such as the human circulatory system) or an electronic circuit (such as a defective television set). Through a set of instructions stored in the computer, so-called algorithms, the computer is called upon to calculate unique responses to varying student inquiries. It is in this manner that the great computational power of a computer has been programmed to play chess with human opponents—to make appropriate moves in response to unpredicted behavior. In other teaching strategies the computer may be programmed to aid the student in the development of logical, algebraic, or geometric proofs, or to play the role of referee and scorekeeper in interactive games between humans, thus providing new insights into group or adversary behavior.

Misconception 2: Since the instructional strategy must be previously programmed in the computer, it must of necessity anticipate all conceivable student responses so as to compare them with "correct" answers stored in the machine. Teaching strategies which do not call for specified student responses are widely used and often of greater value in many fields and at many levels of instruction. For example, students studying geometry may be called upon to "draw" on the Plato graphic display a figure that has specified geometrical properties but need not be of a particular size or in any given location on the screen. In such cases, a set of algorithms in a so-called "judging routine" makes use of the computational power of the machine to assess the validity of the "answer." Other such routines have been assembled to judge open-ended verbal responses and to distinguish between conceptual errors and spelling difficulties. In a sequence for teaching algebraic proofs, the computer helps the student by pointing out or correcting arithmetical or logical errors after each statement, thus allowing the student to concentrate on the central notion of "proof."

Misconception 3: Computer-based instruction may be useful for the transfer of information but is not of value in the development of critical thinking. On the contrary, the development of comprehension calls for individual challenge or attention and is often inconsistent with the "classroom" approach. Computer-based instruction has often been found to be more effective than standard educational procedures in many learning situations that call for judgment, interpretation of complex problems, and evaluation by the student of the validity of his conjectures. In the course of some lessons, for example, the student may use the computer-based system to calculate, analyze, and display. This relieves him of much of the drudgery of "learning" and helps him develop intuition and insight. Although we view computer-based education as a way of enriching rather than replacing human involvement in the teaching process, we do not relegate computer-based education solely to routine tasks.

Misconception 4: A computer system used for computer-based education cannot be used in a time-sharing mode for conventional computer programming. The extent to which this is true is largely dependent on the size and design specifications of the system. In any multiple-access system it is necessary to set aside some reserve time, over and above the statistical "average" time of individual student image, in order to avoid long intervals of waiting at times of peak load. In a large computer system this reserve time may be substantial. For Plato IV the reserve is to be of the order of 40 percent of the total available time, to make sure that the typical waiting time for any student is less than 0.2 second. This reserve capacity may be utilized in various ways for conventional computer programming. As many as 200 or 300 terminals could be used in a true time-sharing computational mode in concurrent operation with the remaining student terminals for purposes of computer-based instruction. Alternatively, this reserve computer time could be used for processing the educational response data from "online" students and could thus provide a mechanism for continuous evaluation of student progress and teaching effectiveness.

One example of a major departure from the tutorial mode of instruction is the so-called "inquiry" mode, which has proved to be of significant value in the development of critical thinking and intellectual comprehension. In this teaching strategy the student is presented with a problem statement that cannot be dealt with by a simple or multiple-choice answer; it may call for a sequential analysis or constructed response that cannot be uniquely anticipated. For example, in one of the chemistry sequences the student is asked to identify an "unknown" organic substance on the basis of any sequence of questions or "tests" he may specify. To make a valid response, the student may find it necessary to gather factual information about the substance's physical properties, to study its interaction with reagents selected by him, to "measure" and display its infrared spectrum, to interpret the data, or to calculate various reaction rates of other properties. While factual data may be stored in the form of dictionaries, tables, or other textual forms, the specific "results" of an experiment are often stored implicitly rather than explicitly. The student decides what tests he wants the computer to perform or what calculations he wants it to carry out. In a similar sequence in medical science, the student is asked to diagnose and prescribe the treatment for a patient's illness. When he proposes a treatment, the computer responds with a report of the expected effect on the simulated patient.

Obviously, we have proceeded far beyond the role of the computer as a bookkeeper, scorekeeper, and guide to selected textual material. Not only is the student helped in acquiring new information but he is aided in fitting this information into a broader context and in gaining new perspective. He may be introduced, even at a very early stage, to an investigative approach to the solution of many problems.

A major computer-based system provides a whole new capability for testing, evaluating, and model building for the learning and teaching process. Educational psychologists were among the first to recognize the potential value of this new medium for research in these areas. Several programs in educational psychology are in progress at the University of Illinois, with the Plato III system as the basic research tool. Obviously, such a system may also be utilized for evaluating specific course materials and, eventually, for measuring and increasing the effectiveness of this new medium.

. . .

Subjective evaluation of Plato by students, teachers, and authors has been unusually positive in a wide variety of exploratory experiments. Several key features help to explain why computer-based education has aroused the enthusiasm of students and teachers alike.

1) The interactive nature of this instructional medium typically absorbs the attention and encourages the total involvement of students at all age and grade levels.

2) The student may proceed at his own pace and can exert considerable choice in the selection of alternative teaching strategies and methods of presentation.

3) The feedback of information is applied not only in the learning process but also in the teaching process; the system provides teacher or author with the means of assessing in detail the progress of the individual student, with a powerful tool for evaluation and modification of lessons, and with a mechanism for measuring overall educational effectiveness.

4) Lesson materials may be written or edited at a student console at any location while other consoles are being used by students. Thus, materials previously prepared elsewhere may be modified by a teacher in a participating institution (for example, a community college or a secondary or elementary school) in response to the particular needs of his own students.

. . .

Two conclusions seem justified: (i) that computer-based education is a plausible approach to improved individualized instruction in a very wide array of courses or subject-material areas; (ii) that the nature of educational testing and evaluation calls for, and will be radically and substantially affected by, the availability of large computer-based education systems; a valid measure of effectiveness calls for a much larger sampling of data and a longer period of comparison than has heretofore been available.

This expanded view of what is educationally possible is made feasible by several unique features of the Plato III system. First, a highly flexible software system has made it easy for educational innovators to use their intuitive notions to develop wholly new sets of teaching or testing strategies; the capacity of a large central computer makes possible a very wide variety of such teaching strategies, even in a single lesson. Second, the flexible software design has provided compatibility not only with CAI systems devleoped by other manufacturers and designers but also with the next generation of such machines; educational materials developed elsewhere can be readily incorporated. Third, although the software system has become increasingly sophisticated and permits an experienced author to develop very complex teaching strategies and lessons, it is not necessary for an author to become, or to be dependent on, a systems programmer. Teachers and authors can begin to prepare, edit, or modify lesson materials after a few hours of familiarization with the Tutor language, with no previous experience. Finally, it is possible for messages to be transmitted from a given student station to any other student station; thus, teachers or authors may act as participants in the system or monitor the progress of individual students.

What is the role of computer-based instruction in the context of the conventional classroom setting? Just as the printed page or the textbook has distinctly different uses at various educational levels, we postulate different uses for computer-based education at the various stages from preschool to graduate education and beyond. At the elementary grade level, in view of the important role of teacher and pupil interactions during most of the day, it seems reasonable to anticipate that computer-based instruction will occupy a relatively small fraction (perhaps 1 hour per day) of the pupil's time. Interestingly, our experience at this level indicates a unique cooperative relationship between teacher and pupil when the individual members of the class are at their Plato consoles. The teacher is called upon only when the pupil needs special help; when this occurs, help can be provided on the basis of a precise indication of the nature of the difficulty as exhibited by the particular sequence in which the problem was encountered. Applications at the grade school level include individual drill and practice in arithmetic and the development of reading skills, and they provide periodic rest intervals for the human teacher.

At the opposite end of the utilization scale we might envisage entire courses given at professional schools, at remotely located guidance centers, and in continuing adult education programs. The individualize approach to education that the Plato systems provide would be uniquely suited to the updating of professional skills or the development of new skills for adults at the non-professional level.

We visualize a particularly valuable role for computer-based education at the undergraduate level at universities, 4-year colleges, and community colleges. As to the degree of utilization, one may expect that the fraction of the instructional load that can be taken over by computer-based education would vary widely. In certain instances—such as introductory courses in computer science, mathematics, basic anatomy, or genetics—a Plato-type system might well assume the entire load. This would be particulary attractive for well-qualified students who wished to register in an advanced seminar without devoting an entire semester or two to a prerequisite survey course. Such students might well take the entire course and a proficiency examination within a week or two. Students who are less well qualified might by this means take remedial work at all levels to aid in their preparation for more advanced courses. In addition, there would be many courses in which the computer-based system and human teachers would share the load more or less equally. Faculty instructors could spend more of their available time in advanced or interdisciplinary seminars in which the discussion of human values or the development of new ideas would occupy the entire time available for interchange between teacher and students.

Computer-based education would make a unique contribution at the community college level, not only because of the shortage of adequately prepared instructors in many fields but also because of the value of such a system in orienting students who transfer to other colleges or universities after 1 or 2 years. They might, by this means, share, prior to transfer, an educational experience with students at the other institution.

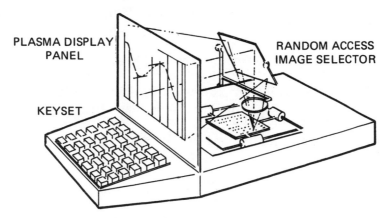

PLASMA DISPLAY PANEL

RANDOM ACCESS IMAGE SELECTOR

KEYSET

FIGURE 13–29   Schematic diagram of the Plato IV student console. See also Figure 13–28.

Some Implications

The cumulative and overwhelming trend of our exploratory research results with the Plato III system suggests that this new medium will be educationally effective and enthusiastically received by students at all levels of age and experience. There is every evidence thus far that this enthusiasm is shared by teachers and authors as well. Supporting this appraisal is the corresponding experience of educators working in the field of computer-assisted instruction at other institutions, for the most part with computer-based equipment far less flexible than Plato III. Most such educators are increasingly persuaded that this medium provides a powerful means of meeting heretofore unmet needs in the entire range of the educational process. If there has been informed skepticism or concern about the potentiality of computer-assisted instruction, it has largely been addressed to the issue of economics.

Some of the possibilities that may well be realized through the application of computer-based education are the following:

1) Gradual abolishment of lock-step schedules and narrowly specified curricula in formal education. Students could proceed at a pace determined by their own capacity and motivation.

2) Provision of remedial instruction or tutorial assistance during regularly scheduled courses for students with insufficient preparation.

3) Reduction in the number of large lecture classes at the college level, in favor of small instructional groupings and seminars.

4) Special instruction at home for physically handicapped students.

5) Development of arithmetical or other skills, at the elementary level, away from the exposed and often competitive environment of the classroom.

6) Effective job training or retraining for any employee group especially affected by expanding technology.

7) Continuing education for professional personnel, permitting the updating of knowledge and skills in their own offices and on their own schedules.

. . .

The introduction of a major new technology into the educational process will undoubtedly raise questions on the part of some educators concerning the possible negative impact of an inanimate tutor on the very human processes of learning and teaching. Similar questions may well have been raised when the printing press and inexpensive paper were introduced into the educational process in the 15th century. It was not long, however, before the technology of the printed page became so identified with education that the library became the universal symbol of educational excellence. We believe that the resulting explosion of knowledge and of information has made the introduction of computer-based education all the more needed in a rapidly changing world.

The Plato program has called for a unique combination of educational and engineering talents. The program has benefited from cooperation among experts in many disciplines and among educators in universities, community colleges, high schools, and elementary schools. Finally, it has depended in a critical way on cooperation among educational institutions, industrial corporations, and government agencies. These features may be indicative of a new level of interinstitutional relationships which would accompany the incorporation of computer-based systems in the educational process.

Elementary and high schools spend about $2 billion annually on instructional material in the US. About $70 million goes for computer-based equipment. By 1985, it is expected that $300 million will be expended on instructional computers. This growth is due to the availability of medium-cost mini-computer based systems.[56]

France is using microcomputers in secondary schools for CAI. It expects to have 10,000 computers in school use by 1984.[53]

One future CAI system may incorporate the benefits of a minicomputer with a videodisk player. A single videodisk can store 108,000 television picture frames which can be used as elements of a motion picture or sequential slides. The cost per frame for videodisk systems is about 100 times cheaper than printing.[54] If a $10,000 microcomputer–videodisk system is amortized over five years and 20 students use each system in a classroom the cost per student would be $50 annually.

The computer will be a library, simulator and tutor in the future. However, the cost of the computer is only a minor part of the total cost, which includes programming costs and course development and maintenance costs.

In the following selection, Professor Seymour Papert describes a scenario for the future based on his experience with the LOGO project, which deals with the use of computers in the education of children:*

> I see the computer as an agent for exposing the child to a set of possibilities for acculturation, whether in mathematics, in science, or in language itself.
>
> This image of learning suggests a critique of what a school is all about and even raises the question if such demarcated institutions as schools make any sense. I sympathize with Ivan Illich's vision of a deschooled and decentralized society[4] but think that his proposals are totally utopian without a look at education through the prism of the computer culture. The presence of the computer is what will make a deschooled society possible and even necessary, because if my vision of the way computers will be used is realized, it will come into conflict with the rational structure of schools on every level, from the epistemological to the social.
>
> My attitude toward Illich extends also to many other educational visionaries. Dewey, Montessori, Neill, all propose to educate children in a spirit that I see as fundamentally correct but that fails in practice for lack of a technological basis. The computer now provides it; it is time to reassess the practical possibilities for instituting what previous generations have dismissed as romantic. I have said enough at least to raise serious doubt about whether Jenck's gloomy conclusions would

*Seymour Papert, "Computers and Learning," *The Computer Age*, MIT Press, Cambridge, Massachusetts, pg. 85.

extend to a reform of education based on a widespread computer presence with LOGO as a model. These doubts should become even stronger when we look at the probable impact of something that we know is happening even now—the proliferation of the personal computer. Already the advent of the microprocessor, the "computer on a chip," has made possible the presence of at least 15,000 computers in the living rooms of American families.

The next few years will see an explosion in the numbers of privately owned computers. Much more significantly, they are about to cross a power threshold that will support the LOGO-like use of them. When this happens, there will be for the first time a viable alternative to schools and the possibility that education will once more become a private act. What I envisage is private in many more senses than a return to an eighteenth-century tutor and pupil model. The tutor served an aristocracy, and the knowledge he transmitted fostered socialization into an elite as much as and together with the "content" of the lessons. The computer has the potential of serving everybody—it will soon be as inexpensive as a television set.

Although the sinister possibility exists that only an elite will appropriate the new computers, this need not happen; I hope it will not. But it is a plausible, even very likely scenario that over the coming decade a significant number of families will come to see the private computer as viable alternative to public school, less expensive and more effective than private school.

CHAPTER 17 PROBLEMS

P13–1. Draw an algorithmic flow chart for a computer system which will monitor an alarm for a patient under treatment for a coronary disease (heart attack).

P13–2. What advantages and disadvantages does the use of a computer-based law enforcement system have for the law-abiding citizen?

P13–3. Design a block diagram, similar to Figure 13–6, for the computer guidance and control of a mass transit railway system such as the Bay Area Rapid Transit System (BART) or the New York City Subway System.

P13–4. Develop a block diagram, similar to Figure 13–11, for computer control of the heating plant at your college.

P13–5. Digital minicomputers are being developed for the control of an individual automobile's speed and fuel. Using some recent articles about automobile computers, design a block diagram of a computer control for the speed and fuel of an automobile.

P13–6. Write a small CAI program in FORTRAN or BASIC which will provide a drill and practice routine for addition of numbers from 1 to 1000 based on the flow chart of Figure 13–23.

P13–7. Computers are radically altering the printing, publishing and newspaper industries. Many newspapers and publishers have replaced their hot metal typesetting systems with minicomputer text-editing and typesetting systems.[57] Visit your local newspaper or printing plant and determine the characteristics of computer typesetting systems. List the advantages of such a system.

P13–8. Computer hardware failure can present some important problems for systems like air traffic control or mass transit control. What characteristics of these systems would you require in order to avoid catastrophic problems?

P13–9. Computerized tomography provides x-ray images of a cross section of the human body.[12] Contact a local hospital—preferably a large hospital associated with a university—and determine the staff's opinion of the use of tomography. Visit the computer tomography center, if possible.

CHAPTER 13 REFERENCES

1. H. Schwartz, *Computers and Medicine*, Artech House, Dedham, Massachusetts, 1979.
2. H. C. Redman and A. E. Fisch, *Computer Tomography of the Body*, Saunders Publishing Co., Philadelphia, 1979.
3. M. Nichols, "Medical Database Speeds Diagnoses, Cuts Staff Costs," *MIS Week*, August 27, 1980, p. 16.
4. "Saving Druggists in a Paper Storm," *Business Week*, June 2, 1980, pp. 84–86.
5. "Mayo's Medical Mini-Micro," *Datamation*, March 1980, pp. 207–216.
6. T. Estrin and R. C. Uzgales, "Information Systems for Patient Care," *Computer*, November 1979, pp. 4–6.
7. H. Roth, "Computerized Device Will Aid Handicapped," *Electronic Engineering Times*, August 18, 1980, pg. 10.
8. M. L. Dertouzos and J. Moses, *The Computer Age*, MIT Press, Cambridge, Massachusetts, 1980.
9. R. G. Rittenhouse, "The Market for Wired City Services," *Computers and Society*, Fall, 1979, pp. 2–13.
10. W. J. Dixon and M. B. Brown, *Biomedical Computer Programs*, University of California Press, Berkeley, 1980.

11. H. R. Warner, *Medical Decision Making in the Computer Age*, Academic Press, New York, 1980.
12. H. C. Redman, *Computed Tomography of the Body*, Saunders Co., Philadelphia, 1979.
13. H. Schwartz, *Computers and Medicare*, Artech House, Dedham, Massachusetts, 1980.
14. B. Niblett, *Computer Science and the Law*, Cambridge University Press, New York, 1980.
15. T. D. Sterling, "Computer Ombudsman," *Society*, February 1980, pp. 31–35.
16. "Clogged Courts Try the Electronic Cure," *US News and World Report*, April 28, 1980, pg. 96.
17. D. J. Sykes, "Positive Personal Identification," *Datamation*, November 1, 1978, pp. 179–186.
18. C. Evans, *The Micro Millennium*, Viking Press, New York, 1980.
19. A. G. Oettinger, "Information Resources: Knowledge and Power in the 21st Century," *Science*, July 4, 1980, pp. 191–209.
20. "A Bigger Load for Rail Computers," *Business Week*, February 4, 1980, pp. 89–90.
21. T. H. Bird and R. R. Sheahan, "Trends in the Automation of Planetary Spacecraft," *Astronautics and Aeronautics*, May 1979, pp. 32–35.
22. E. Teicholz, "Processing Satellite Data," *Datamation*, June 1978, pp. 117–142.
23. E. A. Torrero, "Unjamming Traffic Congestion," *IEEE Spectrum*, November 1977, pp. 77–79.
24. M. Feazel, "FAA Expands Flow Control Use," *Aviation Week*, May 18, 1980, pp. 25–27.
25. "BART Battles to Keep Automatic Control," *Business Week*, December 2, 1972, pp. 80–82.
26. W. F. Arnold, "Accelerating Need for Chips," *Electronics*, August 30, 1979, pp. 44–46.
27. S. Groves, "Controllers Come of Age," *Computer Design*, May 1980, pp. 86–100.
28. D. Whieldon, "Computers Spearhead the Energy Counteroffensive," *Computer Decisions*, June 1980, pp. 24–35.
29. B. Schultz, "Data Lags Cited in Nuclear Mishap," *Computerworld*, July 21, 1980, pg. 2.
30. M. Stephens, *Three Mile Island*, Random House, Inc., New York, 1981.
31. R. C. Dorf, *Energy, Resources and Policy*, Addison-Wesley Publishing Company, Reading, Massachusetts, 1977.
32. G. J. Agin, "Computer Vision Systems for Industrial Inspection and Assembly," *Computer*, May 1980, pp. 11–20.
33. R. C. Dorf, *Modern Control Systems*, 3rd Edition, Addison-Wesley Publishing Co., Reading, Massachusetts, 1980.

34. C. B. Besant, *Computer Aided Design and Manufacture*, Halsted Press, New York, 1980.
35. W. K. Pratt, *Digital Image Processing*, Wiley and Sons, Inc., New York, 1978.
36. G. Halevi, *The Role of Computers in Manufacturing Processes*, Wiley and Sons, Inc., New York, 1980.
37. M. P. Groover, *Automation, Production Systems, and Computer Aided Manufacturing*, McGraw-Hill Book Co., New York, 1980.
38. R. Paul, "Robots, Models and Automation," *Computer*, July 1979, pp. 19-27.
39. E. J. Kompass, "The Long Term Trends in Control Engineering," *Control Engineering*, September 1979, pp. 53-64.
40. M. Marshall, "VLSI pushes Super CAD Techniques," *Electronics*, July 31, 1980, pp. 73-80.
41. J. K. Krouse, "CAD/CAM—Bridging the Gap From Design to Production," *Machine Design*, June 12, 1980, pp. 117-125.
42. D. C. Allen, "Techniques: Computer-Integrated Manufacturing," *Datamation*, March 1980, pp. 187-190.
43. J. Orr, "Interactive Computer Graphics Systems," *Mini-Micro Systems*, December 1979, pp. 68-78.
44. W. M. Newman and R. F. Sproull, *Principles of Interactive Computer Graphics*, 2nd Edition, McGraw-Hill Book Co., New York, 1979.
45. P. Kirby, "Desktop Graphics," *Datamation*, May 1979, pp. 162-170.
46. R. W. Decker, "Computer Aided Design and Manufacturing at GM," *Datamation*, May 1978, pp. 159-165.
47. K. D. Wise *et. al.*, *Microcomputers: A Technology Forecast*, Wiley and Sons, Inc., New York, 1980.
48. A. Bork, "Learning with Computer Simulations," *Computer*, October 1979, pp. 75-84.
49. R. M. Aiken and L. Braun, "Into the 80s with Microcomputer-Based Learning," *Computer*, July 1980, pp. 11-16.
50. "Spurt in Computer Graphics," *Business Week*, June 16, 1980, pp. 104-105.
51. S. D. Milner, "Teaching Teachers about Computers," *Phi Delta Kappan*, April 1980, pp. 544-546.
52. J. A. Chambers and J. W. Sprecher, "Computer Assisted Instruction: Current Trends and Critical Issues," *Communications of the ACM*, June 1980, pp. 332-341.
53. J. Hebenstreit, "10,000 Microcomputers For French Secondary Schools," *Comuputer*, July 1980, pp. 17-21.
54. J. I. Lipson, "Technology in Science Education: The Next Ten Years," *Computer*, July 1980, pp. 23-27.
55. R. M. Aiken, "Computer Science Education in the 1980s," *Computer*, January 1980, pp. 41-46.

56. L. R. Gallese, "Textbook Publishers Enter Computer Age with Products Aimed at Classroom Market," *Wall St. Journal*, September 8, 1980, pg. 24.

57. A. Smith, *Goodbye Gutenberg: The Newspaper Revolution of the 1980s*, Oxford University Press, New York, 1980.

57. V. Zonana, "A $1.3 Million Transit Improvement in Which Man Emerges Triumphant," *Wall Street Journal*, September 8, 1980, pg. 24.

58. *Computer Applications in Medical Care*, IEEE Computer Society, New York, 1980.

59. J. Nievergelt, "A Pragmatic Introduction to Courseware Design," *IEEE Computer*, September 1980, pp. 7–21.

60. C. Machover, "The Coming Decade in Computer Graphics," *IEEE Computer Graphics*, January 1981, pp. 1–12.

14

CYBERNETICS, ARTIFICIAL INTELLIGENCE AND THE SOCIAL CONSEQUENCES OF COMPUTERS

14.1 CYBERNETICS AND ARTIFICIAL INTELLIGENCE

The collaboration of man and machine has been a fact of western civilization since the industrial revolution. One illustration of the man-machine relationship is shown in Figure 14-1. With the development of the digital computer after World War II, there has been increasing study of the relationships among computers, the human nervous system, and the human's thinking process. The origination of this field of study is usually attributed to Norbert Wiener (1894-1964). Wiener invented the word *cybernetics* to describe the field of control and communication in machines and in living organisms. The word cybernetics is taken from the Greek *kybernetes*, meaning "steersman." From the same Greek word, through the Latin corruption *gubernator*, came the term *governor*, which has been used for a long time to designate a control mechanism. *Governor* was also the title of a brilliant study written by James Clerk Maxwell. The basic concept which both Maxwell and the investigators of cybernetics describe, by the choice of this term, is that of a feedback mechanism, or self-control device, which is especially well represented by the steering engine of a ship and described below.[1]

Feedback is used to control various industrial systems as well as CAI systems and others. (The use of a computer to control an industrial process or to provide

FIGURE 14–1   Man and Machine. Charlie Chaplin in *Modern Times. The Museum of Modern Art/Film Stills Archive, New York City.*

a man-machine system was discussed in Chapter 13.) If we have a goal or objective in mind, we can use feedback to make sure we reach our goal, because feedback is self-correction. It keeps us on the path to our goal. When feedback is added to digital computer processes, we have all that we need to simulate almost any action of an organism in its environment.

The self-correcting process includes the desired output, which the computer compares with the actual output. The difference, or error, is used by the computer to cause the regulated process to respond in the desired way. The steering engine of a ship is one of the earliest forms of feedback mechanisms.

When you reach for the salt cellar, the distance and direction of that object from your hand is the desired-result input to your brain. By an astonishing series of observations and measurements, carried out unconsciously and at lightning speed, your brain measures the difference between where your hand is and where the salt cellar is, returning that information as feedback to your brain. Your brain keeps your arm and hand moving until that feedback is zero, at which point it switches from the MOVE HAND procedure to the CLUTCH and LIFT procedures.

A block diagram of a computer feedback system is shown in Figure 14–2. The system shown incorporates a *negative* feedback mechanism, since the *error* is the difference between the desired and the measurement of the actual. This type of feedback system may also be called a *trial and error* system. The basic hypothesis of cybernetics is that the chief mechanism of the human nervous system is one of negative feedback. Also, cybernetics includes the hypothesis that the negative feedback mechanism explains purposive and adaptive behavior.[2] Thus, one definition of cybernetics is:

CYBERNETICS   The theory of control and communication which can be applied to machines and animals.

The analogy of the computer to the human brain has been used to study the process of thinking and the action of the human nervous system. John Van Neumann commented on the digital nature of human nerve functioning.[3]

The most immediate observation regarding the nervous system is that its functioning is *prima facie* digital.

The basic component of this system is the nerve cell, the neuron, and the normal function of a neuron is to generate and propa-

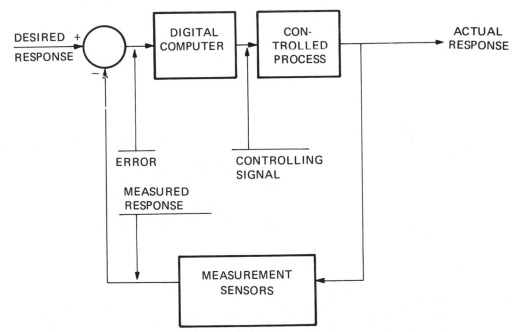

FIGURE 14–2   A negative feedback control process. The error is the difference between the desired and the measured actual response.

gate a nerve impulse. This impulse is a rather complex process, which has a variety of aspects—electrical, chemical and mechanical. It seems, nevertheless, to be a reasonably uniquely defined process; *i.e.* nearly the same under all conditions; it represents an essentially reproducible, unitary response to a rather wide variety of stimuli.

The use of process-control computers has led to a discussion of whether computers may be said to possess intelligence and engage in the process of thinking. This subject of discussion and research is called the field of artificial intelligence (AI). Other fields within AI include problem solving using computers, computers that learn, and neurological information-processing models. One definition of artificial intelligence is:

ARTIFICIAL INTELLIGENCE   The characteristic of a computer system capable of thinking, reasoning and learning (functions normally associated with human intelligence).

There have been several attempts to set up a learning program in a machine so that the machine modifies its own performance on the basis of experience gained.[34,41] A computer has been programmed to learn from its successes and failures at the game of checkers to improve its own play so that eventually it beats the person who programmed it. We may be many years yet from the time when computer-learning techniques have wide commercial application. Probably we shall need new technical developments to improve the computer's ability to recognize patterns.

A considerable range of human behavior can be explained in terms of information processing theories. Within the theories of artificial intelligence, comparisons can be made between men and machines in that range of activities we describe as thinking. If there is objection to the use of the word *thinking*, then *ability to process information* or some similar term can be used. But it must be admitted that there exists some field of behavior in which men and machines coexist and in which they can be compared. It has been noted that one often regards an action as "intelligent" until he understands it. In explaining the action, it often becomes routine and mechanistic rather than intelligent.

As Christopher Evans points out, intelligence is an amalgam of different faculties.[50] These factors include:
1. Data capture ability
2. Data storage capability
3. Processing speed
4. Software flexibility
5. Software efficiency
6. Software range

These factors can also be used to measure machine intelligence.

One important goal of artificial intelligence research is to devise machines to perform various tasks normally requiring human intelligence. Proving mathematical theorems, translating languages, playing good games of chess, and learning to improve its own performance are a few of the kinds of things such a machine is expected to perform. Can a computer be programmed to be intelligent? Marvin Minsky illustrates several computer programs which he contends meet the definition of artificial intelligence.[4] Many AI investigators believe that there is nothing a human can do that cannot in principle be done by a computer.[11,23,41] Herbert Simon, a pioneer in the field of AI, believes that computers that "think" eventually could help solve some of mankind's pressing problems. Simon's program called BACON, after Sir Francis Bacon, recently "discovered" a law of planetary motion first conceived by Kepler in the 17th Century.

The question of whether a computer can think or can possess an intelligence has occupied the thoughts of several philosophers.[37] To determine whether a computer can think, a definition of thinking must be developed to be used as a criterion. Professor A. M. Turing, one of the first computer scientists, was challenged by the problem of developing a criterion of thinking which could be used with a computer to test its ability to exhibit an intelligence like that of a human. Professor Turing published an article in *Mind* in 1950 attacking the problem of machine intelligence. The first two pages of that article clearly outline the qualities which Turing suggests might be used to distinguish intelligence. They appear below.*

CAN A MACHINE THINK?

By A. M. Turing

1. The Imitation Game

I propose to consider the question, 'Can machines think?' This should begin with definitions of the meaning of the terms 'machine' and 'think.' The definitions might be framed so as to reflect so far as possible the normal use of the words, but this attitude is dangerous. If the meaning of the words 'machine' and 'think' are to be found by examining how they are commonly used it is difficult to escape the conclusion that the meaning and the answer to the question, 'Can machines think?' is to be sought in a statistical survey such as a Gallup poll. But this is absurd. Instead of attempting such a definition I shall replace the question by another, which is closely related to it and is expressed in relatively unambiguous words.

*from *Mind*, 1950, pp. 2099–2123, with permission.

The new form of the problem can be described in terms of a game which we call the 'imitation game.' It is played with three people, a man (A), a woman (B), and an interrogator (C) who may be of either sex. The interrogator stays in a room apart from the other two. The object of the game for the interrogator is to determine which of the other two is the man and which is the woman. He knows them by labels X and Y, and at the end of the game he says either 'X is A and Y is B' or 'X is B and Y is A.' The interrogator is allowed to put questions to A and B thus:

C: Will X please tell me the length of his or her hair?

Now suppose X is actually A, then A must answer. It is A's object in the game to try and cause C to make the wrong identification. His answer might therefore be:

'My hair is shingled, and the longest strands are about nine inches long.'

In order that tones of voice may not help the interrogator the answer should be written, or better still, typewritten. The ideal arrangment is to have a teleprinter communicating between the two rooms. Alternatively the question and answers can be repeated by an intermediary. The object of the game for the third player (B) is to help the interrogator. The best strategy for her is probably to give truthful answers. She can add such things as 'I am the woman, don't listen to him!' to her answers, but it will avail nothing as the man can make similar remarks.

We now ask the question, 'What will happen when a machine takes the part of A in this game?' Will the interrogator decide wrongly as often when the game is played like this as he does when the game is played between a man and a woman? These questions replace our original, 'Can machines think?'

As well as asking, 'What is the answer to this new form of the question,' one may ask, 'Is this new question a worthy one to investigate?' This latter question we investigate without further ado, thereby cutting short an infinite regress.

The new problem has the advantage of drawing a fairly sharp line between the physical and the intellectual capacities of a man. No engineer or chemist claims to be able to produce a material which is indistinguishable from the human skin. It is possible that at some time this might be done, but even supposing this invention available we should feel there was little point in trying to make a 'thinking machine' more human by dressing it up in such artificial flesh. The form in which we have set the problem reflects this fact in the condition which prevents the interrogator from seeing or touching the other competitors, or hearing their voices.

Some other advantages of the proposed criterion may be shown up by specimen questions and answers. Thus:

> Q: Please write me a sonnet on the subject of the Forth Bridge.
> A: Count me out on this one. I never could write poetry.
> Q: Add 34957 to 70764.
> A: (Pause about 30 seconds and then give as answer) 105621.
> Q: Do you play chess?
> A: Yes.
> Q: I have K at my K1, and no other pieces. You have only K at K6 and R at R1. It is your move. What do you play?
> A: (After a pause of 15 seconds) R-R8 mate.

The question and answer method seems to be suitable for introducing almost any one of the fields of human endeavour that we wish to include. We do not wish to penalise the machine for its inability to shine in beauty competitions, nor to penalise a man for losing in a race against an aeroplane. The conditions of our game make these disabilities irrelevant. The 'witnesses' can brag, if they consider it advisable, as much as they please about their charms, strength or heroism, but the interrogator cannot demand practical demonstrations.

The game may perhaps be criticised on the ground that the odds are weighted too heavily against the machine. If the man were to try and pretend to be the machine he would clearly make a very poor showing. He would be given away at once by slowness and inaccuracy in arithmetic. May not machines carry out something which ought to be described as thinking but which is very different from what a man does? This objection is a very strong one, but at least we can say that if, nevertheless, a machine can be constructed to play the imitation game satisfactorily, we need not be troubled by this objection.

It might be urged that when playing the 'imitation game' the best strategy for the machine may possibly be something other than imitation of the behaviour of a man. This may be, but I think it is unlikely that there is any great effect of this kind. In any case there is no intention to investigate here the theory of the game, and it will be assumed that the best strategy is to try to provide answers that would naturally be given by a man.

Considering the lucid criterion given above for determining whether a machine is thinking, we can progress to the question of whether modern computers are able to exhibit the qualities of intelligence.* In the following article the famous author Arthur Clarke reflects on several of the often-mentioned consequences of computers possessing an intelligence.[6]

*An excellent discussion of the Turing test or game appears in reference 27.

ARE YOU THINKING MACHINES?**

By Arthur C. Clarke

"Are you serious? Do you really believe that a machine thinks?"—It will not be accepted universally, but there is one very straightforward answer to this question that originally was posed in the opening line of Ambrose Bierce's classic, *Moxon's Master*. It can be maintained that every man is perfectly familiar with at least one thinking machine, because he has a late-type model sitting on his shoulders. For if the brain is not a machine, what is it?

Critics of this viewpoint (who are probably now in the minority) may argue that the brain is in some fundamental way different from any non-living device. But even if this is true, it does not follow that its functions cannot be duplicated, or even surpassed, by a nonorganic machine. Airplanes fly better than birds, though they are built of very different materials.

For obvious psychological reasons, there are people who never will accept the possibility of artificial intelligence, and would deny its existence even if they encountered it.

We no longer become upset because machines are stronger, or swifter, or more dexterous than human beings, though it took us several painful centuries to adapt to this state of affairs. How our outlook has changed is well shown by the Ballad of John Henry; today, we should regard a man who challenged a steam hammer as merely crazy—not heroic. I doubt if contests between calculating prodigies and electronic computers will ever provide inspiration for future folk songs. But I'll be happy to donate the theme to Tom Lehrer.

It is, of course, the advent of the modern computer that has brought the subject of thinking machines out of the realm of fantasy into the forefront of industrial research. One could not have a plainer answer to the question that Bierce posed three-quarters of a century ago than this quotation from MacGowan and Ordway's recent book, *Intelligence in the Universe:* "It can be asserted without reservation that a general-purpose digital computer can think in every sense of the word. This is true no matter what definition of thinking is specified; the only requirement is that the definition of thinking be explicit."

The last phrase is, of course, the joker, for there must be almost as many definitions of thinking as there are thinkers; in the ultimate analysis, they all boil down to "Thinking is what *I* do."

One neat way of avoiding this problem is a famous test proposed by the British mathematician Alan Turing, even before the digital computer existed. Turing visualized a "conversation" over a teleprinter circuit with an unseen entity "X." If, after some hours of talk, one could not decide whether there was man or a machine at the other end of the line, it would have to be admitted that X was thinking.

There have been several attempts to apply this test in restricted areas—say, in conversations about the weather. One clever program (DOCTOR) has even allowed a computer to conduct a psychiatric interview, with such success that 60% of the patients refused to believe afterward that they were not "conversing" with a flesh-and-blood psychiatrist.

For the Turing test to be applied properly, the conversation should not be restricted to a single narrow field but should be allowed to range over the whole arena of human affairs. ("Read any good books lately?" "Has your wife found out yet?," etc.) We certainly are nowhere near building a machine that can fool many of the people for much of the time; sooner or later, today's models give themselves away by irrelevant answers that show only too clearly that their replies are, indeed, "mechanical," and that they have no real understanding of what is going on.

As Oliver Selfridge of MIT has remarked sourly: "Even among those who believe that computers *can* think, there are few these days, except for a rabid fringe, who hold that they actually *are* thinking."

.   .   .

To quote another MIT scientist—Marvin Minsky, professor of electrical engineering: "As the machine improves . . .we shall begin to see all the phenomena associated with the terms 'consciousness,' 'intuition' and 'intelligence' itself. It is hard to say how close we are to this threshold, but once it is crossed, the world will not be the same. . . . It is unreasonable to think that machines could become *nearly* as intelligent as we are and then stop, or to suppose that we will always be able to compete with them in wit and wisdom. Whether or not we could retain some sort of control of the machines, assuming that we would want to, the nature of our activities and aspirations would be changed utterly by the presence on earth of intellectually superior beings."

Very few, if any, studies of the social impact of computers have yet faced up to the problems posed by this last sentence—particularly the ominous phrase "assuming that we would want to." This is understandable; the electronic revolution has been so swift that those involved in it have barely had time to think about the present, let alone the day after tomorrow. Moreover, the fact that today's computers are very obviously not "intellectually superior" has given a false sense of security—like that felt by the 1900 buggy-whip manufacturer every time he saw a broken-down automobile by the wayside. This comfortable illusion is fostered by the endless stories—part of the transient folklore of our age—about stupid computers that have had to be replaced by good old-fashioned human beings, after they had insisted on sending out bills for $1,000,000,000.95, or threatening legal action if outstanding debts of $0.00 were not settled immediately. The fact that the *gaffes* are almost invariably due to oversights by human programmers is seldom mentioned.

Though we have to live and work with (and against) today's mechanical morons, their deficiencies should not blind us to the future. In particular, it should be realized that as soon as the borders of electronic intelligence are passed, there will be a kind of chain reaction, because the machines will rapidly improve themselves. In a very few generations—*computer* generations, which by this time may last only a few months—there will be a mental explosion; the merely intelligent machine will swiftly give way to the *ultra*intelligent machine.

One scientist who has given much thought to this matter is Dr. Irving John Good of Trinity College, Oxford—author of papers with such challenging titles as "Can an Android Feel Pain?" (This term for artificial man, incidentally, is older than generally believed. I had always assumed that it was a product of the modern science-fiction magazines, and was astonished to come across "The Brazen Android" in an *Atlantic Monthly* for 1891.) Good has written: "If we build an ultraintelligent machine, we will be playing with fire. We have played with fire before, and it helped keep the other animals at bay." Well, yes—but when the ultraintelligent machine arrives, *we* may be the "other animals"; and look what's happened to them. It is Dr. Good's belief that the very survival of our civilization may depend upon the building of such instrumentalities; because if they are, indeed, more intelligent than we are, they can answer all our questions and solve all our problems. As he puts it in one elegiac phrase: "The first ultraintelligent machine is the last invention that man need make." *Need* is the operative word here. Perhaps 99% of all the men who have ever lived have known only need; they have been driven by necessity and have not been allowed the luxury of choice. In the future, this no longer will be true. It may be the greatest virtue of the ultraintelligent machine that it will force us to think about the purpose and meaning of human existence. It will compel us to make some far-reaching and perhaps painful decisions, just as thermonuclear weapons have made us face the realities of war and aggression, after 5,000 years of pious jabber.

These long-range philosophical implications of machine intelligence obviously far transcend today's more immediate worries about automation and unemployment. Somewhat ironically, these fears are both well grounded and premature.

Although automation already has been blamed for the loss of many jobs, the evidence indicates that so far, it has created many more opportunities for work than it has destroyed. (True, this is small consolation for the particular semiskilled worker who has just been replaced by a couple of milligrams of microelectornics.)

. . .

For the plain fact is that long before that date, the talents and capabilities of the average—and even the superior—man will be as unsalable in the market place as his muscle power. Only a few specialized and distinctly non-white-collar jobs will remain the prerogative of non-mechanical labor; one cannot easily picture a robot handy man, gardener, construction worker, fisherman. . . .These are professions that require mobility, dexterity, alertness and general adaptability—for no two tasks are precisely the same—but not a high degree of intelligence or data-processing power.

And even these relatively few occupations probably will be invaded by a rival and frequently superior labor force from the animal kingdom; for one of the long-range technological benefits of the space program (though no one has said much about it yet, for fear of upsetting the trade unions) will be a supply of educable anthropoids filling the gap between man and the great apes.

It must be clearly understood, therefore, that the main problem of the future—and a future that may be witnessed by many who are alive today—will be the construction of social systems based on the principle not of full employment but rather full *un*employment.

At the very least, we may expect a society that no longer regards work as meritorious or leisure as one of the Devil's more ingenious devices. Even today, there is not much left of the old puritan ethic; automation will drive the last nails into its coffin.

. . .

THE OPTIMUM HUMAN POPULATION

Utopiamongering has been a popular and, on the whole, harmless occupation since the time of Plato; now it has become a matter of life and death—part of the politics of survival. Thinking machines, food production and population control must be considered as the three interlocking elements that will determine the shape of the future; they are not independent, for they all react on one another. This becomes obvious when we ask the question, which I have deliberately framed in as nonemotional a form as possible: "In an automated world run by machines, what is the optimum human population?"

Fred Hoyle once remarked to me that it was pointless for the world to hold more people than one could get to know in a single lifetime. Even if one were President of United Earth, that would set the figure somewhere between 10,000 and 100,000; with a very generous allowance for duplication, wastage, special talents, and so forth, there really seems no requirement for what has been called the Global Village of the future to hold more than 1,000,000 people, scattered over the face of the planet.

If the machines decide that more than 1,000,000 human beings constitutes an epidemic, they might order euthanasia for anyone with an I.Q. of less than 150, but I hope that such drastic measures will not be necessary.

. . .

In some of these fields, the background presence of superior nonhuman mentalities would have a stultifying effect; but in others, the machines could act as pacemakers. Does anyone really imagine that when all the grand masters are electronic, no one will play chess? The humans will simply set up new categories and play better chess among themselves. All sports and games (unless they become ossified) have to undergo technological revolutions from time to time; recent examples are the introduction of fiberglass in pole vaulting, archery, and boating. Personally, I can hardly wait for the advent of Marvin Minsky's promised robot table-tennis player.

These matters are not trivial; games are a necessary substitute for our hunting impulses, and if the ultraintelligent machines give us new and better outlets, that is all to the good. We shall need every one of them to occupy us in the centuries ahead.

Thinking machines will certainly make possible new forms of art and far more elaborate developments of the old ones, by introducing the dimensions of time and probability. Even today, a painting or piece of sculpture that stands still is regarded as slightly passé.

Even if art turns out to be a dead end, there still remains science—the eternal quest for knowledge, which has brought man to the point where he may create his own successor. It is unfortunate that, to most people, "science" now means incomprehensible mathematical complexities; that it could be the most exciting and *entertaining* of all occupations is something that they find impossible to believe. Yet the fact remains that, before they are ruined by what is laughingly called education, all normal children have an absorbing interest and curiosity about the universe that, if properly developed, could keep them happy for as many centuries as they may wish to live.

. . .

The discussion of whether computers are able to exhibit a quality not unlike human intelligence will undoubtedly continue for the next decade. Professor Marvin Minsky in a recent lecture charged that many teachers have been reactionary in telling students and the world about computers. He said that they have engaged in only describing the limitations of computers and stating that "the computer is nothing but. . .a lightning-fast calculator that does what you tell it. . .or a bunch of flip-flops," or whatever. Such oversimplificatons, he noted, could be applied as well to people.[7]

Professor Weizenbaum, in his book *Computer Power and Human Reason*, explores two major questions: whether there are tasks for which computers ought not to be used and whether there is a difference between man and machine.[32] He states that to ask " 'What does a judge (or a psychiatrist) know that we cannot tell a computer?' is a monstrous obscenity." As Weizenbaum points out, a major concern is the moral, not the scientific, issue concerning AI.[32] There are, he says, domains where computers should not intrude. These domains are where such intrusion is an attack on humanity, and the side effects of the action may not be anticipated. Weizenbaum also notes that many people have embraced the machine metaphor as a description of ourselves and our institution and may thus yield the very essence of humanity to a machine.

In 1871, Samuel Butler completed the manuscript of the satire *Erewhon*.[8] Butler saw machines as gradually evolving into higher forms and assuming the capacities and functions of animals and man. As the machine was seen to assume some of the characteristics of man, the discussion grew in range and pitch. In one book, *God and Golem, Inc.,* Weiner states, "No, the future offers very little hope for those who expect that our new mechanical slaves will offer us a world in which we may rest from thinking. Help us they may, but at the cost of supreme demands upon our honesty and our intelligence. The world of the future will be an ever more demanding struggle against the limitations of our intelligence, not a comfortable hammock in which we can lie down to be waited upon by our robot slaves.''[8]

Thus, the question of the intelligence of the computer leads to a challenge of a human intelligence and the question of conscience. In an elaborate treatment of the question of conscience, Mortimer Adler states that when it becomes possible to carry on a discussion with a computer behind a screen, not knowing whether it is a computer or a man—and after a long conversation, thinking the computer is a *man*, we shall then realize that man has nothing to distinguish him substantially from the machine.[9] And yet, who is to make the final decisions—the man or the computer? Perhaps one of the challenges lies in the area of decision-making where it may be a temptation to let the computer decide and thus avoid the matter of conscience.

The use of intelligent computers integrated with machines that perform tasks like a human worker has been foreseen by several authors. Karel Čapek, a Czechoslovakian author, was apparently inspired by the legend of a mechanical man or "golem" of medieval Prague. He called artificial workers *robots*, deriving the word from the Czech noun *robota*, meaning "work." The term won international usage in Čapek's famous play *R.U.R.*[10] Th play concerns a revolt of Rossum's Universal Robots, their destruction of humanity, and their own need to develop a conscience. Čapek expresses this conflict between the machine as worker and the machine without conscience, as the following passage illustrates:[10]

> DOMAIN. So young Rossum said to himself: A man is some-
> thing that, for instance, feels happy, plays the fiddle, likes
> going for walks, and, in fact, wants to do a whole lot of things
> that are really unnecessary. . . .But a working machine must
> not want to play the fiddle, must not feel happy, must not do
> a whole lot of other things. A petrol motor must not have
> tassels or ornaments, Miss Glory. And to manufacture arti-
> ficial workers is the same thing as to manufacture motors.The
> process must be of the simplest, and the product of the best
> from a practical point of view. What sort of worker do you
> think is the best from a practical point of view?
>
> HELENA. The best? Perhaps the one who is most honest and
> hardworking.
>
> DOMAIN. No the cheapest. The one whose needs are the small-
> est. Young Rossum invented a worker with the minimum
> amount of requirements. He had to simplify him. He rejected
> everything that did not contribute directly to the progress of
> work. In this way he rejected everything that makes man more

> expensive. In fact, he rejected man and made the Robot. My dear Miss Glory, the Robots are not people. Mechanically they are more perfect than we are, they have an enormously developed intelligence, but they have no soul.

In the field of the development of robots, there has been some advancement during the past decade. At Disneyland, the technology has been used to create extremely life-like computer-controlled humanoids capable of moving their arms and legs, grimacing, smiling, glowering, simulating fear, joy and a wide range of other emotions. Built of clear plastic, the robots closely resemble human forms. To this technology must be added the technologies being developed in the field of artificial intelligence. A group of research centers are working to develop machines that can act intelligently. Most tasks assigned to these experimental machines involve manipulating objects or moving around a laboratory environment autonomously, carrying out assigned tasks which are incompletely specified. Intelligent machines with a "hand" and "eye" are being controlled by digital computer. One version of a hand/eye robot is shown in Figure 14−3a. The hand is capable of grasping, transporting, and assembling blocks of various shapes with the area of vision of the television camera eye. A digital computer provides the intelligence required to select, recognize, pick up, and place the blocks in the proper sequence to build a structure. A hand-touching sensing system using a six-axis wrist sensor is shown in Figure 14−3b. There are now about 3500 robots at work in the United States.[30]

A mobile automation vehicle has been constructed at Stanford Research Institute in California which exhibits some attributes of intelligence. The mobile vehicle is shown in Figure 14−4. The mobile robot requires the same abilities used by an explorer trained to sense, map, navigate, and use information obtained from an environment unknown to him. The laboratory environment consists of a large well-lighted room strewn with a number of solid objects such as cubes and ramps. In this laboratory setting, the mobile robot is required to sense and recognize objects and room boundaries; to make, store and update representations or models of the environment; to plan sensible routes through available passageways; to navigate in carrying out its route plans and to gather information; and, ultimately, to interact physically with the objects by simple manipulative means.[29,49,50]

The development of intelligent robots will lead to their application in at least two fields. First, the application of robots to control functions in the foundry, mining and other industrial activities will relieve men of very tedious, often dangerous and undesirable jobs. Second, there is a need for machines that can act independently—at least for part if not all of the time. Applications exist such as the exploration of the Moon, planets, space, the deep seas and Arctic wastes which are inhospitable to man and which require very expensive life-support systems for protracted stays by human explorers. Robots are suitable for use in

FIGURE 14–3a   An intelligent hand/eye robot built at Stanford University. A television
                eye, in the upper right of the photo, feeds data to a digital computer
                which instructs the hand to grasp and assemble building blocks into
                structures. *Courtesy of the Artificial Intelligence Project, Stanford
                University.*

hostile, dangerous or remote environments. They are reliable, nonfatiguing and
usually speedy.

Several important US firms are working on producing commercial systems
based on artifical intelligence.[34] Texas Instruments has developed ENTICE
(Easy to Use Novice Oriented TI Computing Environment) to be used with its
computers in the 1980s. Douglas Hofstadter of Indiana University argues that a
computer may one day create and feel. The interwoven qualities of software and
hardware may result in will, intuition and consciousness.[42]

The movie *2001: A Space Odyssey* was based on a book by Arthur C. Clarke
concerned with space travel, toward the planet Jupiter. The star of *2001: A Space
Odyssey* is a computer, HAL, which operates the space ship, monitors the trip,
and communicates with the astronauts in spoken words. HAL appears as a computer panel with a large T.V. eye. Several paragraphs from this book follow.[12]*

> The sixth member of the crew cared for none of these things, for
> it was not human. It was the highly advanced HAL 9000 com-
> puter, the brain and nervous system of the ship.

*Reprinted by permission of The World Publishing Company from *2001: A Space Odyssey* by A. C.
Clarke. A NAL Book. Copyright © 1968 by Polaris Productions, Inc. and Arthur C. Clarke.

FIGURE 14–3b   A hand-touch sensing system with a six-axis wrist sensor, external touch
sensors and a pair of matrix jaw sensors. *Courtesy SRI.*

Hal (for *H*euristically programmed *AL*gorithmic computer, no
less) was a masterwork of the third computer breakthrough.
These seemed to occur at intervals of twenty years, and the
thought that another one was now imminent already worried a
great many people.

Hal had been trained for this mission as thoroughly as his
human colleagues—and at many times their rate of imput, for in
addition to his intrinsic speed, he never slept. His prime task was
to monitor the life-support systems, continually checking oxygen pressure, temperature, hull leakage, radiation, and all the

FIGURE 14-4   The automation vehicle used by SRI in the application of artificial intelligence principles to the development of integrated robot systems. The vehicle is propelled by electric motors and carries a television camera and optical range finder in a movable "head." The vehicle responds to command from a computer. The sensors are the bump detector, the T.V. camera and the range finder. *Courtesy of SRI.*

other interlocking factors upon which the lives of the fragile human cargo depended. He could carry out the intricate navigational corrections, and execute the necessary flight maneuvers when it was time to change course.

Whether Hal could actually think was a question which had been settled by the British mathematician Alan Turing back in the 1940s. Turing had pointed out that, if one could carry out a prolonged conversation with a machine—whether by typewriter or microphone was immaterial—without being able to distinguish between its replies and those that a man might give, then the machine *was* thinking, by any sensible definition of the word. Hal could pass the Turing test with ease.

The computer HAL begins to malfunction and the astronauts attempt to ascertain the difficulty as shown in Figure 14–5. The climax of the controversial part

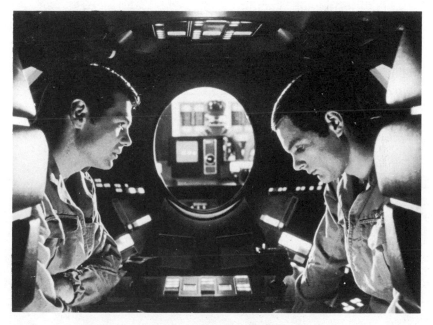

FIGURE 14–5 Astronaut Poole, left and Mission Commander Bowman seek the privacy of a one-man space pod in an effort to confer without being overheard by computer HAL 90000. The computer is able to read their lip movements by means of the T.V. camera input. From *2001: A Space Odyssey* © 1968 by Metro-Goldwyn-Mayer Inc.

of *2001* occurs when HAL, the computer which was programmed to simulate human emotions, kills one astronaut and shuts off the life support systems of the hibernating crew members. The one remaining crew member performs a lobotomy on the brain of the computer, rendering it helpless. The following paragraphs illustrate this portion of the film:

> Here goes, thought Bowman. I never imagined I'd be an amateur brain surgeon—carrying out a lobotomy beyond the orbit of Jupiter.
>
> He released the locking bar on the section labeled COGNITIVE FEEDBACK and pulled out the first memory block. The marvelously complex three-dimensional network, which could lie comfortably in a man's hand yet contained millions of elements, floated away across the vault.
>
> "Hey, Dave," said Hal. "What are you doing?"
>
> I wonder if he can feel pain? Bowman thought briefly. Probably not, he told himself; there are no sense organs in the human cortex, after all. The human brain can be operated on without anesthetics.
>
> He began to pull out, one by one, the little units on the panel marked EGO-REINFORCEMENT. Each block continued to sail onward as soon as it had left his hand, until it hit the wall and rebounded. Soon there were several of the units drifting slowly back and forth in the vault.
>
> "Look here, Dave," said Hal. "I've got years of service experience built into me. An irreplaceable amount of effort has gone into making me what I am."
>
> A dozen units had been pulled out, yet thanks to the multiple redundancy of its design—another feature, Bowman knew, that had been copied from the human brain—the computer was still holding its own.
>
> He started on the AUTO-INTELLECTION panel.
>
> "Dave," said Hal, "I don't understand why you're doing this to me. . . . .I have the greatest enthusiasm for the mission. . . . .You are destroying my mind. . . . .Don't you understand?. . . .I will become childish. . . . .I will become nothing. . . . ."

This is harder than I expected, thought Bowman. I am destroying the only conscious creature in my universe. But it has to be done, if I am ever to regain control of the ship.

"I am a HAL Nine Thousand computer Production Number 3. I became operational at the Hal Plant in Urbana, Illinois, on January 12, 1997. The quick brown fox jumps over the lazy dog. The rain in Spain is mainly in the plain. Dave—are you still there? Did you know that the square root of 10 is 3 point 1622776660168379? Log 10 to the base e is zero point 434294481903252. . .correction, that is log e to the base 10. . . .The reciprocal of three is zero point 333333333333333333333. . .two times two is. . .two times two is. . .approximately 4 point 101010101010101010. . . .I seem to be having some difficulty—my first instructor was Dr. Chandra. He taught me to sing a song, it goes like this, 'Daisy, Daisy, give me your answer, do. I'm half crazy all for the love of you.' "

Thus, the man is able to disconnect the intelligence of HAL, the computer, suggesting that man will always be able to control his robots, if, perhaps, at a great cost.

There are perhaps three options open to AI research. The first is that work on AI should cease. The second is that work on AI should proceed indefinitely, but only on certain lines of inquiry and development. The third option is that work on AI should proceed to the equivalent level of average human intelligence and not beyond.

In order to limit the potential effect of robots, a society might adopt the three Laws of Robotics formulated by the author Isaac Asimov:

1. A robot must not harm, or through inactivity, allow to come to harm, a human being.

2. A robot must obey all commands given to it by a human being except when these conflict with the first law.

3. A robot must preserve itself at all times unless by doing so it contradicts the first two laws.

Richard Brautigan, the San Francisco poet, summarizes a view of the cybernetic machine and its anthropomorphic qualities in his poem which concludes this section.

All Watched Over by Machines of Loving Grace*

Richard Brautigan

I like to think (and
the sooner the better!)
of a cybernetic meadow
where mammals and computers
live together in mutually
programming harmony
like pure water
touching clear sky.

I like to think
    (right now, please!)
of a cybernetic forest
filled with pines and electronics
where deer stroll peacefully
past computers
as if they were flowers
with spinning blossoms.

I like to think
    (it has to be !)
of a cybernetic ecology
where we are free of our labors
and joined back to nature,
returned to our mammal
brothers and sisters,
and all watched over
by machines of loving grace.

The development of robots, machines which exhibit intelligence and which perform formerly reserved for man, has been the subject of many novels.[40] In *Player Piano* by Kurt Vonnegut, Jr. the robots have replaced the working man in Illium, New York, and the computers and engineers are in control. The hero of the novel revolts against the automation and robot age.[13] The conflict against the robots, a theme running from *Erewhon* and *R.U.R* through *Player Piano* and *2001*, assumes that the computer controlled robots exhibit human qualities such as intelligence and emotion. This attribution of human form or qualities to things such as machines or computers is called *anthropomorphism*. Among other novels that reflect on future traits of computers are *Colossus* and *Program for a*

Puppet.[26,33] One artist's image of the anthropomorphic computer appears in Figure 14–6.

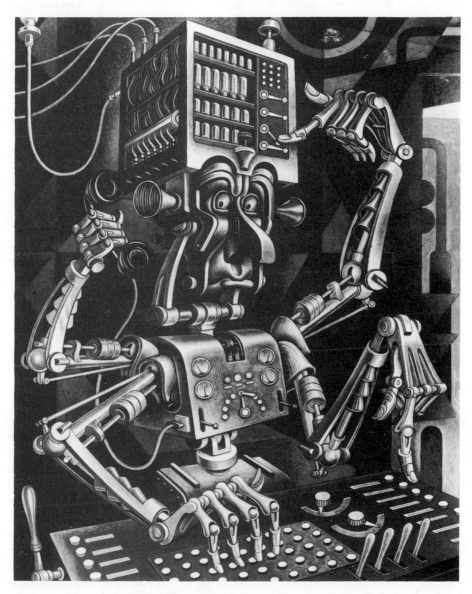

FIGURE 14–6 *Executive of the Future* by Boris Artzybasheff. *Reproduced by permission of the estate of Boris Artzybasheff.*

14.2   THE SOCIAL CONSEQUENCES OF COMPUTERS

The implications of the application of computers to a myriad of industrial, governmental, and educational problems is an issue of great significance. The consequences of the uses of computers to our social structure and to each person's value to himself and his society are currently being explored by many computer scientists and social scientists. Technological change almost always has accompanying social consequences. The automobile has led to changes in family relationships, work location and our cities. In a similar fashion, computers may have led to more effective and efficient government, but also to a loss of privacy. The unforeseen effects on society and the individual are often positive as well as negative. It is the purpose of this section to expose some of the projected consequences of the use of computers and to advocate the application of computers to problems where the social consequences, as well as the short-term solution or profit, are accounted for.

If one were asked to try to capture the essential spirit of the last half of the 20th Century in a single picture, he might well consider as his background a vast chessboard that stretches to the far corners of the world. On one side of the board, he might place a forlorn, hopelessly romantic Don Quixote, the Knight of an age long gone, mounted on a mechanical Rocinante, as shown in **Figure 14–7**. Facing this symbolic relic of the past—whose dispirited lance already droops in foregone defeat—at the other side of the board, there is an enigmatic little black box, the computer. In its calm inscrutability it seems to have crept out of the world of the future. And perhaps it has. One feels instinctively that the confrontation between these two is reflected on the thousand squares and diagonals of which our world is made; and that whatever move the knight makes now, the little black box will make the last one.[14,19]

Computers have already had an impact on man's society and his personality. A striking effect is the extent to which computers have excited the popular imagination. There is widespread belief and appreciation that the computer is beneficial now and will continue to be so in the future. The computer, however, is often seen as an autonomous entity without control by humans. Also, people tend to generalize from the computer's well-known computational accuracy to the idea that the computer is infallible in solving the larger problems for which it may be used. The emergence of the computer has become, for many, a challenge to man's self-concept.[14,42] Some authors see man as threatened by the computer and his applications of the computer and thus out of harmony with himself because he is discontinuous with the machines that he has built. It is fashionable to describe such a state as "alienation." This discontinuity may be a result of a desire of some people to have a problem solved in an incomprehensible fashion by a computer rather than to have to adjust their own value systems and understanding in order for themselves to do something concrete and rational about the problem. In a related matter, H. R. J. Grosch stated, "If the average American has to choose between privacy and a convenient way to charge a purchase, he'll pick convenience."[16]

The computer provides a challenge to activities formerly reserved for humans. For example, as computers are able to reproduce a human activity, such as proving geometry theorems, then people tend to state that the act does not

FIGURE 14-7 Man and his life with a little black box—the computer. This illustration combines allusions to *Don Quixote*, to chess, and to the mechanical part of life—among others. The thoughtful reader may wish to examine the several relationships suggested, beginning with the shadows. *Courtesy of Kaiser Aluminum News.*

define human intelligence. As computers become adept at playng chess, perhaps man will decide that playing chess is not what being human is about. However, the fear is that just as John Henry lost his identity when his physical strength was matched by that of the steam drill, perhaps people whose forte is the kind of tedious rote work done better by computers will lose theirs.[40]

The technological activity in the field of computer development and computer applications is quite rapid and causes social changes. For over twenty years, growth and change in the computer field have been caused by technological advances that made equipment better and cheaper each year. As equipment becomes more diverse, efficient and cheap, more and more applications will become practical. The spread of applications of computers leads to an increased anxiety over the social problems associated with the use of computers. Some comparisons of technological increases in different fields of endeavor are given in Table 14–1. Note that the speed of computation has increased by a factor of 250,000 over the past thirty years. The corresponding increase in speed of travel is only six! This rapid change in computational speed and the resulting social change and adjustment that accompanies it have caused some concern among authors and social scientists. Many have asked if there is a possibility of the formation of a data elite, manipulating society by their manipulation of data on American individuals. The blurring of the private and the public data creates anxiety concerning data banks on individuals and their uses. The origins of depersonalization lie in the high degree of standardization needed to use computers effi-

TABLE 14-1
Comparison of Technological Increase

| Area | Ancient Times | 1880 | 1950 | 1980 | Factor of Increase in | | |
					2000 years	100 years	30 years
Transportation	40 miles/day	200	600	3,500	90	17.5	6
Average Formal Education (U.S.)		1 yr.	10	12	—	12	1.2
Life Expectancy (U.S.)	22 yrs.	45	66	67	3.05	1.48	1.07
Energy per Person	1/2 unit	1.6	10	15	30	9	1.5
Computation Speed	.005	.005	40	10,000,000	2×10^9	2×10^9	250,000

Energy Unit = 1 horsepower for 8-hour day.

Computation Speed Unit = multiplications per second for 8-digit numbers.

ciently. As computer activities spread, individuals tend to feel molded to fit the requirements of the computer system. During several campus riots in the 1970s, major attacks were directed toward computer centers.

A common case of depersonalized treatment by a computer involves dealing with a store that uses a computer for its billing operation. The problems usually arise from the fact that a system's design is made more complicated by provisions for dealing with exceptional circumstances, so they are ignored. This difficulty is compounded if an organization seeks to get by with minimum training of the clerical staff that examines the customer "inputs" of payments and complaints. The usual result is that the customer writes letter after letter into a non-answering void, his resentment growing at each cycle. Meanwhile, the computer is sending him even-nastier demands and recriminations.[18]

Also in the fields of business, we may be confronted with difficulties as our banking system, our mutual funds, our exchanges and other institutions make increasing use of computer records. We have had cases already in which records were destroyed by mistake or were lost. The size of the largest organization in a given field tends to approach the maximum that is manageable. The use of the computer increases the manageable size of a company but also increases the vulnerability of that company if something happens to the computer and the records stored in it. Furthermore, business management may become vulnerable in the corporate decision-making. As a firm relies on data banks and management science, there is a chance that filtering of information by staff personnel will occur before materials are presented to senior management. As the decision-making apparatus becomes more complex, it will be harder for managers to exercise effective personal control.

Some anticipated consequences of technological and scientific developments associated with the field of computers are given in Table 14–2.[19] Several consequences are outlined for each potential development, and the judgment of which are positive and which are negative consequences is left to the reader.

Norbert Wiener wrote his book *Cybernetics* in 1946 and published an article with the same title in *Scientific American* in 1948.[1] Both the article and the book aroused discussion among computer scientists which led to a further article by Wiener on the moral and technical consequences of computer automation.[20] This article was responded to by another computer scientist, Arthur Samuel, then of IBM Corporation, and now at Stanford University. The response was a strong refutation of Wiener's concerns and thesis.[21]

SOME MORAL AND TECHNICAL CONSEQUENCES OF AUTOMATION*

As machines learn they may develop unforeseen
strategies at rates that baffle their programmers.

Norbert Wiener

Some 13 years ago, a book of mine was published by the name of *Cybernetics*. In it I discussed the problems of control and communica-

*N. Wiener, "Some Moral and Technical Consequences of Automation," *Science*, Vol. 131, May 6, 1960, pp. 1355–1358, Copyright 1960 by the American Association for the Advancement of Science.

TABLE 14-2

Some Anticipated Consequences of Technological and Scientific Developments*

Development	Potential Consequence
Laboratory operation of automated language translators capable of coping with idiomatic syntactical complexities.	Increased technical and scientific communications including, perhaps, reorientation of scientific journals.
	Further ethnic separation between countries speaking different languages since there would be fewer linguists and less intimate understanding of vocabulary nuances.
	Decrease in the number of extant languages.
Establishment of a central data storage facility (or several regional or disciplinary facilities) with wide public access (perhaps in the home) for general or specialized information retrieval primarily in the areas of library, medical and legal data.	Individual citizens becoming proficient in law and medicine, through easy availability of the relevant data in the home.
	The rise of new methods of computer-aided crime.
	Information overload; the problem will be to select from the available plethora of information that which is important and relevant to the individual.
Availabilty of complex robots which are programmable and self-adaptive and capable of performing most household chores, such as machines which independently prepare meals and clean or otherwise dispose of dishes.	Reorientation of certain industries (*e.g.*, the electronic industry moving into the home appliance industry *diversifying* into electronics service-mechanisms, etc.
	Development of a counter-trend which places high value in "personally" done housework and menial tasks (*e.g.*, home-cooked vs. robot prepared meals).
Availability of a computer which comprehends standard IQ tests and scores above 150 (where "comprehend" is to be interpreted behavioristically as the ability to respond to questions printed in English and possibly accompanied by (diagrams).	Self replicating computers and more advanced computers designed by other computers.
	The raising of philosophical and speculative questions regarding human significance.
	Development of meaningful, or at least amusing, hardly ever boring, pastimes
Demonstration of man-machine symbiosis enabling man to extend his intelligence by direct electromechanical interaction between his brain and a computing machine.	Elimination of factual eduction, since this data could be stored.
	The creation of robots which would be used to decrease human risk, as in war.

*From *A Forecast of Technological Trends, Their Societal Consequences and Science Policy Strategies of the Future,* Theodore Gordon, *Proceedings of the Hearings of the Committee on Science and Astronautics,* U.S. House of Representatives, Washington, D.C., 1970, pp. 429–470.

tion in the living organism and the machine. I made a considerable number of predictions about the development of controlled machines and about the corresponding techniques of automatization, which I foresaw as having important consequences affecting the society of the future. Now, 13 years later, it seems appropriate to take stock of the present position with respect to both cybernetic technique and the social consequences of this technique.

Before commencing on the detail of these matters, I should like to mention a certain attitude of the man in the street toward cybernetics and automatization. This attitude needs a critical discussion, and in my opinion it should be rejected in its entirety. This is the assumption that machines cannot possess any degree of originality. This frequently takes the form of a statement that nothing can come out of the machine which has not been put into it. This is often interpreted as asserting that a machine which man has made must remain continually subject to man, so that its operation is at any time open to human interference and to a change in policy. On the basis of such an attitude, many people have pooh-poohed the dangers of machine techniques, and they have flatly contradicted the early predictions of Samuel Butler that the machine might take over the control of mankind.

It is true that in the time of Samuel Butler the available machines were far less hazardous than machines are today, for they involved only power, not a certain degree of thinking and communication. However, the machine techniques of the present day have invaded the latter fields as well, so that the actual machine of today is very different from the image that Butler held, and we cannot transfer to these new devices the assumptions which seemed axiomatic a generation ago. I find myself facing a public which has formed its attitude toward the machine on the basis of an imperfect understanding of the structure and mode of operation of modern machines.

It is my thesis that machines can and do transcend some of the limitations of their designers, and that in doing so they may be both effective and dangerous. It may well be that in principle we cannot make any machine the elements of whose behavior we cannot comprehend sooner or later. This does not mean in any way that we shall be able to comprehend these elements in substantially less time than the time required for operation of the machine, or even within any given number of years or generations.

As is now generally admitted, over a limited range of operation, machines act far more rapidly than human beings and are far more precise in performing the details of their operations. This being the case, even when machines do not in any way transcend man in the performance may be delayed until long after the task which they have been set has been completed.

This means that though machines are theoretically subject to human criticism, such criticism may be ineffective until long after it is relevant. To be effective in warding off disastrous consequences, our understanding of our man-made machines should in general develop *pari passu* with the performance of the machine. By the very slowness of our human actions, our effective control of our machines may be nullified. By the time we are able to react to information conveyed by our senses and stop the car we are driving, it may already have run head on into a wall.

GAME-PLAYING

I shall come back to this point later in this article. For the present, let me discuss the technique of machines for a very specific purpose: that of playing games. In this matter I shall deal more particularly with the game of checkers, for which the International Business Machines Corporation has developed very effective game-playing machines.

Let me say once for all that we are not concerned here with the machines which operate on a perfect closed theory of the game they play. The game theory of von Neumann and Morgenstern may be suggestive as to the operation of actual game-playing machines, but it does not actually describe them.

In a game as complicated as checkers, if each player tries to choose his play in view of the best move his opponent can make, against the best response he will have taken upon himself an impossible task. Not only is this humanly impossible but there is actually no reason to suppose that it is the best policy against the opponent by whom he is faced, whose limitations are equal to his own.

The von Neumann theory of games bears no very close relation to the theory by which game-playing machines operate. The latter corresponds much more closely to the methods of play used by expert but limited human chess players against other chess players. Such players depend on certain strategic evaluations, which are in essence not complete. While the von Neumann type of play is valid for games like ticktacktoe, with a complete theory, the very interest of chess and checkers lies in the fact that they do not possess a complete theory. Neither do war, nor business competition, nor any of the other forms of competitive activity in which we are really interested.

In a game like ticktacktoe, with a small number of moves, where each player is in a position to contemplate all possibilities and to establish a defense against the best possible moves of the other player, a complete theory of the von Neumann type is valid. In such a case, the game must inevitably end in a win for the first player, a win for the second player, or a draw.

I question strongly whether this concept of the perfect game is a completely realistic one in the cases of actual, nontrivial games. Great generals like Napoleon and great admirals like Nelson have proceeded in a different manner. They have been aware not only of the limitations of their opponents in such matters as materiel and personnel but equally of their limitations in experience and in military know-how. It was by a realistic appraisal of the relative inexperience in naval operations of the continental powers as compared with the highly developed tactical and strategic competence of the British fleet that Nelson was able to display the boldness which pushed the continental forces off the seas. This he could not have done had he engaged in the long, relatively indecisive, and possibly losing conflict to which his assumption of the best possible strategy on the part of his enemy would have doomed him.

In assessing not merely the materiel and personnel of his enemies but also the degree of judgment and the amount of skill in tactics and strategy to be expected of them, Nelson acted on the basis of their record in previous combats. Similarly, an important factor in Napoleon's conduct of his combat with Austrians in Italy was his knowledge of the rigidity and mental limitations of Würmser.

This element of experinece should reccive adequate recognition in any realistic theory of games. It is quite legitimate for a chess player to play, not against an ideal, nonexisting, perfect antagonist, but rather against one whose habits he has been able to determine from the record. Thus, in the theory of games, at least two different intellectual efforts must be made. One is the short-term effort of playing with a determined policy for the individual game. The other is the examination of a record of many games. This record has been set by the player himself, by his opponent, or even by players with whom he has not personally played. In terms of this record, he determines the relative advantages of different policies as proved over the past.

There is even a third stage of judgment required in a chess game. This is expressed at least in part by the length of the significant past. The development of theory in chess decreases the importance of games played at a different stage of the art. On the other hand, an astute chess theoretician may estimate in advance that a certain policy currently in fashion has become of little value, and that it may be best to return to earlier modes of play to anticipate the change in policy of the people whom he is likely to find as his opponents.

Thus, in determining policy in chess there are several different levels of consideration which correspond in a certain way to the different logical types of Bertrand Russell. There is the level of tactics, the level of strategy, the level of the general considerations which should have been weighed in determining this strategy, the level in which the length of the relevant past—the past within which these considerations may be valid—is taken into account, and so on. Each new level demands a study of a much larger past than the previous one.

I have compared these levels with the logical types of Russell concerning classes, classes of classes, classes of classes of classes, and so on. It may be noted that Russell does not consider statements involving all types as significant. He brings out the futility of such questions as that concerning the barber who shaves all persons, and only those persons, who do not shave themselves. Does he shave himself? On one type he does, on the next type he does not, and so on, indefinitely. All such questions involving an infinity of types may lead to unsolvable paradoxes. Similarly, the search for the best policy under all levels of sophistication is a futile one and must lead to nothing but confusion.

These considerations arise in the determination of policy by machines as well as in the determination of policy by persons. These are the questions which arise in the programming of programming. The lowest type of game-playing machine plays in terms of a certain rigid evaluation of plays. Quantities such as the value of pieces gained or lost, the command of the pieces, their mobility, and so on, can be given numerical weights on a certain empirical basis, and a weighting may be given on this basis to each next play conforming to the rules of the game. The play with the greatest weight may be chosen. Under these circumstances, the play of the machine will seem to its antagonist—who cannot help but evaluate the chess personality of the machine—a rigid one.

LEARNING MACHINES

The next step is for the machine to take into consideration not merely the moves as they occurred in the individual game but the record of games previously played. On this basis, the machine may stop from time to time, not to play but to consider what (linear or nonlinear) weighting of the factors which it has been given to consider would correspond best to won games as opposed to lost (or drawn) games. On this basis, it continues to play with a new weighting. Such a machine would seem to its human opponent to have a far less rigid game personality, and tricks which would defeat it at an earlier stage may now fail to deceive it.

The present level of these learning machines is that they play a fair amateur game at chess but that in checkers they can show a marked superiority to the player who has programmed them after from 10 to 20 playing hours of working and indoctrination. They thus most definitely escape from the completely effective control of the man who has made them. Rigid as the repertory of factors may be which they are in a position to take into consideration, they do unquestionably—and so say those who have played with them—show originality, not merely in their tactics, which may be quite unforeseen, but even in the detailed weighting of their strategy.

As I have said, checker-playing machines which learn have developed to the point at which they can defeat the programmer. However, they appear still to have one weakness. This lies in the end game. Here the machines are somewhat clumsy in determining the best way to give the *coup de grâce*. This is due to the fact that the existing machines have for the most part adopted a program in which the identical strategy is carried out at each stage of the game. In view of the similarity of values of pieces in checkers, this is quite natural for a large part of the play but ceases to be perfectly relevant when the board is relatively empty and the main problem is that of moving into position rather than that of direct attack. Within the frame of the method I have described it is quite possible to have a second exploration to determine what the policy should be after the number of pieces of the opponent is so reduced that these new considerations become paramount.

Chess-playing machines have not, so far, been brought to the degree of perfection of checker-playing machines, although, as I have said, they can most certainly play a respectable amateur game. Probably the reason for this is similar to the reason for their relative efficiency in the end game of checkers. In chess, not only is the end game quite different in its proper strategy from the mid-game but the opening game is also. The difference between checkers and chess in this respect is that the initial play of the pieces in checkers is not very different in character from the play which arises in the mid-game, while in chess, pieces at the beginning have an arrangement of exceptionally low mobility, so that the problem of deploying them from this position is particularly difficult. This is the reason why opening play and development form a special branch of chess theory.

There are various ways in which the machine can take cognizance of these well-known facts and explore a separate waiting strategy for the opening. This does not mean that the type of game theory which I have here discussed is not applicable to chess but merely that it requires much more consideration before we can make a machine that can play master chess. Some of my friends who are engaged in these problems believe that this goal will be achieved in from 10 to 25 years. Not being a chess expert, I do not venture to make any such predictions on my own initiative.

It is quite in the cards that learning machines will be used to program the pushing of the button in a new pushbutton war. Here we are considering a field in which automata of a non-learning character are probably already in use. It is quite out of the question to program these machines on the basis of an actual experience in real war. For one thing, a sufficient experience to give an adequate programming would probably see humanity already wiped out.

Moreover, the techniques of pushbutton war are bound to change so much that by the time an adequate experience could have been accumulated, the basis of the beginning would have radically changed. Therefore, the programming of such a learning machine would have to be based on some sort of war game, just as commanders and staff officials now learn an important part of the art of strategy in a similar manner. Here, however, if the rules for victory in a war game do not correspond to what we actually wish for our country, it is more than likely that such a machine may produce a policy which would win a nominal victory on points at the cost of every interest we have at heart, even that of national survival.

MAN AND SLAVE

The problem, and it is a moral problem, with which we are here faced is very close to one of the great problems of slavery. Let us grant that slavery is bad because it is cruel. It is, however, self-contradictory, and for a reason which is quite different. We wish a slave to be intelligent, to be able to assist us in the carrying out of our tasks. However, we also wish him to be subservient. Complete subservience and complete intelligence do not go together. How often in ancient times the clever Greek philosopher slave of a less intelligent Roman slaveholder must have dominated the actions of his master rather than obeyed his wishes! Similarly, if the machines become more and more efficient and operate at a higher and higher psychological level, the catastrophe foreseen by Butler of the dominance of the machine comes nearer and nearer.

The human brain is a far more efficient control apparatus than is the intelligent machine when we come to the higher areas of logic. It is a self-organizing system which depends on its capacity to modify itself into a new machine rather than on ironclad accuracy and speed in problem-solving. We have already made very successful machines of the lowest logical type, with a rigid policy. We are beginning to make machines of the second logical type, where the policy itself improves with learning. In the construction of operative machines, there is no specific foreseeable limit with respect to logical type, nor is it safe to make a pronouncement about the exact level at which the brain is superior to the machine. Yet for a long time at least there will always be some level at which the brain is better than the constructed machine, even though this level may shift upwards and upwards.

It may be seen that the result of a programming technique of automatization is to remove from the mind of the designer and operator an effective understanding of many of the stages by which the machine comes to its conclusions and of what the real tactical intentions of many of its operations may be. This is highly relevant to the problem of our being able to foresee undesired consequences outside the frame of the strategy of the game while the machine is still in action and while intervention on our part may prevent the occurrence of these consequences.

Here it is necessary to realize that human action is a feedback action. To avoid a disastrous consequence, it is not enough that some action on our part should be sufficient to change the course of the machine, because it is quite possible that we lack information on which to base consideration of such an action.

In neurophysiological language, ataxia can be quite as much of a deprivation as paralysis. A patient with locomotor ataxia may not suffer from any defect of his muscles or motor nerves, but if his muscles and tendons and organs do not tell him exactly what position he is in, and whether the tensions to which his organs are subjected will or will not lead to his falling, he will be unable to stand up. Similarly, when a machine constructed by us is capable of operating on its incoming data at a pace which we cannot keep, we may not know, until too late, when to turn it off. We all know the fable of the sorcerer's apprentice, in which the boy makes the broom carry water in his master's absence, so that it is on the point of drowning him when his master reappears. If the boy had had to seek a charm to stop the mischief in the *grimoires* of his master's library, he might have been drowned before he had discovered the relevant incantation. Similarly, if a bottle factory is programmed on the basis of maximum productivity, the owner may be made bankrupt by the enormous inventory of unsalable bottles manufactured before he learns he should have stopped production six months earlier.

The "Sorcerer's Apprentice" is only one of the many tales based on the assumption that the agencies of magic are literal-minded. There is the story of the genie and the fisherman in the *Arabian Nights*, in which the fisherman breaks the seal of Solomon which has imprisoned the genie and finds the genie vowed to his own destruction; there is the tale of the "Monkey's Paw," by W. W. Jacobs, in which the sergeant major brings back from India a talisman which has the power to grant each of three people three wishes. Of the first recipient of this talisman we are told only that his third wish is for death. The sergeant major, the second person whose wishes are granted, finds his experiences too terrible to relate. His friend, who receives the talisman, wishes first for £200. His next wish is that his son should come back, and the ghost knocks at the door. His third wish is that the ghost should go away.

Disastrous results are to be expected not merely in the world of fairy tales but in the real world wherever two agencies essentially foreign to each other are coupled in the attempt to achieve a common purpose. If the communication between these two agencies as to the nature of this purpose is incomplete, it must only be expected that the results of this cooperation will be unsatisfactory. If we use, to achieve our purposes, a mechanical agency with whose operation we cannot efficiently interfere once we have started it, because the action is so fast and irrevocable that we have not the data to intervene before the action is complete, then we had better be quite sure that the purpose put into the machine is the purpose which we really desire and not merely a colorful imitation of it.

TIME SCALES

Up to this point I have been considering the quasi-moral problems caused by the simultaneous action of the machine and the human being in a joint enterprise. We have seen that one of the chief causes of the danger of disastrous consequences in the use of the learning machine is that man and machine operate on two distinct time scales, so that the machine is much faster than man and the two do not gear together without serious difficulties. Problems of the same sort arise whenever two control operators on very different time scales act together, irrespective of which system is the faster and which system is the slower. This leaves us the much more directly moral question: What are the moral problems when man as an individual operates in connection with the controlled process of a much slower time scale, such as a portion of political history or—our main subject of inquiry—the development of science?

Let it be noted that the development of science is a control and communication process for the long-term understanding and control of matter. In this process 50 years are as a day in the life of the individual. For this reason, the individual scientist must work as a part of a process whose time scale is so long that he himself can only contemplate a very limited sector of it. Here, too, communication between the two parts of a double machine is difficult and limited. Even when the individual believes that science contributes to the human ends which he has at heart, his belief needs a continual scanning and re-evaluation which is only partly possible. For the individual scientist, even the partial appraisal of this liaison between the man and the process requires an imaginative forward glance at history which is difficult, exacting, and only limitedly achievable. And if we adhere simply to the creed of the scientist, that an incomplete knowledge of the world and of ourselves is better than no knowledge, we can still by no means always justify the naive assumption that the faster we rush ahead to employ the new powers for action which are opened up to us, the better it will be. We must always exert the full strength of our imagination to examine where the full use of our new modalities may lead us.

SOME MORAL AND TECHNICAL CONSEQUENCES OF AUTOMATION—A REFUTATION*

Arthur L. Samuel

Abstract. The machine is not a threat to mankind, as some people think. The machine does not possess a will, and its so-called "conclusions" are only the logical consequences of its input, as revealed by the mechanistic functioning of an inanimate assemblage of mechanical and electrical parts.

In an article entitled "Some moral and technical consequences of automation," Norbert Wiener has stated some conclusions with which I disagree. Wiener seems to believe that machines *can* possess originality and that they *are* a threat to mankind. In ascribing a contrary opinion to the man in the street—to wit, "that nothing can come out of the machine which has not been put into it"—he overlooks or ignores the fact that there is a long history of the acceptance of this more reassuring view by scientific workers in the field, from the time of Charles Babbage to the present. Apparently Wiener shares some of the lack of understanding which he ascribes to the public, at least to the extent that he reads im-

*N. Wiener, "Some Moral and Technical Consequences of Automation," *Science*, Vol. 131, May 6, 1960, pp. 1355–1358, copyright 1960 by the American Associates for the Advancement of Science.

plications into some of the recent work which the workers themselves deny.

It is my conviction that machines cannot possess originality in the sense implied by Wiener and that they cannot transcend man's intelligence. I agree with Wiener in his thesis that "machines can and do transcend some of the limitations of their designers, and that in doing so they may be both effective and dangerous." The modern automobile travels faster than its designer can run, it is effective, and the records of highway fatalities attest to the dangerous consequences. However, a perusal of Wiener's article reveals that much more than this is meant, and it is to this extension of the thesis that I wish to take exception.

Wiener's reference to the "Sorcerer's Apprentice," and to the many tales based on the assumption that the agencies of magic are literal-minded, might almost lead one to think that he attributes magic to the machine. He most certainly seems to imply an equality between man and the machine when he states "disastrous results are to be expected not merely in the world of fairy tales but in the real world wherever two agencies essentially foreign to each other are coupled in the attempt to achieve a common purpose." In relationships between man and a machine the machine is an agency, but only an agency of man, entirely subservient to man and to his will. Of course, no one will deny that "we had better be quite sure that the purpose put into the machine is the purpose which we really desire and not merely a colorful imitation of it." If we want our house to be at 70 °F when we get up in the morning, we had better set the thermostat at 70° and not at 32°. But once the thermostat is set at 70° we can go to sleep without fear that the genie in the furnace controls might, for some reason of his own, decide that 32° was a better figure. In exactly the same way and to the same degree we must anticipate our own inability to interfere when we instruct a modern digital computer (which works faster than we do) and when we instruct a thermostat (which works while we sleep).

Wiener's analogy between a machine and a human slave is also quite misleading. He is right in his assertion that "complete subservience and complete intelligence do not go together" in a human slave with human emotions and needs and with a will of his own. To ascribe human attributes to a machine simply because the machine can simulate some forms of human behavior is, obviously, a fallacious form of reasoning.

A machine is not a genie, it does not work by magic, it does not possess a will, and, Wiener to the contrary, nothing comes out which has not been put in, barring, of course, an infrequent case of malfunctioning. Programming techniques which we now employ to instruct the modern digital computer so as to make it into a learning machine *do not* "remove from the mind of the designer and operator an effective understanding of many of the stages by which the machine comes to its conclusions." Since the machine does not have a mind of its own, the "conclusions" are not "its." The so-called "conclusions" are only the logical consequences of the input program and input data, as revealed by the mechanistic functioning of an inanimate assemblage of mechanical and electrical parts. The "intentions" which the machine seems to manifest are the intentions of the human programmer, as specified in advance, or they are subsidiary intentions derived from these, following rules specified by the programmer. We can even anticipate higher levels of abstraction, just as Wiener does, in which the program will not only modify the subsidiary intentions but will also modify the rules which are used in their derivation, or in which it will modify the rules which are used in their derivation, or in which it will modify the ways in which it modifies the rules, and so on, or even in which one machine will design and construct a second machine with enhanced capabilities. However, and this is important, the machine *will not* and *cannot* do any of these things until it has been instructed as to how to proceed. There is (and logically there must always remain) a complete hiatus between (i) any ultimate extension and elaboration in this process of carrying out man's wishes and (ii) the development within the machine of a will of its own. To believe otherwise is either to believe in magic or to believe that the existence of man's will is an illusion and that man's actions are as mechanical as the machine's. Perhaps Wiener's article and my rebuttal have both been mechanistically determined, but this I refuse to believe.

An apparent exception to these conclusions might be claimed for projected machines of the so-called "neural net" type. These machines were not mentioned by Wiener, and, unfortunately, they cannot be adequately discussed in the space available here. Briefly, however, one envisions a collection of simple devices which, individually, simulate the neurons of an animal's nervous system and which are interconnected by some random process simulating the organization of the nervous system. It is maintained by many serious workers that such nets can be made to exhibit purposeful activity by instruction and training with reward-and-punishment routines similar to those used with young animals. Since the internal connections would be unknown, the precise behavior of the nets would be unpredictable and, therefore, potentially dangerous. At the present time, the largest nets that can be constructed are nearer in size to the nervous system of a flatworm than to the brain of man and so hardly constitute a threat. If practical machines of this type become a reality we will have to take a much closer look at their implications than either Wiener or I have been able to do.

One final matter requires some clarification—a matter having to do with Wiener's concluding remarks to the effect that "We must always exert the full strength of our imagination to examine where the full use of our new modalities may lead us." This certainly makes good sense if we assume that Wiener means for us to include the full use of our intelligence as well as of our imagination. However, coming as it did at the end of an article which raised the spectre of man's domination by a "learning machine," this statement casts an unwarranted shadow over the learning machine and, specifically, over the modern digital computer. I would be remiss were I to close without setting the record straight in this regard.

First a word about the capabilities of the digital computer. Although I have maintained that "nothing comes out that has not gone in," this does not mean that the output does not possess value over and beyond the value to us of the input data. The utility of the computer resides in the speed and accuracy with which the computer provides the desired transformations of the input data from a form which man may not be able to use directly to one which is of direct utility. In principle, a man with a pencil and a piece of paper could always arrive at the same result. In practice, it might take so long to perform the calculation that the answer would no longer be of value, and, indeed, the answer might never be obtained because of man's faculty for making mistakes. Because of the very large disparity in speeds (of the order of 100,000 to 1), on a computer we can complete calculations which are of immense economic value with great precision and with a reliability which inspires confidence, and all this in time intervals which conform to the demands of real-life situations. The magnitude of the tasks and the speed with which they are performed are truly breath-taking, and they do tend to impress the casual observer as being a form of magic, particularly when he is unacquainted with the many, many hours of human thought which have gone into both the design of the machine and, more particularly, into the writing of the program which specifies the machine's detailed behavior.

Most uses of the computer can be explained in terms of simulation. When one computes the breaking strength of an airplane wing under conditions of turbulence, one is, in effect, simulating the behavior of an actual airplane wing which is subjected to unusual stresses, all this without danger to a human pilot, and, indeed, without ever having to build the airplane in the first place. The checker-playing program on the I.B.M. 704, to which Wiener referred, actually simulates a human checker player, and the machine learns by accumulating data from its playing experience and by using some of the logical processes which might be employed by a person under similar circumstances. The specific logical processes used are, of course, those which were specified in advance by the human programmer. In these, and in many other situations, the great speed of the computer enables us to test the outcome resulting from a variety of choices of initial actions and so to choose the course with the highest payoff before the march of human events forces us to take some inadequately considered action. This ability to look into the future, as it were, by simulation on a computer is already being widely used, and as time goes on it is sure to find application in more and more aspects of our daily lives.

Finally, as to the portents for good or evil which are contained in the use of this truly remarkable machine—most, if not all, of man's inventions are instrumentalities which may be employed by both saints and sinners. One can make a case, as one of my associates has jokingly done, for the thesis that the typewriter is an invention of the devil, since its use in the nations' war offices has made wars more horrible, and because it has enslaved the flower of our young womanhood. On the whole, however, most of us concede that the typewriter, as a labor-saving device, has been a boon, not a curse. The digital computer is something more than merely another labor-saving device, since it augments man's brain rather than his brawn, and since it allows him to look into the future. If we believe, as most scientists do, that it is to our advantage to increase the rate at which we can acquire knowledge, then we can hardly do otherwise than to assert that the modern digital computer is a modality whose value is overwhelmingly on the side of the good. I rest my case with this assertion.

In July 1979, the computer program BKG 9.8 defeated the world champion backgammon player Luigi Villa of Italy by a score of 7−1 in a match.[43] The program used a PDP−10 computer at Carnegie-Mellon University. However, by 1980 a computer program had not been developed that can consistently defeat a chess Grand Master.

Modern authors state that man feels threatened by the machine and feels out of harmony. He is discontinuous with the machine age. Thus, as Professor Drucker states, we live in an age of discontinuity; an age of the knowledge industry when information is the conveyor of power rather than energy and materials. The fears of man are that the computer provides the following threats:

1. The computer threatens man's identity as a worker and as a producing member of society.
2. The computer adds to the depersonalization of man's relationships.
3. The computer contributes to the pollution of man's environment.
4. The computer makes man himself, as an intelligent being, irrelevant, inadequate or meaningless.
5. The comptuer leads to centralized power.

The potential social impacts of the computer are illustrated in Figure 14−8.

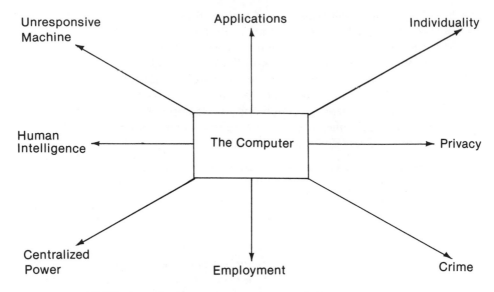

FIGURE 14–8 The potential social impacts of the computer.

In many ways the greatest threat to man is the possibility of forcing upon us the need to find an alternative to work. The possibilities of automation are profound to consider. Perhaps within this century work will no longer exist as we now know it and jobs will not be available for the majority of the population. As William Kuhns recently stated, "For computers will not simply force upon us the need to find an alternative to work; they will offer us that alternative. New ways of registering knowledge, an unbelievably enlarged capacity for information, new possibilities of communication—the computer's potential for a leisure-stricken society is even more phenomenal than its creation of such a world. Yet it is possible, even likely, that men will be hesitant and fearful about the computer, that the radically ambivalent reactions noticeable in man's response to many contemporary environments will be all the more apparent in the final age of the computer."[9]

When a person engages in work, he uses his body and brain in three specific ways. The first is the exercise of physical strength and manual dexterity, called skill. The second is the functioning of the five perceptive senses...and the personal control that is exercised therefrom. The third is the use of the brain, both in its decision-making capacity and in the information storage system we call memory. The computer used in automation systems is a challenge to all three of these ways of man. The computer and automated devices may effectively replace man in a majority of tasks in the future. To this present time, however, the alarm over the potential unemployment caused by computer automation has been premature. The silent conquest of the employment market forseen by Donald Michael and others has not yet become reality.[22,42] Yet computer automation, often called *cybernation* (for *cybernetics* and *automation*), is only in its infancy. Perhaps the exponential growth of unemployment, due to cybernation, has only begun. The profound changes in the size of the agricultural labor force has only begun. The half century and the changes we are to experience due to the computer will not be significant before the end of the twentieth century. It has been estimated that whereas in 1900 eighteen out of twenty worked with their hands, ten of them on the farm, by 1980 only five of twenty earned their living by manual work, just one of them on the farm.

One of the consequences of the introduction of the computers to clerical activities is the industrialization of the office in a pattern amazingly similar to that found on assembly lines. In large banks, insurance companies, and credit billing operations, the paperwork operation is strikingly factory-like, and its managers tend to talk in production-line terminology. Computers can compound errors rapidly without hesitation, as is shown in Figure 14–9. Work tasks are fragmented until they become little more than keying an account number and a dollar amount onto a card. Thus, automation of the functions of the business office has this unforeseen result.[16]

"... and in 1/10,000th of a second, it can compound the programmer's error 87,500 times!"

FIGURE 14–9   © Sidney Harris. Used with permission.

As the computer becomes a partner with man in the intellectual process, one has to consider an additional problem, as Kuhns states:[9]

> . . .the tendency of men to think computationally—What effect will our new concept of information have on the way in which people know? In other words, in a world of immediately accessible information, what will become of knowledge—and of insight, the ratios of knowledge created by the personal mind? The repercussions here are strongest for art and religion, in which insight—the inescapably personal aspect of knowledge—is fundamental. Will computational man be capable of insight, or will insight be capable of enabling men to distinguish between computational and noncomputational thought, even as they distinguish between reality and fantasy?

Computers are man's tools and can be used knowingly to perform needed tasks for society. Alternatively, man's slaves can, when used indiscriminately, cause social consequences of a profound and foreseen nature. A fear of these unforeseen consequences of a delirious nature has caused many to echo Samuel Butler's dictum:[8]

> But the servant glides by imperceptible approaches into the master; and we have come to such a pass that, even now, man must suffer terribly on ceasing to benefit the machines. If all machines were to be annihilated at one moment, and if all knowledge of mechanical laws were taken from him so that he could make no more machines, and all machine-made food destroyed so that the race of man should be left as it were naked upon a desert island, we should become extinct in six weeks. Man's very soul is due to the machines; it is a machine-made thing: he thinks as he thinks, and feels as he feels, through the work that machines have wrought upon him, and their existence is quite as much a *sine qua non* for his, as for theirs. This fact precludes us from proposing the complete annihilation of machinery, but surely it indicates that we should destroy as many of them as we can possibly dispense with, lest they should tyrannize over us even more completely.

Is the answer to destroy as many of the computer systems as we can? Many people believe so. Is there another way to use computers advantageously while overcoming the problems of depersonalization, unemployment due to cybernation, and the inability to comprehend the solutions resulting from rapid calculations? Perhaps the answer for man is to remain man above all else, and not imitate or compete with his tool or slave the comptuer. It is appropriate that Norman Cousins has suggested this course of action and Mr. Cousins' reasoned response to the challenge of the computer serves as a suitable ending to a chapter which cannot answer questions, but only raise the issues. For the consequences of the actions we take with the computer in the present will only by known by those who experience them in the future. But that is, of course, one of the great challenges to man.

THE COMPUTER AND THE POET*

Norman Cousins

The essential problem of man in a computerized age remains the same as it has always been. That problem is not solely how to be more productive, more comfortable, more content, but how to be more sensitive, more sensible, more proportionate, more alive. The computer makes possible a phenomenal leap in human proficiency; it demolishes the fences around the practical and even the theoretical intelligence. But the question persists and indeed grows whether the computer will make it easier or harder for human beings to know who they really are, to identify their real problems, to respond more fully to beauty, to place adequate value on life, and to make their world safer than it now is.

Electronic brains can reduce the profusion of dead ends in involved in vital research. But they can't eliminate the foolishness and decay that come from the unexamined life. Nor do they connect a man to the things he has to be connected to—the reality of pain in others; the possibilities of creative growth in himself; the memory of the race; and the rights of the next generation.

The reason these matters are important in a computerized age is that there may be a tendency to mistake data for wisdom, just as there has always been a tendency to confuse logic with values, and intelligence with insight. Unobstructed access to facts can produce unlimited good only if it is matched by the desire and ability to find out what they mean and where they would lead.

Facts are terrible things if left sprawling and unattended. They are too easily regarded as evaluated certainities rather than as the rawest of raw materials crying to be processed into the texture of logic. It requires a very unusual mind, Whitehead said, to undertake the analysis of a fact. The computer can provide a correct number, but it may be an irrelevant number until judgment is pronounced.

*From July 23, 1966, *Saturday Review.* Copyright 1966, *Saturday Review,* Inc.

To the extent, then, that man fails to make the distinction between the intermediate operations of electronic intelligence and the ultimate responsibilities of human decision and conscience, the computer could prove a digression. It could obscure man's awareness of the need to come to terms with himself. It may foster the illusion that he is asking fundamental questions when actually he is asking only functional ones. It may be regarded as a substitute for intelligence instead of an extension of it. It may promote undue confidence in concrete answers. "If we begin with certainties," Bacon said, "we shall end in doubts; but if we begin with doubts, and we are patient with them, we shall end in certainties."

The computer knows how to vanquish error, but before we lose ourselves in celebration of the victory, we might reflect on the great advances in the human situation that come about because men were challenged by error and would not stop thinking and probing until they found better approaches for dealing with it. "Give me a good fruitful error, full of seeds, bursting with its own corrections," Ferris Greenslet wrote. "You can keep your sterile truth for yourself."

The biggest single need in computer technology is not for improved circuitry or enlarged capacity or prolonged memory or miniaturized containers, but for better questions and better use of the answers. Without taking anything away from the technicians, we think it might be fruitful to effect some sort of junction between the computer technologist and the poet. A genuine purpose may be served by turning loose the wonders of the creative imagination on the kinds of problems being put to electronic tubes and transistors. The company of poets may enable the man who tend the machines to see a larger panorama of possibilities than technology alone may inspire.

A poet, said Aristotle, has the advantage of expressing the universal; the specialist expresses only the particular. The poet, moreover, can remind us that man's greatest energy comes not from his dynamos but from his dreams. The notion of where a man ought to be instead of where he is; the liberation from cramped prospects, the intimations of immortality through art—all these proceed naturally out of dreams. But the quality of a man's dreams can only be a reflection of his subconscious. What he puts into his subconscious, therefore, is quite literally the most important nourishment in the world.

Nothing really happens to a man expect as it is registered in the subconscious. This is where event and feeling become memory and where the proof of life is stored. The poet—and we use the term to include all those who have respect for and speak to the human spirit—can help to supply the subconscious with material to enhance its sensitivity, thus safeguarding it. The poet, too, can help to keep man from making himself over in the image of his electronic marvels. For the danger is not so much that man will be controlled by the computer as that he may imitate it.

The poet reminds men of their uniqueness. It is not necessary to possess the ultimate definition of this uniqueness. Even to speculate on it is a gain.

CHAPTER 14 PROBLEMS

P14-1. Select an area of human thought and discuss if a computer would duplicate the processes involved.

P14-2. Does HAL, the computer of *2001: A Space Odyssey*, think or just mimic thinking? Can a computer have emotions?

P14-3. It has been said, "The steam drill outlasted John Henry as a digger of railway tunnels, but that didn't prove the machine has muscles; it proved that muscles were not necessary for digging railway tunnels.[27] Can one say the same about computers and their "ability to think?"

P14-4. List a foreseeable development of computer use and its potential consequences as illustrated in Table 14-2.

P14-5. Computers will be increasingly used in business and thus will affect the nature of the business world and the consumer as an individual. Discuss the consequences of increased use of computers in business which accrue to the citizens and consumers in the US.

P14-6. Robots are a threat as well as an opportunity to modern man. The Robotics International of SME, Box 930, Dearborn, MI, 48128, is an organization pursuing an investigating the development of robots. Do you believe that robots are evil? Contact the RI and discover the view of that organization.

P14-7. The television series *Six-Million Dollar Man* and the series *Star Trek* are based, in part, on the important role of computers. Do you find the role of computers in these series to be realistic and threatening or helpful to man?

P14-8. In the novels *Terminal Man* and *The Andromeda Strain*, the computer is always infallible and always programmed for the problem at hand. Who are the tools in these stories: the men or the computers? What are the characteristics of the computers involved? Are they the computers of tomorrow?

P14-9. "If robots do our work," some people ask, "how can humans then earn an income?" What answer can you give such queries? Some believe that the service sector will absorb the displaced manufacturing worker. Do you agree?

P14—10. "Knowledge is power" is a commonly-held viewpoint. Is the gap between the people with access to a computer and those without such access growing? What are the effects of computer power available to a segment of our society?

P14—11. List at least five major social consequences that may be brought about by the establishment of Electronic Funds Transfer Systems.[43]

P14—12. How does increasing access to computers operate to encourage more or less conformity (or more less diversity) in our society? Prepare an outline of your posiiton suitable for a debate on the question.

P14—13. How do you get a robot on Mars to find a rock it has just dropped? The time to communicate the fact to an earth control station is 20 minutes, and, even if the command were made up instantly it would take another 20 minutes to return the command to Mars. What level of intelligence is necessary to allow the robot to carry out the task itself without control from Earth? Is it threatening to mankind to have a robot that can "think through" such a task?

CHAPTER 14 REFERENCES

1. N. Wiener, "Cybernetics," *Scientific American*, November, 1948, pp. 348—384.

2. J. O. Wisdom, "The Hypothesis of Cybernetics," *British Journal for the Philosophy of Science*, Vol. 2, No. 5, 1951.

3. J. Von Neumann, *The Computer and the Brain*, Yale University Press, New Haven, Conn., 1958.

4. M. L. Minsky, "Artificial Intelligence," *Scientific American*, September, 1966, pp. 142—148.

5. A. M. Turing, "Can a Machine Think?" *Mind*, 1950, pp. 2099—2123.

6. A. C. Clarke, " Are You Thinking Machines?" *Industrial Research,* March, 1969, pp. 52—55.

7. "The Day They Rated Minsky," *Datamation,* October, 1969, pg. 159.

8. N. Weiner, *God and Golem, Inc.* M.I.T. Press, Cambridge, Massachusetts, 1964.

9. W. Kuhns, *Environmental Man*, Harper and Row, Inc., New York, 1969.

10. K. Čapek, *Rossum's Universal Robots,* English version by P. Selver and N. Playfair, Doubleday, Page and Co., New York, 1923.

11. N. Graham, *The Mind Tool*, West Publishing Co., St. Paul, Minnesota, 1980.

12. A. C. Clarke, *2001: A Space Odyssey*, Signet Books, New York, 1968.
13. K. Vonnegut, Jr., *Player Piano*, Avon Books, New York, 1952.
14. D. Fabun, *Dynamics of Change*, Prentice-Hall, Inc., Englewood Cliffs, New Jersey, 1968.
15. J. Osborne, "At Your Keyboard," *New Republic*, March 22, 1980, pp. 8–10.
16. A. Toffler, *The Third Wave*, Morrow and Company, New York, 1980.
17. N. Bjorn–Andersen, *The Human Side of Information Processing,* North Holland Publishing Co., New York, 1980.
18. S. Turkle, "Computers as Rorschach," *Society,* February 1980, pp. 15–24.
19. R. Kling, "Social Analyses of Computing," *Computing Surveys*, March 1980, pp. 61–110.
20. N. Wiener, "Some Moral and Technical Consequences of Automation," *Science*, Vol. 131, May 6, 1960, pp. 1355–1358.
21. A. L. Samuel, "Some Moral and Technical Consequences of Automation—A Refutation," *Science*, Vol. 132, September 16, 1960.
22. D. N. Michael, "Cybernation: The Silent Conquest," Center for the Study of Democratic Institutions, 1962.
23. B. W. Arden, *What Can be Automated?* M.I.T. Press, Cambridge, Massachusetts, 1980.
24. N. Cousins, "The Computer and the Poet," *Saturday Review,* July 23, 1966.
25. N. Wiener, *The Human Use of Human Beings,* Houghton Mifflin Co., Boston, 1950.
26. D. F. Jones, *Colossus,* Putnam's Sons, Inc., New Yrok, 1968.
27. P. McCorduck, *Machines Who Think,* W. H. Freeman, San Francisco, 1979.
28. T. D. Sterling, "Computer Ombudsman," *Society,* February 1980, pp. 31–35.
29. R. Paul, "Robots, Models and Automation," *IEEE Computer*, July 1979, pp. 19–27.
30. R. Sugarman, "The Blue–Collar Robot," *IEEE Spectrum,* September 1980, pp. 53–57.
31. R. Bernhard, "An Electronic Advisor/Companion," *IEEE Spectrum,* September 1980, pp. 39–43.
32. J. Weizenbaur, *Computer Power and Human Reason: From Judgment to Calculation,* W. H. Freeman and Co., San Francisco, 1976.
33. R. Perry, *Program for a Puppet,* Crown Publishers, New York, 1980.
34. M. Marshall, "Artificial Intelligence: On the Brink," *Electronics,* September 11, 1980, pp. 93–94.
35. G. Bonnot, "The Coming Age of Telematics," *World Press Review,* February 1980, pp. 21–23.
36. H. D. Covvey and N. H. McAlister, *Computer Consciousness: Surveying*

the Autonomous 80s, Addison-Wesley Publishing Co., Reading, Massachusetts, 1980.

37. M. Laver, *Computers and Social Change,* Cambridge University Press, New York, 1980.

38. W. M. Mathews, *The Computer's Impact on Society: Humanistic Perspectives,* Mississippi University Press, 1980.

39. G. A. Silver, *The Social Impact of Computers,* Harcourt Brace Jovanovich, Inc., New York, 1980.

40. A. Mowshowitz, *Inside Information, Computers in Fiction,* Addison-Wesley Publishing Company, Reading Massachusetts, 1977.

41. R. Bellman, *An Introduction to Artificial Intelligence: Can Computers Think?* Boyd & Fraser Publishing Co., San Francisco, 1978.

42. W. Myers, "The Social Implications of Computers," *IEEE Computer,* August 1979, pp. 79−86.

43. H. Berliner, "Computer Backgammon," *Scientific American,* June 1980, pp. 64−72.

44. H. A. Simon, *Models of Thought,* Yale University Press, New Haven, 1979.

45. U. Neisser, "Computers Can't Think," *Creative Computing,* January 1980, pp. 62−67.

46. P. Senker, "Social Implications of Automation," *The Industrial Robot,* June 1979, pp. 58−61.

47. M. L. Dertouzos and J. Moses, *The Computer Ape: A Twenty Year View,* M.I.T. Press, Cambridge, Massachusetts, 1980.

48. P. H. Winston, *Artificial Intelligence,* Addison-Wesley Publishing Co., Reading, Massachusetts, 1978.

49. R. Malone, *The Robot Book,* Harcourt Brace Jovanovich, Inc., New York, 1978.

50. C. Evans, *The Micro Millennium,* The Viking Press, New York, 1980.

51. D. R. Hofstadter, *Godel, Escher and Bach,* Vintage Books, New York, 1980.

15

COMPUTERS AND THE FUTURE

15.1 FUTURE COMPUTERS AND COMPUTER SYSTEMS

Our society is future-oriented; to a great extent computers have contributed to this orientation. As we noted in the last chapter, many feel that the technological determinants of our society give us nothing like a free choice in our future, but rather have already set us on a path that is technologically determined. Yet, if we are to exercise a free choice about the development of large new computers and their uses, we must be informed about existing computers and the potential new machines. Thus, the purpose of this chapter is to portray the new and expected world of the computer during the period from the present until the year 2000.

It has been estimated that the market for computing systems will continue to grow at a rapid rate. For example, the computing systems market in 1985 will be twice the size (in dollars) of the market in 1980. While it is doubtful that this pace of growth can continue for the next three decades, a market for computers which doubles every six or ten years implies a rapid change in technology and equipment.[1] In a sense, computers become obsolete the way automobiles do. The technological and psychological push is toward possessing the latest model with its new and special features. Furthermore, the average performance/price ratio increases by a factor of two every two years, which leads competing industries and firms to upgrade and update their computer equipment. Table 15–1 shows the increase in performance/price ratio during the period 1953–1980.[8,9] As this performance continues to increase, the obsolescence of the old computer is caused by the availability of the new, higher performance computer.

TABLE 15-1
Performance/Price Ratio for the Period 1953-1980

	Year Introduced	Performance/Price Ratio (10,000 Operations/Dollar)
First Generation	1953	1.82
	1956	14.1
	1958	16.6
Second Generation	1959	94.8
	1962	154
	1964	178
Third Generation1968	1966	1920
	1968	4000
	1970	8000
Mini and Microcomputers	1974	40,000
IBM 4300 Models	1979	200,000

The widespread availability of time-sharing computers may result in a national information computer utility with tens of thousands of computer terminals in homes and offices connected to a large central computer. Also, the communication of data will occur, by means of terminals, through the use of telephone and other communication devices. The amount of data transmitted over telephone lines is certain to increase in the next decade. It is estimated that computer data transmissions over telephone lines now account for about 30 percent of the telephone time consumed in the United States. By 1982 it is estimated that data transmission will equal that of all voice communications.[3]

As the size of computers, computer networks and data banks grow during the next several decades, the performance of computers and computer communication systems must be monitored and evaluated. During the past several years, the performance of computers has been studied and several measures of performance have been developed. One measure of performance is the performance/price ratio of operations per dollar as given in Table 15–1. The performance measures of computers assist the computer user in evaluating the relative effectiveness of one computer compared to another. Also, the measures of effectiveness can be used to determine if there are economies of scale in using different computers. In developing an inclusive measure of computer system effectiveness, the cost of personnel and programming costs must be included since they often consume a fair share of the costs of operating a computer center. Man's progress is always measured by indices of his performance in conjunction with his tools. Therefore what is needed is a measure of effectiveness of a computer system including the equipment, the operating personnel and the programming time and cost. Measures of effectiveness are usually numerical, and one problem with computer systems today is the unsophisticated manner of recognizing their important characteristics which can be represented numerically. Real progress in the computer art will be made when it is known what is significant about computer behavior, when numbers are assigned to these effects, and when progress is measured using these numbers. As a theory of computer performance is developed, two kinds of information will become available: knowledge about the *structure of programs* during execution, and knowledge about the *response of computers* to these program structures.

The four performance measures commonly used today for analyzing computer effectiveness are capacity, throughput, speed and ease of use. *Capacity* is the total information work executable per unit when all the accessible resources of a computer are utilized. *Throughput* is the number of useful jobs run per unit time. The *speed* of a computer can be defined as the rate of adding two numbers or a similar index. The *ease* of *use* describes the effort required to prepare a problem for solution by the computer and to operate the computer to solve that problem. All of these measures must be considered in the evaluation of the effectiveness of a computer. The inclusion of the cost of programming in the total measure of effectiveness is critical. In 1980, it cost 4¢ per million computer arithmetic additions. As the cost of the computer arithmetic has decreased, the cost of programming has become relatively important. It has been estimated that in 1980, the cost of equipment consumed 20 percent of the total computer operation cost and the programming costs consumed 80 percent of the total costs.[10] Therefore, in the future, even a drastic reduction in the cost of hardware, or a significant increase in speed at an unchanged price, can have only a minor effect on the cost of computing as a whole. Lower programming cost is what is needed; in order to achieve a significant improvement in the effective low-cost use of computers in the future, it will be necessary to reduce the cost of programming. This is particularly important as industry, business and government progress toward the use of increasingly complex programs.

In order to ease the cost and complexity of programming, it would be advantageous if improved programming languages would be developed. An improved programming language should be easy to learn, use and implement and it should be machine-independent. Also, the language should be applicable to a wide variety of problems. Currently, there are programming languages available for specific purposes such as business and science. What may emerge is a series of languages to fit a range of users from beginner to expert, but all general in application. Some languages may be for big problems and big machines, others for small ones; some for experiments and one-of-a-kind problems, others for production runs.[6]

The use of computers in large complex systems has grown during the past decade and will continue to grow during the next several decades. Many contemporary critics have noted the tendency in the design of large complex systems using computers to underestimate the costs and development time and to exaggerate the expected performance. The most complex subsystem or portion of the complex system is often the computer programming. For example, in the case of the ABM (which is illustrative of complex systems) computer programs that carry out regulatory and control functions are usually much simpler and easier to prepare than computer programs that involve target acquisition, pattern recognition, decoy discrimination, decision-making and problem-solving.

All complex computer programs contain programming errors. No complex program is ever wholly debugged and very few complex programs can ever be run through all possible states or conditions in order to permit the programmers to see that what they think ought to happen actually does happen.

Perhaps, in order to avoid the reprogramming required by a new generation of computers, future computer systems will be modular in design. As is done in the telephone industry, the replacement of modules or subsystems with newly-developed modules will enable an evolutionary growth to occur.

I has been stated that overexpectations and underestimates characterized the application of computers to large-scale complex systems during the past decade. If the expectations were exaggerated, it was the concept of on-line large integrated information systems that was attractive but unfulfilled in practice. During the next decade, computer systems will evolve which will increasingly incorporate the interactive feature required for effective man-computer systems used in process control, CAI and management information systems. The modular development of the evolutionary computer will enable the programmers to develop effective programs to accommodate the changing computer.

Future computers will be more reliable, more fault-tolerant, and more nearly failsafe than any built heretofore. That is, they will retain data and continue operating even if some part of the computer system fails. Future systems may include multiple parallel processors to overcome failures of one CPU. Also they will be based on advance semiconductor technology, and many will use bubble memories. Computer systems with a given power and throughput that cost $200,000 in 1980 may cost only $40,000 in 1985.[1] It will be a desirable goal to reduce the number of failures of any one computer system to one per year. Also, we can expect that, by 1985, much of the input data to a computer will be collected automatically by sensors.[10]

The large, high-speed computer of the last few years of the decade of the 1960s and the 70s was built to satisfy a need for time-sharing computers or large complex system computers which could operate in real time. The IBM System 3033 is an example of a presently available large computer. The 3033 can be used for a complex airline reservation systems, or coast-to-coast time-sharing networks. Other applications include extensive scientific studies, such as global weather forecasting and space exploration. The central processing unit possesses a cycle time of 20 nanoseconds for accessing data stored in its core storage. The computer uses a 64-bit word and integrated circuit memory components, and is reported to provide an increase in its performance/price ratio of approximately five over the IBM System/370 Model 168. The large computer, the 3033, is designed to mix computer programs, a fact that has widespread implications for improving throughput.

The Control Data Corporation 7600 computer is another large computer built to accomplish large complex tasks. The cycle time of the 7600 is 27.5 nanoseconds; the computer utilizes a 65-bit word.

The Illiac IV computer is one of the world's fastest. Essentially 64 computers operating in parallel and handling more than ten million instructions per second, the Illiac IV was developed at the University of Illinois to solve large scientific problems. It uses 64-bit words, and it has an all-semiconductor memory.[5] Illiac IV is now operating at NASA-Ames Center in Mountain View, California.

One of the world's fastest computers, built by Texas Instruments, is operating at the National Oceanic and Atmospheric Administration Laboratory at Princeton, New Jersey. Called the Advanced Scientific Computer, it is capable of 50 million additions per second. Its central memory can store one million words. This large capacity is necessary for the solution of weather prediction problems.

The price for computing performance for a given performance has declined steadily over the past 25 years, as is shown in Figure 15–1. The IBM Series 4300,

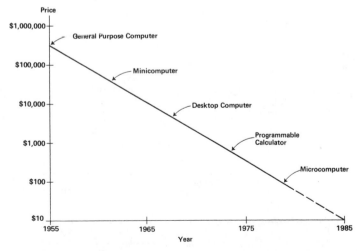

FIGURE 15–1   Constant performance of a computer plotted for price of the computer
for 1955 to 1985.

announced in 1979, provided a 6 to 1 improvement in price/performance over the IBM 303X series. The 4331 has a one million byte memory. It is capable of 239,000 multiplications per second. The price versus performance of these IBM computers is shown in Figure 15–2.

The Amdahl 470 V/8 system is a 1980 high-performance computer; it is shown in Figure 15–3.

The world's largest "supercomputers" are the Cray Research-1 and the Control Data Corporation Cyber 205. The Cray-1 performs 100 million floating-point operations per second; it sells for about 10 million dollars. The Cyber 205 can perform 800 million floating-point operations per second; it sells for $16 million. The evolution of large high-speed computers is illustrated by Figure 15–4.[12]

The development of a computer using optical principles and utilizing a laser is proceeding toward a practical product. One company recently reported that it is developing a laser computer which incorporates 10^{10} bits of storage and operates with a storage access time of 20 nanoseconds. In addition, it planned that this laser computer will involve a storage cost of 10^{-7} cent per bit and average fewer than one error in 10^9 bits.[4]

The computer of the future will be modular in design and faster than present

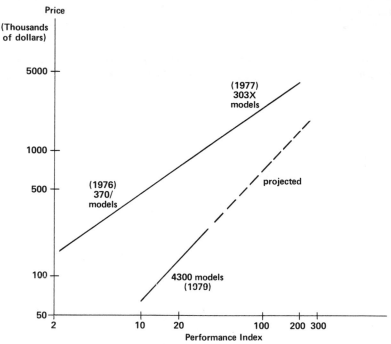

FIGURE 15–2   The price versus performance evolution for IBM general purpose computers in the 1970s.

FIGURE 15–3   The Amdahl 470 V/8 is capable executing 8.5 million instructions per second. It has a 26 nanosecond machine cycle time. This is a large, powerful computer useful for business purposes. *Courtesy of Amdahl Corporation.*

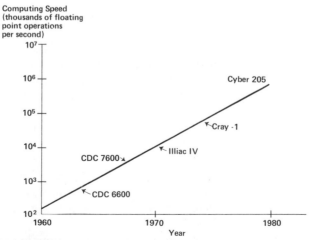

FIGURE 15–4   The evolution of high-speed large computers

machines. Also, the computer will be designed toward improved equipment and hardware to serve the functions often previously relegated to a program. The number of program instructions in basic software available with a computer has grown ten times every 5.5 years during the period 1952—1980.[3] With the growth in importance and cost of programming software, the hardware portion of the computer must assume some of the tasks previously allocated to software.

The computer industry will tap the vast small-business market in the next few years. The use of small minicomputers and microcomputers in a wide range of industries will expand rapidly. Distributed processing in business will expand, and point-of-sale retail systems should become common by 1985. Electronic funds transfer systems (EFTS) promise to connect every individual who possesses a plastic money card to a nation-wide computer banking system. Microcomputers used in games, autos, and applications by hobbyists will increase rapidly in sales in the late 1980s.

Pattern recognition by computer may become common for electrocardiogram analysis, picture processing, speech recognition and robot automation in the 1980s.

15.2 COMPUTERS AND INFORMATION SYSTEMS IN THE YEARS 1971-2000

In this section we present some specific predictions and estimates for the period 1980 to 2000. Many of these predictions will undoubtedly prove to be in error, but predictions still provide us with an arrow pointing toward the future. While we cannot clearly visualize the path to be followed, one can indicate the direction of the evolving field of computer science; that is the objective of this section.

Future generations of computers will be classified as communication-and-control systems, using on-line data collection. The computers will be directed to user requirements. The user will participate more in the design of the computer in order to assure that the computers are built with the objectives of applications. For example, computers will be designed to shift the emphasis in industry *from* administrative record-keeping in the plant production environment *toward* a system involving the real-time monitoring of men, machines, and material throughout the working day. One possible technical approach to controlling plant operations involves on-line use of a computer with programs structured to provide continuous information on the operation as well as summary input to the administrative record-keeping system. Computer utilities, or networks of computers, will be developed. Networks of computers, particularly those designed for sharing data bases, open tremendous possibilities for the users, as in scale-time management information systems.

The future potential for computers and their applications is great indeed. In the future the emphasis on replacing clerical routines by computer programs will continue, but new applications for computers will be developed. The challenge is to design and to assist in the operation of a company, institution or process. The computer will be readily used in devices and machines ranging from automobiles to microwave ovens.

For any nation, the ability to utilize computer and communication technology and to realize its benefits should be considered nothing less than a national resource.[7] As yet, no fundamental limit to the reduction in cost and the increase in computing power of a computer has emerged.[8] More powerful microcomputers and large general-purpose computers can be expected to be developed. The use of distributed processing systems and multiple processor-based systems is expected to grow rapidly over the next five years. The limit to progress may be in the development of reliable, useful and cost-efficient programs and software.[10] A national marketplace for computing and information services has been developing continually in the 1970s. The linking of computers by communications systems may transform the structure of society.

Some of the challenge of the next decade lies in the need for improved standards for hardware and software. Improved program validation techniques are also required.

Some of the computer devices that will become available during the next decade can be envisaged as logical extensions of technologies presently in the laboratory. These laboratory technologies will be designed for volume production and produced at a commercial price. We can expect that low-cost minicomputers will become available in many sizes and forms and in special purpose units which will extend their use in dozens of ways. The low-cost minicomputer will cost approximately $1,000, which may become practical for the home and the hobby shop. The minicomputer can be used for such practical home functions as storing and processing budget and account information, recipes, menus, and calendar schedules. The minicomputer will also be available for such plant uses as segmented process control and automated testing, for communication-system data handling, and for general business calculating and record-keeping chores in, say, a fair-sized neighborhood retail store. The three stages of computer development are shown in Figure 15−5. The rapid spread of microcomputers during the 1970s will continue through the 1980s.

Within the decade, computers may play a major role in data storage and retrieval. A large time-sharing system similar to a telephone network would alter the nature of our society. The availability of a library stored in the computer, and computer-aided instruction to subscribers, could be of significant value to the citizens of the United States. For example, the *New York Times's* Information Bank, which went into operation in 1974, makes indexed data and topical summaries from the paper's files avilable as a subscriber service. Users punch in requests on keyboards in their own offices and receive either CRT readings or printouts.

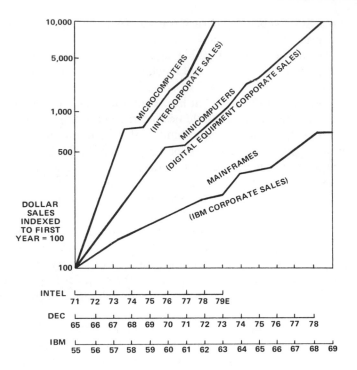

Revolution	Computer Type	Leading Company	Typical System Cost ($)
First	Mainframe - General Purpose	IBM	Millions
Second	Minicomputer	Digital Equipment	Thousands
Third	Microcomputer	INTEL	Tens

FIGURE 15–5   Three computer revolutions.

The combination of artificial intelligence and mechanical devices may lead to general use of practical robot devices within the next decade. The computer-controlled hand and eye laboratory robot has led to the production of robots in 1982. These robots serve as a limited substitute for humans in a variety of dangerous or undesirable industrial operations. Perhaps other types of cybernetic machines (*e.g.*, robots) will be serving in factories and in the home.

In the future, programs will be generally sold as hardware rather than software.[13] That is, programs may be replaced by dedicated microcomputer elements. A computer user may be able to purchase a new program from a catalog and may then be able to insert the module into his or her computer system. Computers will be better able to tolerate faults than present computing machinery. Also, we can expect the computer to be used more readily than at present in the schools, in business, factories and even the home. Computerized encyclopedias, electronic mail, robots, and the paperless office will be items of the next two decades. Automated factories may be designed to produce products tailored specifically to each customer by a computer that controls the manufacturing for each product.

A handheld computer terminal device will become generally available in the mid-1980s. The alphanumeric keypad, with a flat-panel display, will enable speech recognition, language translation, time keeping, memory and communications capability for data and other information as shown in Figure 15–6.

By reviewing the progress and problems of the next computer decade, we can visualize the problems and promise of the third computer decade. The discussion about the value of various programming languages will continue in the next decade, for instance, and we can expect to find several new programming languages available. Also, the basic education of the computer scientist is now a subject for debate because it is generally not systematic. Perhaps the education of the future computer scientist will begin to occur on a systematic basis in the 1980s as graduate programs in computer science, at many universities, become further developed. The graduates of these programs will become the teachers of our future programmers, operators, computer scientists and engineers at all levels of

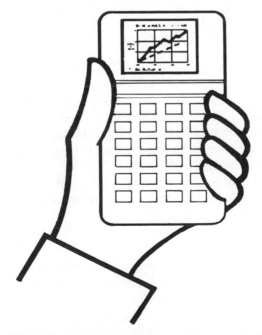

FIGURE 15–6   A handheld computer terminal.

study. Perhaps we will even find the study of computers regularly available to the high school student at an introductory level.

During the late 1980s, we can expect the emergence of a profession of computer science as the qualifications and educational standards become accepted and standardized. As the critics point out, the computer allows one to automate and mass produce inaccuracies and incorrect programs. The nation will look to the professionalism of the computer scientist for leadership, contol and a solution to the problems of the second decade of computers which will be solved in the third decade of computers.

A forecast of the applications of computers and developments within the computer field for the years 1968–2000 was recently published by Parsons and Williams, Inc., a consulting firm of Denmark.[14] The forecast was prepared by the use of the Delphi procedure to obtain a concensus among computer scientists and users.

In a Delphi forecast, a group of experts use a two-step questionnaire to come to a consensus about when technical events will occur. The first step usually results in widely divergent opinions; those at the extremes are asked to justify their views. In the second part, the experts are told how the first survey came out, and the reasons for extreme positions. They are then asked to reconsider their views. The second part usually shows a closer range of opinions. The questionnaire was mailed to 174 computer experts registered for an international conference on information processing. The size of the panel questioned was one of the largest ever used in a Delphi forecast. Most of the computer scientists involved in the conference were Europeans; thus the forecast tends to an international view of the future of computers.

By 1985, predicts this group of experts, employers will record income on terminals and automatically transfer this information to the tax authorities. (Many of the experts argued that by then direct taxes will be obsolete.) In general, the prospect of automated tax collection was viewed with dismay. Book libraries for factual information, not for literature, will be obsolete by 1992. Also, computer-aided instruction will have widespread use by 1982 and central files of scientific data will be common around 1983.

One day, there may even be a computer linkup in every home—a teletype terminal connected to a large data bank, but compulsory ownership of a terminal is not foreseen by this Delphi panel.[15]

Some of the specific forecasts of the Delphi panel are summarized as follows:*

> There will continue to be a rapid development of advanced computer applications which will result in much more influence on society than is the case today.

---

*With the permission of Lt. Col. Joseph P. Martino and *The Futurist*, published by the World Future Society, P. O. Box 19285, Washington, D. C. 20036. The material originally appeared in *Forecast 1968-2000 of Computer Development*, Parson and Williams, Inc.

Widespread automation may even create new forms of democracy in the future with widespread participation through remote computer terminals.

By the late 1980s there will be a 50% reduction in the working force in present industries, partly compensated for by shorter working hours and new industries. However, unemployment is expected to be a serious problem.

By the year 2000 all major industries will be controlled by computers. Small industries will not be automated to the same extent, but not many will exist by then.

The money and check system of today will, to a large extent, be taken over by a network of terminals and computers by the early 1990s. Around 1985 a majority of employers will have terminals where income is recorded and taxes automatically transferred to the appropriate government agencies.

Large urban traffic flow will be controlled by computers after 1973 and policing of individual vehicles by combined radar detection and computer record of violations will be normal between 1980 and 1986. In the late 1990s there will be a widespread use of automobile autopilots.

Around 1975 patients in major hospitals will be monitored by computers; and in the beginning of the 1980s, a majority of doctors will have computer terminals for consultation. By then computers will give reliable diagnoses when the physician presents the computer with the patient's symptoms.

These predictions are summarized in Figure 15–7, which shows the median estimate as well as the range of estimates. The range of estimated dates of occurrence of predicted events spreads as the predicted date of occurrence is further in the future.

If the forecast is reasonably accurate, the computer will have penetrated the sectors of industry, the hospital, and the home significantly by the year 2000. Widespread participation in the political process by means of the computer could significantly alter the process of government, possibly causing governing bodies to be more responsive to the desires of the governed.

The forecast predicts the work force in the present industries will be reduced by 50 percent. Of course, that reduction, due to automation, can be partially accounted for by a shorter work week and an early retirement age.

However, automation and cybernation are likely to create as many jobs as they eliminate by contributing to the increase of productivity and economic growth. The net effects on employment, hours worked and productivity are dif-

Computers and the Future*

The horizontal bars indicate the interquartile range (where 50% of the responses lay). The vertical bar indicates the median estimate. The last two events had upper quartiles falling later than the year 2000.

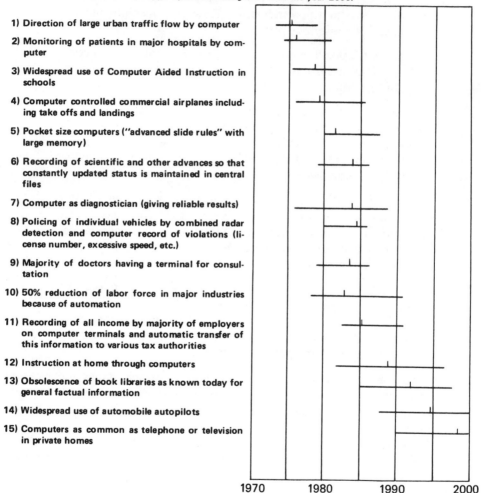

1) Direction of large urban traffic flow by computer

2) Monitoring of patients in major hospitals by computer

3) Widespread use of Computer Aided Instruction in schools

4) Computer controlled commercial airplanes including take offs and landings

5) Pocket size computers ("advanced slide rules" with large memory)

6) Recording of scientific and other advances so that constantly updated status is maintained in central files

7) Computer as diagnostician (giving reliable results)

8) Policing of individual vehicles by combined radar detection and computer record of violations (license number, excessive speed, etc.)

9) Majority of doctors having a terminal for consultation

10) 50% reduction of labor force in major industries because of automation

11) Recording of all income by majority of employers on computer terminals and automatic transfer of this information to various tax authorities

12) Instruction at home through computers

13) Obsolescence of book libraries as known today for general factual information

14) Widespread use of automobile autopilots

15) Computers as common as telephone or television in private homes

1970   1980   1990   2000

FIGURE 15–7

*With the permission of Lt. Col. Joseph P. Martino and the World Future Society, Washington, D.C. 20036. Also with the permission of Parsons and Williams, Inc., publishers of *Forecast 1968–2000 of Computer Development.*

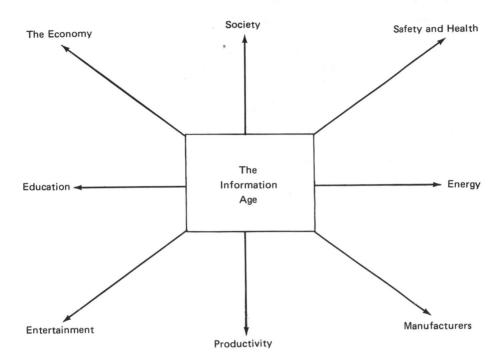

FIGURE 15–8   The impacts of the Information Age

ficult to predict because society may choose to invest in increased production or increased leisure in some unknown proportion. In this era of a post-industrial United States, many predict widespread cybernation and a lesser emphasis on efficiency as a criteria for industry and society. Whatever the exact consequences of a cybernated society are to a person in 2000 A.D., we can estimate that our society will experience a change in attitude about work, leisure and the value of time.

The 1980s are a period of transition to a knowledge-based information society. The impacts of such a transformation are summarized in Figure 15–8. With the combination of computing, voice, video and telecommunications systems we can expect changes in the workplace and the home. Alvin Toffler foresees the evolution to the 'electronic cottage' where work will take place in the home.[2] By 1990 we may expect electronic funds transfer, speech recognition and English-language programming to enable a person to use a computer-communications network for work and recreation. Computers will become as common as electric motors.

Despite the fact that 300,000 computer programmers are working in the United States in 1980, the demand for skilled programmers is for another 200,000 in the 1980s. This is an excellent opportunity for today's graduate.

A recent survey conducted in the United States and West Germany showed that people remain optimistic about the benefits the computer can bring to society.[14]The respondents felt that the computer will improve education, law enforcement and health care. They were less optimistic about the benefits of computer use for storing credit information and personal records. Furthermore, a significant proportion of respondents felt that computer polls and predictions tend to influence the outcome of elections and to dehumanize society by treating everybody as a number.

Whatever the outcome of the future development of computers and computer applications, man remains the architect of his own destiny. All the functions and activities of computer science relate to the larger problems and needs of man and his economic, political, social and religious dimensions. Computers will help to make life more livable for man if their limitations, applications and implications are fully understood. That is the objective of this book and computer science.

CHAPTER 15 PROBLEMS

P15–1.   Determine the performance/price ratio of the computer available for your use and compare it with those listed in Table 15–1.

P15–2.   Determine the throughput of the computer available for your use and compare it with another computer near your location.

P15–3.   Establish another class at your college as a Delphi panel and using two cycles of inquiry and feedback determine their estimates for the statements given in Figure 15–1.

CHAPTER 15 REFERENCES

1. J. F. Magee, "Into the Information Era," *Design News*, August 4, 1980, pg. 11.

2. A. Toffler, *The Third Wave*, William Morrow and Company, New York, 1980.

3. "Putting Up the Chips in the World's Fastest Industry," *Technology Review*, November 1979, pp. 76–77.

4. S. Fedida and R. Malik, *The Viewdata Revolution*, Wiley and Sons, Inc., New York, 1979.

5. N. Mokhoff, "A Computer Center for the Homeowner," *IEEE Spectrum*, September 1980, pp. 73–77.

6. F. G. Withington, "Transformation of the Information Industries," *Datamation*, November, 1978, pp. 9–14.

7. D. Bell, "Communications Technology—For Better or for Worse," *Harvard Business Review*, June 1979, pp. 20–42.

8. B. Uttal, "How the 4300 Fits IBM's New Strategy," *Fortune*, July 30, 1979, pp. 58–64.
9. M. Marshall, "New Direction Predicted for IBM," *Electronics*, March 27, 1980, pp. 93–94.
10. "Missing Computer Software," *Business Week*, September 1, 1980, pp. 46–56.
11. C. Evans, *The Micro Millenium*, Viking Press, New York, 1980.
12. R. Sugarman, "Superpower Computers," *IEEE Spectrum*, April 1980, pp. 28–34.
13. R. Bernhard, "The No-Downtime Computer," *IEEE Spectrum*, September 1980, pp. 33–37.
14. "Forecast 1968–2000 of Computer Developments and Applications," Parsons and Williams, Inc., Copenhagen, Denmark, 1969.
15. J. Martino, "What Computers May Do Tomorrow," *The Futurist*, October, 1969, pp. 134–135.
16. S. M. Lipton, "Making the Digital Signature Legal," *Data Communications*, February 1978, pp. 41–52.
17. M. L. Dertouzos and J. Moses, *The Computer Age: A Twenty-Year View*, MIT Press, Cambridge, Massachusetts, 1980.
18. R. Johansen *et. al.*, *Electronic Meetings*, Addison-Wesley, Inc., Reading, Massachusetts, 1979.
19. K. D. Wise *et. al.*, *Micro-Computers: A Technology Assessment to the Year 2000*, Wiley and Sons, Inc., New York, 1980.

A DATA PROCESSING GLOSSARY

Access time. (1) The time interval between the instant at which data are called for from a storage device and the instant delivery is completed; that is, the read time. (2) The time interval between the instant at which data are requested to be stored and the instant at which storage is completed; that is, write time.

Accounting machine. (1) A keyboard-actuated machine that prepares accounting records. (2) A machine that reads data from external storage media, such as cards or tapes, and automatically produces accounting records or tabulations, usually on continuous forms.

Accumulator. A register in which the result of an arithmetic or logic operation is formed.

Accuracy. The degree of freedom from error; that is, the degree of conformity to truth or to a rule. Accuracy is contrasted with precision. For example, four-place numerals are less precise than six-place numerals. Nevertheless, a properly computed four-place numeral might be more accurate than an improperly computed six-place numeral.

Acronym. A word formed from the first letter or letters of the words in a name, term, or phrase; for example, SAGE from semi-automatic ground environment, and ALGOL from algorithmic language.

Adder. (1) A device whose output is a representation of the sum of the quantities represented by its inputs. (2) (See "half-adder.")

Address. An identification, as represented by a name, label, or number, for a register, location in storage, or any other data source or destination.

Address register. A register in which an address is stored.

Add time. The time required for one addition, not including the time required to get and return the quantities from storage.

ADP. Automatic data processing.

ALGOL. Algorithmic–oriented language. An international procedure–oriented language.

Algorithm. A prescribed set of well–defined unambiguous rules or processes for the solution of a problem in a finite number of steps; for example, a full statement of an arithmetic procedure for evaluating *sin x* to a stated precision.

Algorithmic language. A language designed for expressing algorithms.

Alphameric. Generic term for alphabetic letters, numerical digits, and special characters which are machine–processable. Pertaining to a character set that contains both letters and digits, and, usually other characters, such as punctuation marks.

Alphanumeric. Synonymous with "alphameric."

Analog data. Data represented in a continuous form, as contrasted with digital data represented in a discrete (discontinuous) form. Analog data are usually represented by means of physical variables, such as voltage, resistance, rotation, etc.

Analysis. (1) The methodical investigation of a problem, and the separation of the problem into smaller related units for further detailed study. (2) (See "numerical analysis.")

Analyst. A person who defines problems and develops algorithms and procedures for their solution.

AND. A logic operator having the property that if P is a statement, Q is a statement, R is a statement, ..., then the AND of P, Q, R, ... is true if all statements are true, false if any statement is false. P AND Q is often represented by P·Q, or PQ or P ∧ Q.

AND gate. A gate that implements the logic AND operator.

Argument. An independent variable. For example, in looking up a quantity in a table, the number, or any of the numbers, identifying the location of the desired value.

Arithmetic operation. Any of the fundamental operations of arithmetic. For example, the binary operations of addition, subtraction, multiplication and division, and the unary operations of negation and absolute value.

Arithmetic unit. The unit of a computing system that contains the circuits that perform arithmetic operations.

Array. An arrangement of elements in one or more dimensions.

Artificial intelligence. The capability of a device to perform functions that are normally associated with human intelligence, such as reasoning, learning, and self–improvement. Related to machine learning.

Artificial language. A language based on a set of prescribed rules that are established prior to its usage. (Contrast with "natural language.")

Assemble. To prepare a machine language program from a symbolic language program by substituting absolute operation codes for symbolic operation codes and absolute or relocatable addresses for symbolic addresses.

Assembler. A program that assembles.

Automatic. Pertaining to a process or device that, under specified conditions, functions without intervention by a human operator.

Automatic data processing. (1) Data processing largely performed by automatic means. (2) By extension, the discipline which deals with methods and techniques related to data processing performed by automatic means. (3) Pertaining to data processing equipment such as EDP equipment.

Automation. (1) The implementation of processes by automatic means. (2) The theory, art, or technique or making a process more automatic. (3) The investigation, design, development, and application of methods rendering processes automatic, self–moving, or self–controlling. (4) The conversion of a procedure, a process, or equipment to automatic operation.

Auxiliary equipment. Equipment not under direct control of the central processing unit.

Auxiliary storage. A storage that supplements another storage.

Base. (1) A reference value. (2) A number that is multiplied by itself as many times as indicated by an exponent. (3) (See "radix.")

BASIC. Beginner's All–purpose Symbolic Instruction Code. BASIC is a procedure–oriented computer language.

Batch processing. (1) Pertaining to the technique of executing a set of programs such that each is completed before the next program of the set is started. (2) Loosely, the execution of programs serially.

BCD. (See "binary coded decimal notation.")

Binary. (1) Pertaining to a characteristic or property involving a selection, choice, or condition in which there are two possibilities. (2) Pertaining to the numeration system with a radix of two.

Binary code. (1) A code that makes use of exactly two distinct characters, usually 0 and 1.

Binary–coded decimal notation. A positional notation in which the individual decimal digits expressing a number in decimal notation are each represented by a binary numeral; for example, the number twenty–three is represented by 0010 0011 in the 8–4–2–1 type of binary–coded decimal notation and by 10111 in binary notation. (Synonymous with BCD.)

Binary digit. (1) In binary notation, either of the characters 0 or 1. (2) (Same as "bit.")

Binary to decimal conversion. Conversion of a binary number to the equivalent decimal number; that is, a base two number to a base ten number.

Bit. (1) A binary digit. (2) (See "check bit" and "parity bit.")

Bit. Contraction of "binary digit," the smallest unit of information in a binary system. A bit may be either a one or a zero.

Bit density. A measure of the number of bits recorded per unit of length or area.

Bit rate. The speed at which bits are transmitted, usually expressed in bits per second.

Boolean. (1) Pertaining to the processes used in the algebra formulated by George Boole. (2) Pertaining to the operations of formal logic.

Bps. Bits per second. In serial transmission, the instantaneous bit speed within one character, as transmitted by a machine or a channel.

Branch. (1) A set of instructions that are executed between two successive decision instructions. (2) To select a branch as in (1). (3) Loosely, a conditional jump.

Branchpoint. A place in a routine where a branch is selected.

Buffer. (1) A routine or device used to compensate for a difference in rate of flow of data, or time of occurrence of events, when transmitting data from one device to another. (2) An isolating circuit used to prevent a driven circuit from influencing the driving circuit.

Bug. A mistake or malfunction.

Business data processing. (1) Use of automatic data processing in accounting or management. (2) Data processing for business purposes. For example, recording and summarizing the financial transactions of a business. (3) (Synonymous with "administrative data processing.")

Byte. A sequence of adjacent binary digits operated upon as a unit and usually shorter than a word. In most cases, a byte is eight bits long.

Calculator. (1) A data processor especially suitable for performing arithmetic operations which require frequent intervention by a human operator. (2) A device capable of performing arithmetic. (3) A calculator, as in (2), that requires frequent manual intervention. (4) Generally and historically, a device for carrying out logic and arithmetic digital operations of any kind.

Card hopper. A device that holds cards and makes them available to a card feed mechanism.

Card punch. A device to record information in cards by punching holes in the cards to represent letters, digits, and special characters.

Card reader. A device which senses and translates into internal form the holes in punched cards.

Carry. (1) One or more characters, produced in connection with an arithmetic operation on one digit place of two or more numerals in positional notation, that are forwarded to another digit place for processing there.

Cathode ray tube display. (1) A device that presents data in visual form by means of controlled electron beams. (Abbreviated "CRT display.")

Central processing unit (CPU). A unit of a computer that includes circuits controlling the interpretation and execution of instructions.

Character. (1) A letter, digit, or other symbol that is used as part of the organization, control, or representation of data. A character is often in the form of a spatial arrangement of adjacent or connected strokes.

Character reader. An input device which reads printed characters directly from a document.

Check bit. A binary check digit; for example, a parity bit.

Clear. (1) To place a storage device into a prescribed state, usually that denoting zero or blank.

Clock. (1) A device that generates periodic signals used for synchronization. (2) A device that measures and indicates time. (3) A register whose content changes at regular intervals in such a way as to measure time.

Closed Loop Control System. A control system which utilizes measurements of the system output to compare with the desired output in order to control the process by ma-

nipulating the input to the process. (Contrast with Open Loop Control System.)

Closed shop. Pertaining to the operation of a computer facility in which most productive problem programming is performed by a group of programming specialists rather than by the problem originators. The use of the computer itself may also be described as closed shop if full–time trained operators, rather than user/programmers, serve as the operators. (Contrast with "open shop.")

COBOL. Common business–oriented language. A business data processing language.

Code. (1) A set of unambiguous rules specifying the way in which data may be represented; for example, the set of correspondences in the standard code for information interchange. (2) In data processing, to represent data or a program in a symbolic form that can be accepted by a data processor. (3) To write a routine. (4) Same as "encode."

Command. (1) A control signal. (2) Loosely, an instruction in machine language. (3) Loosely, a mathematical or logic operator.

Communication. Transmission of intelligence between points of origin and reception without alteration of sequence or structure of information content.

Communication link. The physical means of connecting one location to another for the purpose of transmitting and receiving information.

Compile. To prepare a machine language program from a computer program written in another programming language by making use of the overall logic structure of the program, or generating more than one machine instruction for each symbolic statement, or both, as well as performing the function of an assembler.

Compiler. A program that compiles.

Complement. A number that can be derived from a specified number by subtracting it from a specified number. For example, in radix notation, the specified number may be a given power of the radix or one less than a given power of the radix. The negative of a number is often represented by its complement.

Component. A basic part. An element.

Computer. (1) A data processor that can perform substantial computation, including numerous arithmetic or logic operations, without intervention by a human operator during the run. (2) A device capable of solving problems by accepting data, performing described operations on the data, and supplying the results of these operations. Various types of computers are calculators, digital computers, and analog computers.

Computer–assisted instruction. An interactive system of a student and a computer using a natural language such as English to produce long-lasting changes in the cognitive domain (intellectual knowledge) of the student.

Computer process control system. A system which utilizes a computer connected to sensors which monitor a process, in order to control the process for handling matter or energy, and its modification, in order to produce a product at a profit.

Computer program. A series of instructions or statements in a form acceptable to a computer, prepared in order to achieve a certain result.

Computer word. A sequence of bits or characters treated as a unit and capable of being stored in one computer location.

Conditional transfer. (1) A transfer from one portion of a program to another specified portion of the program if a specified criterion is satisfied. (2) A computer instruction which, when reached in the course of a program, will cause the computer either to continue with the next instruction in the original sequence or to transfer program control to another location depending on a predetermined condition.

Console. That part of a computer used for communication between the operator or maintenance engineer and the computer.

Constant. A fixed or invariable value or data item.

Control unit. In a digital computer, those parts that effect the retrieval of instructions in proper sequence, the interpretation of each instruction and the application of the proper signals to the arithmetic unit and other parts in accordance with this interpretation.

Conversational mode. Communication between a terminal and the computer in which each entry from the terminal elicits a response from the computer and vice versa.

Core storage. A form of high–speed storage using magnetic cores.

Counter. A device such as a register or storage location used to represent the number of occurrences of an event.

Cybernetics. That branch of learning which brings together theories and studies on communication and control in living organisms and machines.

Cycle time. The time required to complete one loop. It is the basic time unit of computer operation.

Data. (1) A representation of facts, concepts, or instructions in a formalized manner suitable for communication, interpretation, or processing by humans or automatic means. (2) Any representations such as characters or analog quantities to which meaning is, or might be, assigned.

Data bank. (1) A comprehensive collection of libraries of data. For example, one line of an invoice may form an item, a complete invoice may form a record, a complete set of such records may form a file, the collection of inventory control files may form a library, and the libraries used by an organization are known as its data bank. (2) An on–line storage unit retaining large masses of data.

Data, digital. Information represented by a code consisting of a sequence of discrete elements.

Data logging. Recording of data about events that occur in time sequence.

Data processing. The execution of a systematic sequence of operations performed upon data. (Synonymous with "information processing.")

Data reduction. The transformation of raw data into a more useful form; for example, smoothing to reduce noise.

Debug. To detect, locate, and remove mistakes from a routine or malfunctions from a computer.

Decimal. (1) Pertaining to a characteristic or property involving a selection, choice, or condition in which there are ten possibilities. (2) Pertaining to the numeration system with a radix of ten.

Decimal digit. In decimal notation, one of the characters 0 through 9.

Deck. A collection of punched cards.

Digit. (1) A symbol that represents one of the non–negative integers smaller than the radix. For example, in decimal notation, a digit is one of the characters from 0 to 9.

Digital. Pertaining to data in the form of digits. (Contrast with "analog.")

Digital computer. (1) A computer in which discrete representation of data is used principally. (2) A computer that operates on discrete data by performing arithmetic and logic processes on these data.

Digital data. Data represented in discrete, discontinuous form, as contrasted with analog data represented in continuous form. Digital data is usually represented by means of coded characters; for example, numbers, signs, symbols, etc.

Digitize. To use numeric characters to express or represent data. For example, to obtain from an analog representation of a physical quantity a digital representation of the quantity.

Direct memory access. Direct communication between memory and peripherals. In computers where this is not inherent, a device that bypasses the CPU.

Disk storage. A storage device which uses magnetic recording on flat rotating disks.

Display. A visual presentation of data.

Document. (1) A medium and the data recorded on it for human use; for example, a report sheet, a book. (2) By extension, any record that has permanence and that can be read by man or machine.

Documentation. (1) The creating, collecting, organizing, storing, citing, and disseminating of documents, or the information recorded in documents. (2) The recording of procedures and programs.

Double precision. Pertaining to the use of two computer words to represent a number.

Drum storage. A storage device which uses magnetic recording on a rotating cylinder. A type of addressable storage associated with some computers.

Edit. To modify the form or format of data; for example, to insert or delete characters such as page numbers or decimal points.

EDP. Electronic data processing.

Electronic Digital Computer. An information processing device that accepts and processes data represented by discrete symbols, and is constructed primarily of devices which operate by means of electrical or electronic phenomena.

Error. (1) Any discrepancy between a computed, observed, or measured quantity and the true, specified, or theoretically correct value of condition.

Error message. An indication that an error has been detected.

Exclusive OR. A logic operator having the property that if P is a statement and Q is a statement, then P exclusive OR Q is true if either but not both statements are true, false if both are true or both are false. P exclusive OR Q is often represented by $P \oplus Q$ or $P \vee Q$. (Contrast with "OR.")

Exponent. In a floating–point representation, the numeral (of a pair of numerals representing a number) that indicates the power to which the base is raised.

External storage. A storage device outside the computer which can store information in a form acceptable to the computer; for example, cards and tapes.

Feedback. The return of part of the output of a machine, process, or system to the computer as input for another phase, especially for self–correcting or control purposes.

Field. In a record, a specified area used for a particular category of data; for example, a group of card columns used to represent a wage rate or a set of bit locations in a computer word used to express the address of the operand.

File. A collection of related records treated as a unit. (See "Data bank.")

File maintenance. The activity of keeping a file up to date by adding, changing, or deleting data.

First generation computer. A computer utilizing vacuum tube components.

Fixed–point. Pertaining to a numeration system in which the position of the point is fixed with respect to one end of the numerals, according to some convention.

Fixed storage. A storage device that stores data not alterable by computer instructions. For example, magnetic core storage with a lockout feature, or a photographic disk. (Synonymous with "nonerasable storage," "permanent storage," and "read only memory.")

Fixed word length computer. A computer in which data is treated in units of a fixed number of characters or bits (as contrasted with variable word length).

Flag. (1) Any of various types of indicators used for identification. For example, a wordmark. (2) A character that signals the occurrence of some condition, such as the end of a word. (3) (Synonymous with "mark" and "tag.")

Flip–flop. A circuit or device containing active elements, capable of assuming either one of two stable states at a given time.

Floating point. A notation in which numbers are expressed as a number of significant digits together with the exponent of the base 10 which indicates the location of the decimal point.

Flow chart. A graphic representation of the definition, analysis, or solution of a problem, in which symbols are used to represent operations, data, flow, equipment, etc.

Format. A specific arrangement of data.

FORTRAN. Formula translating system. A family of programming languages of which FORTRAN IV is the latest version.

GAME. (1) An activity among two or more independent decision makers seeking to achieve their objectives in some limiting context. (2) A contest with rules among several adversaries who are attempting to win specified objectives.

Gang–punch. To punch all or part of the information from one punched card into succeeding cards.

Gate. (1) A device having one output channel and one or more input channels, such that the output channel state is completely determined by the contemporaneous input channel states, except during switching transients. (2) A combinational logic element having at least one input channel, such as an AND gate or an OR gate.

General purpose computer. A computer that is designed to handle a wide variety of problems.

Graphic. A symbol produced by a process such as handwriting, drawing or printing.

Half–adder. A combinational logic element having two outputs, S and C, and two inputs, A and B, such that the outputs are related to the inputs according to the following table:

Input		Output	
A	B	S	C
0	0	0	0
0	1	1	0
1	0	1	0
1	1	0	1

S denotes "sum without carry," C denotes "carry." Two half–adders may be used for performing binary addition.

Hard copy. A printed copy of machine output in a readable form; for example, printed reports, listings, documents, summaries, etc.

Hardware. Physical equipment, as opposed to the program or method of use; for example, mechanical, magnetic, electrical, or electronic devices. (Contrast with "software.")

Heuristic. Pertaining to exploratory methods of problem solving in which solutions are discovered by evaluation of the progress made toward the final result. (Contrast with "algorithm.")

Hexadecimal. (See "sexadecimal.")

Hollerith. (1) A particular type of code or punched card utilizing 12 rows per column and usually 80 columns per card. (2) An inventor of punched–card computing equipment.

Hybrid computer. A computer for data processing using both analog and discrete representation of data.

I/O. Input/output. Input or output, or both.

Information. (1) The meaning assigned to data by the known conventions used in its representation. (2) The aggregation of data that are presented in various forms.

Information retrieval. The technique and process of accumulating, classifying, storing, and searching large amounts of data, extracting and reproducing or displaying the required information contained within the data.

Initialize. To set counters, switches and addresses to zero or other starting values at the beginning of, or at prescribed points in, a computer routine.

Input data. Data to be processed.

Input device. The device or collective set of devices used for conveying data into another device.

Input/output. (1) Commonly called I/O. A general term for the equipment used to communicate with a computer. (2) The data involved in such communication. (3) The media carrying the data for input/output.

Inquiry. A request for information from storage; for example, a request for the number of available airline seats or a machine statement to initiate a search of a data bank.

Instruction. A statement that specifies an operation and the values or locations of its operands. In this context, the term "instruction" is preferable to the terms "command" or "order," which are sometimes used synonymously.

Integrated circuit. A combination of interconnected circuit elements inseparably associated on or within a continuous layer of material, called a substrate.

Interface. A shared boundary. An interface might be a hardware component to link two devices or it might be a portion of storage or registers accessed by two or more programs.

Internal storage. Addressable storage directly controlled by the central processing unit of a digital computer.

Interpreting. Printing, on paper tape or cards, the meaning of the holes punched on the same tape or cards.

Interrupt. To stop a process in such a way that it can be resumed.

Iterate. To execute a loop or series of steps repeatedly; for example, a loop in a routine.

Job. A specified group of tasks prescribed as a unit of work for a computer. By extension, a job usually includes all necessary programs, linkages, files, and instructions to the Operating System.

Job control statement. A statement in a job that is used in identifying the job or describing its requirements to the Operating System.

Jump. (1) A departure from the normal sequence of executing instructions in a computer. (Synonymous with "transfer" - 1.) (2) (See "conditional jump.")

Justify. To align data about a specified reference.

K. An abbreviation for the prefix "kilo."

Label. One or more characters used to identify an item of data.

Language. (1) A set of words and rules for constructing sentences that can be used for communicating. Each language has a *syntax*; that is, a grammar, rules of formulation and word relationship. (2) (See "algorithmic language," "artificial language," "machine language," "natural language," "object language," "problem–oriented language," "procedure–oriented language," "programming language," and "source language.")

Language translator. A general term for any assembler, compiler, or other routine that accepts statements in one language and produces equivalent statements in another language.

Large–scale integration. A term used to describe the technology which consists of putting together arrays of logic cells to realize a complete function.

Library. A collection of organized information used for study and reference. (See "Data bank.")

Library routine. A proven routine that is maintained in a program library.

Line feed character. A format effector that causes the printing or display position to be moved to the next printing or display line. Abbreviated LF.

List. An ordered set of items.

List processing. A method of processing data in the form of lists. Usually, chained lists are used so that the logical order of items can be changed without altering their physical location.

Load. In programming, to enter data into storage or working registers.

Logic element. A device that performs a logic function.

Loop. A sequence of computer instructions which are executed repeatedly, but usually with index (or counter) modification until the index attains the terminating condition.

Machine–independent. Pertaining to procedures or programs created without regard for the actual devices which will be used to process them.

Machine language. A language that is used directly by a machine.

Magnetic card. A card with a magnetic surface on which data can be stored by selective magnetization of portions of the flat surface.

Magnetic core. A configuration of magnetic material that is, or is intended to be, placed in a spatial relationship to current–carrying conductors and whose magnetic properties are essential to its use. It may be used to concentrate an induced magnetic field as in a transformer, induction coil, or armature, to retain a magnetic polarization for the purpose of storing data, or for its nonlinear properties as in a logic element. It may be made of such material as iron, iron oxide, or ferrite and in such shapes as wires, tapes, toroids (doughnut–shaped solids), or thin film.

Magnetic disc. A flat circular plate with a magnetic surface on which data can be stored by selective magnetization of portions of the flat surface.

Magnetic drum. A right circular cylinder with a magnetic surface on which data can be stored by selective magnetization of portions of the curved surface.

Magnetic ink. An ink that contains particles of a magnetic substance whose presence can be detected by magnetic sensors.

Magnetic storage. A storage device that utilizes the magnetic properties of materials to store data; for example, magnetic cores, tapes, and films.

Magnetic tape. A tape with a magnetic surface on which data can be stored by selective polarization of portions of the surface.

Main frame. The central processing unit of a computer plus the input/output unit and the random–access and read–only memories. The mainframe is the computer without peripherals.

Management information system. (1) A computer system integrating equipment, people and procedures in such a way as to deliver analysis-supporting and analytical information pertinent to management decisions. (2) A system of people, equipment, procedures, documents, and communications that collects, validates, operates on, transforms, stores, retrieves, and presents data for use in planning, budgeting, accounting, controlling, and other management processes for various top executives of a firm.

Management science. A mathematical or quantitative study of the management of resources of business, usually with the aid of a computer.

Mark. (See "flag.")

Mark–sense. To mark a position on a punched card with an electrically conductive pencil, for later conversion to machine punching.

Mathematical model. A mathematical representation of a process, device, or concept.

Matrix. (1) In mathematics, a two–dimensional rectangular array of quantities. Matrices are manipulated in accordance with the rules of matrix algebra. (2) In computers, a logic network in the form of an array of input leads and output leads with logic elements connected at some of their intersections. (3) By extension, an array of any number of dimensions.

Memory. (See "storage.")

Microsecond. One–millionth of a second.

Millisecond. One–thousandth of a second.

Mnemonic symbol. A symbol chosen to assist the human memory; for example, an abbreviation such as MPY for "multiply."

Model. A qualitative or quantitative representation of a process or endeavor that shows the effects of those factors which are significant for the purposes being considered.

Module. (1) A program unit that is discrete and identifiable with respect to compiling, combining with other units, and loading; for example, the input to, or output from, an assembler, compiler, linkage editor, or executive routine. (2) A packaged functional hardware unit designed for use with other components.

Monitor. Software or hardware that observes, supervises, controls, or verifies the operations of a system.

Multiprocessing. (1) Pertaining to the simultaneous execution of two or more programs or sequences of instructions by a computer or computer network. (2) Loosely, parallel processing.

Multiprogramming. Pertaining to the concurrent execution of two or more programs by a single computer.

NAND. A logic operator having the property that if P is a statement, Q is a statement, R is a statement, ... , then the NAND of P, Q, R, ... is true if at least one statement is false, false if all statements are true. (Synonymous with "NOT–AND.")

Nanosecond. One–thousand–millionth (one billionth) of a second.

Natural language. A language whose rules reflect and describe current usage rather than prescribed usage. (Contrast with "artificial language.")

Nest. To imbed subroutines or data in other subroutines or data at a different hierarchical level such that the different levels of routines or data can be executed or accessed recursively.

Nondestructive read. A read process that does not erase the data in the source.

NOR. A logic operator having the property that if P is a statement, Q is a statement, R is a statement, ... , then the NOR of P, Q, R, ... is true if all statements are false, false if at least one statement is true. P NOR Q is often represented by a combination of OR and NOT symbols.

NOT. A logic operator having the property that if P is a statement, then the NOT of P is true if P is false, false if P is true. The NOT of P is often represented by $\bar{P}$.

Notation. A representational system which utilizes characters and symbols in positional relationships to express information.

Number. (1) A mathematical entity that may indicate quantity or amount of units. (2) Loosely, a numeral. (3) (See "binary number" and "random numbers.")

Number system. A system for representing numbers. Each number system contains a base or radix, which is the number of distinct symbols used in the system.

Numerical analysis. The study of methods of obtaining useful quantitative solutions to problems that have been expressed mathematically, including the study of the errors and bounds on errors in obtaining such solutions.

Object code. Output from a compiler or assembler which is itself executable machine code or is suitable for processing to produce executable machine code.

Object language. The language in which the output from a compiler or assembler is expressed.

Object program. A fully compiled or assembled program that is ready to be loaded into the computer.

Octal. (1) Pertaining to a characteristic or property involving a selection, choice or condition in which there are eight possibilities. (2) Pertaining to the numeration system with a radix of eight.

Offline. Pertaining to equipment or devices not under direct control of the central processing unit.

Online. Pertaining to equipment or devices under direct control of the central processing unit. Pertaining to a user's ability to interact with a computer.

Open Loop Control System. A control system which utilizes manipulation of the input variables to control the process and achieve the desired output. (Contrast with Closed Loop Control System.)

Open shop. Pertaining to the operation of a computer facility in which most productive problem programming is performed by the problem originator rather than by a group of programming specialists. The use of the computer itself may also be described as open shop if the user/programmer, rather than a full–time trained operator, also serves as the operator. (Contrast with "closed shop.")

Operating system. Software which controls the execution of computer programs and which may provide scheduling, debugging, input/output control, accounting, compilation, storage assignment, data management and related services.

Operations research. A scientific approach to decision making that involves the operations of organizational systems.

Optical scanner. (1) A device that scans optically and usually generates an analog or digital signal. (2) A device that optically scans printed or written data and generates their digital representations.

OR. (1) A logic operator having the property that if P is a statement, Q is a statement, R is a statement, ... , then the OR of P, Q, R, ... is true if at least one statement is true, false if all statements are false. P OR Q is often represented by P + Q.

Order. To put items in a given sequence.

OS. Operating System.

Output. (1) Data that has been processed. (2) The state or sequence of states occurring on a specified output channel. (3) The device or collective set of devices used for taking data out of a device. (4) A channel for expressing a state of a device or logic element. (4) The process of transferring data from an internal storage to an external storage.

Overflow. (1) That portion of the result of an operation that exceeds the capacity of the intended unit of storage. (2) Pertaining to the generation of overflow as in (1).

Paper tape reader. A device that senses and translates the holes in perforated tape into electrical signals.

Parallel computer. (1) A computer having multiple arithmetic or logic units that are used to accomplish parallel operations or parallel processing. (Contrast with "serial computer.") (2) Historically, a computer, some specified characteristic of which is parallel; for example, a computer that manipulates all bits of a word in parallel.

Parameter. A variable that is given a constant value for a specific purpose or process.

Parity bit. A binary digit appended to an array of bits to make the sum of all the bits always odd or always even.

Peripheral equipment. In a data processing system, any unit of equipment, distinct from the central processing unit, which may provide the system with outside communication.

Permanent storage. (See "fixed storage.")

PL/I. Programming Language/I, a high–level programming language.

Plot. To map or diagram. To connect the point–by–point coordinate values.

Precision. (1) The degree of discrimination with which a quantity is stated; for example, a three–digit numeral discriminates among 1000 possibilities. (2) The amount of detail used in representing the data. (3) (See "double precision.")

Printer. A device which expresses coded characters as hard copy.

Problem–oriented language. A programming language designed for the convenient expression of a given class of problems.

Procedure–oriented language. A programming language designed for the convenient expression of procedures used in the solution of a wide class of problems.

Program. (1) A detailed and explicit set of instructions for accomplishing some purpose, the set being expressed in some language suitable for input to a computer. (2) A plan for the automatic solution of a problem. A complete program includes instructions for transcription of the data, coding for the computer and output of the results.

Program library. A collection of available computer programs and routines.

Program testing. The process whereby the programmer assures himself that his program solves the problem he proposed to solve, and will continue to solve it as the data change.

Programmer. A person mainly involved in designing, writing and testing programs.

Programming language. A language used to prepare computer programs.

Punched card. (1) A card punched or intended to be punched with a pattern of holes to represent data.

Punched tape. A tape on which a pattern of holes or cuts is used to represent data.

Radix. In positional representation, the integral ratio of the significances of any two specified adjacent digit positions. For example, if the radix is five, then 142.3 means 1 times 5 to the second power, plus 4 times 5 to the first power, plus 3 times 5 to the zero power, plus 2 times 5 to the minus one power. (Synonymous with "base.")

Random access. (1) Pertaining to the process of obtaining data from, or placing data into, storage where the time required for such access is independent of the location of the data most recently obtained or placed in storage. (2) Pertaining to a storage device in which the access time is effectively independent of the location of the data. (3) (Synonymous with "direct access.")

Random numbers. (1) A series of numbers obtained by chance. (2) A series of numbers considered appropriate for satisfying certain statistical tests. (3) A series of numbers believed to be free from conditions which might bias the result of a calculation.

Raw data. Data which has not been processed or reduced.

Read. To acquire or interpret data from a storage device, a data medium, or any other source.

Reader. A device which converts information in one form of storage to information in another form of storage.

Read–only memory (ROM). A memory in which the information is stored at the time of manufacture. The information is available at any time, but it can be modified only with difficulty.

Real time. (1) Pertaining to the actual time during which a physical process transpires. (2) Pertaining to the performance of a computation during the actual time that the related physical process transpires in order that results of the computation can be used in guiding the physical process.

Record. A collection of related items of data, treated as a unit. For example, one line of an invoice may form a record. A complete set of such records may form a file.

Recording density. The number of bits in a single linear track measured per unit of length of the recording medium.

Reel. A mounting for a roll of tape.

Register. A device capable of storing a specified amount of data, such as one word.

Reliability. The quality of freedom from failure, usually expressed as the probability that a failure will not occur in a given amount of usage.

Remote access. Pertaining to communication with a data processing facility by one or more stations that are distant from that facility.

Remote station. Data terminal equipment for communicating with a data processing system from a location that is time, space, or electrically distant.

Reproduce. To prepare a duplicate of stored information, especially for punched cards, punched paper tape, or magnetic tape.

Round. To adjust the least significant digits retained in truncation to partially reflect the dropped portion. For example, when rounded to three digits, the decimal number 3.14563 becomes 3.15.

Rounding error. An error due to roundoff. (Contrast with "truncation error.")

Routine. An ordered set of instructions that may have some general or frequent use.

RPG. Report program generator.

Run. A single, complete execution of a computer program.

Sampling. (1) Obtaining the values of a function for discrete, regularly or irregularly spaced values of the independent variable. (2) In statistics, obtaining a sample from a population.

Segment. (1) (Verb). To divide a computer program into parts such that the program can be executed without the entire program being in internal storage at any one time. (2) (Noun). A part of a computer program as in (1).

Semi-conductor. A solid–state element which contains properties between those of metal or conductor and those of a poor conductor of electrons such as insulator.

Sequential computer. A computer in which events occur in time sequence, with little or no simultaneity or overlap of events.

Sequential operation. The consecutive or serial execution of operations without any simultaneity or overlap. This is the normal mode of digital computer operation.

Serial. (1) Pertaining to the sequential or consecutive occurrence of two or more related activities in a single device or channel. (2) Pertaining to the time–sequencing of two or more processes. (3) Pertaining to the time–sequential processing of the individual parts of a whole, such as the bits of a character or the characters of a word, using the same facilities for successive parts. (4) (Contrast with "parallel.")

Serial access. (1) Pertaining to the sequential or consecutive transmission of data to or from storage. (2) Pertaining to the process of obtaining data from, or placing data into, storage where the time required for such access is dependent upon the location of the data most recently obtained or placed in storage. (Contrast with "random access.")

Sexadecimal. (1) Pertaining to a characteristic or property involving a selection, choice, or condition in which there are sixteen possibilities. (2) Pertaining to the numeration system with a radix of sixteen. (3) (Synonymous with "hexadecimal.")

Sign bit. A binary digit occupying the sign position.

Significant digit. A digit that is needed for a certain purpose, particularly one that must be kept to preserve a specific accuracy or precision.

Sign position. A position, normally located at one end of a numeral, that contains an indication of the algebraic sign of the number represented by the numeral.

Simulation. The use of models and the actual conditions of either the thing being modeled or the environment in which it operates, with the models or conditions in physical, mathematical, or some other form. The purpose of simulation is to explore the various results which might be obtained from the real system by subjecting the model to representative environments which are equivalent to, or in some way representative of, the situations it is desired to understand or investigate.

Skip. To ignore one or more instructions in a sequence of instructions.

Smooth. To apply procedures that decrease or eliminate rapid fluctuations in data.

Software. (1) A set of programs, procedures, rules and possibly associated documentation concerned with the operation of a data processing system. For example, compilers, library routines, manuals, circuit diagrams. (2) (Contrast with "hardware.")

Solid state component. A component whose operation depends on the control of electric or magnetic phenomena in solids; for example, a transistor, crystal diode, ferrite core.

Sorter. A person, device or computer routine that sorts.

Source language. A language that is an input to a given translation process.

Source program. A program written in a source language.

Special purpose computer. A computer that is designed to handle a restricted class of problems.

Stacked job processing. A technique that permits multiple job definitions to be grouped (stacked) for presentation to the system, which automatically recognizes the jobs, one after the other. More advanced systems allow job definitions to be added to the group (stack) at any time and from any source. They also honor priorities.

Statement. In computer programming, a meaningful expression or generalized instruction in a source language.

Step. (1) Noun. One operation in a computer routine. (2) Verb. To cause a computer to execute one operation.

Storage. (1) Pertaining to a device into which data can be entered, in which it can be held, and from which it can be retrieved at a later time. (2) Loosely, any device that can store data. (3) (Synonymous with "memory.")

Storage capacity. The amount of data that can be contained in a storage device.

Storage cell. An elementary unit of storage; for example, a binary cell, a decimal cell.

Storage device. A device into which data can be inserted, in which it can be retained, and from which it can be retrieved.

Storage register. A device for holding a unit of information.

Stored program computer. A computer controlled by internally stored instructions that can synthesize, store and in some cases alter instructions as though they were data, and that can subsequently execute these instructions.

String. A linear sequence of entities, such as characters or physical elements.

Subroutine. A routine that can be part of another routine.

Symbol. (1) A representation of something by reason of relationship, association or convention. (2) (See "flow chart symbol," "logic symbol," and "mnemonic symbol.")

Synchronous computer. A computer in which each event, or the performance of any basic operation, is constrained to start on, and usually to keep in step with, signals from a clock. (Contrast with "asynchronous computer.")

Syntax. (1) The structure of expressions in a language. (2) The rules governing the structure of a language.

System. (1) An assembly of methods, procedures, or techniques united by regulated interaction to form an organized whole. (2) An organized collection of men, machines and methods required to accomplish a set of specific functions.

Systems analysis. The analysis of an activity to determine precisely what must be accomplished and how to accomplish it.

Table look-up. A procedure for obtaining the function value corresponding to an argument from a table of function values.

Tabulate. (1) To form data into a table. (2) To print totals.

Tag. One or more characters attached to an item or record for the purpose of identification.

Tape drive. A device that moves tape past a head. (Synonymous with "tape transport.")

Tape unit. A device containing a tape drive, together with reading and writing heads and associated controls.

Teleprocessing. A form of information handling in which a data processing system utilizes communication facilities.

Teletype. Trademark of Teletype Corporation, usually referring to several different kinds of teleprinter equipment such as tape punches, reperforators, page printers etc., utilized for communication systems.

Temporary storage. In programming, storage locations reserved for intermediate results. (Synonymous with "working storage.")

Terminal. A point in a system or communication network at which data can either enter or leave.

Ternary. (1) Pertaining to a characteristic or property involving a selection, choice, or condition in which there are three possibilities. (2) Pertaining to the numeration system with a radix of three.

Throughput. A measure of system efficiency; the rate at which work can be handled by a system.

Time sharing. Participation in available computer time by multiple users via terminals. Characteristically, the response time is so short that the computer seems dedicated to each user.

Transistor. A small solid–state semiconducting device, using germanium or silicon, that performs dynamic functions such as amplification or switching.

Translate. To convert from one language to another language.

Truncate. To terminate a computational process in accordance with some rule; for example, to end the evaluation of a power series at a specified term.

Truncation error. An error due to truncation. (Contrast with "rounding error.")

Truth table. A table that describes a logic function by listing all possible combinations of input values and indicating, for each combination, the true output values.

TTY. Teletypewriter equipment.

Turing machine. A mathematical model of a device that changes its internal state and reads from, writes on, and moves a potentially infinite tape, all in accordance with its present state, thereby constituting a model for computer–like behavior.

Turnaround time. The elapsed time between submission of a job to a computing center and the return of results.

Underflow. Pertaining to the condition that arises when a machine computation yields a non–zero result that is smaller than the smallest non–zero quantity that the intended unit of storage is capable of storing.

Unit record. Historically, a card containing one complete record. Currently, the punched card.

Update. To modify a master file with current information according to a specified procedure.

User. Anyone utilizing the services of a computing system.

Variable. A quantity that can assume any of a given set of values.

Verify. (1) To determine whether a transcription of data or other operation has been accomplished accurately. (2) To check the results of keypunching.

Word. A character string or a bit string considered as an entity.

Word length. A measure of the size of a word, usually specified in units such as characters or binary digits.

Write. To record data in a storage device or a data medium. The recording need not be permanent, such as on a cathode ray tube display device.

INDEX